Second Edition

INTERNET
Systems and Applications

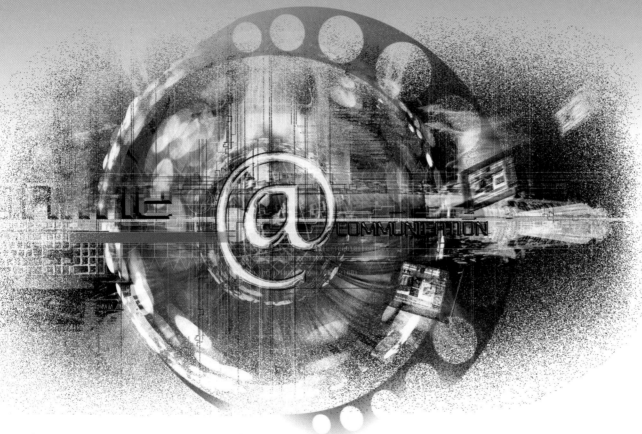

Alec Fehl

Asheville-Buncombe Technical Community College
Asheville, North Carolina

John Marshall Baker

Computer Technology Consultant

Paradigm PUBLISHING

St. Paul • Los Angeles • Indianapolis

Senior Developmental Editor:	Christine Hurney
Production Editor:	Bob Dreas
Proofreader:	Laura M. Nelson Publishing Services
Indexer:	Schroeder Indexing Service
Cover Designer:	Leslie Anderson
Composition House:	Parkwood Composition

Care has been taken to verify the accuracy of information presented in this book. However, the authors, editors, and publisher cannot accept responsibility for Web, e-mail, newsgroup, or chat room subject matter or content, or for consequences from application of the information in this book, and make no warranty, expressed or implied, with respect to its content.

Trademarks: Some of the product names and company names included in this book have been used for identification purposes only and may be trademarks or registered trade names of their respective manufacturers and sellers. The authors, editors, and publisher disclaim any affiliation, association, or connection with, or sponsorship or endorsement by, such owners.

Photo and Screen Image Credits: Photo and Screen Image Credits continue following Index.

We have made every effort to trace the ownership of all copyrighted material and to secure permission from copyright holders. In the event of any question arising as to the use of any material, we will be pleased to make the necessary corrections in future printings. Thanks are due to the aforementioned authors, publishers, and agents for permission to use the materials indicated.

ISBN 978-0-76383-189-9 (text)
ISBN 978-0-76383-193-6 (text and CD)

Printed in the United States of America

16 15 14 13 12 11 10 09   2 3 4 5 6 7 8 9 10

CONTENTS

PREFACE

In less than a single generation the Internet has become a ubiquitous part of daily life for many people around the world. People use the portion of the Internet known as the World Wide Web to send and receive messages, shop, make travel reservations, research information, listen to radio and watch videos, download programs, play games, make phone calls, and much more. *Internet: Systems and Applications, Second Edition* teaches the essential skills necessary to take full advantage of the Internet and the World Wide Web, using simple but informative explanations and step-by-step exercises that are rich with illustrative screen captures and detailed instructions. After completing this book, students will have a thorough understanding of how the Internet works, and will be able to use the skills they have learned to enjoy everything it has to offer.

Organization of the Text

The chapters that compose *Internet: Systems and Applications, Second Edition* are organized into three different units covering related material. Unit 1, *Using the Internet*, begins with Chapter 1, *Understanding the Internet*, which introduces the Internet and the World Wide Web and explains their relationship and how they work. Chapter 2, *Accessing the Internet*, describes the various methods that can be used to access the Internet. Coverage of Network Interface Cards (NICs) has been expanded in this edition. Chapter 3, *Ensuring Internet Security*, deals with the different security threats to the Internet and describes the steps that can be taken to counter threats. New coverage has been added about Vista's parental control features.

Unit 2, *Accessing Information on the Web*, begins with Chapter 4, *Using a Web Browser*, which teaches students Web browser fundamentals using exercises based on Microsoft Internet Explorer. This chapter provides in-depth coverage of the Internet Explorer 7 interface. Chapter 5, *Accessing Information Resources*, teaches skills and strategies that can be used to mine the information available on the Web. Chapter 6, *Downloading and Storing Information*, provides instruction on downloading material from the Web to a computer or network, as well as the different methods that can be used for saving information. Information related to FTP site usage in Internet Explorer 7 and Vista is included.

Unit 3, *Communications Technology*, begins with Chapter 7, *Experiencing Multimedia*, which describes the various multimedia formats available for use on the Web, including coverage of Vista's new Windows Media Player. Chapter 8, *Using E-mail*, provides a thorough explanation of e-mail clients using Microsoft Windows Mail as an example. Chapter 9, *Asynchronous Communications*, teaches students how to use various forms of asynchronous communication methods such as mailing lists, newsgroups, Web logs, and so on. Chapter 10, *Synchronous Communications*, teaches students how to use synchronous communication methods such as Internet Relay Chat, instant messaging clients, and Voice over Internet Phone (VoIP). The chapter is enhanced with coverage of Vista Remote Assistance and Vista Remote Desktop.

The book concludes with an Appendix covering the downloading and use of the popular Mozilla Firefox Web browser as well as a complete glossary listing definitions for all of the chapter's key terms.

Chapter Features

All of the chapter features are designed to engage the students and help them learn the concepts and skills presented.

- **Learning Objectives** introduce the chapter and list specific learning goals to focus student study of the material.
- **Living on the Net** provides a realistic, practical portrayal of how the Internet is being used. These engaging scenarios allow students to connect with the concepts that will be covered in more depth in the chapter.
- **Key Terms** are bolded in context of the text discussion and are supported with margin definitions. All of the chapter's terms are also listed, with page numbers, at the end of each chapter. Chapter-specific as well as book-level glossaries are available on the Encore CD.
- **Sidebars** provide the student with more information about a subject explored in the chapter.
- **Concept Reviews** list questions to assist the student in reviewing each section's material.
- **Skills Reviews** are step-by-step, hands-on exercises allowing the student to practice or explore the concepts introduced in each section.

End-of-each chapter materials include the following elements to help students review what they have learned and assess achievement.

- A chapter summary outlining key concepts
- Key terms list including the terms found in the margins of the chapter displayed with a page reference
- Net Check section of 10 multiple choice and 10 true/false questions designed to reinforce key concepts and topics
- Virtual Perspectives discussion questions challenging students to think beyond the scope of the text and to research upcoming trends and advances in technology
- Internet Lab Projects that allow the student to demonstrate proficiency with hands-on assessments
- Internet Research Activities that invite students to use the Web to further explore Internet-related topics and to summarize their findings

• Net Challenge a concluding activity that allows advanced students to demonstrate their mastery of advanced skills

Student Courseware

Included with the textbook is a multimedia CD that adds an experiential and interactive dimension to the text. For every chapter, the Encore CD includes the following features.

- **Tech Demos:** These brief, animated Flash segments bring key topics to life. To highlight them for the instructor and student, the text includes a margin note and Encore CD icon next to the related chapter discussion.
- **Quizzes:** The Encore CD includes a rich bank of multiple-choice quizzes available in both practice and reported modes. In the practice mode, students receive immediate feedback on each quiz item and a report of his or her total score. In the reported mode, the results are e-mailed to both the student and instructor. Book-level and chapter-specific quizzes are available.
- **Glossary:** Key terms and definitions are combined with related illustrations from the text.
- **Image Bank:** Illustrations of concepts are accompanied by the related terms and definitions.
- **Flash Cards:** Flash cards are a fun way to learn Internet concepts. Each chapter is supported by this interactive, game-like feature.

Students will find other useful learning aids on the Internet Resource Center at **www.emcp.net/Internet2e**. At this site, students can access chapter-specific Study Notes documents, PowerPoint presentations, interactive chapter quizzes, a complete glossary, and the end-of-chapter exercises. The Internet Resource Center also includes Windows Vista and Internet tutorials; tips for communicating online, taking tests, and achieving course success; resources for creating Web pages; and other valuable resources.

www.emcp.net/Internet2e

Instructor Resources

Instructor resources include course planning tools such as a grading sheet, course objectives, and syllabus suggestion; teaching hints for each chapter; answers to the Concept Review questions; Net Check answers; PowerPoint teaching slides; and chapter quizzes and unit tests. All of these instructor resources are furnished on both the password-protected instructor pages of the Internet Resource Center at **www.emcp.net/Internet2e** and on the Instructor Resources CD. These resources also come pre-loaded on WebCT and Blackboard Class Connections.

This edition is also supported by an ExamView test generator. Instructors can use the bank of 500 multiple choice and true/false items to create customized, Web-based, or print tests.

UNIT 1

Using the Internet

- **Understanding the Internet**
- **Accessing the Internet**
- **Ensuring Internet Security**

Chapter 1

Understanding the Internet

Learning Objectives

- Define open architecture philosophy and explain its importance to the development of the Internet.

- Describe circuit and packet switching and explain how they work.

- Define the role and function of TCP/IP.

- Describe IP addresses and domain names.

- Explain the function of HTML in creating Web pages.

- Describe how hyperlinks work.

- Explain the concepts behind computer networking and how they relate to the development of the Internet.

- Differentiate between an intranet and an extranet.

- Explain wireless networking and describe its advantages and disadvantages.

- Examine and evaluate Internet2's role in the development of new Internet technologies and applications.

Living on the Net

A soft buzzing from his alarm clock tells Bob Wagoner that it is time to get up for work. After eating breakfast, he turns on his personal computer (PC) to check his e-mail before going to work. He is excited to see a message from his girlfriend, Carolyn. She is in Rome on business and writes to tell him how much she misses him. He types a short message to her, letting her know the feeling is mutual, and then clicks the Send button to transmit his reply. Before shutting down his computer, Bob checks the CNN and BBC Web sites to read the latest news, and checks his investments at his broker's Web site. Soon Bob realizes he may be late for work, so he shuts off his computer and heads out the door.

One of the first items on Bob's agenda after arriving at work is a Web conference to discuss some new product developments with affiliates located in Southeast Asia. Once the conference concludes, Bob checks his work e-mail account and communicates with customers located around the world. Because he has so much work to do, Bob decides to eat lunch at his desk. Suddenly, he remembers that he needs to get some additional tax forms from the IRS so that he can file his tax return on time. The IRS Web site offers the forms he needs via download. Bob downloads the forms and attaches them to a message that he sends to his personal e-mail account, so he can later print the forms at home.

The afternoon passes quickly, and Bob is ready to call it a day. While driving he realizes that he did not receive an e-mail message he had been expecting from a supplier. Rather than waiting until he gets home to access his e-mail account, Bob pulls over and uses his Web-enabled cellular phone to check his work e-mail account again. Seeing that there is still no reply, he sends a short message reminding the supplier to send a response. Soon Bob is back home, where he relaxes by tuning into a Swedish Internet radio station that uses streaming technology to broadcast jazz over the Internet. Before going to bed, he sends one more e-mail to Carolyn.

The events in Bob's day provide just a few examples of the many ways that the Internet can make life easier. In the relatively few years that the Internet has been available to the public, the increase in both the number of different applications available and the number of Internet users has been nothing short of astounding. Before learning more about using the Internet, study how the Internet developed to understand how it works.

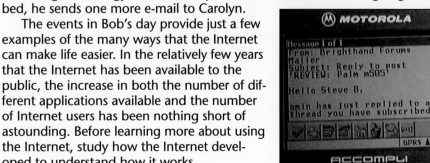

Development of the Internet

The concept of the Internet is generally attributed to a Massachusetts Institute of Technology (MIT) professor named J.C.R. Licklider, who in 1962 described a future "Galactic Network" of linked computers that would enable everyone access to computer resources. While the wisdom of this idea seems obvious now, at the time many computer industry experts thought that sharing computers was a waste of valuable resources and thus did not support Licklider's visionary idea. Fortunately, Licklider had a chance to develop his ideas thanks to the Advanced Research Projects Agency (ARPA). ARPA was established under the control of the U.S. Department of Defense in 1958 to help the United States win the "space race" that began with the Soviet Union's successful 1957 launch of Sputnik, the world's first man-made satellite.

In 1962, J.C.R. Licklider went to work for ARPA as head of the computer research program, where he continued to promote his computer network ideas. A few years later, a former MIT researcher named Lawrence G. Roberts joined ARPA, and in 1967 he published his plan for a computer network called the ***ARPANET***. The ARPANET became a reality in 1969, when four computer networks were linked through telephone lines, creating the precursor of what we now know as the Internet. Figure 1.1 shows the original hand-drawn schematic diagram for the ARPANET.

Shortly after the ARPANET's inception, its developers made an important decision by adopting what they termed an open architecture philosophy to encourage other computer networks to link to the ARPANET. At the time, most of the big players in the computer industry operated under a closed architecture philosophy and deliberately made their local networks incom-patible with competitors' networks to lock customers into relying on a particular system. The open architecture philosophy adopted by the ARPANET did not require changes to internal network operations and thus facilitated connection to the ARPANET. Thanks to the adoption of open architecture philosophy, over 200 computers were connected to the ARPANET by 1981.

By the 1980s other large networks not connected with the ARPANET appeared. For example, BITNET connected mainframe computers at educational institutions across the country. The arrival of personal computers (PCs) in the 1980s accelerated the spread of computer networking. Eventually, the National Science Foundation (NSF) created NSFnet to connect non-ARPANET networks. In 1984, security concerns saw the ARPANET split in two—MILNET for military operations and ARPANET for research. In 1989, the last ARPANET node was shut down, and the NSFnet became the sole backbone for the fledgling Internet. A ***backbone*** is a high-speed line that forms the major pathway for a network. NSFnet was restricted initially to noncommercial purposes, but the NSF lifted that restriction in 1991.

ARPANET the first packet-switched computer network

backbone a high-speed line that forms the major pathway for a network

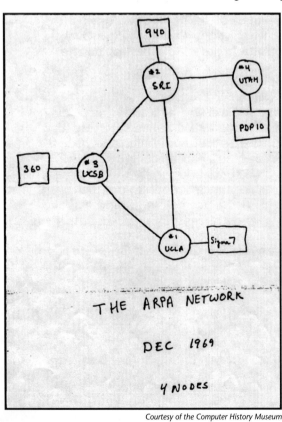

Courtesy of the Computer History Museum

Figure 1.1 Original ARPANET Schematic Diagram

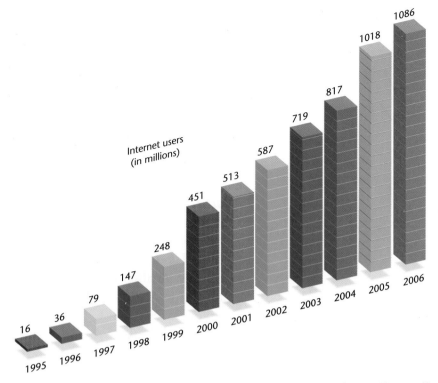

Figure 1.2 Internet Growth Statistics

Source: www.internetworldstats.com

In 1995, the NSF made the decision to stop supporting the backbone, transferring the responsibility for providing Internet access to private-sector organizations. The same year, large nationwide dial-up Internet providers such as AOL, CompuServe, and Prodigy emerged. Once network access was unrestricted, Internet growth increased exponentially, and the Internet became the information superhighway that we know today. Figure 1.2 shows the growth in Internet users between 1995 and late 2006.

Successfully implementing the ARPANET concept involved overcoming a number of technical hurdles, and the solutions to those hurdles provide the basic technical principles underlying today's Internet. The solutions include the packet switching concept used for the transmission of data over the Internet, the paired TCP/IP protocols that enable computers on different networks to communicate, the IP address system used to identify computers connected to the Internet, and the Domain Name System (DNS) that lets computers locate each other using domain names mapped to IP addresses.

Packet Switching

A pre-ARPANET attempt at networking computers over telephone lines proved that Licklider's networking concept was viable but found that the circuit-switched telephone service was not up to the task.

ARPA or DARPA?

You may have seen ARPA sometimes referred to as DARPA, or vice versa. If you are confused, you are not alone. Known as ARPA at its founding in 1958, the agency's name was changed to the Defense Advanced Research Projects Agency (DARPA) in 1972. In 1993, the government decided that DARPA should once again be known as ARPA, but three years later changed the name back to DARPA. What has not changed is the agency's responsibility, "for the direction or performance of such advanced projects in the field of research and development as the Secretary of Defense shall, from time to time, designate by individual project or by category." The agency was created to promote thinking "outside the box," but its efforts are not always as successful as the ARPANET. A former director noted that 85 to 90 percent of the agency's projects failed to meet their objectives.

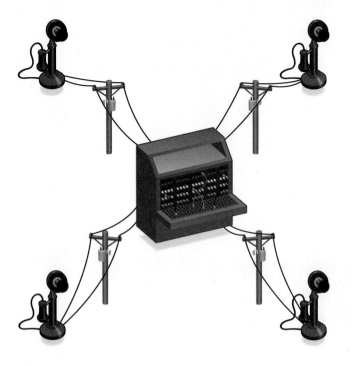

Figure 1.3 Circuit-Switched Line

In ***circuit switching***, single telephone circuits (lines) are connected through a central switchboard as shown in Figure 1.3. Because this type of connection depends on a single link, it is vulnerable to interruptions due to any number of causes, such as downed lines, electrical interference, switchboard problems, and so on. Circuit switching is also inefficient because the circuit in use cannot be used by others.

Packet switching provided the solution to the obstacles circuit switching presented to networking computers. Packet switching separates data into small packets that can be routed individually through a number of circuits, rather than sending the data in one continuous stream through a single circuit. A header in each packet identifies its source, its destination, and its relationship to other packets. Devices known as routers use sets of rules known as routing algorithms to determine the best route for packets and then forward the packets on their way. When packets reach their destination, they are examined and reassembled in their original format as shown in Figure 1.4. If any packets are missing, the system sends a notice requesting that the missing packet be resent.

The fact that packet switching is not dependent on a single path for success provides a significant advantage. If a circuit is defective or unavailable, the network can send a packet through another circuit. Packet switching is also more efficient than circuit switching because circuits can be filled to capacity with a continuous stream of packets.

circuit switching a method for transmitting data using single telephone circuits (lines) connected through a central switchboard

packet switching a data transmission method where large chunks of data are divided into packets that can travel along any number of different circuits until the packets are collected and the data reassembled in its original form at the destination

protocol a set of rules that enables computers to communicate

TCP/IP

The ARPANET needed a method to reconcile the different protocols and data transmission methods used by member networks. A ***protocol*** is a set of rules that enables computers to communicate. The Network Control Protocol (NCP) used by the ARPANET was not designed with open architecture in

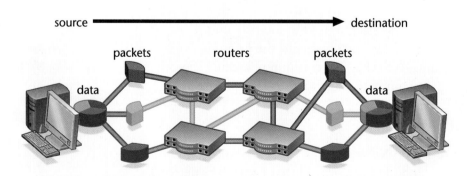

Figure 1.4 Packet Switching

mind so a replacement protocol was required. In 1983, NCP was supplanted by a new set of paired protocols called *TCP/IP (Transmission Control Protocol/ Internet Protocol)*. The IP part of the protocol handles the breakdown of data into packets, while the TCP part ensures that the packets are delivered and reassembled in the correct order. TCP/IP remains the protocol used by the Internet to this day.

Internet Protocol (IP) Address

TCP/IP provided the many computers and devices connected to the ARPANET with a way to identify and locate each other. A network using the TCP/IP protocol assigns a unique identifying number known as an *Internet Protocol (IP) address* to every computer or device on the network. The IP address identifies the node and the network to which the computer is attached, so different computers can find each other and communicate. Although computers process data using the binary numbering system composed of ones and zeroes, IP addresses use a decimal format referred to as dotted decimal notation. Each IP address in dotted decimal notation consists of four numbers separated by a period (or dot), such as 192.168.1.0. Each of the four numbers composing the address is called an octet because in binary form each number occupies eight positions. For example, in binary form 192.168.1.0 is 11000000.10101000.00000001.00000000.

Under Internet Protocol Version 4 (IPv4), IP addresses are 32-bit numbers, determined by adding all the IP address positions (8+8+8+8=32). In decimal form, each octet can contain any value from 0 to 255, and the total number of unique values possible is 4,294,967,296.

In addition to identifying the network and node, the octets in an IP address also identify the class the address belongs to, which is why this system is sometimes referred to as classful. There are five classes:

- Class A: large networks (begins with 0–127 decimal or 0 binary)
- Class B: medium-sized networks (begins with 128–191 decimal or 10 binary)
- Class C: small networks (begins with 192–223 decimal or 110 binary)
- Class D: multicast addresses (begins with 224–239 decimal or 1110 binary)
- Class E: experimental (begins with 240–254 or 1111 binary)

The first octet in any IP address identifies its class. For example, the IP address used as an example in the previous paragraph (192.168.1.0) belongs to Class C because it begins with 192.

Octets also determine the parts of an address that identify the network and node attached to the network. For example, in a Class A IP address (beginning 0–127), the first octet identifies the network, while the remaining three octets identify the node. In a Class B IP address, the first two octets identify the network and the remaining two identify the node, and in a Class C IP address, the first three octets identify the network and the remaining octet identifies the node. Figure 1.5 shows this concept in graphic form.

Class A: NNNNNNNN.nnnnnnnn.nnnnnnnn.nnnnnnnn

Class B: NNNNNNNN.NNNNNNNN.nnnnnnnn.nnnnnnnn

Class C: NNNNNNNN.NNNNNNNN.NNNNNNNN.nnnnnnnn

Figure 1.5 IP Address Network and Node Breakdown (N=Network, n=Node)

TCP/IP (Transmission Control Protocol/Internet Protocol) paired protocols that handle the breakdown of data into packets and ensure that packets are delivered and then reassembled in the correct order

Internet Protocol (IP) address an address that identifies the node and the network to which a device is attached so that other computers and devices can find it and communicate

The developers of the IP address system perhaps thought that it contained more than enough numbers (a few more than 4.2 billion) to handle all the computers connected to networks around the world for quite a long time. Unfortunately, IP address availability problems have arisen because nobody anticipated the Internet expanding to the size it is today. Even more importantly, IP addresses were allocated inefficiently because the body allocating IP addresses granted large blocks to organizations that often used only a small portion of the IP addresses they were awarded.

Several workarounds have been developed to try to prevent the Internet from running out of IP addresses. One method, ***subnetting***, sets aside special IP addresses for intranets—private TCP/IP networks used within companies or organizations. The reserved IP addresses are not permitted on the Internet. When packets need to be sent from the intranet to the Internet, a program known as a ***network address translator (NAT)*** converts the private IP addresses into permitted IP addresses that can travel on the Internet. Subnetting reduces the need for IP addresses because only a small percentage of IP addresses used on intranets communicate with the Internet. Thus, the same reserved IP addresses can be used on internal networks operated by different organizations, thereby reducing the number of IP addresses that need to be allocated.

Another method for conserving IP addresses called Classless InterDomain Routing (CIDR) or supernetting eliminates the classful IP address system. A CIDR address will contain a slash, such as */8* for Class A or */16* for Class B.

Subnetting and supernetting serve as short term solutions to the problem of dwindling IP address availability. A more permanent solution will arrive with the full implementation of Internet Protocol Version 6 (IPv6), which features 128-bit addresses using hexadecimal (16-digit) numbers. Under IPv6, also referred to as IP next generation (IPng), there will be enough addresses for every person on earth to have more than a billion IP addresses even under a worst case scenario. IPv6 will gradually replace IPv4, but the two systems will coexist for some time. In appearance, IPv6 addresses differ from current IPv4 addresses by using colons instead of dots, and hexadecimal digits instead of decimal digits.

Domain Name System (DNS)

While IP addresses allow networked computers and devices to be identified, the long strings of numbers are difficult for most users to remember. The ***Domain Name System (DNS)*** created in 1983 addresses this problem by mapping a domain name to an IP address. For example, the domain name for the CNN Web site IP address 64.236.29.120 is www.cnn.com. For most people remembering www.cnn.com is a lot easier that remembering 64.236.29.120. Domain name servers are used to convert domain names back into IP addresses that can be understood by other servers.

Domain names are hierarchical and read from right to left, with the rightmost portion of the domain name referred to as a ***top-level domain (TLD)***, or sometimes as an extension. In the www.cnn.com example, *.com* is the top-level domain. Table 1.1 lists the limited number of generic top-level domains in use. In addition to the limited number of generic TLDs, every country has its own country code TLD, such as .au for Australia, .ca for Canada, and so on.

subnetting a method that sets aside special IP addresses for intranets

network address translator (NAT) a program used to change private IP addresses into permitted IP addresses that can travel on the Internet

Domain Name System (DNS) a system for mapping a domain name to an IP address

top-level domain (TLD) the rightmost portion of the domain name (for example, .com), sometimes referred to as an extension

A country code TLD does not necessarily mean that a domain originates in the country indicated by its TLD. Some countries have residency requirements for those wishing to use their country code TLD, while others permit registration by anybody showing up with the required fees.

Every network has a DNS server that locates IP addresses to make a connection. If a local DNS server does not know the location of an IP address, it passes the IP address to a root DNS server that knows the location of the top-level DNS servers. The root DNS server then passes the request on to the appropriate DNS server handling the top-level domain specified in the IP address, such as .com. The top-level DNS server next passes on the request to the DNS server handling the requested IP address. That DNS server then notifies the DNS server originating the request that it knows the IP address and a network connection can be made. Redundancy built into the system ensures that if one server fails, others will take its place to resolve an address. DNS servers also save IP addresses so a DNS server need not contact other DNS servers for an address it handled recently.

Since 1997, the Internet Corporation for Assigned Names and Numbers (ICANN) has been responsible for managing the Domain Name System, ensuring that each domain name maps to the correct IP address. ICANN also is responsible for accrediting domain name registrars, bodies that enable users to register for and receive a domain name. ICANN maintains a list of approved registrars as shown in Figure 1.6.

Table 1.1 Top-Level Generic and Country Code Domains

Top-Level Domain	Reserved For
.aero	global aviation industry
.biz	businesses
.cat	Catalan linguistic and cultural community
.com	commercial
.coop	cooperatives
.edu	educational institutions
.gov	United States government
.info	unrestricted use
.jobs	human resource management community
.mil	United States military
.mobi	consumers and providers of mobile products and services
.museum	museums
.name	individuals
.net	service providers
.org	nonprofit organizations
.pro	licensed professionals
.travel	travel industry
.cc (country code), e.g., .nz for New Zealand	countries

Figure 1.6 ICANN Top-Level Domain Registrars

www.icann.com

1. Describe how packet switching works.
2. What role does TCP/IP play in the Internet?
3. What is dotted decimal notation?
4. How does an IP address identify the class to which it belongs?
5. How do DNS servers locate an IP address?
6. Explain the relationship between domain names and IP addresses.

Skill
Review 1 **Conduct a Domain Name Search** •

1. If necessary, connect to the Internet.
2. Start Internet Explorer.
3. Open the Network Solutions Whois Web site (www.networksolutions.com/whois) by typing the URL in the Internet Explorer Address bar and then pressing the Enter key. *(Note: If the URL fails to work, try a Google search using the key terms* **Network Solutions.***)*

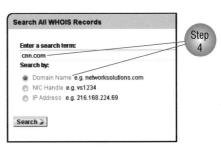

4. Type **cnn.com** in the *Enter a search term* text box. Make sure the *Domain Name* option is selected and then click the Search button.
5. Use the information you find to type or write answers to the following questions:
    a. Who is the domain name cnn.com registered to?
    b. What is the name of the current domain name registrar for cnn.com?
    c. What is the IP address for cnn.com?

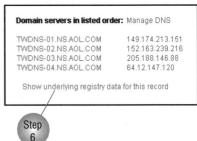

6. Click the Show underlying registry data for this record link to obtain additional registration data and answer the following questions:
    a. When was the cnn.com domain name first registered?
    b. When does the registration expire?

Development of Internet Applications

File Transfer Protocol (FTP) a program developed for the ARPANET that provided a standard means of transferring files

graphical user interface (GUI) a computer interface (window element) that uses graphics instead of text

Developers soon created applications to take advantage of the opportunities afforded by the ARPANET. (An application is a computer program that performs a specific task or function.) One of the first, electronic mail (e-mail), was soon followed by Telnet, an application that enabled users to access remote computers. Shortly after Telnet made its appearance, *File Transfer Protocol (FTP)* made it possible to use an FTP client to upload and download files from remote computers. Perhaps most importantly, in 1991 the World Wide Web (the Web or WWW) emerged. By enabling the use of *graphical user interface (GUI)* browser programs, the Web made accessing information a simple task that even nonprofessionals could perform. A GUI computer interface presents information and enables navigation via graphics instead of text.

E-mail (Electronic Mail)

Computers linked by the ARPANET could talk to each other, but network users could only communicate with other users if they were both logged onto the same mainframe computer. Somewhat surprisingly, there was no way for one user to leave a message for another if the person with whom they wanted to communicate was not logged on. The first program for leaving messages, called SNDMSG, could not be used to communicate from one computer to another. In 1971, a researcher named Ray Tomlinson modified SNDMSG so that it could be used to send and receive mes-

Figure 1.7 First Computers to Send and Receive E-mail

sages from computer to computer, creating what we now know as e-mail (electronic mail). The first e-mail message was sent through the ARPANET between two mainframe computers located next to each other as shown in Figure 1.7. E-mail became one of the first of many unanticipated benefits of the Internet. Within six months, e-mail became the most popular service on the ARPANET, a rank it still holds today on the Internet.

TELNET and FTP

In 1972, a protocol called Telnet was introduced on the ARPANET. Telnet enabled users to access a remote computer (host) and work with files and programs stored there, and very quickly became a popular method for listing library card catalogs online as shown in Figure 1.8. Telnet suffered from one drawback—it did not enable users to send (upload) or receive (download) files. That capability came in 1973 when File Transfer Protocol (FTP) was developed to provide a standard means of transferring files on the ARPANET. Users could upload and download files from one computer to another by using

```
                    WELCOME to ALICE              OU:All Locations
            The Ohio University Libraries On-Line Catalog
       Serving Athens, Chillicothe, Eastern, Lancaster, Southern,
                      and Zanesville Campuses
       You may search for Library materials by any of the following:
              A > AUTHOR
              T > TITLE
              B > AUTHOR/TITLE
              S > LIBRARY OF CONGRESS SUBJECT
              M > MeSH (Medical) SUBJECT
              C > CALL NUMBERS
              O > OTHER indexes
              W > KEYWORDS
              P > Repeat PREVIOUS Search
              R > RESERVE Lists
              D > Library INFORMATION
              U > Search OHIOLINK Central Catalog
              V > VIEW your circulation record
              X > DISCONNECT
              Choose one (A,T,B,S,M,C,O,W,P,R,D,U,V,X) █

                         FOR ASSISTANCE:
             Athens Alden Library ask at the Reference Desk.
       Chillicothe, Eastern, Lancaster, Southern & Zanesville ask at Circ Desk.
```

Figure 1.8 Telnet Screen Showing Library Card Catalog

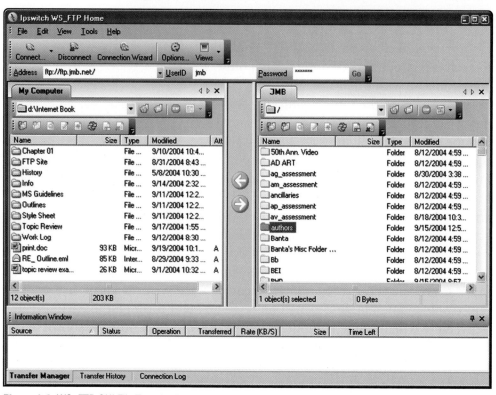

Figure 1.9 WS_FTP GUI File Transfer Protocol Program

an FTP program that implemented the protocol. In those early days prior to graphical user interfaces (GUIs), Telnet and FTP required users to know and enter different commands at a command prompt, making them less than user friendly by today's standards. FTP is still the dominant method for transferring files on the Internet. GUI FTP programs such as WS_FTP shown in Figure 1.9 make using FTP very easy. Most Internet applications involving file transfers have an FTP program running in the background.

World Wide Web (WWW)

The creation of the World Wide Web by Tim Berners-Lee in 1991 marks the most important milestone in the development of the Internet so far. The Web's system of hyperlinked (linked) documents accessible through a browser (a software program that enables users to view Internet resources) vastly expanded the utility of the Internet and made using the Internet a simple point-and-click activity. As Berners-Lee later noted, "The Web made the net useful because people are really interested in information (not to mention knowledge and wisdom!), and don't really want to have to know about computers and cables" (www.w3.org). Berners-Lee developed a document authoring language called Hypertext Markup Language (HTML) and the concept of Uniform Resource Locators (URLs) to make hyperlinks possible.

**Tech Demo 1-1
URL Structure**

Hypertext Markup Language (HTML)

Tim Berners-Lee was a consultant working at CERN (*Conseil Européen pour la Recherche Nucléaire* or European Organization for Nuclear Research) when he became frustrated with the difficulty he had retrieving his list of phone numbers, daily planner listings, and documents that were stored in databases

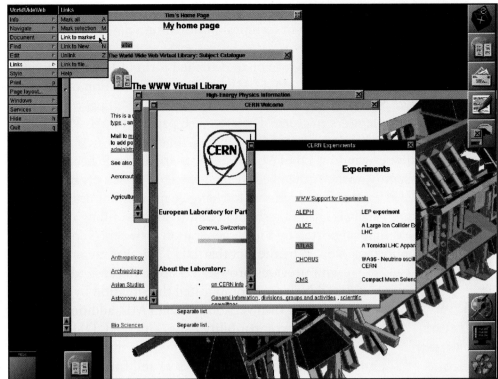

Figure 1.10 The Earliest Example of a Web Page

Source: www.w3.org

located in different computer databases. In his words, "I wanted a program that could store random associations between arbitrary pieces of information" (www.w3.org). The end result of his efforts was a browser he named WorldWideWeb. WorldWideWeb was a GUI point-and-click browser that could download and display documents, images, animations, sound files—in short just about anything on the Internet. Figure 1.10 shows the earliest known screenshot of a Web page in a browser window, created when Berners-Lee was developing the Web.

To make his WorldWideWeb browser work, Berners-Lee created a new protocol enabling communication between a client (a host or node computer on a network) and file servers (the computers that store information on a network) called *HyperText Transfer Protocol (HTTP)*. He also created the *HyperText Markup Language (HTML)* for designing Web documents, and the Uniform Resource Locator (URL) method for locating documents that incorporates domain names. Berners-Lee derived HTML from a metalanguage known as Standard Generalized Markup Language (SGML). SGML is a very powerful and complex text markup system originally developed for electronic publishing.

In an HTML document, HTML tags applied to the text tell a browser program how to display the marked up text. Each HTML tag is enclosed by paired angle brackets (< >), and the tags are generally used in pairs, with the second or closing tag containing a forward slash before the tag name. To display the sentence *This is an example of italicized text*, paired <i> tags would enclose the sentence to instruct browsers to italicize the text, for example `<i>This is an example of italicized text</i>`.

In its early days HTML was not standardized, and the various interpretations of HTML led to compatibility problems. To address this issue, Tim Berners-Lee formed the World Wide Web Consortium (W3C) in 1994 to

HyperText Transfer Protocol (HTTP) protocol enabling communication between a client and file servers

HyperText Markup Language (HTML) computer language used to design Web documents

develop and maintain open standards for the Web. The W3C Web page (www.w3.org) contains a wealth of technical information related to the World Wide Web.

Many Web pages today make use of an extended form of HTML known as **Dynamic HTML (DHTML)**. DHTML utilizes a combination of HTML, **Cascading Style Sheets (CSS)** a method for formatting Web pages, and **JavaScript** to enable users to create dynamic Web pages. HTML Web pages are static, meaning that page content does not change unless a new page is loaded in a browser window. DHTML Web pages are dynamic because they can change instantly, without the need to change pages. When created via DHTML, a Web page can enable users to change page content using mouse clicks to do things such as changing slides in a slide show or filling out forms.

DHTML was first supported by fourth generation browsers (version 4.*x*), but initial adoption was slowed by the fact that DHTML was incompatible with previous browser versions. Because Microsoft and Netscape complicated the situation by developing their own versions of DHTML, additional cross-browser compatibility issues emerged. DHTML usage increased dramatically with the gradual disappearance of pre-4.*x* browsers and Internet Explorer's almost total dominance of browser market share.

HTML is being phased out slowly in favor of **eXtensible HTML (XHTML)**. The W3C plans no more enhancements to the most recent version of HTML (4.01) and instead will create HTML enhancements starting with XHTML 1.0. The W3C calls XHTML the "next step in the evolution of the Internet." XHTML combines HTML 4.01 elements with the syntax used by XML, an SGML-derived metalanguage. Because HTML was designed to display data and XML was designed to describe data, proponents say combining the two into XHTML results in an enhanced markup language that will serve as a transition to eventual full implementation of XML, although no target date has been set for the switchover.

The Origin of Hypertext

The key principle behind the Web is the concept of hypertext. Many people credit a former science advisor to President Roosevelt named Vannevar Bush with originating the idea of hypertext. In a 1945 article in the *Atlantic Monthly*, he described his idea for a mechanized desk he called the Memex that would enable users access to hundreds or even thousands of microfilmed documents and files at the tap of a keyboard. Although Bush did not call it hypertext, his description of the ability to move between or within documents using text links provided the concept for what later became known as hypertext,

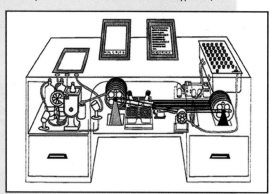

text that contains links (hyperlinks) to other documents. In 1960, a computer visionary named Ted Nelson began Project Xanadu, an ambitious project that would make the document-linking concepts behind Vannevar Bush's Memex a reality. Unfortunately, Nelson's Project Xanadu was never completed, although many of its goals were achieved with the appearance of the World Wide Web.

Source: Bush, Vannevar. "As We May Think." The Atlantic Monthly 176:1 (1945): 101-108.

Uniform Resource Locators (URLs)

Uniform Resource Locators (URLs) are addresses that provide the path to a document or location on the Internet. As shown in Figure 1.11, a URL contains the protocol to be used (http:// for Web pages), the domain name, and the path to the linked document or location. In the path portion of a URL forward slashes (/) set off folder names, and the last portion of a URL contains the file or object name, such as apple.html for a Web page or grand_canyon.jpg for an image. When the user enters a URL into a browser address bar as shown in Figure 1.11, the browser will use the information contained in the URL to locate a document and display it in the browser window. If a file name is not included in a URL, the browser will locate and a load a file named index.html (or sometimes .htm) that is usually a home page. A home page is the gateway or index document for a Web site.

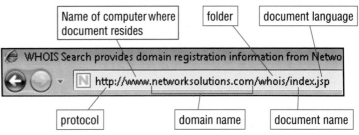

Figure 1.11 Uniform Resource Locator (URL)

Hyperlinks (Links)

Clicking a hyperlink in a document can take a user to another document located on a nearby computer, or to a document or object located on a server thousands of miles away. Links in HTML are created using HTML starting and ending anchor tags and href attributes as shown in Figure 1.12. The paired anchor tags surround the text or object (such as an image file name) that will become a link. The href attribute directs a browser to the link target by specifying a path to the link target's location. For example, `<a href="page_2.htm"> Page Two</a>` makes a link out of the enclosed Page Two text. Clicking the Page Two link displayed in the browser window directs a browser to find and open the link target

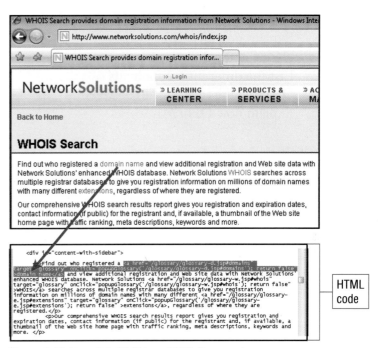

Figure 1.12 Hyperlink (Link) in an HTML Document

in the browser window, in this case a document named page_2.htm. This type of path is called a ***document relative path*** and is used to link to documents that are located in the same folder as the document containing the hyperlink. Document relative paths do not contain a protocol and also omit any portion of a path that is the same for the linking document and the target document. For example, a document in a folder could be linked to another document in the same folder using a relative path consisting only of the target document's file name, such as report.html.

A link to a document located on another server must use an ***absolute document path***. Absolute document paths resemble relative paths except that they include the complete URL for a linked document or object as well as the protocol to be used. A link containing an absolute path to the Network Solutions Web site would look like this: `<a href="http://www.networksolutions. com">NetworkSolutions</a>`. You will learn more about URLs and hyperlinks in the HTML chapters of this textbook.

Figure 1.13 shows an HTML document (Web page) displayed in a browser with hyperlinks in underlined blue text. This is the traditional format for hyperlinks, but

document relative path document path used to link to documents that are located in the same folder as the document containing the hyperlink

absolute document path document path containing all the information needed to link to a document located on another server, beginning with the protocol and ending with the file name

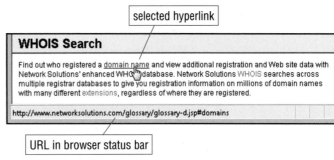

Figure 1.13 A Selected Hyperlink

many Web page designers have moved away from underlining links. Placing the mouse pointer over a link causes it to change into a hand shape, causes the URL to change color, and displays the URL for the link in the browser status bar if it is enabled as shown in Figure 1.13. Clicking the link directs the browser to locate and display the document or object indicated by the URL.

Concept Review 2 Development of Internet Applications

1. Explain how hyperlinks work.
2. Describe the difference between relative and absolute paths.
3. List the different components of a typical URL.
4. Describe the relationship between SGML, HTML, and XHTML.
5. Explain how DHTML works.

Skill Review 2 Discover Hypertext and Hyperlinks

1. If necessary, connect to the Internet.
2. Start Internet Explorer.
3. Open the CNN home page (www.cnn.com).
4. Click the right mouse button and then click View Source from the shortcut menu that appears. *(Hint: Take care to right-click on a blank portion of the web page or on text. Do not right-click on a picture or you will get a different shortcut menu.)*

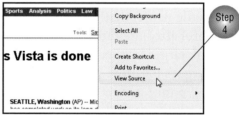

5. Click the Maximize button in the Notepad window to expand Notepad and view the HTML source code for the Web page.
6. Find and then select the code from the starting tag to the ending tag. Copy the code for the hyperlink by right-clicking and then clicking Copy in the shortcut menu. *(Hint: Use the Notepad search function to search for and find an href attribute by clicking Edit on the menu bar and then Find and typing href. Look to the left of the href attribute to find the starting anchor tag [<a] and to the right of the href attribute to find the closing anchor tag [</a].)*

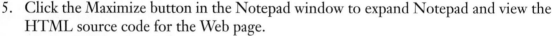

7. Paste the code into a Word document by right-clicking and then clicking Paste or by clicking Edit on the menu bar and then clicking Paste. Print the document. Circle and identify the anchor tags, href attribute, and the hyperlink.

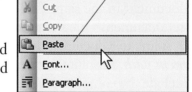

8. Exit Word and Notepad without saving the documents.

Web Browsers

In a very altruistic move, Tim Berners-Lee declared that he was not interested in personally profiting from his invention, and to promote the development of the Web he placed the WWW concepts and protocols in the public domain. This enabled others to make modifications and improvements to the WWW.

In 1993, a graduate student at the University of Illinois (Urbana) National Center for Supercomputing Applications (NCSA) named Marc Andreesen was involved in creating a new browser based on the Mosaic browser he helped develop while at the NCSA, shown in Figure 1.14. Mosaic incorporated significant improvements over Berners-Lee's original browser and successor browsers, making Mosaic easier to install and use. Perhaps most importantly, Mosaic could display in-line images, whereas previous browsers opened images in separate windows. Mosaic was free and available for the Unix, Windows, and Apple MacIntosh operating systems.

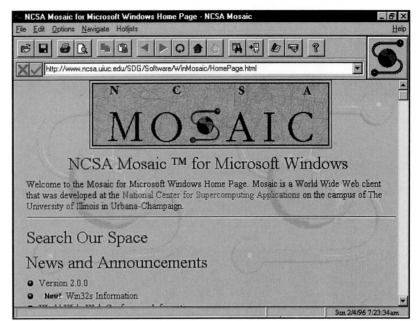

Figure 1.14 Mosaic Browser Window

Andreesen named his new browser Netscape after a losing legal battle with the NCSA over the rights to the name Mosaic. Netscape introduced now-common browser features such as frames, Java, JavaScript, and plug-ins. By 1995, Netscape captured 80 percent of the market share for browsers. In the same year, Microsoft launched Windows 95 and its own Web browser, Internet Explorer, and the "Browser Wars" were on. While Netscape was available for a fee, Microsoft offered Internet Explorer for free, and it soon came included with Windows. Netscape began playing catch up, and by 1998 when Netscape decided to give away its browser, it had already lost the lead to Internet Explorer. The browser market currently includes a number of different offerings in addition to the ubiquitous Internet Explorer, including Opera, Mozilla, Netscape Navigator, and most recently Mozilla Firefox.

Concept Review 3 Web Browsers ●

1. Why did Tim Berners-Lee decide not to profit from his invention of the WWW?
2. Describe the origin of the Netscape browser.
3. Name some of the now-common browser features that Netscape introduced.
4. Which Web browser currently has the largest market share?

Skill Review 3 Explore the World Wide Web

1. If necessary, connect to the Internet.
2. Start Internet Explorer.
3. Go to the World Wide Web Consortium (W3C) home page (www.w3.org).
4. Type **short web history** in the Google *Search W3C* text box and then click the Go button.
5. Click the search titled <u>The World Wide Web: A very short personal history</u> and then read the short history.

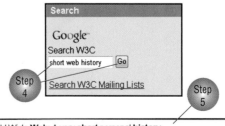

6. Click the <u>Back to main bio</u> link at the bottom of the page and then read the page.
7. Click the <u>Frequently Asked Questions</u> link on the Main Bio page to learn more about the Web.
8. After you have read the FAQ, write or type short answers to the following questions:
   a. What does Tim Berners-Lee think about domain squatting?
   b. Did he invent the Internet?
   c. What is the difference between the Net and the Web?
   d. What is metadata?
   e. What was Viola?

See also
Longer Bio
Research at MIT-CSAIL
Talks
Design Issues: web architecture
World Wide Web Consortium
Frequently Asked Questions
Kids' Questions
blog
Weaving the Web - the book

Step 7

Computer Networks

Understanding the different types of networks that make up the Internet is essential to understanding how the Internet works. A computer network refers to two or more computers linked together so that they can communicate and share resources. Two or more networks joined together are referred to as an internet (lowercase i). The Internet (uppercase I) is the global network of networks that connects computers around the world. While many people think that the World Wide Web (WWW or the Web) and the Internet are one and the same, the Web is actually just one of many Internet applications.

While computers directly linked together form ***peer-to-peer networks***, more often they are linked to form ***client/server networks***, where computers known as clients and other network devices such as printers connect to a central computer known as a server. A server provides services to other computers, such as handling requests and sharing resources that may be located on the server. A computer or device connected to a network is also known as a node or host. Clients also can act as hosts to other clients. Computer networks can connect computers in an office or university, a city, a state, or even a country. Figure 1.15 presents a simplified diagram of a client/server network.

peer-to-peer network a network in which computers are linked directly to one another

client/server network a network in which computers or devices (clients) are linked to a central computer known as a server

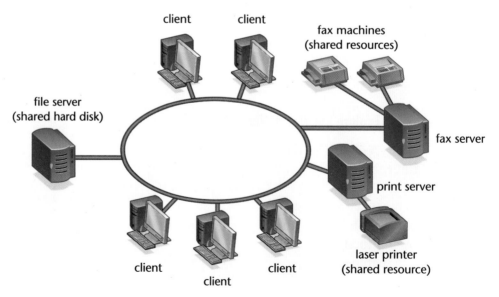

Figure 1.15 Client/Server Network

Computer networks are generally classified in terms of the area they cover or distance they extend. For example, a *local area network (LAN)* is usually defined as a network within a single building or adjacent buildings, with a maximum coverage area of approximately half a mile. A *wide area network (WAN)* links LANs and extends over a much wider geographic area, which could be a city, a state, or even a country. The Internet is the largest example of a WAN. Other distance-based network classifications fall between the LAN/WAN dichotomy, such as metropolitan area network (MAN), used to describe networks connecting a metropolitan area, or personal area network (PAN), in which infrared or wireless technology connects computer devices used by an individual. Figure 1.16 contains a simplified hierarchical network diagram.

While the first networks physically connected devices using cables or wires, wireless networks use radio waves to communicate. The area-based network classifications also describe wireless networks when prefixed with *wireless*, such as wireless local area network (WLAN), wireless metropolitan area network (WMAN), and so on.

local area network (LAN) a network within a single building or adjacent buildings with a maximum coverage area of approximately half a mile

wide area network (WAN) a network that links LANs and extends over a much wider geographic area, which could be a city, state, or even country; the Internet is the largest example of a WAN

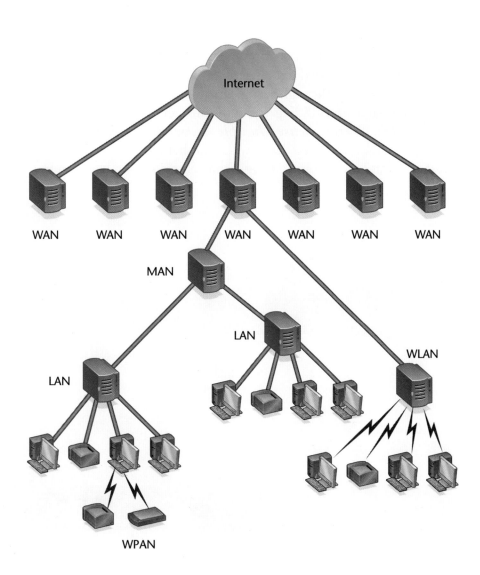

Figure 1.16 Network Hierarchy

LANs

Local area networks (LANs) first appeared in the early 1970s with the development of **Ethernet** technology, a method for networking computers. LANs enabled communication and data sharing among the different computers connected to the LAN, as well as the ability to share resources such as printers and backup systems. Ethernet remains the most widely used LAN technology today. Ethernet networks initially used coaxial cables as a medium or connecting method. Category 5, 5e (enhanced), or 6 cables are the cable types most frequently used in wired networks today. Category 5e supports connection speeds 10 times as fast as category 5. Category 6 benefits from reduced signal crosstalk and packet loss resulting in speeds faster than category 5e. Coaxial cables support high bandwidth and are resistant to interference because they contain a grounded shield as shown in Figure 1.17. Today's LANs can communicate via a variety of different mediums, including radio frequencies.

The Ethernet protocol differs from the TCP/IP protocol used on the Internet and other internets in that it uses frames to send data through a single medium. Each frame traveling through a medium contains information about its origin and destination as shown in Figure 1.18. Nodes in an Ethernet network examine the address information in a frame and ignore the frame if it is addressed to another node. Ethernet networks offer an interesting feature known as broadcast addresses, which can be used to deliver data to all the nodes on the network.

Because frames travel through a single medium, Ethernet requires a method to prevent frames from colliding with one another if nodes transmit frames at the same time. **Carrier-Sense Multiple Access with Collision Detection (CSMA/CD)** enables a node to detect when another node is transmitting frames, so that it can wait before transmitting frames. If a collision between frames

Ethernet a networking technology used to create LANs

Carrier-Sense Multiple Access with Collision Detection (CSMA/CD) access method used by Ethernet networks to avoid frames colliding with each other if nodes transmit frames at the same time

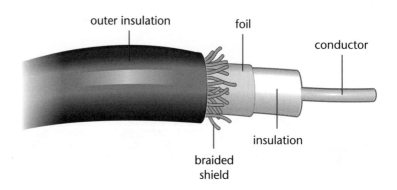

Figure 1.17 Coaxial Cable

Figure 1.18 Ethernet Frame

occurs, the nodes on the network will wait until the medium is clear before resending any frames. The waiting time is random to reduce the chances that nodes will resend frames at the same time as other nodes.

Computers (sometimes referred to as workstations) are connected to a LAN using a *network interface card (NIC)*. Many of the personal computers available today come with NICs preinstalled, making the job of setting up a network easier. A NIC enables a computer to communicate with the LAN server, the computer that coordinates requests from other computers and shares some of its own resources in a client/server network.

WANs

Wide area networks (WANs) connect LANs and can extend over a very wide geographical area, including states, countries, and even the world. For example, the computers in different campus LANs could be connected to a campus WAN that is connected to a regional WAN, which is in turn is connected to the global WAN known as the Internet.

Intranets and Extranets

Intranets and extranets form a subset of LANs and WANs. An *intranet* is a company or organization network for internal use only. To allow for access to the Internet, intranet creators typically install a *firewall*, a hardware or software buffer that prevents unauthorized access to the internal network (intranet). Users accessing an intranet from remote computers are required to log on using user names and passwords as a security measure.

An intranet that shares a portion of its resources with users outside the intranet is known as an *extranet*. Typically an extranet links a company's intranet with its suppliers, vendors, or customers—but not the general public. Figure 1.19 shows the DHL.com Web site, an excellent example of an intranet.

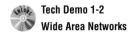

Tech Demo 1-2
Wide Area Networks

- - - - - - - - - -

network interface card (NIC) computer card used to connect a computer or device to a network

intranet a private TCP/IP network used within companies or organizations

firewall hardware and software buffers that prevent unauthorized access to a network

extranet an intranet that shares a portion of its resources with users outside the intranet

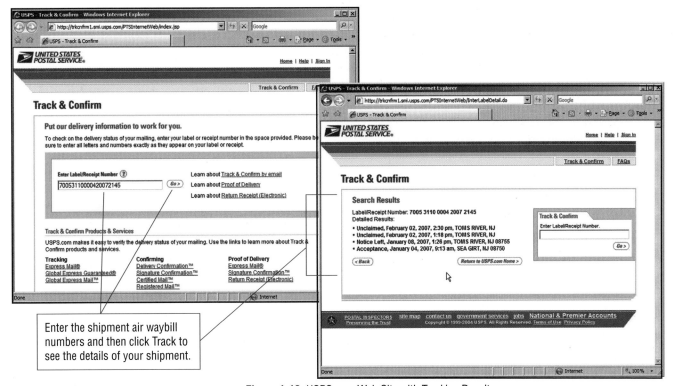

Figure 1.19 USPS.com Web Site with Tracking Results

Customers can use the site to track shipments. The customer enters a tracking number, and the site responds with the real-time location of the shipment, as well as delivery details. While many extranets are carried across dedicated phone lines known as leased lines because they are leased rather than owned, an increasing number use virtual private networks (VPNs), which operate through the Internet using encryption to maintain privacy and security.

Wireless Networks

Wireless networking uses radio waves to connect computers equipped with wireless NICs. While there are a number of different wireless standards in use, most wireless hardware available today supports one or more of the IEEE 802.11 series of specifications (IEEE 802.11a, IEEE 802.11b, and IEEE 802.11g). IEEE stands for the Institute of Electrical and Electronic Engineers, a standards-setting body. IEEE 802.11 networks are often referred to as *Wireless Fidelity (Wi-Fi)*, a term created by the Wi-Fi Alliance, a nonprofit association that promotes the interoperability of wireless products based on IEEE 802.11 specifications. Any product marked Wi-Fi Certified is certified by the Wi-Fi Alliance to be interoperable with other similarly marked products as shown in Figure 1.20.

Wireless networking can be used to connect computers directly to each other in a peer-to-peer network, or to connect computers to an access point that can be used to connect to a wireless LAN or even the Internet as discussed in Chapter 2, *Accessing the Internet*.

Because wireless networks use radio waves to network computers they offer many advantages

Bluetooth

One of the headaches involved with setting up any personal computer system is the clutter of cables needed to connect peripheral devices such as printers and scanners. Besides being unsightly, the need to physically connect devices means that longer cables will probably need to be purchased for any device located more than a few feet from the computer. The Bluetooth wireless standard provides a solution to this problem by allowing almost any type of electronic device to be connected wirelessly, eliminating the need for cable connections. The heart of the system is a relatively inexpensive radio chip that was originally conceived by the Swedish telecommunications giant Ericsson, but is now supported by the Bluetooth Special Interest Group, a trade association formed to develop and promote the technology whose membership includes IBM, Intel, Microsoft, Motorola, Nokia, and Toshiba.

Bluetooth-enabled devices operate on the same 2.4 gHz frequency used by baby monitors and garage door openers and have a range of approximately 10 meters, although some high-powered devices can operate to a range of up to 100 meters. Up to seven devices can be networked at a time in a Bluetooth personal area network referred to as a piconet. To prevent the possibility that any of the devices in a piconet will share the same frequency Bluetooth employs a technique known as frequency-hopping spread-spectrum (FHSS). With FHSS, each device changes frequencies 1,600 times per second to avoid any frequency overlap problems. In theory Bluetooth-enabled devices should locate each other and communicate automatically, but in practice getting the devices to recognize each other and communicate may require some user input.

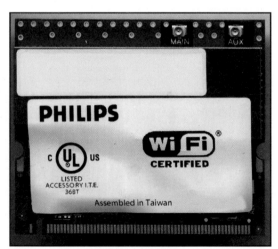

Figure 1.20 Wi-Fi Certification Label

over traditional hard-wired networks. Older buildings may make it impossible or very expensive to set up network connections using cables. Wireless technology can penetrate walls and make such networking straightforward and affordable. Computers and other equipment in a network can be rearranged without the need to move or change cable connections.

Tech Demo 1-3
Wireless Access Point

Concept
Review 4 Computer Networks

1. Describe the various types of computer network classifications.
2. What is wireless networking, and how does it work?
3. What does Wireless Fidelity (Wi-Fi) refer to?
4. Describe the difference between an intranet and an extranet.
5. What is the difference between internet and Internet?

Skill
Review 4 Explore the World of Wireless

1. If necessary, connect to the Internet.
2. Start Internet Explorer.
3. Open the Google search engine Web site (www.google.com).
4. Use Google to search for information that will help you write or type short answers for the following questions:
   a. What are the differences between the IEEE 802.11a, IEEE 802.11b, and IEEE 802.11g specifications?
   b. How do Bluetooth-enabled devices work?
   c. Compare the price and capabilities of two different brands of wireless NICs.

Future of the Internet

A number of efforts aim to expand Internet possibilities. One such initiative is known as **Internet2**, a university-led research and development consortium founded in 1996 to develop new technologies and applications for the Internet. In addition to university members, the consortium includes participants from the private sector and government organizations. The Internet2 is designed to serve as a test bed, not as a replacement for the Internet. Ideally, technologies and applications developed for Internet2 will trickle down to the Internet once they are perfected.

The backbone for Internet2 is known as Abilene and extends nationwide as shown in Figure 1.21. Internet2 members connect to the Abilene backbone via network access points called gigaPOPs (gigabit Point of Presence) that support data transfer

Internet2 a university-led research and development consortium founded in 1996 to develop new technologies and applications for the Internet

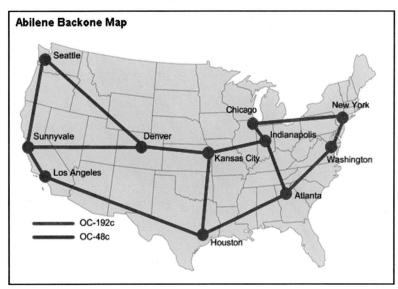

Figure 1.21 Abilene Backbone Map

rates of 10 gigabits per second (Gbps), a speed 15,000 times faster than the typical household broadband connection. The eventual goal is to have Abilene supporting 100 megabits (Mbps) per second to each connected desktop.

One of the more interesting Internet2 projects currently under development involves ***multicasting***, a technique for increasing the data delivery efficiency on a network. The Internet sends data in ***unicast*** mode; a copy of the source data must be created for each recipient, a method that uses a lot of bandwidth. A bandwidth value expresses the maximum amount of data that can be transmitted through a communications link over a given timeframe, such as 2.5 Mbps (megabits per second). With multicast, copies of source data are made as close to the recipient as possible, thereby conserving bandwidth. Multicast benefits applications that are bandwidth hungry, such as streaming video. Internet2 currently uses multicast to transmit better-than-TV-quality video to multiple viewers on the network. So, for example, academic settings could use multicasting to improve distance learning.

Tele-immersion is another Internet2 project. Tele-immersion enables an individual to experience being somewhere other than his or her actual location, or as someone once put it, "Being there without being there." A step beyond virtual reality, tele-immersion will require innovative vision and sensing technologies to overcome current limitations. Tele-immersion is an ideal project for Internet2 because it will require the improvement of existing Internet infrastructure and applications, including the need for vast amounts of bandwidth. If the goals of tele-immersion proponents become a reality, doctors will some day be able to perform surgery on patients many miles away, vacationers will be able to visit exotic locations from the comfort of their homes, and technicians will be able to safely work in hazardous environments—just to name a few possibilities. Researchers predict that commercial tele-immersion will be available within 10 years.

New Internet technologies and applications will almost certainly emerge from sources other than organized research initiatives such as Internet2. We should not forget that many of today's major Internet services, such as e-mail and the Web, were unanticipated when the Internet first came into being. With that history in mind, we should not be surprised if in a few years new Internet services and applications appear that nobody is even dreaming of at present.

multicast data transmission method in which copies of source data are made as close to the recipient as possible, thereby conserving bandwidth

unicast data transmission method in which a copy of the source data must be created for each recipient, a process that uses a lot of bandwidth

Space: The Next Frontier

Vinton Cerf, an Internet pioneer sometimes called the "Father of the Internet," works today to extend the Internet beyond the Earth's atmosphere. Since 1998, he has been working with the NASA Jet Propulsion Lab's Interplanetary Network (IPN) to extend the Internet into outer space so that it can be used to communicate with spacecraft. The challenging environment of outer space requires several layers of protocols, and two layers are already on board the Spirit and Opportunity rovers on Mars. If all goes well, an Internet backbone will eventually extend into outer space.

Sources: http://news.bbc.co.uk/2/hi/technology/3832527.stm, www.ibiblio.org/pioneers/cerf.html

Concept Review 5 Future of the Internet

1. Write a brief description of Internet2.
2. What is Abilene, and how does it relate to Internet2?
3. Compare multicast to unicast, and explain the advantage of multicast.
4. Why is tele-immersion an ideal project for Internet2?

Skill Review 5 Examine the Future of the Internet

1. If necessary, connect to the Internet.
2. Start Internet Explorer.
3. Open the Google search engine Web site (www.google.com).
4. Use Google to search for information that will help you write or type a short essay (one to two double-spaced pages) describing what you think the Internet will look like 10 years from now. Use your own ideas as well as those you learn from your research.

Chapter Summary

- Building on J.C.R. Licklider's idea of a "Galactic Network," in 1969 the ARPANET linked four computer networks through telephone lines, creating the precursor of what we now know as the Internet.

- The developers of the Internet adopted what they termed an open architecture philosophy in order to encourage other computer networks to link to the ARPANET.

- Due to inefficiency and vulnerability to interruptions, circuit switching gave way to packet switching, which separates data into packets instead of sending it in one chunk or stream through a single circuit.

- The paired protocols called TCP/IP (Transmission Control Protocol/Internet Protocol) reconcile the different protocols and data transmission methods used by Internet member networks.

- Several workarounds, such as subnetting, Classless InterDomain Routing (CIDR), and IPv6, have been developed to prevent the Internet from running out of IP addresses.

- The Domain Name System (DNS) maps a domain name to an IP address. Every network has a DNS server that functions to locate IP addresses in order to make a connection.

- The development of Internet applications introduced e-mail, Telnet, File Transfer Protocol (FTP), and perhaps most importantly, the World Wide Web (WWW).

- The Web's system of hyperlinked (linked) documents accessible through a browser vastly expanded the utility of the Internet and made using the Internet a simple point-and-click activity.

- Tim Berners-Lee formed the World Wide Web Consortium (W3C) in 1994 to develop and maintain open standards for the Web.

- Many Web pages use an extended form of HTML known as Dynamic HTML (DHTML), which combines HTML, Cascading Style Sheets (CSS—a method for formatting Web pages), and JavaScript to let users create dynamic Web pages.

- HTML is being phased out slowly in favor of eXtensible HTML (XHTML).

- HTML links are created using HTML starting and ending anchor tags and an HREF attribute.

- Document relative paths do not contain a protocol and also omit any portion of a path that is the same for the linking document and the target document.

- Absolute document paths are similar to relative paths except that they include the complete URL (including folder and file name) for a linked document or object as well as the protocol to be used.

- Mosaic was one of the first successful browsers. It featured the ability to display in-line images, whereas previous browsers opened images in separate windows.

- Netscape, a Mosaic-based browser, introduced now-common browser features such as frames, Java, JavaScript, and plug-ins.

- Computers can be linked together to form networks, such as local area networks (LANs), wide area networks (WANs), metropolitan area networks (MANs), and personal area networks (PANs).

- Local area networks first appeared in the early 1970s with the development of Ethernet technology.

- The Ethernet protocol differs from the TCP/IP protocol used on the Internet and other internets in that it uses frames to send data through a single medium.

- An intranet is a company or organization network that is for internal use only.

- An extranet is an intranet that shares a portion of its resources with outside users.

- While many extranets are carried across leased lines, an increasing number use virtual private networks (VPNs), which operate through the Internet using encryption to maintain privacy and security.

- Wireless networking uses radio waves to connect computers equipped with wireless network interface cards (NICs).

- While there are a number of different wireless standards in use, most wireless hardware available today supports one or more of the IEEE 802.11 series of specifications commonly referred to as Wireless Fidelity (Wi-Fi).

- The Internet2 is designed to serve as a test bed for new Internet technologies and applications, not as a replacement for the Internet. Ideally, technologies and applications developed for Internet2 will trickle down to the Internet once they are perfected.

Key Terms

Numbers indicate the pages where terms are first cited in the chapter. An alphabetized list of key terms with definitions can be found on the Encore CD that accompanies this book. In addition, these terms and definitions are included in the end-of-book glossary.

absolute document path, *15*

ARPANET, *4*

backbone, *4*

Carrier-Sense Multiple Access with Collision Detection (CSMA/CD), *20*

Cascading Style Sheets (CSS), *14*

circuit switching, *6*

client/server network, *18*

document relative path, *15*

Domain Name System (DNS), *8*

Dynamic HTML (DHTML), *14*

Ethernet, *20*

eXtensible HTML (XHTML), *14*

extranet, *21*

File Transfer Protocol (FTP), *10*

firewall, *21*

graphical user interface (GUI), *10*

HyperText Markup Language (HTML), *13*

Net  **Check**

Additional quiz questions are available on the Encore CD that accompanies this book as well as on the Internet Resource Center for this title at www.emcp.net/Internet2e.

Multiple Choice

Indicate the correct answer for each question or statement.

1. The Internet is an example of a
   a. WAN.
   b. LAN.
   c. PAN.
   d. MAN.

2. A network in which computers are linked directly together is known as a(n) _____ network.
   a. client/server
   b. peer-to-peer
   c. Ethernet
   d. Wi-Fi

3. The protocol used to send packets over the Internet is
   a. NCP.
   b. IPv4.
   c. TCP/IP.
   d. IPv6.

4. IP addresses are expressed in a decimal format known as _____ numbers.
   a. hexadecimal
   b. binary
   c. decimal
   d. dotted decimal notation

5. This protocol enables users to transfer files on the Internet.
   a. Telnet
   b. FTP
   c. GUI
   d. e-mail

6. The ARPANET encouraged other networks to join it by adopting
   a. Network Control Protocol (NCP).
   b. NSFnet.
   c. open architecture philosophy.
   d. classful domain names.

7. IPv4 allows this number of unique IP addresses.
   a. 4 million
   b. 7.5 million
   c. 4.2 billion
   d. an infinite number

8. IPv6 is also referred to as
   a. IP next generation (IPng).
   b. CIDR.
   c. subnetting.
   d. supernetting.

9. Two methods used to extend the number of IP addresses available under IPv4 are
    a. CIDR and NET.
    b. subnetting and supernetting.
    c. Domain Name System (DNS) and IP address system.
    d. TCP and IP.

10. The concept underlying hyperlinks is known as
    a. hypertext.
    b. hypermedia.
    c. HTML.
    d. Memex.

True/False

Indicate whether each statement is true or false.

1. WWW is another name for the Internet.

2. Circuit switching is a method used to send data over the Internet.

3. The ARPANET was the forerunner of the Internet.

4. Packet switching uses frames to transmit data.

5. Routers determine where packets should go and send them on their way.

6. An algorithm is a set of rules that allows computers to work with wireless networks.

7. A client is a server on a network.

8. TCP/IP reconciles the different protocols and data transmission methods used by Internet member networks.

9. The numbers separated by dots in an IP address are known as octets.

10. Tim Berners-Lee formed the World Wide Web Consortium (W3C) in 1994 to develop and maintain open standards for the Web.

Virtual Perspectives

1. The Internet operates without a central controlling authority. While many people think that this is one of the Internet's positive points, others think it is a drawback because it makes it difficult to control some of the questionable activities that take place on the Internet. Where do you stand on this issue? What are the pros and cons of having a central authority?

2. Internet accessibility is an important issue for the millions of people with disabilities. Research this issue and then discuss whether or not you think that creating accessible Web pages is necessary for everyone. There are laws requiring accessibility for government Web sites. Do you think these laws should be expanded to cover all Web sites?

3. Tim Berners-Lee decided not to profit from his invention of the World Wide Web. Discuss how the Internet might be different today if Berners-Lee had decided to patent or trademark his invention. Do you think his decision was a wise one or a foolish one?

Internet Lab Projects

Project 1 Create and Send a Postcard or Greeting Card

1. Use Google or another search engine to find information about Web sites offering free e-mail greeting cards or postcards.
2. Review the search results and visit the sites that seem most promising.
3. When you have decided on a site, follow the site's instructions to create and send a greeting card or postcard to an e-mail address specified by your instructor.

Project 2 Use Currency Converters

1. Use Google or another search engine to find a Web site providing currency conversions.
2. Convert US$5 into euros, UK pounds, Thai baht, Mexican pesos, and South African rand. Write down the results for each currency conversion.
3. Open a different currency converter and do the same conversions. Write down the results for each currency conversion.
4. Create a table comparing the currency conversion results for the two Web sites. Print the comparison table.

Project 3 Navigate a Travel Web Site

1. Open the Expedia Web site (www.expedia.com).
2. Create an itinerary for a round-trip to a place of your choice for two adult passengers and two children.
3. Print out page 1 of your flight details for the round trip. *(Note: Do not proceed to Booking, do not create an account, and do not actually purchase the tickets.)*

Internet Research Activities

Activity 1 Research Ethernet

Search the Internet for more information about Ethernet. Write a short paper outlining the history of Ethernet, describe how it works, and point out any similarities and differences between Ethernet networks and TCP/IP internets or the Internet.

Activity 2 Explain Wireless Router Components

A wireless router or access point can be used to let computers share an Internet connection. Research wireless routers and then write a paper describing the equipment needed to allow two computers to share an Internet connection.

Activity 3 Examine Bluetooth Technology

Bluetooth is a wireless method for connecting devices in a personal area network (PAN). Research Bluetooth and then write a short paper describing how Bluetooth works. Include information about any hardware or software necessary to connect Bluetooth devices to a computer. Also include technical information such as the operating range and the frequency used by Bluetooth. Describe some of the devices available with Bluetooth technology and their price range.

Activity 4
Net Challenge

In 1982, the French government offered an online service called Minitel that found widespread public acceptance. Research Minitel and then write a short paper describing how it worked and what it could be used for. Compare Minitel to the Internet, and point out any similarities and differences.

Chapter 2
Accessing the Internet

Learning Objectives

- Describe how the last mile connects users to the Internet.

- Examine the difference between bandwidth, throughput, and latency.

- Explain the different hardware and software requirements for connecting to the Internet.

- Contrast the different types of wired and wireless Internet connection methods.

- Evaluate Internet Service Providers and determine best practices.

Living on the Net

When Carolyn returned from her business trip, she decided to ask Bob for help in finding and setting up a better Internet connection. With the dial-up service she used, it seemed to take longer each day to download materials. Carolyn found it frustrating that she could not view video, and when she tried to listen to Internet radio, the sound stream often skipped or stopped. She also was not impressed with the technical support provided by her Internet Service Provider (ISP). Whenever she had a problem with her connection, it took several days to reach someone from the ISP who could help her.

Carolyn used the Web to research the different ways to connect to the Internet, but what she had learned had confused her. She had difficulty comparing services because she was not familiar with some of the terms used, such as bandwidth, throughput, or ISDN. Although Carolyn had a vague understanding of bits and bytes, she noticed that the way 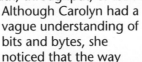 data transmission speeds were measured differed from the way file size was measured. Carolyn's research also made her realize that she had a poor understanding of how the Internet worked. She found the variety of different methods that could be used to connect to the Internet overwhelming—dial-up connections, ISDN, cable, DSL, leased lines, satellite—which one was right for her? To ensure she would make an informed choice, Carolyn decided to tap into Bob's expertise to learn more before she made any decisions about a new Internet connection.

Carolyn's Internet connection was not slowing down. As Web pages increase in size, slow Internet connections seem even slower. A 56 Kbps dial-up connection that was once adequate for most purposes now cannot support new uses such as streaming audio and video. Carolyn was smart to learn more about the Internet and how it works before making any decisions. Now that she has armed herself with that knowledge, she can analyze her needs and then find an Internet connection that will meet her requirements, as well as fit her pocketbook.

Internet Infrastructure

As illustrated in Figure 2.1, in a typical wired Internet connection, end users connect to a telephone company's central office over telephone lines referred to as the "last mile." From the central office, the connection continues to an Internet Service Provider (ISP) or Internet Access Provider (IAP) and then taps into an Internet backbone via a network access point (NAP). The following sections explain how each of these segments function in a wired Internet connection.

The Last Mile

last mile telephone company term referring to the last portion of any telephone connection from a central office (CO) to an end user

twisted-pair cable two insulated copper wires twisted around each other in a continuous spiral to form a single telephone line, commonly used in POTS last mile service

The *last mile* is a figurative telephone company term referring to the last portion of any telephone connection from a central office (CO) to an end user. In reality, the last mile may be as much as three to four miles in length. The standard telephone service found in last mile connections to most homes is referred to as plain old telephone service (POTS). POTS uses *twisted-pair cables* consisting of two insulated copper wires twisted around each other in a continuous spiral as shown in Figure 2.2. Twisting the wires rather than running them side-by-side helps to reduce signal interference. Some twisted-pair wires covered by a ground layer are known as shielded twisted-pair, but ordinary telephone connections use unshielded twisted-pair wires. Bundles of twisted-pair wires are wrapped together in a cable sheath. Standard twisted-pair POTS only supports Internet connection speeds up to 56 Kbps, but newer last mile technologies

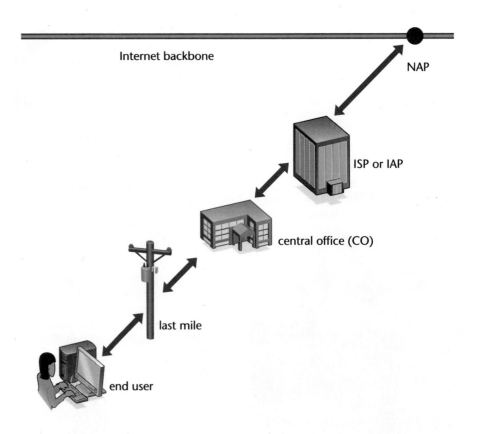

Figure 2.1 Internet Schematic Diagram

such as xDSL and ISDN provide much higher speeds, as will be described later in this chapter.

The last mile often presents a stumbling block for fast and reliable Internet connections because it typically uses technology originally designed for voice service, and the hardware in the CO it is connected to may be equally out of date. Even the distance a user is located from a CO can play a role in the performance of some Internet connection methods such as xDSL and ISDN. The last mile is usually the slowest portion of any Internet connection, and any Internet connection will only be as fast as the slowest portion of the link. The last mile and CO connects users with an Internet Service Provider or Internet Access Provider.

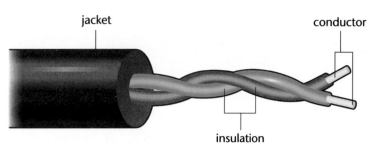

Figure 2.2 Twisted-Pair Cable

Internet Service Providers (ISPs) and Internet Access Providers (IAPs)

An Internet Service Provider (ISP) is a company or organization that provides Internet access and other services such as Web development and hosting, while an Internet Access Provider (IAP) generally refers to a company or organization that only provides access to the Internet. The distinction between these two has, in many cases, become blurred, and you will often see the two terms used interchangeably. ISPs and IAPs connect to an Internet backbone through *network access points (NAPs)*. Smaller ISPs or IAPs may connect to a larger ISP or IAP, which is in turn connected to an Internet backbone.

The Internet Backbone

The *Internet backbone* consists of high-speed lines that form the core network of the Internet. As described in Chapter 1, *Understanding the Internet*, the first backbones for the Internet were supported by the ARPANET and later the NSFnet. In 1995, the NSF stopped supporting the backbone and opened it up to the private sector. A number of different companies currently support the links that make up the Internet backbone. Figure 2.3 shows a map of the backbone provided by a company called Level 3 Communications. Internet backbone high-speed lines include T1, T3, OC-1, and OC-3 cables. T1 cables contain two twisted-pair wires with a bandwidth of 1.544 megabits per second (Mbps). T3 lines contain 28 T1 lines and have a bandwidth of 44.736 Mbps.

OC-1 and OC-3 are *fiber-optic cables* (Optical Carrier or OC) and

network access point (NAP) connection that allows ISPs or IAPs to connect to an Internet backbone

Internet backbone the core or central network that forms the Internet

fiber-optic cable cable composed of strands of optically pure glass or plastic used to transmit data through beams of light that bounce off the reflective walls of the cable

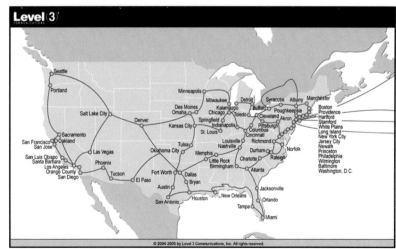

Figure 2.3 Example of an Internet Backbone for Level 3 Communications

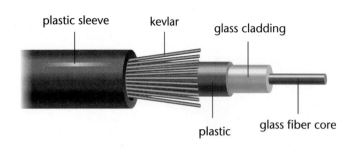

plastic sleeve   kevlar   glass cladding

plastic   glass fiber core

Figure 2.4 Fiber-Optic Cable

Figure 2.5 Fiber-Optic Beam

support capacities of 51.84 Mbps and 155.52 Mbps, respectively. A fiber-optic cable contains strands of optically pure glass or plastic approximately the diameter of a human hair as shown in Figure 2.4. The cables transmit data using beams of light that bounce off the reflective walls of the cable as they travel toward their destination as shown in Figure 2.5. A transmitter sends light signals through the fiber-optic cable, and an optical receiver decodes the signals at the destination. The purity of the glass or plastic used determines how far a signal can travel before it loses quality (degrades). Optical regenerators placed at intervals along the cable path boost degraded signals.

Concept Review 1 Internet Infrastructure

1. Why do the last mile and the hardware in a central office (CO) often present a stumbling block to fast and reliable Internet connections?
2. What is the difference between an ISP and an IAP?
3. Describe how fiber-optic cables work.
4. What is a network access point (NAP)?

Skill Review 1 Research the Last Mile and Internet Backbones

1. Open the Google search engine Web site (www.google.com).
2. Use Google to search for information that will help you write or type short answers for the following questions:
   a. Describe in detail the different components that make up the last mile.
   b. Make a list of some of the local (not national) Internet Service Providers in your area and describe the types of Internet connection methods that are available where you live.
   c. What Internet backbone or backbones do the ISPs in your area use to connect to the Internet? *(Hint: Call the ISPs if you cannot find the information on their Web site.)*

Table 2.1 Nominal Download Times by Internet Connection Type

File Type	Dial-Up 56 Kbps	ISDN 128 Kbps	Residential Satellite 500 Kbps	DSL/ 1 Mbps+	T1 1.54 Mbps	Cable 2.2 Mbps	OC-1 51.84 Mbps
text document (1 page) 4 KB	< 1 second	< 1 second	< 1 second	< 1 second	< 1 second	< 1 second	< 1 second
Web page with graphics (1 page) 50 KB	7 seconds	3 seconds	< 1 second	< 1 second	< 1 second	< 1 second	< 1 second
single-spaced Word document (20 pages) 115 KB	16 seconds	7 seconds	1 second	1 second	< 1 second	< 1 second	< 1 second
80% quality JPEG image 1.3 MB	3 minutes 14 seconds	1 minute 25 seconds	17 seconds	10 seconds	7 seconds	5 seconds	< 1 second
MP3 song file (4 minutes) 4 MB	10 minutes	4 minutes 22 seconds	52 seconds	31 seconds	21 seconds	15 seconds	< 1 second
full-Length DVD 5 GB	8 days 21 hours 2 minutes 38 seconds	3 days 21 hours 2 minutes 24 seconds	18 hours 38 minutes 28 seconds	10 hours 51 minutes 2 seconds	7 hours 43 minutes 37 seconds	5 hours 25 minutes 31 seconds	13 minutes 48 seconds

Source: Bandwidth.com File Download Time calculator, ComScore Networks Q1 2004 Average Bandwith Survey

Note: Actual bandwidth can vary considerably from stated or potential bandwidth. The figures listed in this table are nominal figures for comparing the different connection types and may vary from the actual bandwidth available where you live.

Bandwidth, Throughput, and Latency

The term *bandwidth* expresses the theoretical maximum amount of data that an Internet connection can transmit in one second. Table 2.1 lists the typical bandwidth for each type of Internet connection, along with typical download times for different file sizes. Figure 2.6 graphically illustrates relative bandwidths.

Internet bandwidth is measured in bits per second, and although bits (from **bi**nary dig**its**) are usually expressed using the binary numbering system, when used for measuring bandwidth they are expressed in decimal format. One bit is a single digit, either 0 or 1, and represents the smallest unit of computer data. A kilobit is 1,000 bits, a megabit is 1,000 kilobits, and a gigabit is 1,000 megabits. When used to indicate bandwidth, these terms include an appended *ps* for per

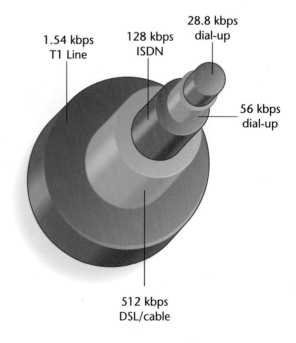

Figure 2.6 Relative Bandwidth Size

Table 2.2 Data Transfer Measurement (Decimal)

Data Transfer in Bits	Is Equivalent To
1 bit per second (bps)	1 binary digit (0 or 1) per second (bps)
1 kilobit per second (Kbps)	1,000 bits per second (bps)
1 megabit per second (Mbps)	1,000 kilobits per second (Kbps)
1 gigabit per second (Gbps)	1,000 megabits per second (Mbps)

Table 2.3 Data Storage or File Size Measurement (Binary)

Data Storage in Bytes	Is Equivalent To
1 byte (B)	8 bits (b)
1 kilobyte (KB)	1,024 bytes (B) or 8,192 bits (b)
1 megabyte (MB)	1,024 kilobytes (KB) or 8,388,608 bits (b)
1 gigabyte (GB)	1,024 megabytes (MB) or 8,589,934,592 bits (b)

bandwidth a value that expresses the maximum amount of data that can be transmitted through a communications link over a given time frame, such as 2.5 Mbps.

symmetrical an Internet connection that offers the same bandwidth for uploading and downloading

asymmetrical an Internet connection that offers different bandwidths for uploading and downloading, usually offering slower uploading bandwidth

throughput the actual amount of user data that a network can transmit per second

second, as in Kbps, Mbps, and Gbps as shown in Table 2.2.

Do not confuse bandwidth measurements with file size measurements, usually listed in bytes and expressed in binary format as shown in Table 2.3. One byte equals eight bits, and a kilobyte (KB) equals 1,024 bytes. Thus, the size of a file or Web page will be referred to in bytes, such as 50 KB (kilobytes), 150 KB, and so on. The *B* representing bytes is capitalized to avoid confusion with bits, thus the Kb in Kbps stands for kilobits, while KB stands for kilobytes.

Bandwidth can be symmetrical (even) or asymmetrical (uneven) depending on the technology used to connect to the Internet. Technologies offering the same bandwidth speeds whether uploading or downloading data are *symmetrical*, while technologies with differing bandwidths for uploading and downloading are referred to as *asymmetrical*. Asymmetrical technologies almost always make more bandwidth available for downloading compared to uploading. For example, an Asymmetrical Digital Subscriber Line (ADSL) connection may offer 256 Kbps of bandwidth for downloading data and only 128 Kbps for uploading data as shown in Figure 2.7. This uneven division is a compromise that meets the needs of most Internet users because most people download data far more frequently than they upload it.

It is important to realize that bandwidth measures the capacity of an Internet connection, stating only the maximum theoretical data transmission capacity of the connecting medium. Network overhead typically prevents a connection from achieving its theoretical maximum. Network overhead means that the network itself uses a certain percentage of available bandwidth to support data transmission. For example, the TCP/IP protocol requires some bandwidth when packaging and addressing data.

Throughput provides a better measure of Internet connection speed than bandwidth. Throughput rates the actual amount of user data the network can transmit per second, rather than the theoretical rate of data transmission capacity measured by bandwidth. Throughput measures only useable data transmitted and does not include data used for network overhead. An Internet connec-

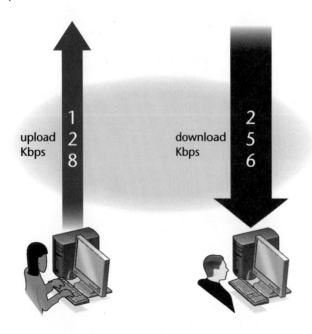

Figure 2.7 Asymmetrical Bandwidth

tion throughput speed of 80 to 85 percent of the theoretical bandwidth available is considered typical and anything approaching 90 percent would be ideal.

Even an Internet connection with high bandwidth and/or high throughput could be slow due to latency. *Latency* refers to the time between the transmission and reception of data across a network, usually expressed in milliseconds (ms). For example, a dial-up modem's latency is approximately 100 to 200 ms, whereas DSL connection latency ranges from 10 to 20 ms. A number of factors contribute to the delays caused by latency, including device delays and network congestion. Satellite Internet connections offer an excellent example of the effect of latency on Internet connection speed. Although the bandwidth and throughput for a satellite Internet connection may be high, the long route that the satellite signals must travel between earth and outer space can cause delays (latency) of more than 750 ms. A user can check latency using a utility program called Ping. Ping sends a small data packet to a host and then measures the time it takes for the packet to go to the host and return. Table 2.4 contains average latency figures for different types of Internet connections.

Table 2.4 Latency Rates by Internet Connection Type

Connection Type	Latency Rate
dial-up modem	100–200 ms
ISDN	15-30 ms
DSL/cable	10-20 ms
satellite	500-750 ms
T1	2-5 ms

latency the time between the transmission and reception of data across a network, usually measured in milliseconds (ms)

Concept Review 2 Bandwidth, Throughput, and Latency

1. How do bandwidth, throughput, and latency differ from each other?
2. What kind of Internet connection is most affected by high latency rates?
3. How are bandwidth, file storage, and latency measured?
4. Explain the difference between symmetrical and asymmetrical Internet connections.

Skill Review 2 Measure the Bandwidth of Your Internet Connection

1. Use a search engine to find a Web site that measures bandwidth, such as www.speakeasy.net/speedtest. *(Hint: Use the keywords **bandwidth speed test**. Ask your instructor if he or she recommends a particular site.)*
2. Conduct a bandwidth speed test and print the results. Retest two more times during the day. If you have an Internet connection at home, conduct tests in the morning and the evening.
3. Compare the results to see if your connection speed differs according to the time of day, and to see how the results compare with your service provider's stated bandwidth.

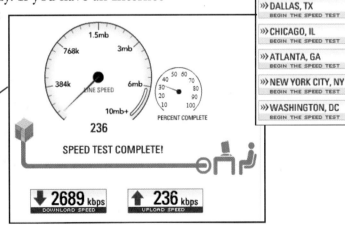

Hardware and Software Requirements for Connecting to the Internet

Connecting to the Internet requires a computer, a modem, a cable for connecting the modem to the Internet connection jack, and special software. The specific hardware and software required varies depending on the type of Internet connection that will be used, so before choosing a particular Internet connection method users should check hardware and software requirements with an Internet Service Provider to ensure that their system will support the service.

Modems send and receive signals over telephone, digital, and cable lines. The term *modem* is derived from *mo*dulator-*dem*odulator, which describes how the original modems worked. Modems modulate (adapt or vary) digital computer data into analog data that can be sent over an analog phone line and demodulate received analog data back into digital data. Newer modems may not even transmit data over lines; for example, satellite modems transmit data using radio waves. ISDN modems, xDSL modems, and cable modems enable computers to go online via ISDN, xDSL, and cable Internet connections, respectively. The different modem types are not interchangeable, so it is important to make sure that a modem supports the type of Internet connection used. Internal modems are installed inside a computer or device, and external modems connect to a computer via a cable.

For high-speed Internet connections such as cable or DSL, a computer typically uses an internal network interface card (NIC) to connect to the external cable modem or DSL modem. The NIC looks similar to an internal modem, but it has a slightly larger port than that found on an internal modem. (An internal modem accepts telephone cable with RJ-11 jacks while a NIC accepts Ethernet cable with RJ-45 jacks.) For computers lacking a NIC, some cable and DSL modems allow a connection over USB, provided the computer has an available USB port. Figure 2.8 shows examples of internal and external modems and an internal network interface card. Software also plays a vital role in enabling Internet connections. Current computer operating systems such as Windows Vista, Linux, or Mac OS X typically include support for the TCP/IP Internet protocol (usually included in an OS), a Web browser for viewing

Network Interface Card

Internal Modem

External Modem

Figure 2.8 Network Interface Card and Internal and External Modems

Web pages on the Internet, and an e-mail program for Internet communications. Older operating systems may require some of these components to be installed separately. In addition, most modems require (and include) driver software for installation, and ISPs often provide installation software to facilitate setting up the Internet connection.

The range of Internet connection options has vastly expanded from the days when the only option for most people was a slow dial-up connection using a regular POTS telephone line. Many people in the United States can now choose from among several connection options. Internet connection services can be broadly divided into two categories: wired and wireless connections. The remainder of this chapter will cover the specific Internet connections that fall under each category.

Concept
Review 3 Hardware and Software Requirements for Connecting to the Internet

1. Describe how a modem works.
2. What kind of software is needed to connect to the Internet?
3. Describe the basic hardware requirements for connecting to the Internet.

Skill
Review 3 Explore Hardware and Software Requirements

1. Type **www.thelist.com** in the browser Address bar and then press Enter. *(Note: The List of ISPs is a Web site that allows you to enter your area code to find information about ISPs in your area. To find similar sites, conduct a search using the terms* **Internet Service Providers**.*)*

2. Use the List of ISPs Web site to find a list of ISPs in your area and visit the Web site of an ISP of your choice.

3. Locate the ISP's Web page that lists the minimum and/or recommended hardware and software requirements for a 56 Kbps dial-up connection and print or record the information. *(Hint: Select the information, right-click, and then click Print. If a dialog box appears, click the* **Selection** *option and then click OK to print only the selected information. Ask your instructor for help if this does not work on the system you are using.)*

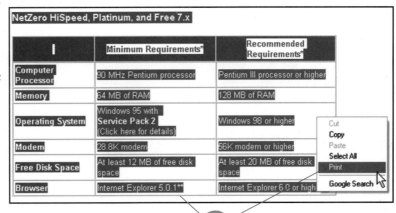

4. Repeat Step 3 for three more ISPs.

5. Use the information you have gathered to create a table comparing the different recommendations.

Wired Internet Connections

Wired Internet connections include any method that uses cable or wires to connect to the Internet. Dial-up connections offering bandwidth of up to 56 Kbps are still commonly used for accessing the Internet in the United States,

Tech Demo 2-2
DSL vs Cable Modem

but greater bandwidth enables the user to truly enjoy all that the Internet has to offer. Popular wired Internet connection methods offering greater bandwidth than dial-up POTS service include ISDN, xDSL, cable, and leased lines. Another wired Internet connection method, broadband over power line (BPL), is struggling to overcome technical and regulatory obstacles that currently prevent its wider use. If these obstacles are overcome, BPL may offer a competitive alternative to xDSL and cable services, especially in rural or remote areas.

Dial-up Internet Access

Dial-up Internet access refers to Internet connections made using a standard telephone modem over POTS telephone lines to an ISP or IAP. Most dial-up connections offer bandwidth between 28.8 and 56 Kbps, although actual bandwidth may be less than stated due to latency and network overhead. Dial-up connections are sometimes referred to as narrowband as opposed to broadband services offering higher bandwidth. A 56 Kbps dial-up connection enables users to surf the Web and access e-mail, but Web pages with multimedia content such as audio and video will be very slow to load, if they load at all. Dial-up users use software to log on (connect to) and to log off (disconnect from) the Internet.

In some areas, accelerated dial-up Internet service is available. Like regular dial-up connections, ***accelerated Internet*** uses standard modems and POTS lines to connect to the Internet, but employs compression and caching technologies to increase throughput and provide Web page loading speeds up to five times faster than standard dial-up connections. Compression technologies reduce text and image file sizes, while caching avoids the need to reload Web content that remains unchanged. Filters weed out pop-up ads, such as the one shown in Figure 2.9, and other undesired Web content that can hog bandwidth and slow down a connection. To use this service, if available, the user only needs to install new software to use with his or her current hardware. Accelerated dial-up cannot accelerate all types of Web content, and will not improve loading for streaming audio and video, secure Web pages, audio and image attachments, and downloads.

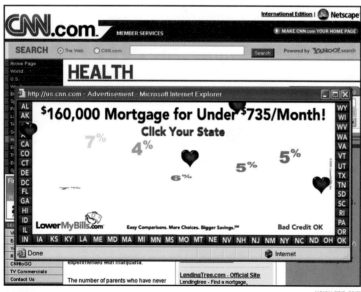

Figure 2.9 Pop-up Ad

www.cnn.com

Integrated Services Digital Network (ISDN)

Newer telephone company phone lines can support digital connections, including ***Integrated Services Digital Network (ISDN)*** Internet service. ISDN integrates voice and data services by creating multiple digital channels using the same telephone wire, enabling the simultaneous use of multiple devices at the same time. For example, with an ISDN connection users can talk on the phone and surf the Internet simultaneously over a single telephone wire, avoiding the need to install separate phone lines to support those activities. ISDN Internet connections offer higher bandwidth than ordinary dial-up connections, usually with speeds of 64 Kbps or 128 Kbps, although higher speeds are possible depending on the medium (connection) used. ISDN service is distance related, and users must be located within 18,000 feet of a telephone company's central office (CO) to take advantage of ISDN. Even within that range, the closer a user is to a CO, the faster the connection speed. To enable a user to use ISDN, the phone company must install a special ISDN phone line to the user's location. In addition to paying the phone company a monthly fee for the line, the user needs an account with an ISP that supports ISDN access. ISPs often charge by the minute for ISDN service, which can be expensive. In recent years, ISDN service has been supplanted by faster and cheaper xDSL and cable modem Internet services.

xDSL

Digital Subscriber Line (DSL) technologies can provide high speed Internet service using POTS twisted-pair cable. Because a number of DSL versions exist, DSL is often collectively referred to as xDSL, with the *x* representing the different members of the family of DSL services available, listed in Table 2.5. Some xDSL service providers use their own trademarked terms to refer to the xDSL services they offer. The most commonly available version of xDSL in the United States is *Asymmetric Digital Subscriber Line (ADSL)*, meaning that download and upload bandwidth speeds differ to match the requirements of most users, who as a group download much more data than they upload. You will often see or hear ADSL referred to as DSL. Like ISDN, xDSL has a service range, and the closer a user is to a CO the faster the connection speed.

American Broadband Use Exceeds 50 Percent Barrier

Broadband Internet connectivity rose to more than 50 percent of all Internet users in the United States in August 2004 according to the Internet survey group Nielsen/NetRatings. The survey results also revealed that the majority of those Americans still using dial-up services connected using 56 Kbps modems, but surprisingly slightly more than 6 percent used 28/33.3 Kbps modems and 2.6 percent used archaic 14.4 Kbps modems. Broadband (as defined by Nielsen/NetRatings) includes any connection speed above 56 Kbps, a somewhat liberal interpretation given that many industry observers define broadband connections at 256 Kbps or even higher. The survey also found broadband use increasing by more than 1 percent per month and that the percentage of workers with access to broadband connections through their workplace was greater than 80 percent.

Nielsen/NetRatings uses software meters installed in the homes of 40,000 to 50,000 survey participants to measure connection speeds. Monthly bandwidth reports can be found on the WebSiteOptimization.Com Web site at www.websiteoptimization.com/bw/.

Source: www.websiteoptimization.com/bw/0408/

Digital Subscriber Line (DSL) an Internet technology capable of providing high-speed Internet service using POTS twisted-pair wires

Asymmetric Digital Subscriber Line (ADSL) DSL connection providing differing bandwidth rates for downloads and uploads

Table 2.5 xDSL Technologies

xDSL Type	Downstream	Upstream	Distance from CO	Lines
ADSL	9 Mbps	1 Mbps	18,000 feet	1
DLS Lite	1.5 Mbps	512 Kbps	19,000–26,000 feet	1
HDSL	1.5 Mbps	1.5 Mbps	12,000 feet	2
RADSL	7 Mbps	7 Mbps	18,000 feet	1
SDSL*	3 Mbps	2.3 Mbps	22,000 feet	1
VDSL	52 Mbps	16 Mbps	1,000–4,000 feet	1

SDSL does not support simultaneous voice transmission.

Note: Speeds and distances are nominal and actual results may vary greatly.

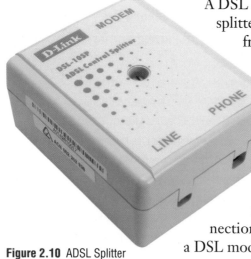

Figure 2.10 ADSL Splitter

A DSL line can carry simultaneous voice and data transmission if a splitter is installed. A splitter is a filter used to separate the low-end frequencies used to carry voice signals from the higher frequencies used for DSL signals. An example of a splitter is shown in Figure 2.10.

The biggest difference between xDSL and ISDN is that xDSL provides vastly higher bandwidth, up to 9 Mbps compared to the 128 Kbps offered by the typical ISDN connection. Unlike ISDN connections (which connect and disconnect as required by the user's Internet use), DSL connections are always on.

xDSL requires special devices at either end of any DSL connection. At the user end, a DSL transceiver, popularly referred to as a DSL modem, connects the computer to a phone line. Another device known as a DSL Access Multiplexer or DSLAM, as pictured in Figure 2.11, receives customer connections at the CO and concentrates them into a single connection to an Internet backbone.

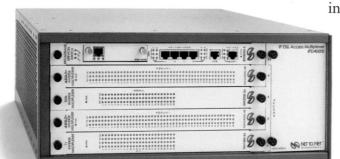

Figure 2.11 DSL Access Multiplexer (DSLAM)

An ordinary POTS line carries voice signals on low frequencies between 0 hertz (Hz) to 4.0 kilohertz (kHz), although it is capable of carrying much higher frequencies. DSL works by making use of the higher frequencies found on an ordinary twisted-pair telephone line, enabling up to 99 percent more capacity. While multiple DSL standards exist, the most commonly used is known as ***Discrete Multitone (DMT) Modulation***. DMT divides the frequencies in a twisted-pair cable into 256 frequency bands of 4.3125 kHz each, as illustrated in Figure 2.12. Bands handle different tasks, such as upstream or downstream use, and the equipment can shift signals from one channel to another if impairments are detected.

Discrete Multitone (DMT) Modulation a method of dividing the frequencies in a twisted-pair wire into 256 frequency bands of 4.3125 kHz

Very High Bit-Rate DSL (VDSL) DSL technology that provides download speeds of up to 52 Mbps

Some of the equipment used on some POTS lines such as bridge taps or load coils can impede DSL, so before a line can be used for DSL it must be qualified by the service provider. Additionally, most xDSL technologies will not work over fiber-optic cables. The service provider will qualify a line by checking to see that the user is located within the service area and by checking to see if there are any impairments on the line.

While ADSL can provide bandwidth speeds of up to 9 Mbps, ***Very High Bit-Rate DSL (VDSL)*** offers download speeds of up to 52 Mbps. Like ADSL, VDSL is asymmetric. VDSL works by converting data received by a DSL modem into pulses of light that can travel through fiber-optic cables using a

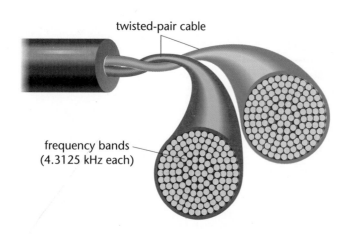

twisted-pair cable

frequency bands
(4.3125 kHz each)

Figure 2.12 Discrete Multitone (DMT) Modulation

device known as a VDSL gateway. VDSL gateways also convert fiber-optic pulses back into digital data for the return trip to the DSL modem. A drawback to VDSL is that its effective range is from 1,000 to 4,000 feet, far less than the range offered by ADSL.

Not all xDSL technologies are asymmetrical. ***High Bit-Rate DSL (HDSL)*** provides symmetrical communication using two phone lines. ***Symmetric DSL (SDSL)*** also provides identical upload and download bandwidth, but cannot support simultaneous voice transmission. Due to a different regulatory environment, SDSL is more popular in Europe than ADSL. ***Rate Adaptive DSL (RADSL)*** enables modems to adjust their speed according to the length and quality of the line in order to improve transmission quality. RADSL supports both symmetric and asymmetric bandwidth.

Cable

Cable Internet service utilizes the coaxial cable used to provide cable television service to connect users to the Internet. The user attaches an external or internal cable modem to his or her computer and then uses coaxial cable from the modem to the cable wall jack that conveys the television and Internet signals as shown in Figure 2.13. Coaxial cable carries television signals in 6 megahertz (MHz) channels, and a single coaxial cable can support hundreds of channels. Downstream and upstream Internet data are carried in a single 6-MHz channel.

A cable modem performs a number of different functions. It contains a tuner that sends and receives signals to and from a modulator and demodulator. A diplexer assigns downstream and upstream traffic to certain frequencies asymmetrically. Some cable modems used on cable systems with limited channel capacity use telephone lines for upstream data and are known as telco-return

High Bit-Rate DSL (HDSL) DSL technology that provides symmetrical Internet data transmission using two phone lines

Symmetric DSL (SDSL) DSL technology that provides identical upload and download bandwidth, but cannot support simultaneous voice transmission

Rate Adaptive DSL (RADSL) DSL technology that enables modems to adjust their speed according to the length and quality of a telephone line in order to improve transmission quality

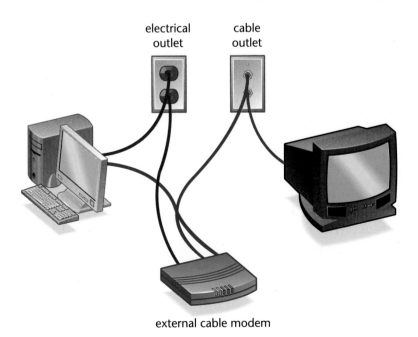

electrical outlet   cable outlet

external cable modem

Figure 2.13 Cable Modem Connection

dedicated line a telephone line that is separate from the public telephone network and is for the exclusive use of the organization leasing the line

cable modems. A media access card (MAC) handles the interface between network protocols, and a microprocessor assists the MAC in performing its functions.

At the cable TV office, a cable modem termination system (CMTS) connects up to 1,000 users to the Internet through a single 6-MHz channel. This means that all cable Internet users share bandwidth with other users. When a lot of customers use the Internet at the same time, bandwidth per customer drops dramatically. To prevent this from happening, cable TV companies use other channels to keep the number of users per channel to a manageable figure.

Cable Internet provides an always-on asymmetric Internet connection with bandwidth exceeding 1.5 Mbps, depending on the Internet connection made through the CMTS at the cable TV office. Distance affects cable Internet less than xDSL, so users can be located as far as 30 to 40 miles away from a cable TV office. Cable Internet often works as a cooperative arrangement between a local cable TV provider and an ISP. When problems occur, this arrangement can sometimes lead to confusion in determining where the fix lies—with the cable TV company or the ISP.

Leased Lines

Businesses with intensive Internet service requirements may lease dedicated lines to handle their needs. A *dedicated line* remains separate from the public telephone network. The organization leasing the line uses the line's entire bandwidth, without affect from other users, as is the case with other Internet connection methods. A leased line with a direct connection to an Internet backbone offers always-on symmetrical bandwidth, with identical speeds for data uploads and downloads.

Leasing a line involves installation costs and high monthly fees, but for many businesses, leasing a line is more economical than using other Internet connection methods. The most commonly leased lines are T1 and T3 lines, but some very large businesses may lease an optical carrier line such as an OC-3. With fractional T1 leasing, a business can lease only a portion of the channels available in a T1 line. Fractional T1 is usually scalable, so the organization can lease additional channels to handle increased usage. Although fractional T1 leasing offers lower bandwidth, with its corresponding lower price it may offer a better fit for organizations whose Internet requirements would not absorb the full bandwidth of a T1 line. Only very large businesses can afford to lease a costly OC-3 line. Competition in the industry has driven down the cost of leasing high-speed lines.

Broadband over Power Line (BPL)

The ***broadband over power line (BPL)*** Internet connection method delivers Internet data over electrical power lines and into homes. BPL offers speeds ranging from 500 Kbps to 3 Mbps. Figure 2.14 shows a schematic diagram of a BPL system using a combination of BPL and wireless technologies to connect homes to the Internet. BPL modems contain silicon chipsets to separate data from the electrical current flowing through the lines. Some BPL systems deliver Internet signals from electrical power lines to houses using wireless technology.

BPL is already available on a very limited basis in a few areas of the United States and Canada as well as in Europe. BPL's future in the United States is uncertain at the moment because there is a dispute about its potential to interfere with other radio signals. Because electrical wiring and cables are unshielded, the data signals they contain could potentially interfere with portions of the radio spectrum. Both the U.S. and Canadian governments support BPL as a method for making the Internet available to underserved areas. Due to concerns that BPL will interfere with broadcasts, shortwave radio enthusiasts support efforts opposing BPL through their national association known as the American Amateur Radio League (ARRL). The Federal Communications Commission (FCC) has given tentative approval to BPL and research is still going on to determine the threat, if any, that BPL poses to the radio spectrum. If BPL passes these hurdles, it may become a major player in the Internet connection market as it promises to offer cheaper service than xDSL and cable services, while offering comparable bandwidth.

broadband over power line (BPL) an Internet connection technology that delivers Internet data over electrical power lines and into homes

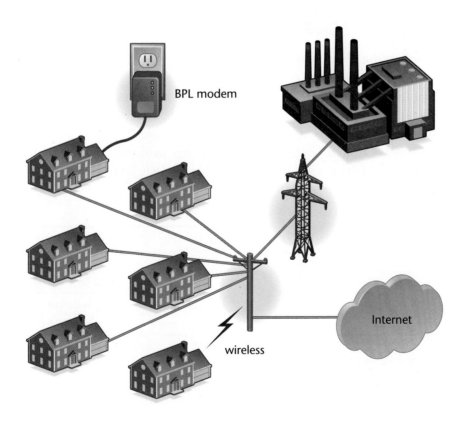

Figure 2.14 Broadband over Power Line (BPL) System

Concept
Review 4 **Wired Internet Connections** •

1. Is there a fixed or agreed-upon definition for the term broadband Internet?
2. Describe the differences between the different types of DSL technologies.
3. Explain how a cable modem Internet connection works.
4. Explain how accelerated Internet works.

Skill
Review 4 **Discover More about Wired Internet Connections** • • • • • • • • • • • • • • • • •

1. Open the Google search engine Web site (www.google.com).
2. Use Google to search for information that will help you write or type answers for the following questions:
   a. Find the best prices for leasing T1, T3, and OC-3 lines. *(Note: Restrict your research to information you can find on the Web. If a provider requires you to provide information skip them and look for providers that offer quotes without any requirements.)*
   b. Make a table comparing the service packages offered by local cable modem and xDSL service providers in your area. Compare installation and equipment costs, monthly or annual charges, bandwidth speeds, and any other relevant considerations.
   c. State your preferred wired Internet connection method and explain the factors that led you to choose that method.

Wireless Internet Connections

As discussed in the "Wireless Networking" section of Chapter 1, wireless networking uses radio waves to connect computers equipped for wireless. While there are a number of different wireless standards in use, most wireless hardware available today support one or more of the IEEE 802.11 series of specifications commonly referred to as Wi-Fi as shown in Table 2.6. Some of the 802.11 specifications are not compatible with each other as shown in Table 2.7, but some wireless dual-band cards support all three IEEE 802.11 specifications.

Table 2.6 IEEE Wireless 802.11 Specifications

	802.11a	802.11b	802.11g
Frequency	5 GHz	2.4 GHz	2.4 GHz
Bandwidth	54 Mbps	11 Mbps	54 Mbps
Indoor Range	100–150 feet	100–150 feet	100–150 feet
Outdoor Range	up to 1,000 feet	up to 1,000 feet	up to 1,000 feet

Table 2.7 IEEE Wireless 802.11 Compatibility

	802.11a	802.11b	802.11g
802.11a	✔	X	X
802.11b	X	✔	✔
802.11g	X	✔	✔

To operate wirelessly, a computer must have a wireless network interface card (NIC) or adapter installed or come factory-equipped with wireless technology. Adapters and cards come in several different formats to fit laptop and desktop computers as shown in Figure 2.15. Some computers such as the Apple PowerBook series or computers equipped with Intel's Centrino package come pre-equipped with wireless capability and do not require the installation of wireless NICs or adaptors.

A more recent IEEE wireless specification, IEEE 802.16, known as WiMAX (Worldwide Interoperability for Microwave Access) promises to extend the reach of wireless broadband to over 30 miles. Promoters say that WiMAX will complement Wi-Fi by connecting Wi-Fi hotspots, the areas covered by Wi-Fi broadcasts, to create wireless metropolitan area networks (WMANs). WiMAX operates using 11GHz radio signals in contrast to the 2.4 GHz signals used by Wi-Fi. Intel foresees notebook computers incorporating WiMAX technology by 2006.

In the United States, an ambitious plan to provide nationwide wireless Internet access was launched in late 2002. The Cometa network supported by Intel, IBM, and AT&T planned a network of over 20,000 hotspots across the United States. Unfortunately, Cometa was undercapitalized, and in mid-2004 it ceased operations. This does not mean the end to the idea of a nationwide wireless hot zone, only a delay. Most Internet observers expect that some day the entire world will be covered by a wireless hot zone, making hard-wired Internet connections a thing of the past.

Wireless USB Adapter   Wireless Desktop Card   Wireless PCMCIA Card

Photos courtesy of Linksys®

Figure 2.15 Wireless Adaptors and Cards

Users may employ one of a number of ways to connect a computer wirelessly to the Internet. Most are terrestrial (land-based) such as fixed wireless services, wireless LAN connections to a wired Internet connection, and cellular phone Internet connections, but satellite Internet involves the transmission of radio waves to outer space and back.

Wireless connections can be open or secure. An open connection allows anyone with a wireless NIC access to the connection. Wireless connections can be made secure by using a 128-bit encryption system known as *Wired Equivalency Privacy (WEP)*. Wireless access points have WEP disabled by default. If WEP is enabled, users need to use a WEP key to gain access to the wireless connection.

Wired Equivalency Privacy (WEP) 128-bit encryption method used to ensure wireless security

fixed wireless Internet service wireless Internet connection that broadcasts signals from a tower to an end user's antenna at a fixed location

Fixed Wireless Service

In many areas of the United States, ISPs offer *fixed wireless Internet service*. The ISP's network operations center (NOC) connects to an Internet backbone and broadcasts data in the form of microwave frequencies from a tower or series of towers as shown in Figure 2.16. An antenna installed at the user's location picks up the microwave frequencies. The antenna connects to a transceiver, which in turn connects to a modem and the user's system. Broadcasting range is up to 35 miles, but fixed wireless service is a line-of-sight technology, so buildings, trees, or hills in between the ISP's transmission tower and the antenna will block signals. Wireless ISP Internet service offers between 256 Kbps

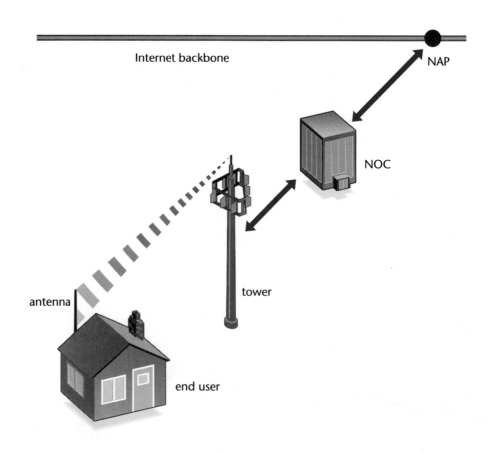

Figure 2.16 Fixed Wireless Service

and 1 Mbps of download bandwidth and 512 Kbps of upload bandwidth. This type of Internet connection suffers from a few drawbacks, including high installation costs, monthly service rates, and the need to be within direct sight and range of a transmission tower.

Wireless Local Area Network to Wired Internet Service

Wireless LAN (WLAN) technology can connect a computer or series of computers to an ADSL or cable modem to access the Internet. The user connects the ADSL or cable modem to a transceiver known as a wireless access point that converts the modem signals into wireless signals and vice versa. The computer's wireless NIC or adapter then picks up the wireless signals. Manufacturers now offer access points that integrate router capabilities (wireless broadband routers). A wireless router enables other wireless-enabled computers on the network to share the Internet service as shown in Figure 2.17. Most wireless routers offer the option of connecting computers through Ethernet cables or wirelessly, so computers on a wired LAN also can share the broadband connection with the wireless devices. Some devices on the market offer dual functions such as modem/router combinations, and Toshiba recently announced a device that combines modem, router, and access point functions. You can use the wireless equipment to provide wireless Internet access for a home or business (and for a single computer or a network) or to create a public hotspot. Public *hotspots* are increasingly being installed in locations such as airports, restaurants, hotel

hotspot a public location with readily accessible wireless networks coverage

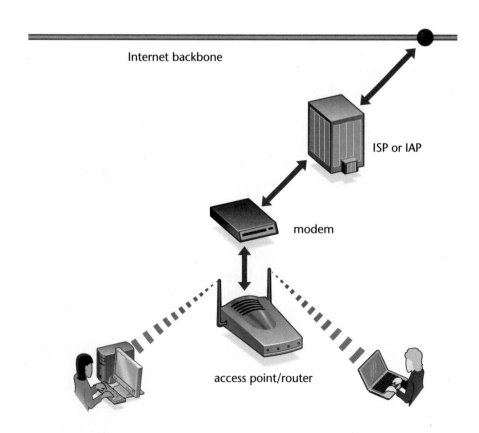

Figure 2.17 Wireless LAN to Wired Internet Connection

Figure 2.18 Hotspot Users

lobbies, and shopping malls as shown in Figure 2.18. Hotspots can be accessed by anyone with a portable computer or device equipped with a wireless NIC as long as they are within the area covered by the WLAN. Some public hotspot providers offer free access, while others require a subscription or the use of a prepaid card. The popular Starbucks was one of the first coffee-shop chains to equip its locations with wireless hotspots so that their customers can use their portable computers while enjoying a cup of coffee.

Cellular Phone Internet Access

Cellular phone networks work by dividing geographic regions into a grid of cells, with each cell containing a radio transmitter and control equipment to carry phone signals. When cellular phone users travel through one cell to another cell their conversation is seamlessly passed along, a process known as handoff.

The first cellular networks (first generation cellular or 1G) were ***analog*** networks, meaning that signals were sent in a continuous stream, and could

Figure 2.19 SMS (Text) Message

only carry voice traffic. Second generation cellular (2G) introduced ***digital*** technology that divided data up before sending it in bursts. 2G cellular phones can carry voice as well as limited data communications such as short message service (SMS) text messages as shown in Figure 2.19. A number of different cellular radio technologies are in use in the United States, including TDMA, CDMA, and GSM. Devices must be compliant with a network's frequency in order to access the network.

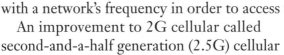

analog electronic signals that are sent in continuous waves, as opposed to digital signals that contain binary data consisting of ones and zeroes

digital electronic signals contain binary data consisting of ones and zeroes, as opposed to analog signals that are continuous waves

Wireless Application Protocol (WAP) an Internet protocol designed for the small screens found on hand-held devices

Wireless Markup Language (WML) the language used to display information displayed in microbrowsers

An improvement to 2G cellular called second-and-a-half generation (2.5G) cellular uses packet switching and offers greater bandwidth (56 Kbps). Cellular networks can update their software to support 2.5G without the need to invest in new equipment or licenses. 2.5G supports limited Internet capability such as e-mail and simple Web browsing through the ***Wireless Application Protocol (WAP)***. WAP is an Internet protocol designed for the small screens found on hand-held devices such as Personal Digital Assistants (PDAs) and cell phones. The WAP display (see Figure 2.20) is known as a microbrowser, and the information displayed on microbrowsers is written in a programming language called ***Wireless Markup Language (WML)*** derived from XML (eXtensible Markup Language), an SGML markup language related to HTML. Latency for cellular Internet connections is very high.

Figure 2.20 WAP Microbrowser

The latest version of cellular technology is known as third generation cellular (3G). 3G cellular was first rolled out in Japan and Korea in 2001, and is now available in some areas of Europe and the United States. Supporters claimed that 3G cellular would be capable of providing high-speed data rates (144 Kbps to 2+ Mbps, depending on whether the user is mobile or stationary) therefore supporting full Internet access, including streaming video. Research has shown that currently actual speeds are some 20 to 40 percent slower than claimed. The costs of implementing 3G are very high due to the need for new equipment, expensive government licenses (costing billions of dollars),

Figure 2.22 PCMCIA Cell Phone Card

Figure 2.21 Cell Phone Cable and Software Package

and the need for new handsets, so the rollout has proceeded slower than expected. The need to recoup heavy investment costs also means that service fees are generally higher than fees for 2G service. As with 2G, 3G service is available in more than one frequency, so to work with a network, a cell phone or computer card must be compliant with the network's frequency.

Digital cellular phone service (2G, 2.5G, and 3G) can link a computer or device to the Internet using cables, a cellular PC card, or Bluetooth wireless technology. Many cellular service providers offer connection kits consisting of a cable and software (see Figure 2.21) so that subscribers can connect their cell phones to a computer or device.

A PCMCIA card with built-in cell phone capability (see Figure 2.22) enables a computer or device to connect to the Internet via cellular service. The card fits in a portable computer or device's PCMCIA slot and contains a small antenna to transmit and receive signals. Purchased through a cellular phone service provider, the card usually includes a SIM card like the one found in a cell phone, and the user has to establish a second cellular service account (for Internet use) in addition to his or her normal phone account. In some cases, a user could remove the SIM from their cell phone and use it in a PCMCIA cell phone card, but most people would find this inconvenient. With a headset, the PCMCIA card can be used to make and receive calls using the computer, but as the card does not have its own power supply, it will not work unless it is attached to the computer and the computer is on.

Bluetooth wireless technology also can connect a cell phone with a computer if both are Bluetooth equipped. The Bluetooth wireless personal area net-

Fourth Generation Cellular (4G)

Although much touted, the rollout of third generation (3G) cellular phone service has not gone smoothly in the United States. Infrastructure and licensing costs for 3G were very high, and many consumers did not feel the added functionality justified the increased prices for handsets and services. Cellular companies excitedly claimed that data services would account for up to 30 percent of their revenues within a few years of the 3G rollout but reality has been harsh, and data services revenues have been as low as 1 to 2 percent for some companies. Now some cellular phone companies are hoping that the fourth generation of cellular technology (4G) will be different. 4G promises a nominal bandwidth speed of 1.5 Mbps, equivalent to a T1 line, which would provide a true broadband Internet experience to cell phone users. In the United States, Nextel has already begun a trial rollout of 4G. If the 4G trials prove successful, some cellular phone companies may bypass 3G in favor of 4G.

working technology uses radio waves to connect devices directly without the need for an access point within a range of 30 feet, although some high-powered Bluetooth devices have a range of up to 300 feet.

Satellite Internet Access

Satellite Internet offers broadband Internet to those who are unable to connect to the Internet through land-based Internet services such as xDSL or cable, and for that reason is popular in rural or remote areas. To connect to the Internet by satellite, users need a small dish, a satellite modem, and a coaxial cable connection between the dish and the modem as shown in Figure 2.23. The dish must be pointed south, so a clear view in that direction is required. Satellite Internet connections are asymmetric, with typical uplink (upload) speeds of up to 128 Kbps and downlink (download) speeds of up to 512 Kbps. One-way satellite service requires a telephone line connection to an ISP for uplinking, while two-way satellite service handles both uplinking and downlinking without the need for a telephone line and ISP. Like DSL and cable Internet service, two-way satellite Internet is an always-on Internet connection.

Satellite service installation and equipment costs can add up to hundreds of dollars. Monthly service charges are also higher than those for DSL and cable

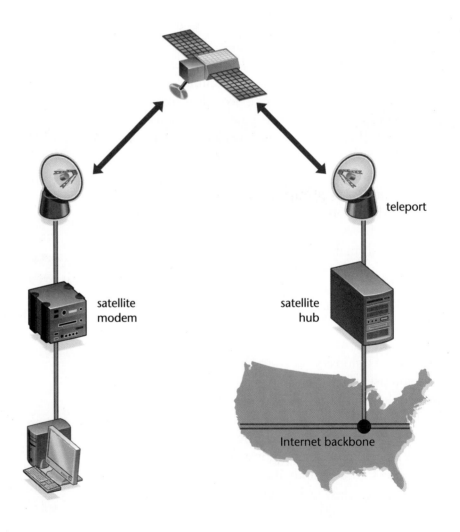

satellite modem

teleport

satellite hub

Internet backbone

Figure 2.23 Satellite Internet Connection

Internet service. Because the satellites are located 23,000 miles above the equator, latency figures are much higher than those for land-based Internet connections, making satellite Internet unsuitable for applications that require rapid back and forth interaction, such as online gaming. Satellite reception can also be affected by adverse weather such as rain and snow.

Concept
Review 5 Wireless Internet Connections

1. Describe how a wireless local area network (WLAN) can be connected to a wired Internet service.
2. Describe how a satellite Internet connection works.
3. Discuss the different methods that can be used to access the Internet using cellular service.

Skill
Review 5 Research Wireless Broadband

1. Open the Google search engine Web site (www.google.com).
2. Use Google to search for information that will help you write or type short answers for the following questions:
   a. What items would you purchase to set up a wireless LAN Internet connection in your home? Describe the items by brand name and list the best price you found for each item.
   b. If fixed wireless Internet is available in your area, describe the service package available from a local service provider.
   c. What level of cellular phone service is available where you live (e.g., 2G, 2.5G, 3G)?
   d. How are service fees calculated for using the Internet through a cell phone?

Choosing an Internet Service Provider

The first step in choosing an Internet Service Provider (ISP) begins with a needs assessment. If you are already using the Internet, you should analyze the way you are using it, and if you have never used the Internet before, you should think about how you plan to use it. For example, if you primarily use e-mail and surf the Web on occasion, you probably do not need an Internet service offering large amounts of bandwidth or disk storage space for hosting Web sites. On the other hand, if you frequently use the Internet to view streaming video, upload or download large files, or play online games, you will need a service that can provide you with the bandwidth you need.

You also should analyze how many hours per week or per month you use or plan to use the Internet. Many ISPs and IAPs offer flat monthly or annual rates, but some offer packages that charge for an initial hourly package and bill for any hours that exceed that amount. Knowing the number of hours you are likely to use the Internet per week or per month will help you determine whether a flat rate or hourly package makes sense for you.

If you want your ISP to host your Web site, you will need to assess how much disk storage, if any, your ISP offers with an account, as well as the price for additional MB of storage. Many accounts include multiple e-mail addresses,

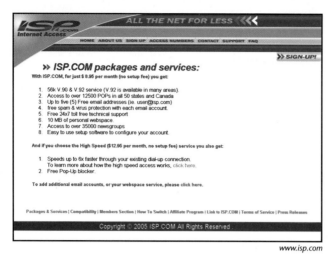

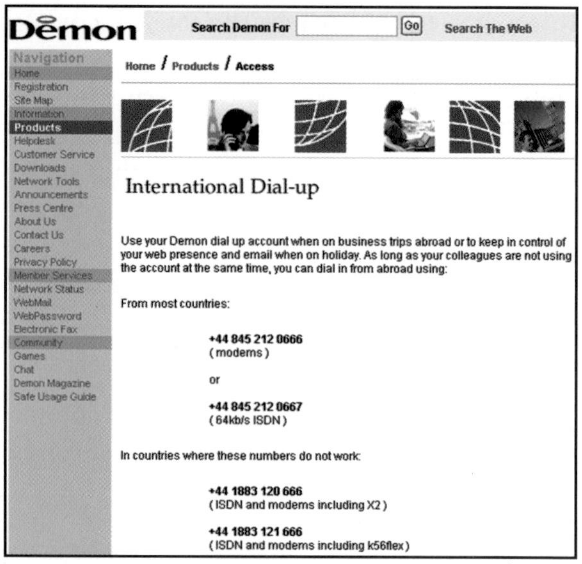

www.isp.com

Figure 2.24 ISP Web Storage and E-mail Address Offer

www.demon.com

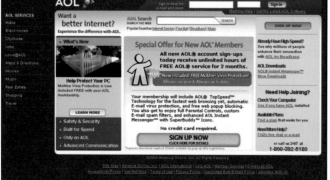

Figure 2.25 International Access Numbers

online service provider (OSP) a type of Internet service provider that offers content and services only to members and usually requires special software that is unique to the OSP, for example AOL and CompuServe

so if you need more than one address, look for that account feature as well as shown in Figure 2.24.

If you want to use your account while traveling, you will need to assess how you can access your account when you are on the road, and what kind of surcharges or rates may be involved if you access your account while you are away. Some ISPs offer 800-number access with a per-minute surcharge. Many providers also offer Web mail service that allows users to check their e-mail accounts using any Internet connection. If you travel overseas, you will want to check to see if the ISP offers International access numbers like those shown in Figure 2.25.

www.juno.com

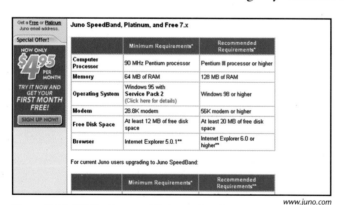

Figure 2.26 ISP Hardware and Software Requirements

Once you have narrowed down your search, you should check with a service provider to see what minimum hardware and software is required and whether there is a cost for any required hardware or software. The Web sites of most ISPs offer information on these requirements, as shown in Figure 2.26. You also should check to see whether you will pay any installation or equipment rental fees. For example, the equipment and installation for a satellite Internet connection typically costs hundreds of dollars.

Many Internet users opt for the convenience of using a type of ISP known as an ***online service provider (OSP)***, such as America Online (AOL) or CompuServe. In addition to Internet access, OSPs offer content and services available only to subscribers and usually provide special software that is unique to the OSP. Figure 2.27 shows some of the price plans and extra services offered by AOL to its members.

Many ISPs offer free trial periods to let you determine whether or not a service is right for

www.aol.com

Figure 2.27 AOL Service Offers

Figure 2.28 Free Internet Service Offer

www.netzero.com

you before spending any money. Some ISPs even offer free Internet service as shown in Figure 2.28. These free accounts usually include only a limited number of usage hours and are offered in the hope that users will sign up for premium accounts.

Support services are a very important factor in choosing an ISP. Some ISPs offer 24/7 support and live telephone or online help, while others offer little or no support. Most users will require help at some point, so the type of help available and when it is available should not be overlooked.

Check with friends or acquaintances to find out the service reputation of an ISP before signing up for an account. Numerous Web sites devoted to explaining different Internet connection methods also describe and rate the service packages provided by different providers. Figure 2.29 shows a Web site that offers advice on choosing cable modem service and offers subscriber ratings for different ISPs.

Figure 2.29 ISP Rating Web Site

http://isprank.com

Concept Review 6 Choosing an Internet Service Provider

1. What is the first thing you should do before evaluating what kind of Internet service is best for you?
2. What is an OSP, and how does an OSP differ from an ISP or IAP?

Skill Review 6 Create an ISP Comparison Table

Create a table that can be used to compare the services offered by different ISPs. Your table should include all the information necessary for someone to make a decision about which service to use.

Chapter Summary

Check your knowledge of chapter concepts by using the flash cards available on the Encore CD that accompanies this book as well as on the Internet Resource Center for this title at www.emcp.net/Internet2e.

- The last mile is often a stumbling block for fast and reliable Internet connections because it often uses technology originally designed for voice service.

- The standard telephone service found in last mile connections to most homes (POTS) uses twisted-pair cables consisting of two insulated copper wires twisted around each other in a continuous spiral.

- ISPs and IAPs connect to the Internet by tapping into Internet backbone access points known as network access points (NAPs).

- Fiber-optic cables transmit data through beams of light that bounce off the reflective walls of the cable as they travel toward their destination.

- Technologies offering bandwidth that is the same whether uploading or downloading data are referred to as symmetrical, while technologies with differing bandwidth for uploading and downloading are referred to as asymmetrical.

- Network overhead means that a certain percentage of available bandwidth will be used to support the transmission of data.

- Throughput is the actual amount of user data that can be transmitted per second rather than the theoretical amount of data transmission capacity measured by bandwidth.

- Modems modulate (adapt or vary) digital data into analog data compatible with an analog phone line and demodulate data back into digital data compatible with computer systems.

- Accelerated Internet uses standard modems and POTS lines to connect to the Internet, but employs compression and caching technologies to increase throughput and provide speeds up to five times faster than standard dial-up connections.

- ISDN integrates voice and data services by creating multiple digital channels in a single telephone wire, allowing the simultaneous use of several devices at the same time.

- Digital Subscriber Line (DSL) technologies are capable of providing high-speed Internet service using POTS twisted-pair cables.

- The most commonly available version of xDSL in the United States is ADSL, with the *A* standing for *asymmetric*.

- While there is more than one DSL standard, the most commonly used is known as Discrete Multitone (DMT) Modulation.

- Some of the equipment used to improve voice signals on POTS lines impede DSL, such as bridge taps or load coils.

- Cable Internet service utilizes the coaxial cable used to provide cable television service to connect users to the Internet.

- Internet-enabled TV set-top boxes handle all the computer functions required to access the Internet, and are in essence another form of a computer.

- A dedicated line is separate from the public telephone network and is for the exclusive use of the organization leasing the line.

- Wireless networking uses radio waves to connect computers equipped for wireless.

- Most wireless hardware available today support one or more of the IEEE 802.11 series of specifications commonly referred to as Wi-Fi.

- In many areas of the United States, ISPs offer fixed wireless Internet service. The ISP's network operations center (NOC) is connected to an Internet backbone and broadcasts data in the form of microwave frequencies from a tower or series of towers.

- Wireless technology can also be used to connect a computer or series of computers to an ADSL or cable modem to access Internet service.

- Digital cellular phone service (2G, 2.5G, and 3G) can be used to link a computer or device to the Internet using cables, a cellular PC card, or Bluetooth wireless technology.

- An alternative to using a cable to connect a cell phone to a computer or device is provided by a PCMCIA card with built-in cell phone capability.

- Bluetooth wireless technology also can be used to connect a cell phone with a computer if both are Bluetooth equipped.

- Satellite Internet offers broadband Internet to those who are unable to connect to the Internet through land-based Internet services such as xDSL or cable.

- The first step in choosing an Internet Service Provider (ISP) begins with a needs assessment.

- You should check with a service provider to see what minimum hardware and software is required, and whether or not any needed hardware or software is provided for free or for a charge.

- Many Internet users opt for the convenience of using a type of ISP known as an online service provider (OSP). OSPs offer content and services that are available only to members, and usually require special software that is unique to the OSP.

Key Terms

Numbers indicate the pages where terms are first cited in the chapter. An alphabetized list of key terms with definitions can be found on the Encore CD that accompanies this book. In addition, these terms and definitions are included in the end-of-book glossary.

accelerated Internet, *42*

analog, *52*

Asymmetric Digital Subscriber Line (ADSL), *43*

asymmetrical, *38*

bandwidth, *38*

broadband over power line (BPL), *47*

dedicated line, *46*

dial-up Internet access, *42*

digital, *52*

Digital Subscriber Line (DSL), *43*

Discrete Multitone (DMT) Modulation, *44*

fiber-optic cable, *35*

fixed wireless Internet service, *50*

High Bit-Rate DSL (HDSL), *45*

hotspot, *51*

Integrated Services Digital Network (ISDN), *42*

Internet backbone, *35*

last mile, *34*

latency, *39*

network access point (NAP), *35*

online service provider (OSP), *56*

Rate Adaptive DSL (RADSL), *45*

satellite Internet, *54*

Symmetric DSL (SDSL), *45*

symmetrical, *38*

throughput, *38*

twisted-pair cable, *34*

Very High Bit-Rate DSL (VDSL), *44*

Wired Equivalency Privacy (WEP), *50*

Wireless Application Protocol (WAP), *52*

Wireless Markup Language (WML), *52*

Net ✓ Check

Additional quiz questions are available on the Encore CD that accompanies this book as well as on the Internet Resource Center for this title at www.emcp.net/Internet2e.

Multiple Choice

Indicate the correct answer for each question or statement.

1. An Internet Service Provider that offers content and services available only to subscribers is known as an
   a. IAP.
   b. ISP.
   c. ILP.
   d. OSP.

2. Bandwidth measures
   a. latency.
   b. the theoretical maximum amount of data that an Internet connection can transmit in one second.
   c. the time it takes to connect to the Internet.
   d. the number of channels in a twisted-pair cable.

3. When used to measure bandwidth a kilobit contains
   a. 1,024 bits.
   b. 1 gigabyte.
   c. 1,000 bits.
   d. Kilobits are not used to measure bandwidth.

4. Which of the following Internet connection methods offers the most bandwidth?
   a. dial-up access
   b. ISDN
   c. accelerated Internet
   d. cable Internet

5. Throughput measures the
   a. nominal or stated bandwidth of an Internet connection method.
   b. actual amount of user data that can be transmitted per second using an Internet connection.
   c. latency rate of an Internet connection.
   d. None of the above

6. Latency rates for satellite Internet connections range between
   a. 2–5 ms.
   b. 10–20 ms.
   c. 15–30 ms.
   d. 500–750 ms.

7. Internet services offering over 56 Kbps of bandwidth are sometimes referred to as
   a. narrowband.
   b. wireless Internet.
   c. broadband.
   d. terrestrial Internet systems.

8. Accelerated Internet uses which of the following to speed Web page loading?
   a. compression technologies and caching
   b. compression technologies and NOC
   c. text-based browsers
   d. cable modems with wireless access points

9. Which of the following Internet connection methods does not allow simultaneous voice and data transmission?
   a. dial-up access
   b. ISDN
   c. DSL
   d. satellite Internet

10. This xDSL technology allows modems to adjust their speed according to the length and quality of a telephone line.
    a. RADSL
    b. ADSL
    c. VDSL
    d. SDSL

True/False

Indicate whether each statement is true or false.

1. Satellite Internet service is not affected by adverse weather conditions.
2. Cable and DSL Internet connections have a range of about 18,000 feet.

3. ADSL uses twisted-pair wires to transmit Internet data.
4. ISDN Internet connections do not allow simultaneous voice and data transmission.
5. Satellite Internet connections have high latency rates.
6. A cable Internet modem that uses a telephone wire for uploads is known as a telco-return cable modem.
7. Modems only work over telephone lines.
8. Asymmetrical Internet technologies almost always have more bandwidth available for downloading compared to uploading.
9. Network overhead refers to the costs associated with running an ISP.
10. WiMax wireless will have a range of up to 30 miles.

Virtual Perspectives

1. Which type of Internet connection method do you think offers the best value for the money? What factors would you take into consideration when choosing an Internet connection method?

2. Would you be interested in TV set-top box Internet access? If yes, explain why you would be interested. If no, describe the type of person who might be interested in using this type of Internet service. Discuss whether you think this type of service has a future, or whether it may be eclipsed by other Internet access methods.

3. Discuss the advantages and disadvantages of using an OSP as compared to using an ISP. Which type of service would you prefer? Provide reasons for your preference.

Internet Lab Projects

Project 1
Measure Latency

1. Use a search engine to find a ping utility such as www.fifi.org/services/ping. *(Hint: Ask your instructor if you need to change your Network Connections setting to allow incoming echo requests. Your instructor may recommend a ping Web site.)*
2. Enter the URL for a Web site and ping it. Print the results.
3. Ping the same URL four more times over a 10-minute period and print the results each time.
4. Compare the results to see the best and worst latency speeds. Compare your results with the average latency rates in Table 2.4.

Project 2
Determine Your Computer's System Information

1. Click Start, click All Programs, click Accessories, click System Tools, and then click System Information to open the System Information window.
2. Select *System Summary* from the list located at the left side of the System Information window and record the following system information:
   - OS Name
   - Version
   - Processor
   - Available Physical Memory
   - Available Virtual Memory
   - Page File Space

(Hint: You can click File on the System Information window menu bar and then Print to print all the System Summary information. Circle the items listed previously on the printout.)

3. Click the plus sign to the left of Components from the list located at the left side of the System Information window, click the plus sign to the left of Network, then click Adapter from the expanded list.

4. You may have several adapters listed, each starting with Name and ending with Driver. Scroll through the list until you find one where the Adapter Type is 802.3 or 802.11. Record or print and circle the following information:
   * Name
   * Adapter Type
   * IP Address

Internet Research Activities

Activity 1
Examine the Issues Surrounding BPL

Supporters of broadband over power line (BPL) claim that it is a revolutionary Internet connection method that will bring Internet access to underserved areas. Research BPL and write a short paper discussing the arguments for and against BPL, as well as the current legal status of BPL in the United States.

Activity 2
Write a Step-by-Step Checklist Describing How to Choose an Internet Connection Method

Use the information you have learned in this chapter as well as information you gather from Internet research to create a checklist outlining the steps that should be followed when deciding which Internet connection method to use.

Activity 3
Net Challenge

Expand on the bandwidth and latency measuring activities described in Skill Review 2 and in Internet Lab Project 1 by conducting a longer-term experiment to measure both of these variables. Over a one-week period (or longer) record bandwidth speeds at the same time each morning and evening. Measure latency rates for two different Web hosts twice a day at the same times. Create a table to compare the results. Analyze the data and write a short paper showing any patterns you observe, such as times or days when bandwidth or latency is usually low or high. Use what you have learned from this chapter and research you conduct on the Internet to explain what may be causing any patterns you observe.

Chapter

Ensuring Internet Security 3

Learning Objectives

- Differentiate between the different types of malware.

- Explain how antivirus programs work.

- Describe how a firewall works.

- Explain the role service patches and updates play in maintaining computer security.

- Explain phishing and 419 scams.

- Compare and contrast DoS, DDoS, and brute force attacks.

- Change Internet Explorer security settings.

- Summarize how encryption works.

- Explain the difference between adware and spyware and discuss the implications of each.

- Describe how cookies work.

- Describe methods that can be used to block spam.

- Explain the procedures designed to avoid adware and spyware.

Living on the *Net*

After her return from Europe, Carolyn noticed that her computer seemed to be running more slowly than when it was new. Programs and files that used to open in the blink of an eye now appeared after a noticeable and irritating delay. She also observed an increasing number of pop-up windows when she browsed the Web, and Web pages loaded more slowly as well. Carolyn suspected that the problems might be due to a computer virus. She had a close friend named Peter who ran a computer repair service, so Carolyn gave him a call and made an appointment to drop off her computer the next day.

Later that week, Carolyn received a call informing her that her computer was ready to be picked up. She was so eager to get her computer back that she rushed to get it during her lunch break. Before Peter could say anything, Carolyn asked him why the antivirus program on her computer had failed to prevent a virus or viruses from infecting her computer. She was shocked when he told her that her problems were not caused by a virus. Instead, her system had been cluttered by adware and spyware programs that had surreptitiously installed themselves. Because such programs are not intentionally malicious they are not considered viruses, but they often cause virus-like symptoms similar to those that Carolyn experienced. Peter explained that better antivirus programs and increased awareness had reduced the number of systems infected with viruses to the point that he now spent much more time repairing adware and spyware problems than he did on virus problems. Peter noted that like Carolyn, most of his customers had no idea that adware and spyware programs were installed on their computers.

Carolyn's experience is not unusual. Drawbacks in the form of increased exposure to irritating or even harmful activities often accompany the Internet's benefits. The Internet also can expose a user to criminal acts and compromise his or her privacy. Just as a person must be aware of threats in everyday life, an Internet user must learn to be aware of threats that might deliver harm via the Internet. Learning about the different threats is the first step in combating them.

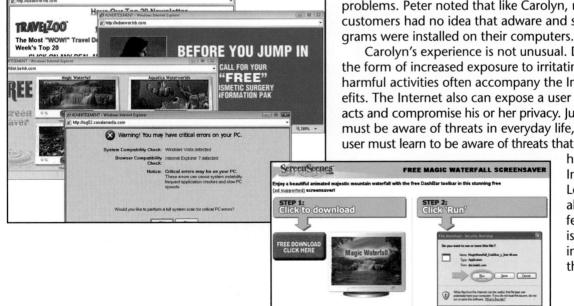

Malware

malware short for *malicious software*, malware refers to any program or computer code deliberately designed to harm any portion of a computer system

Tech Demo 3-1
E-Mail Viruses

Malware (*mal*icious soft*ware*) refers to any program or computer code deliberately designed to harm any portion of a computer system. In 2004, industry experts estimated that malware caused up to $192 billion in damage to computer systems worldwide. This figure does not include the billions of dollars spent protecting against the threat posed by malware. A threat is any event that could potentially violate the security of your computer system. Victims of malware may lose valuable data and spend considerable time and money repairing the damage. The three most common forms of malware are viruses, worms, and Trojan horses. Sometimes the different malware types are used in combination in what are known as blended threats. Figure 3.1 shows a Microsoft decision tree used to help distinguish the different types of malware.

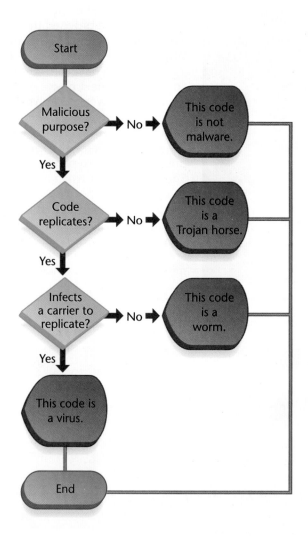

Figure 3.1 Microsoft Malware Decision Tree

Viruses

A *virus* is a self-replicating form of malware that is spread from computer to computer using another file or program as a host. In the early days of personal computing, viruses entered computer systems through transferable media such as floppy disks or files downloaded from computer bulletin board services. The Internet now provides the route for most virus transmissions. Once a user downloads a virus-infected file or program and the virus executes on the user's computer system, the virus can release its *payload*—the malicious action that will be performed by the virus. Virus actions can range from pranks, such as a message that will appear periodically on a computer screen, to extremely damaging events such as the corruption or loss of data. In worst-case scenarios, a virus may delete the entire contents of a hard drive. Even seemingly benign virus payloads are potentially damaging because they consume system resources and Internet bandwidth when they replicate. They also have the potential to corrupt data, even if that was not the intent of the person who created the virus.

Virus payloads can take a number of different forms, including backdoor payloads that allow unauthorized access to a computer, data corruption or deletion payloads that damage or even remove data from a computer, and information theft payloads that steal information from a computer. A virus payload can activate automatically, be activated manually by an unwitting user, or activate after a predetermined time or event such as a date or a keystroke sequence.

The Love Bug Virus

One of the worst malware attacks in recent years was a blended threat known as the Love Bug. The Love Bug combined Trojan horse and worm features. Users received an e-mail with an attachment named I Love You. When the user opened the attachment, the Love Bug's payload would hijack the user's Outlook Express Address Book to mail itself to every contact in the book. Recipients of the e-mails would then think that the Love Bug e-mail was coming from a trusted source and open the attachment, thus repeating the cycle. This method of propagation enabled the Love Bug to spread around the world in a matter of hours. Government institutions such as the U.S. State Department and the UK House of Commons were affected, as well as private-sector organizations such as Silicon Graphics and DaimlerChrysler. Unlike the earlier Melissa virus, the Love Bug was very destructive because it was programmed to overwrite music and image files. Investigators eventually determined that the Love Bug was created by a hacker in the Philippines who used pre-paid phone cards and hacked computer accounts in an effort to cover his tracks. Because the Philippines had no laws covering this type of activity, he went unpunished. By the time it was all over, more than 45 million computers around the world had been infected and total damages were estimated in the billions of dollars. The Address Book hijacking method used by the Love Bug is still popular, as attested by the more recent Bugbear, Sobig, and Mydoom attacks.

Worms

A *worm* is a form of malware that spreads through network connections without the need for a host program. The first widely known instance of Internet-spread malware was a worm. In 1988 the Morris worm, named for its creator, infected over 6,000 computers using the UNIX operating system. As is sometimes the case, the author of the Morris worm did not intend to do damage, but a coding error caused the worm to loop and repeatedly infect computers until they slowed down to the point where they were unusable. The number of computers that were eventually infected with the Morris worm amounted to almost 10 percent of the computers connected to the Internet, and the eventual damage that the Morris worm caused was estimated at up to $100 million.

The Morris worm served as a wake-up call to computer professionals. One of the positive outcomes of this incident was the formation in 1988 of the Computer Emergency Response Team, now known as CERT Coordination Center, or CERT/CC. After the Morris worm incident, DARPA established CERT/CC to coordinate efforts to deal with similar threats to computer security and to build security issue awareness among Internet users. The

virus a self-replicating form of malware that is spread from computer to computer using another file or program as a host

payload the malicious action that will be performed by the virus

worm a form of malware that spreads through network connections without the need for a host program

Figure 3.2 CERT/CC Home Page

CERT/CC Web site shown in Figure 3.2 is a valuable source of information on the latest computer security threats.

Trojan Horses

A *Trojan horse* is a type of malware that disguises itself as a harmless or legitimate program to persuade people to download and run it. Therefore, a Trojan horse does not need to self-replicate like a virus or worm. A Trojan horse program may use a name that entices a user to download and open it, such as FreeMP3.exe or Kiss.exe. Running the Trojan horse executable (.exe) file then enables it to unleash its payload, which can take any number of forms. The typical Windows configuration often prevents users from seeing the file extension, so a user might not know he or she is about to run an executable program file. Using the example of the Kiss.exe Trojan horse mentioned above, its full file name might be Kiss.txt.exe, but it may appear as Kiss.txt in Windows. That could mislead users to think that it is a harmless file because text files are not known to spread viruses. One common Trojan horse payload disconnects a dial-up user from his or her normal ISP and reconnects the user to a number charging exorbitant rates as high as $150 an hour. This activity is known as stealth dialing because users are usually unaware of what is going on until they receive an inflated phone bill.

> **Trojan horse** a type of malware that hides disguises itself as a harmless or legitimate program

Concept Review 1 Malware

1. What are the key distinguishing characteristics of viruses, worms, and Trojan horses?
2. What is a backdoor payload?
3. What is a malware payload?

Skill Review 1 Perform a System Vulnerability Scan

(Note: Ask your instructor if you have permission to download and save files to your computer network location. If you do have permission, ask your instructor where you should save the file you download for this exercise.)

1. Open the Microsoft Security Tools Web page by typing **http://www.microsoft.com/technet/security/tools/default.mspx** in the browser Address bar and then pressing Enter.
2. Scroll down the page and then click the <u>Microsoft Baseline Security Analyzer (MBSA) 2.0</u> hyperlink.
3. Microsoft still offers older versions of the MBSA tool. Read the description of each version to determine which is appropriate for your system. You will most likely need version 2.0. Click the MBSA 2.0 link.
4. Scroll down the MBSA 2.0 page and then click the <u>Download Now</u> hyperlink.

Security Update Detection Solutions

> Step 2 → **Microsoft Baseline Security Analyzer (MBSA) 2.0**
> MBSA 2.0 scans for missing security updates and comm_ an improved user experience, expanding product suppo_

> Step 3 → **MBSA 2.0**
> MBSA 2.0 offers an intuitive user i_ versions. Using the new Windows

On This Page
> Step 4 →
> ↓ Download Now
> ↓ Detailed Information
> ↓ Frequently Asked Questions (FAQ)

5. Click the appropriate language version when the next page appears.

6. Before the download begins, Microsoft validates your copy of Windows as being "genuine". If you have not validated your copy of Windows previously, you will have to click Continue to start the validation process, then follow the onscreen instructions.

7. After the validation completes and a new page opens, scroll down to the download section and click the Download button for your language. (EN for English.)

8. Click Save when the File Download - Security Warning dialog box appears.

9. Once the MBSA file is downloaded, close your web browser, locate the MBSA file on your hard drive, and install the program on your computer or network. *(Note: Ask your instructor where the analyzer should be installed.)*

10. Click Start, point to All Programs, and then click Microsoft Baseline Security Analyzer 2.0 to open it.

11. Click the Scan a computer hyperlink.

12. Click the Start scan hyperlink at the bottom of the next page to start the scan. *(Hint: The scan may take a few minutes to complete.)*

13. If desired, click the Print button located on the left side of the security report page to print a copy of the report.

14. Close the Microsoft Baseline Security Analyzer when you are finished.

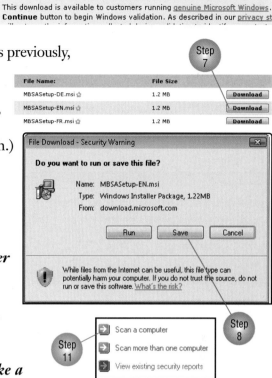

Malware Countermeasures

Internet users can use various countermeasures to protect against threats to computer security. Fortunately, countermeasures to guard against malware are highly developed today, and a properly configured computer system should be able to ward off most threats.

Installing an antivirus program designed to detect viruses, worms, Trojan horses, and other forms of malware serves as the first line of defense. Software and/or hardware firewalls can add another layer of protection to a computer or network. Installing the latest security patches and software updates to rectify any operating system vulnerabilities remains vital. Finally, using passwords to prevent unauthorized access to your computer and e-mail program provides another important barrier in guarding against threats. The combination of these four countermeasures along with user vigilance and common sense will not guarantee security, but will ensure that potential threats are kept to a minimum.

Tech Demo 3-2
Security Measures

Antivirus Programs

Antivirus programs (virus protection software) scan computers or computer systems to detect any malware that may be present. Most antivirus programs also offer proactive features to help prevent malware from gaining a foothold

antivirus program software that can be used to scan a computer to detect any malware that may be present

Figure 3.3 Online Antivirus Scanning

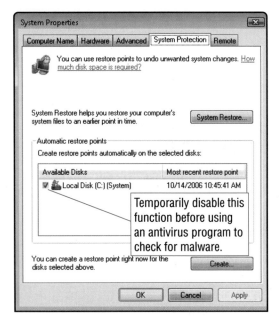

Figure 3.4 Disabling the Windows Vista System Restore Function

in any computer system. Users can purchase antivirus programs as retail CD-ROMs or as downloads. Programs such as Norton Antivirus, PC-Cillin, and McAfee VirusScan are among the most popular antivirus programs available. Software companies increasingly offer online antivirus scanning as shown in Figure 3.3.

When an antivirus program detects an infected file, the program typically offers three different options for dealing with the infected file: cleaning, deleting, or quarantining. The user can set the default mode (choosing one of those three options) or manually override the default if desired. If an antivirus program cannot clean an infected file, the file may be quarantined or deleted. Files in quarantine will not cause further damage, as they are safely isolated. Future (downloadable) updates to the antivirus program may enable the program to clean and release quarantined files at a later date.

Windows Vista includes a System Restore function that can be used to revert to computer settings from a previous point in time in the event of any harmful or unwanted changes in settings or operation. Unfortunately, System Restore can allow viruses to remain in backup files where they cannot be cleaned or deleted by antivirus programs. For that reason it is a good idea to temporarily disable this function before using an antivirus program to check for malware. Once an antivirus scan is completed, you should re-enable the System Restore function. The Windows System Restore function can be disabled by using the following steps:

1. Click Start and then click Control Panel. If using Classic View, switch to Control Panel Home via the link in the left sidebar.
2. Click System and Maintenance.
3. Click System.
4. Click Advanced System Settings from the left sidebar.
5. If Windows Vista's User Account Control is enabled and you are prompted to click Continue, please do so.
6. Click the System Protection tab.
7. If a drive's checkbox is checked as shown in Figure 3.4, System Restore is enabled for that drive. To disable System Restore for a drive, click the checkbox to remove the check.

Antivirus programs usually employ three different methods to detect malware: signature scanning looks for virus signatures, heuristic scanning looks for malware characteristics, and behavior blocking looks for behavior patterns that suggest malware activity.

Signature Scanning

virus signature a string of binary code that is unique to a virus, also known as its fingerprint or pattern

A *virus signature* is a string of binary code unique to a particular virus. Virus signatures are also known as fingerprints or patterns. Antivirus software keeps a dictionary of known virus signatures, often referred to as *virus definitions,* to identify and protect against known viruses. Because new viruses appear all the time, the virus definitions must be updated frequently to maintain the program's ability to defend against threats. Many antivirus programs will automatically inform users when a new virus definition update is available for download as shown in Figure 3.5.

There are several drawbacks to signature scanning. Polymorphic viruses change with each replication. The constantly changing signature of a polymorphic virus makes it more difficult to detect using definition files alone. Signature scanning also is ineffective against new viruses for which definition updates do not yet exist. Perhaps the biggest drawback is that signature scanning is a reactive method, meaning that it detects malware only after it has infected a computer system. Fortunately, other methods such as heuristic scanning and behavior blocking can be used to detect malware. Both of these proactive methods work to prevent malware from infecting a computer system.

Figure 3.5 Virus Signature Update

Heuristic Scanning

Heuristic scanning looks for general malware characteristics rather than specific characteristics such as a signature. Heuristic problem solving relies on previous experience or knowledge. An antivirus program that uses heuristic scanning examines file size, architecture, or code behavior. Heuristic scanning can produce false positives and negatives. For example, it might report a legitimate software program as malware on the basis that it shares some characteristics with known malware programs. Just as with signature scanning, heuristic scanning software requires periodic updates to ensure that the catalog of suspicious characteristics is up to date.

virus definitions a dictionary file used by antivirus software to identify known viruses.

heuristic scanning antivirus program tool that looks for general malware characteristics rather than specific characteristics such as a signature

behavior blocking antivirus program tool that looks for behaviors that are typical of malware

Behavior Blocking

To supplement signature checking and heuristic scanning detection features, antivirus programs also look for suspicious behavior. *Behavior blocking* looks for typical malware behaviors, such as attempts to change computer settings, the opening and or alteration of files, network communications initiation, attempts to open computer ports, and so on. Ports are computer doorways used for various activities, and an open or unguarded port can be the entryway for malware. Behavior blocking is becoming an increasingly popular method for detecting malware because hackers face greater difficulty in changing malware behavior than changing a virus signature.

Firewalls

As illustrated in Figure 3.6, a firewall is a hardware or software barrier located between the Internet and a computer or computer network. Many routers available nowadays contain built-in firewalls. Microsoft Vista features a software firewall that can be enabled by users as shown in Figure 3.7. A firewall filters data arriving

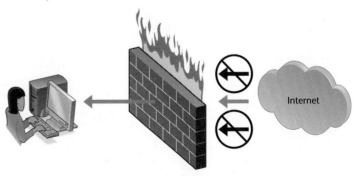

Figure 3.6 Firewall Protection

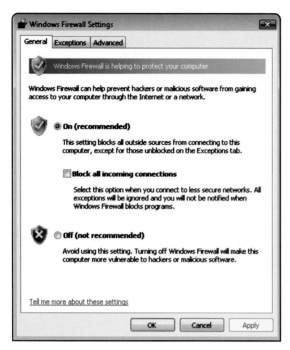

Figure 3.7 Windows Vista Firewall Options

proxy server a firewall function that handles page and data requests so that the requesting computer or computer network never comes into direct contact with remote computer systems

through the Internet to protect the system from any threats. Firewalls can be configured to reject incoming packets based on the IP address or domain name they originate from. This prevents the entry of data from sites known to harbor threats. A user can configure a firewall to allow or disallow the use of different protocols. For example, a network administrator may wish to restrict the use of the File Transfer Protocol (FTP) to prevent unauthorized file transfers from taking place. Firewalls also can filter incoming packets for text they might contain. This type of filtering ability might typically enable a computer network to reject any incoming content of an adult nature.

Many firewalls make use of a **_proxy server_** function. A proxy server handles page and data requests so that the requesting computer or computer network never comes into direct contact with remote computer systems, thereby adding another level of threat protection. A proxy server also can speed up Internet access by saving frequently visited Web pages so that the proxy server can reload the pages directly rather than retrieving them from a remote computer.

Start with the highest level of security when you configure a firewall. If the highest security level creates problems by denying access to legitimate data, adjust the configuration until an appropriate balance between security and convenience is achieved. While a firewall can help prevent malware from entering a computer system, it is not the same as an antivirus program, and the two should always be used in conjunction to provide the highest level of security. Firewalls play a particularly important role in preventing unauthorized access via always-on Internet connections such as xDSL or cable.

Service Patches and Updates

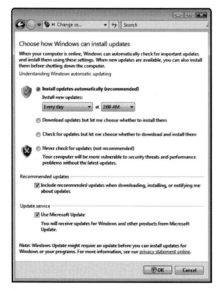

Figure 3.8 Microsoft Windows Vista Automatic Updates Dialog Box

The Microsoft Windows operating system versions have been much criticized for containing vulnerabilities that make them susceptible to security threats. As a result, Microsoft offers security updates or patches to repair system vulnerabilities when discovered. Because new security updates appear fairly frequently, you should ensure that your computer has the latest security patches and software updates installed. The default Windows Vista configuration periodically checks for new security patches or updates when they become available and then automatically downloads and installs them. To open the Automatic Updates dialog box, click Start and then click Control Panel. In the Control Panel window, click Security, locate the section titled Windows Update, and click the link _Turn automatic updating on or off_ to open the Automatic Updates dialog box shown in Figure 3.8. By default, Automatic Updates will check for and download updates on a daily basis, but you can change the frequency if desired. A surprising percentage of people using Microsoft Windows operating systems fail to install security patches and software updates, unnecessarily exposing their computer systems to security threats.

Password Protection

Passwords serve as an important method for ensuring that unauthorized parties do not obtain access to your confidential data. Password protection is particularly important if you share your computer with others or if your computer is part of a network. To protect your computer against unauthorized use, you can create passwords to protect your user account on Windows Vista. After you assign a password to your account, Windows will prompt you to enter your password whenever you start Windows or log on to your account as shown in Figure 3.9.

Figure 3.9 Windows Vista User Logon

Concept Review 2 — Malware Countermeasures

1. What can be done to protect your computer against malware?
2. Explain the different methods that antivirus programs use to detect malware.
3. What does a firewall do?

Skill Review 2 — Create a Windows Vista Firewall Security Log

(Note: Before starting this exercise, ask your instructor if your system is using the Windows Vista firewall, and if so, whether you are permitted to change configuration settings to create a security log.)

1. Open the Windows Firewall dialog box by clicking Start, Control Panel, System and Maintenance, Administrative Tools.
2. Double-click Windows Firewall with Advanced Security and choose Continue if prompted by the Vista User Account Control dialog box.
3. Under the Public Profile section, click the link Windows Firewall Properties.
4. Click the tab for the profile you want to change. If you are connected to a home network, you will most likely want the Private Profile tab.
5. Click the Customize button in the *Security Logging* section to open the Customize Logging Settings dialog box.

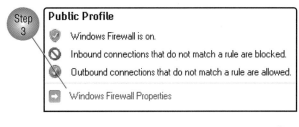

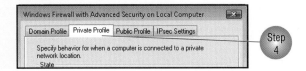

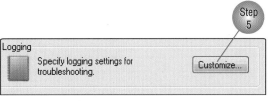

6. Set the *Log dropped packets* drop-down menu to Yes.

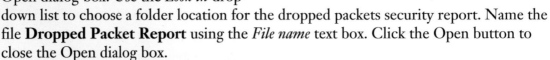

7. Click the Browse button to open the Open dialog box. Use the *Look in* drop-down list to choose a folder location for the dropped packets security report. Name the file **Dropped Packet Report** using the *File name* text box. Click the Open button to close the Open dialog box.

8. Click the OK button to close the Customize Logging Settings dialog box.

9. Click the OK button to close the Properties dialog box.

10. Click the Close button on the Windows Firewall with Advanced Security window to close it. Continue closing the Administrative Tools window and the Control Panel window.

11. After using the Internet for two or more hours, locate the **Dropped Packet Report.log** file in the folder you indicated in the Open dialog box and open the file. Look at the report to see if any packets were dropped.

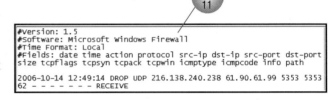

The #Fields lines at the top of the report lists headings that explain what the numbers mean. Print a copy of the report when you are finished.

Cyber Crime

Cyber crime is a relatively new term that refers to crimes committed using the Internet. Unfortunately, the very factors that make the Internet a success make it attractive to criminals. Through the Internet, criminals around the world can gain access to people and information with the click of a mouse. Many cyber crimes originate from countries with poor or lax law enforcement, making those crimes difficult to prosecute even if the perpetrators are identified. The nature of the Internet can also make it easy for savvy criminals to destroy evidence that any crime was committed by erasing Web logs and other records that could be used to track them. Many instances of cyber crime go unreported because the victims are embarrassed at having been so naïve, or feel that nothing can be done to catch the perpetrators. Because cyber crime often transcends local and national boundaries, unclear jurisdiction can make law enforcement a nightmare. The issues raised by cyber crime mean that the law enforcement framework worldwide is still being updated to deal with the reality of crimes committed over the Internet.

Lawbreakers use a number of techniques to commit crime using the Internet, and the following sections describe some of the most popular methods in use today. In addition to making sure that your computer is configured to provide maximum threat protection, awareness can help you defend yourself. Many cyber crimes require the cooperation of gullible targets in order to succeed, so the more you know about cyber crime, the lower the likelihood that you will become a cyber crime victim.

Phishing

With *phishing*, an online scammer sends a user an e-mail that appears to be from a legitimate and well-known company to try to trick the user into sending confidential information. The practice of disguising an e-mail or a Web site so that it appears to belong to a well-known company such as eBay, American Express, or others is called *spoofing*. The e-mail typically lists a URL that will direct victims to a spoofed Web site that gives every appearance of being the legitimate Web site of a familiar company. The sender of a phishing attack wants victims to provide passwords, credit card numbers, banking details, or other confidential information.

In one popular phishing variant, scammers say that they are updating account details and ask recipients to update their account information as shown in the spoofed eBay e-mail displayed in Figure 3.10. Victims are directed to a spoofed Web site so that they can provide the requested confidential information via a legitimate-looking form. The scammers use the gathered information to plunder bank accounts or run up credit card bills. Victims may never realize that the theft was accomplished using the confidential information they unwittingly provided to the cyber criminals, and even if they do, the perpetrators are long gone by the time the crime is uncovered.

Many users recognize phishing attempts by noticing obvious spelling or grammatical errors. In the spoofed eBay e-mail shown in Figure 3.11, note the awkward sentence construction and incorrect capitalization. As criminals become more adept at spoofing e-mail addresses and Web sites, their ability to deceive victims increases. While current phishing attacks are estimated to have a 3 percent success rate, some experts think that sophisticated attacks might someday raise that rate as high as 50 percent.

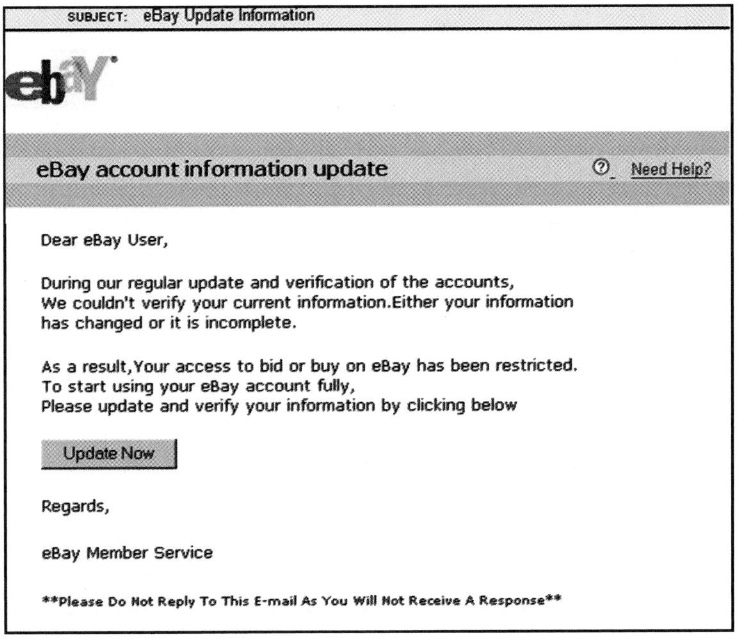

phishing an online scam that tricks Internet users into believing that they are being contacted by a legitimate and well-known company

spoofing disguising an e-mail or Web site so that it appears to come from a well-known or trusted company

Figure 3.10 Spoofed eBay E-mail

Reverse 419 Scams

The popularity of the 419 scam has led to so-called reverse 419 scams in which individuals attempt to turn the tables on the 419 scammers by wasting their time in amusing ways. The often hilarious results are then posted on the Web sites of the reverse 419 scammers. Reverse 419 scammers frequently dupe the scammers into posing for ridiculous photos in order to establish their legitimacy. In one incident, a 419 scammer posed for a photo with his shirt off and a letter painted on his chest to show that he had completed a ritual that the reverse scammer had proposed in order to establish the 419 scammer's legitimacy. Reverse 419 scammers sit back and laugh as the 419 scammers offer earnest replies to silly scenarios that the reverse scammers have concocted. Some have even completely turned the table by tricking the 419 scammers into advancing them money. While the efforts of the reverse scammers have increased awareness of this type of cyber crime, law enforcement authorities take a dim view of this activity. Those behind the 419 scams are often very dangerous people, and some victims who have traveled to meet the scammers have been murdered. The best thing to do if you receive a 419 scam e-mail is to ignore it, or to forward it to the local field office of the U.S. Secret Service.

419 Scams

The 419 scam, or advance fee fraud, is a very popular cyber crime committed using e-mail. The scam gets its name from a section of the Nigerian penal code, because the vast majority of this type of crime originates in that country. The 419 scam depends on the gullibility and greed of victims to succeed. The crime begins with the victim receiving an e-mail purporting to be from someone, often a government official, who has access to a large amount of money but is unable to smuggle it out of the country. The scammers say that in return for the victim assisting them in smuggling the money out of the country, the victim will get a percentage of the total, often amounting to millions of dollars. The scammers make their money by tricking their victims into paying advance fees to facilitate the smuggling. These fees can amount to thousands of dollars before victims finally realize that there is no pot of gold at the end of the rainbow. Almost anyone who has an e-mail account has received at least one 419 e-mail such as that shown in Figure 3.11. No one can estimate the true amount of damage done by 419 scams, as victims are usually reluctant to step forward because the role they thought they were playing in the scam was unethical.

Denial-of-Service (DoS) Attacks

Denial-of-service (DoS) attacks paralyze computer networks by bombarding them with traffic in the form of packets of useless information. Network servers targeted by a DoS attack slow down as they become overwhelmed dealing with packets and can eventually grind to a halt. The goal of DoS attackers is to deny service to those they oppose for economic or political reasons, or sometimes just for

denial-of-service (DoS) attack
attack that paralyzes a computer network by bombarding it with traffic in the form of packets of useless information

Mr. A. John
Inter continental bank Plc.
Eko branch,
Lagos, Nigeria.

For the attention of: The C.E.O

Compliment of the day and how is life generally with you? Of course it is my humble wish to solicit and crave your indulgence to make this project request for a joint business transaction, which I hope, will not come to you as a surprise, hence I plead for your pardon.

I am Mr. Aboh John, the manager in the Intercontinental bank Plc above. I have an urgent and confidential business proposal for you.

On June 8, 1998, an Australian oil consultant/contractor with via Nigerian National Petroleum cooperation (NNPC) Mr. Uzter Khan made a numbered time (fixed) deposit for twelve calendar months valued at US$18,000.00(Eighteen Million US Dollars) in my branch.

On maturity, I sent a routine notification to his forwarded address in Nigeria but got no reply. After months we sent a reminder and finally we discovered from his contract employee (Nigerian National Petroleum Corporation) that Mr. Uzter Khan died from an auto crash accident in Nigeria. All attempts by the Australian to trace his next of kin were fruitless.

Figure 3.11 419 Scam E-mail

fun. Past victims of DoS attacks include Microsoft, the U.S. government, Yahoo, Amazon, and CNN.com.

Because a DoS attack involves sending thousands of messages in a short period of time a new type of attack called a ***distributed denial-of-service (DDoS) attack*** has been developed. In a DDoS attack, a Trojan horse is used to download a small program onto an unsuspecting Internet user's computer. The program transforms the computer into a zombie that is used to send messages to the target of a coordinated DDoS attack. Hundreds or even thousands of zombie computers can be used in a single attack, for the most part without the computer owners' even being aware of their involvement. A DDoS attack is very difficult to combat because of the sheer number of computers used and the fact that the owners have no idea that their machines have been hijacked.

Even more insidious than a normal DDoS attack is a form of DDoS attack known as a pulsing zombie. A pulsing zombie attack intermittently degrades rather than shuts down a service. The intermittent nature of the attack makes it even more difficult to detect and combat because it may be some time before a service's operators realize that an attack is underway. Corporations and governments are usually technically capable of preventing their computers from being used in staging DDoS attacks, but home users with inadequate safeguards in place are vulnerable.

distributed denial-of-service (DDoS) attack DoS attack that uses a Trojan horse to download a small program onto an unsuspecting Internet user's computer so that the computer can be one of many computers used to take part in a DDoS attack

brute force attack an attack that aims to overcome a password-protected computer or network by systematically trying different combinations of letters and numbers until the correct password is discovered

Brute Force Attacks

A ***brute force attack*** aims to overcome a password-protected computer or network by systematically trying different combinations of letters and numbers until the correct password is discovered. Some computer experts, known as hackers, attempt to break into computer systems or networks just to see if they can, while others have more sinister intent. Hackers sometimes refers to those who wish to do damage as crackers, but the distinction between hackers and crackers is not recognized by many outside of the hacker community because damage can result from a break-in even if it was unintentional. The fact that many computer users create passwords using common words, word combinations, or word and number combinations makes many systems vulnerable to brute force attacks. With this in mind, hackers consult dictionaries of commonly used password combinations to increase the likelihood of a successful attack. Because brute force attackers can target many systems at the same time, even a small success rate can be worthwhile. To make the job of brute force attackers even more difficult, Internet users should never use passwords based on simple or easily deduced word or number combinations.

Concept Review 3 Cyber Crime

1. How would you define cyber crime?
2. Describe some of the different types of cyber crime.
3. What is spoofing, and what role does it play in cyber crime?

1. Use the Internet to find at least one real-life example for at least four different types of cyber crime.
2. Research United States legislation that can be used to combat the types of cyber crime you discovered in the previous step.
3. Research cyber crime statistics.
4. Use the information you gathered in the previous steps to write a short paper which includes the following:
   - Profiles the cyber crime cases you discovered
   - Uses some of the cyber crime statistics you discovered to give your readers a feeling for the extent of the problem
   - Describes what kind of legislation is used to combat cyber crime

Cyber Crime Countermeasures

The same measures used to protect your computer against malware can play a role in protecting against cyber crime. However, antivirus programs, firewalls, and passwords alone are not enough. Two additional tools can supplement the role played by the methods mentioned above in protecting against cyber crime. Internet Explorer enables users to tailor security settings for Web sites, and encryption can be used to authenticate and protect communications, including confidential transactions.

Internet Explorer Security Settings

To configure Internet Explorer security settings, click Tools on the Internet Explorer Command Bar and then click Internet Options to open the Internet Options dialog box. Clicking the Security tab displays the Internet Explorer security settings.

Internet Explorer enables users to assign Web sites to different Web content security zones depending on how trusted the sites are. The default Internet Explorer security setting places all Web sites in an Internet zone and assigns them a medium security level as shown in Figure 3.12. The Medium security level means that Internet Explorer will prompt you to take action to confirm a download from a Web site in the Internet Zone (Figure 3.13) and will not allow unsigned ActiveX controls to be downloaded.

You can choose one of four security level choices for each security zone: Low, Medium-low, Medium, and High. Move the level slider up or down to see a description of each level and how it operates as shown in Figure 3.12. The higher the security level, the more restrictive it is. The Medium level is the recommended

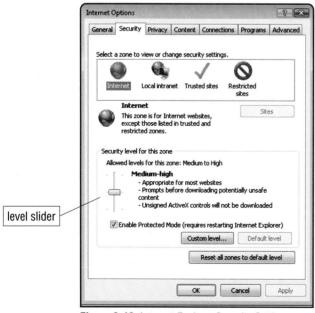

level slider

Figure 3.12 Internet Explorer Security Settings

compromise, but Internet users who desire the highest level of security can set the slider setting to High.

Internet Explorer users also can assign Web sites to the Restricted sites or Trusted sites zones. Web sites placed in the Restricted sites zone have a default security setting of High, while the Trusted site zone has a security setting of Low. Only Web sites that you are confident you can trust should be placed in the Trusted sites zone. Use the Restricted sites zone for Web sites with a high potential for danger. Web sites cannot be added to the Internet zone because it includes all Web sites with the exception of those contained in the Trusted, Restricted, or Intranet zones.

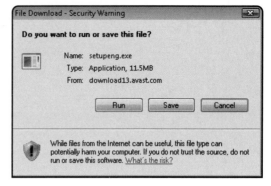

Figure 3.13 File Download Warning Message

Encryption and Authentication

When you use e-mail to send messages across the Internet, it is possible for those messages to be intercepted and read by others without your knowledge. This fact becomes particularly worrying if a message contains valuable information, such as a credit card number or other form of confidential data. To protect against this possibility, you can apply powerful mathematical formulas known as algorithms to encrypt a message so that it is difficult, if not impossible, for unauthorized parties to decrypt and read the message. *Encryption* refers to the process of using an algorithm to scramble text or data into an unreadable format that cannot be unscrambled without the use of a key.

Because the Internet is not a form of face-to-face communication, encryption also provides a method for authenticating personal identity and protecting the integrity of documents and Web sites. *Authentication* refers to the process of verification. Encryption technology underpins digital certificates for verifying an identity, digital signatures for verifying that a document was signed by the person purporting to sign the document and that the document has not been altered since it was signed, and Secure Sockets Layer (SSL) technology for ensuring secure Web transactions.

encryption the process of scrambling text or data into an unreadable format that cannot be unscrambled without the use of a key

authentication refers to the process of verification

Symmetric Encryption/Asymmetric Encryption

Figure 3.14 is a simple example illustrating the message encryption process. An encryption method could scramble a word by using a key that shifts each letter in the word forward three places in the alphabet. Using this key, the word THE would be spelled WKJ when encrypted. Anyone in possession of the key used to encrypt THE can easily decrypt WKJ back to THE, but anyone without the key would have a difficult time figuring out what WKJ represented. In symmetric encryption the message sender and recipient both use the same private key to encrypt and decrypt their communication. This method can be used on the Internet, but the sender and the recipient must know and trust each other, as each party must possess the same key. Both parties must maintain strict security to ensure that the key does not fall into the wrong hands.

Because the public nature of Internet communications makes it difficult to ensure the confidentiality of private keys, a method for sharing keys called asymmetric or public key encryption is used instead. Asymmetric encryption uses paired private and public keys to encrypt and decrypt data as shown in

Figure 3.15. While the paired keys are mathematically related, knowledge of the content of one key cannot be used to determine the content of the other key. To exchange encrypted messages, both parties need to possess unique paired private and public keys. The users can exchange public keys through a public forum such as a public key ring or registry. If Bill wants to send Jenny a confidential message, he would use Jenny's public key to encrypt the message. Jenny would then use her private key to decrypt the message. To respond to Bill's message, Jenny would then use Bill's public key to encrypt her response, and Bill would use his private key to decrypt it. If a third party somehow gained access to any of the encrypted messages Bill and Jenny were exchanging, the third party would be unable to decrypt the messages because the third party would not have access to the required private keys. Asymmetric encryption thus enables Internet users to communicate securely, without the need to use secure channels to exchange private keys.

Because asymmetric encryption works much more slowly than symmetric encryption, the two methods are often combined. The user encrypts a symmetric key using asymmetric encryption, and sends the encrypted key along with symmetrically encrypted data. The recipient decrypts the encrypted symmetric key using his or her private key and then uses the decrypted symmetric key to decrypt the data.

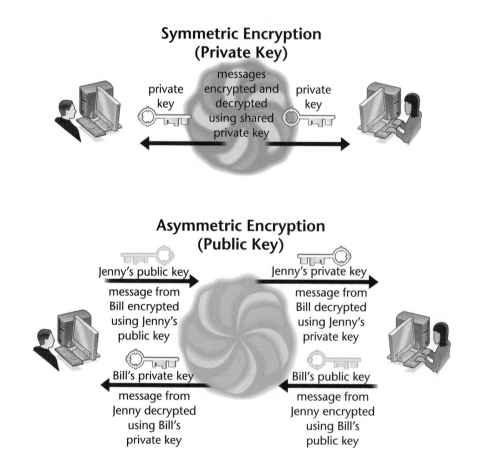

Figure 3.14 Symmetric and Asymmetric Encryption

Digital Certificates

Digital certificates provide a means of verifying that a public key belongs to the person who claims to own it. Without a digital certificate, it could be possible for someone to create a private/public key pair in another user's name and then use the public key to impersonate the user and deceive others. A digital certificate acts as a form of credential that enables others to verify that an identity attached to a public key is correct.

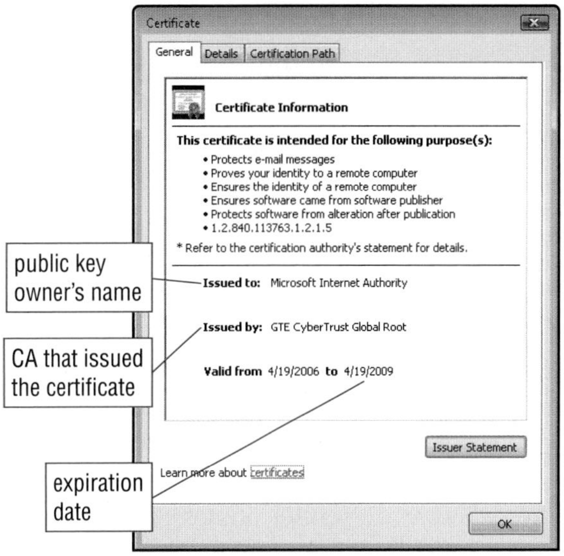

Digital certificates are issued by independent certification bodies known as certification authorities (CA). The CA confirms the identity of anyone applying for a digital certificate. A personal certificate confirms an identity, while a Web site certificate (sometimes known as an SSL certificate) confirms that a Web site is secure and genuine. At a minimum, a personal certificate will contain the public key owner's name, an expiration date, and the name of the CA that issued the certificate, as shown in Figure 3.15, as well as a serial number, and a digital signature for the CA. The certificate also contains a copy of the public key being certified. A user can apply for and receive a personal certificate using the Internet as shown in Figure 3.16. Some CAs provide personal certificates free of charge to noncommercial users. Once the user receives a personal digital certificate, he or she can install the certificate in a browser such as Internet Explorer and use the certificate to create digital signatures and to encrypt messages.

Figure 3.15 Digital Certificate

digital certificate a means of verifying that a public key belongs to the person who claims to own it

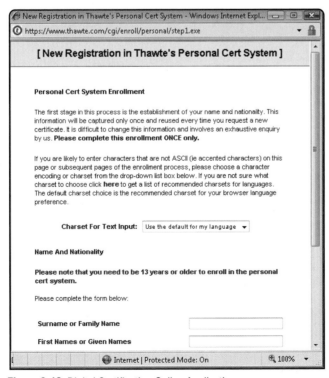

Figure 3.16 Digital Certification Online Application

Digital Signatures

Digital signatures use encryption as shown in Figure 3.17 to help a message recipient confirm that a digitally signed message originates from the person claiming to have sent it and that the message contents have not been altered. To create a digital signature, the contents of a message are reduced to a few lines using a mathematical process known as ***hashing***. The result is known as a message digest. Creating the message digest is a one-way process, so the message digest cannot be used to recreate the message in its original form. The sender encrypts the message digest using his or her private key, resulting in a digital signature that is then attached to the message.

When a recipient receives a digitally signed message, the recipient uses the sender's public key to decrypt the signature back into a message digest. If this is successful, it offers proof that the sender signed the document, as only the sender possesses the private key used to encrypt the signature. If a certificate accompanies the public key, the recipient can check the certificate with the Certifying Authority to confirm the identity of the sender.

To verify that the contents of the message have not been altered, the recipient uses the same hashing process to hash the message and create a message digest. The recipient can then compare the resulting message digest to the decrypted message digest from the digitally-signed message. Matching message digests assure the recipient that the message has not been tampered with

digital signature encryption method that allows an Internet user to confirm that a digitally signed message originates from the person claiming to have sent it, and that the contents of the message have not been altered

hashing a mathematical process (used during digital signature creation) that condenses the contents of a message to a few lines called a message digest

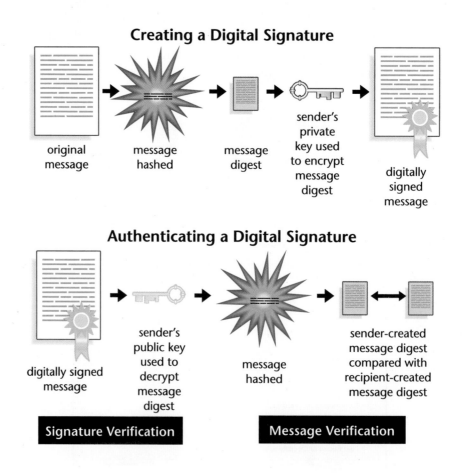

Figure 3.17 Digital Signature Process

Figure 3.18 Web Site Certificate and SSL Closed Padlock Icon

or corrupted. Software performs the entire process outlined previously for the sender and receiver.

Secure Sockets Layer (SSL) Protocol

The *Secure Sockets Layer (SSL)* protocol ensures the security of confidential information such as that contained in financial transactions conducted over the Internet. Servers and clients involved in an SSL transaction use Web site certificates to verify their identity and confirm that any data exchanged will be encrypted in a process known as an SSL handshake. The URL for a Web site that requires a secure connection will begin with *https*, which stands for Hypertext Transfer Protocol over Secure Socket Layer. Internet Explorer also displays a closed padlock icon at the right end of the browser window status bar as shown in Figure 3.18. Hover the mouse pointer over the padlock icon to display a ToolTip identifying the level of encryption employed. Current Secure Sockets Layer protocols use 128-bit encryption, which is virtually impossible to crack. Double-clicking the padlock icon opens the certificate for the Web site as shown in Figure 3.18.

Biometric Authentication

Biometric authentication is a cutting-edge technology that uses biological features such as fingerprints, speech, or even iris patterns to verify identity. Biometric authentication can replace or supplement passwords and other authentication methods currently in use. Fingerprint readers, such as the one from Microsoft shown in Figure 3.19, are already available in the retail marketplace. A fingerprint reader optically scans the user's finger

Secure Sockets Layer (SSL) an encryption protocol used to ensure the security of financial transactions and other private activities conducted over the Internet

biometric authentication a cutting-edge technology that enables a computer to use biological features such as fingerprints, speech, or even iris patterns to verify a user's identity

Figure 3.19 Microsoft Fingerprint Reader

and compares the fingerprint to patterns stored in a database to confirm the user's identity. Current fingerprint scanners are not foolproof, and a picture or mold of someone's fingerprint might be enough to deceive some scanners. However, rapid progress in biometric technology almost certainly will make biometric authentication methods increasingly popular in the years to come.

Concept Review 4 Cyber Crime Countermeasures

1. How can using Internet Explorer security zones protect a computer or network?
2. How does asymmetric encryption work?
3. Describe the process of creating a digital signature.

Skill Review 4 Configure Internet Explorer Web Site Security Settings

1. Open Internet Explorer.
2. Click Tools on the Command Bar and then click Internet Options.
3. Click the Security tab in the Internet Options dialog box to display the different security zones.
4. Click the different zone icons to read their description and security level setting.
5. Click the *Restricted sites* zone icon and then click the Sites button to view a list of restricted Web sites in the Restricted sites dialog box. (*Note: If you or a previous user have not entered any sites into the Restricted zone, the* **Web sites** *text box will be empty.*)
6. Enter the URL for a Web site of your choice in the *Add this Web site to the zone* text box in the Restricted sites dialog box. Click the Add button to add the site to the list of restricted sites. (*Hint: Ask your instructor for a site recommendation.*)
7. Select the newly added URL in the *Web sites* list box and then click the Remove button to remove the URL. Click OK to close the Restricted sites dialog box.
8. Click the *Internet* zone icon and move the slider up to *High*. Click Apply and then OK to close the Internet Options dialog box.
9. Open a Web page in the browser. Place the insertion point on a hyperlink on the page, right-click, and then click Save Target As in the shortcut menu that appears. Because you raised the Internet security zone setting to *High*, a message will appear stating that you are not allowed to download the page.

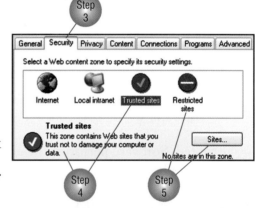

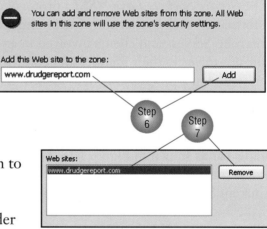

10. Open the Internet Options dialog box and click the Default button to restore the Internet zone security level to its default setting.
11. Repeat Step 9. You should be able to download the page now because of the lowered security level. *(Note: You do not need to complete the download.)*

Threats to Privacy

In addition to the threats posed by malware and cyber crime, Internet users increasingly find their personal privacy in jeopardy. Spam, spyware, adware, cookies, and inappropriate content all erode the privacy most people desire. While these different Internet activities are not specifically intended to do harm, the damage these activities do to our ability to enjoy using the Internet can have almost the same effect. While spyware and adware are not technically considered malware, this state of affairs may change as evidence mounts that these types of programs can degrade the performance of computer systems.

Spam

Spam is the online equivalent of the junk mail delivered by the U.S. Postal Service. Most Internet users routinely find spam offering any number of questionable goods or services in their e-mail Inbox as shown in Figure 3.20. While many wonder how anyone could ever respond to a junk mail solicitation, the fact that millions of spam messages can be broadcast at little expense means that even an infinitesimal response rate as low as one in 10,000 can be profitable for the spam sender.

From	Subject
On Lycos	On Lycos: Burn CDs for Only 49¢ a Track!
NETHERLOTTO CORPO...	AWARD NOTIFICATION; FINAL NOTICE
MusicSites	Earn up to 5% Cash Back -- Get Blue Cash
nelson odili	ACQUISITION OF ESTATES

Figure 3.20 Spam Messages

Spammers (the senders of spam) find e-mail addresses in a number of ways: by combing through newsgroups and chat rooms, by checking Web sites, and by using software that surreptitiously gathers name lists from ISP directories. Spammers also trick users into providing e-mail addresses via pop-up ads saying the user has won a prize or something similar. For many Internet users, spam has become more than a minor irritation, given the difficulty and time required to sort legitimate e-mail messages from spam.

spam the online equivalent of the junk mail delivered by the postal service

spyware any program that is used to gather user information without their knowledge

Adware/Spyware

Adware is short for *advertising supported software*. Creators of shareware and freeware software programs often agree to include adware in a program. Because users of shareware programs pay little or no fees for the software, the fee paid by the adware advertisers helps the shareware or freeware programmer remain a viable business entity. An adware program will typically display a banner, open a pop-up window, and so on. Shareware users often can disable the adware by purchasing the shareware product or an enhanced version of that product. *Spyware* is a term used to describe any program that is used to gather user information without their knowledge. Adware that includes a reporting function is considered a type of spyware. Tracking software enables the spyware to report statistical data and viewing habits back to a database. Spyware creators usually promise that any information reported will not be used to identify users, but this is impossible to verify and users have no control over the reporting function. The reporting feature of spyware makes it very controversial, and some experts think that it should be illegal. Adware and spyware are also controversial because the way they function can create problems that are just as serious as those caused by malware. While adware and spyware are frequently installed on computers when shareware or freeware programs are installed, it is also possible for a computer to become infected with adware and spyware just by visiting a Web site that installs these programs without the user's knowledge.

Symptoms of adware and spyware infestation include the repeated appearance of pop-up windows, unauthorized changes to the default browser home page and/or changes to the default browser search engine, the appearance of new toolbars, being directed to advertising Web sites, and so on. Most importantly, adware and spyware can dramatically slow down computer performance. As noted in the case study for this chapter, most computer users are surprised to find out that adware and spyware programs are installed on their computers.

Cookies

Cookies are very small text files that Web sites can place on a computer to help a Web site server recognize previous visitors so that the viewing experience can be customized. For example, the top image in Figure 3.21 shows how the CNN.com Web site allows a user to enter his or her ZIP Code in a text box to view weather information for that specific ZIP Code. CNN.com creates a viewer ID cookie recording the ZIP Code preference in a small text file stored on the user's computer. The next time the user visits the CNN.com home page, the CNN.com Web server searches the user's system for the CNN.com cookie and then loads the CNN.com Web page with the specified weather information. The information stored in a cookie can allow automatic logins, customized page viewing, and other convenient features.

Cookie files are usually less than 150 bytes. A cookie is not a program and can only be read by the Web site that created it. As text files, cookies cannot harbor viruses nor can they access information on a hard drive. Temporary or session cookies are only stored as long as you are browsing the Web and are deleted when you close your browser. Persistent cookies remain on your computer even after your browser is closed. First-party cookies are cookies that are placed on your computer by the Web site you are visiting, while third-party cookies originate from another Web site. Third-party cookies are usually advertising related. Advertisers such as DoubleClick also use cookies to tailor banner ads to individual viewers. This practice is controversial, and some Internet users object to cookies on the grounds that they constitute an invasion of privacy.

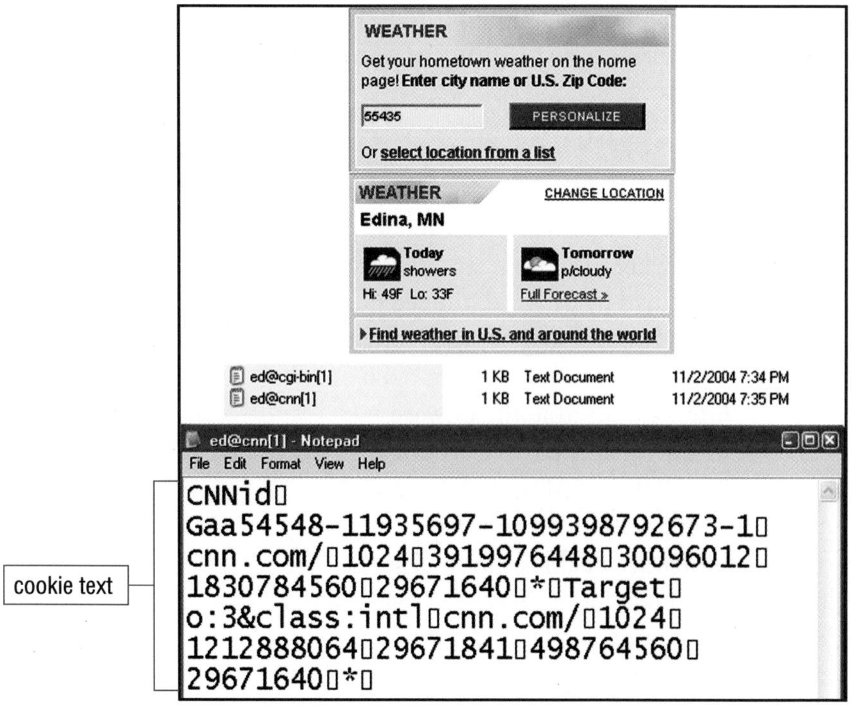

cookie a small text file that Web sites can place on a computer to help a Web site server recognize previous visitors in order to customize the viewing experience

cookie text

Figure 3.21 CNN Weather Information Preference Cookie

Google Desktop Search Tool Controversy

In late 2004, Google introduced a new feature called Desktop Search. Once a user downloads and installs Desktop Search, the user searches the contents of his or her computer as if using the Google search engine to search the contents of the Web. Desktop Search works by automatically recording the different materials viewed on a computer, such as Outlook and Outlook Express e-mail messages, Web pages, AOL Instant Messenger chat conversations, and Microsoft Office documents. The privacy of individual users is protected because Google cannot access the stored material. However, the Desktop Search feature can pose a danger to those using shared computers, because sensitive material viewed by one user could be retrieved by another user. For this reason, security experts advise those using shared computers to look for the *Google Desktop Search* icon in the lower right corner of the desktop to see if the program is running. If it is, the user can right-click the icon to disable the feature. In the long run, many security experts are urging Google to incorporate multiuser privacy and security features into their new Desktop Search tool.

Concept Review 5 Threats to Privacy

1. What is spam, and how do spammers find e-mail addresses to send spam to?
2. What is the difference between adware and spyware?
3. Describe how cookies work.

Skill Review 5 Research Spyware

1. Use the Internet to conduct research to find the names of shareware programs that are known to contain spyware.
2. Create a table to list your results alphabetically.
3. Conduct additional research to find arguments for and against spyware.
4. Use the research you conducted in Step 3 to write or type a short paper describing spyware pros and cons, and explain why some people voluntarily sign up for shareware programs known to contain spyware.

Privacy Countermeasures

Working to reduce spam, spyware, adware, cookies, and inappropriate content to acceptable levels involves a combination of behavior modification and software control methods. As a first step, Internet users should avoid certain behaviors that are likely to attract privacy violations. An Internet user also should configure his or her browser to provide the desired level of privacy. As is the case with fighting malware, setting privacy levels involves finding the right balance between privacy and convenience. Finally, a user can install programs that provide an additional defense, such as programs blocking spam, adware, and spyware as well as parental control software.

Spam Blocking Methods

Many Internet users unwittingly engage in activities that make it easy for spammers to gather their e-mail addresses. Avoiding these activities is simple. Following the tips listed below can reduce the amount of spam a user receives:
- Never buy a product advertised in a spam message.
- Never reply to a spam message.
- Do not forward chain letters or mass mailings.

Figure 3.22 Web Site Privacy Statement

www.cnn.com

- Be careful when subscribing to anything. Check for a privacy statement like the one shown in Figure 3.22 to see if your e-mail address will be shared with advertisers.
- Avoid Web sites without privacy policies. When signing up for anything, look for check boxes placing you on mailing lists or making your e-mail addresses available to advertisers. Check or uncheck these boxes as appropriate.
- You can prevent programs called spam harvesters from gathering your e-mail address whenever you post it on Web pages, in chat rooms, or other public locations by camouflaging it. For example, johnsmith@emcp.net could be camouflaged by adding [] to the address, as in johnsmith[]@emcp.net. While an alert human reader would know that the [] portion of the address should be removed before using the address, a harvester would not.
- Do not post your e-mail address in Internet e-mail directories.
- Set up a free mail service e-mail address such as a Hotmail or Yahoo address, and use it for Internet transactions in order to protect your normal e-mail address.
- Disable automatic image downloading in HTML e-mail because spammers can track your e-mail address when the image is downloaded from their server. Disabling HTML mail entirely is an even safer option.

In addition to following these suggestions, you can install spam filtering software, such as ChoiceMail, MailWasher, or McAfee SpamKiller to reduce the amount of spam cluttering your Inbox. These programs incorporate a number of different tools to identify and delete spam messages. Programs blocking spam may also block wanted messages. To reduce that possibility, spam filtering software enables the user to create a list of trusted or friendly e-mail addresses, so messages from those addresses will not be blocked. Like antivirus programs, spam filtering programs must be updated periodically to maintain their effectiveness.

Spyware/Adware Avoidance

Modifying online behavior also can decrease the chances that adware and or spyware will find their way onto a user's computer. The following list describes some of the activities to avoid in order to reduce the risk posed by adware and spyware:

- Be wary when considering downloading and installing freeware or shareware. If you do download this type of product, read any software disclaimers carefully to make sure the product does not include adware and/or spyware.

- Before installing any freeware or shareware, search the Web for the program's name and the key terms adware or spyware to see if the program has been identified as containing adware or spyware.
- Avoid surfing sites that are notorious for adware and spyware, such as adult sites.
- Close any unexpected or unfamiliar dialog boxes. The best way to close these is by clicking the Close button (X) at the right end of the Title bar, because the No and Cancel buttons in the dialog box may be deliberately nonfunctional.
- Change your browser security settings to prevent the unauthorized download and installation of ActiveX controls. (Directions for disabling ActiveX controls will be discussed in Chapter 10, *Experiencing Multimedia*.)
- Delete spam without opening it.
- Never click on links inside pop-up windows, even if the link says *Close*. Use the Close button on the title bar to close the window.
- Activate or install browser anti-pop-up window features.

Most current antivirus programs include spyware and adware detection and removal capabilities. You also can use a program specifically developed to detect, remove, and block adware and spyware, such as Spyware Doctor, shown in Figure 3.23. Other popular adware and spyware removal programs include Spy Sweeper, Spybot, and Ad Aware. Many users report that they must use more than one of these programs to remove all the adware and spyware on their computers. These programs can usually be downloaded from the developer's Web site or from a download site such as Tucows or Download.Com.

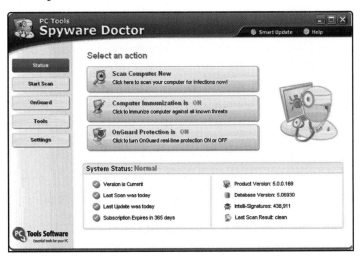

Figure 3.23 Spyware Doctor Adware and Spyware Removal Program

Microsoft is currently offering a free beta (trial) version of its AntiSpyware program, Windows Defender, that can be downloaded from the Microsoft Web site and installed by Windows users. The free Yahoo add-on browser toolbar also contains a spyware removal program. There are fake antispyware programs available on the Web that actually load more adware and spyware onto computers, so users should be very careful to use only reputable products.

Internet Explorer 7 includes a built-in pop-up window blocker that is activated by default. To configure the blocker, click Tools on the Internet Explorer Command Bar, point to Pop-up Blocker, and then click Pop-up Blocker Settings. Google offers a free downloadable toolbar that includes a pop-up blocker, among other features. When the Google pop-up blocking feature is active, it displays the number of pop-up ads that have been blocked as shown in Figure 3.24.

Proposed legislation would criminalize the installation of spyware without the express approval of computer owners. Whether the legislation would be sufficient to deal with the problem is unclear. Many shareware programs already contain disclaimers, but many of these disclaimers are confusing or so long that consumers are unlikely to fully understand them. One license agreement for spyware covers over 50 screen pages and contains more than 6,000 words.

Figure 3.24 Google Toolbar Showing Blocked Pop-up Ads

Cookie Blocking

Internet Explorer 7 Settings users can use the browser's custom privacy settings to enable different levels of cookie management as shown in Figure 3.25. Privacy settings range from accepting all cookies to blocking all cookies. To select a privacy setting, as shown in Figure 3.25, open the Internet Options dialog box and then click the Privacy tab. The slider shown in Figure 3.25 can then be used to change cookie settings. To create custom settings for a particular site, click the Sites button and select settings as shown in Figure 3.26. Some Web sites or Web site features require cookies; blocking a required cookie prevents the Web site from displaying those pages or features. For example, blocking all cookies would prevent the display of the customized weather function of the CNN.com site.

Changing privacy settings does not affect cookies that are already stored on the system. To ensure that new settings affect all cookies, the user should delete existing cookies. To do so, click Tools from the Command Bar, then choose Delete Browsing History. When the Delete Browsing History window opens, click the Delete Cookies button. A user who removes all the cookies from his or her system will need to reregister and reset Web page preferences for some Web pages because the deleted cookies handled those functions.

parental control software software that enables parents to control the Internet content that children can access to prevent the children from viewing inappropriate content

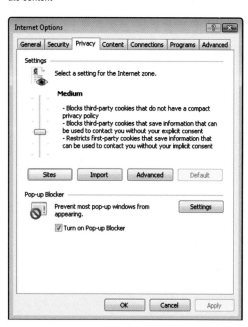

Figure 3.25 Internet Explorer Custom Privacy Settings

Inappropriate Content and Parental Control Software

There is no single standard for judging the appropriateness of Web page content, so individual users must form their own opinions about what is appropriate or inappropriate.

Most parents want to shield their children from Web sites or chat rooms containing sexual or violent content, and many adults do not wish to view that type of material either. The nature of the Internet makes it difficult for people to avoid seeing material that they feel is inappropriate. Many X-rated Web sites use spam and pop-up windows to advertise their wares, so an Internet user inadvertently views such material until he or she can close the browser window displaying the offending items. It is also impossible for Web site and chat room operators to verify the age of people viewing their material. The disclaimers requiring people accessing Web pages or chat rooms to acknowledge that they are over 18-years-old are a legal tool to protect the owners against charges of deliberately catering to minors, but those disclaimers contain no verification features.

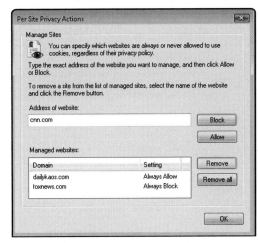

Figure 3.26 Internet Explorer Privacy Settings for Specific Sites

Windows Vista comes with built-in parental controls, Figure 3.27, that limit a specific user's access to the Internet. To access the controls, click Start, then Control Panel. Find the User Accounts and Family Safety category and click the link *Set up parental controls for any user*. From here, you can choose to allow access to only specified web sites, block file downloads, or control times when specific accounts can log on to Windows. For example, you can configure these settings to allow a specific user to log on Monday through Friday between the hours of 4:00pm and 8:00pm. If they try to use the computer outside of the specified hours, they will not be able to log on. Additionally, you can disallow the account access to web sites except for specific sites, like Disney.com or PBS.org.

Figure 3.27 Windows Vista Parental Controls for the account named *student*

Concept Review 6 Privacy Countermeasures

1. Describe the different ways that Internet Explorer can be configured to block cookies.
2. What measures can Internet users undertake to reduce the amount of spam they receive?
3. What can Internet users do to avoid unwanted adware and spyware programs?

Skill Review 6 Change Internet Explorer Privacy Settings

1. Open the CNN.com home page by typing **www.cnn.com** in the browser Address bar and then pressing Enter.
2. Look for the *Weather* section and enter your ZIP Code in the text box. Click the PERSONALIZE button to enter your preference. The CNN.com page will automatically refresh and display weather information for the ZIP Code you specified. *(Note: If this function does not work, ask your instructor for help. The privacy settings on your computer may be set too high to allow this functionality.)*

3. Click Tools on the Internet Explorer Command bar and then click Internet Options.

4. Click the Privacy tab in the Internet Options dialog box to display the different privacy settings.

5. Move the *Privacy* slider up to the *Block All Cookies* level. This setting blocks all cookies and prevents Web sites from reading existing cookies. Click the Apply button and then click OK to enable the setting. *(Note: If a **Custom** level has been set, click the Advanced button, remove the check mark from the **Override automatic cookie handling** check box, and then click OK to restore the slider function.)*

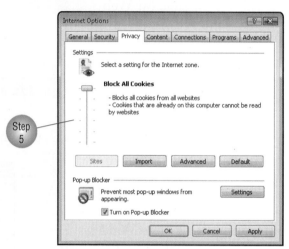

6. Click the Refresh button on the Internet Explorer toolbar to refresh the CNN.com

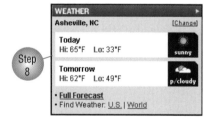

page. Notice that the weather for the ZIP Code you entered no longer appears. The privacy setting you changed blocks the CNN.com site from reading the cookie enabling the weather function.

7. Reopen the Internet Options dialog box, click the Privacy tab, and use the slider to change the privacy setting to *Medium*. Close the dialog box when you are finished.

8. Refresh the CNN.com page. The Weather box should once again display the weather for the ZIP Code you entered previously. The Medium privacy level once again allows the CNN.com site to read the cookie you created to enable the Weather function.

Chapter Summary

- The three most common forms of malware are viruses, worms, and Trojan horses.

- Victims of malware may lose valuable data and must spend considerable time and money repairing the damage that malware can do.

- Once a virus-infected program downloads from the Internet and runs on a computer system, the virus can release a malicious payload.

- Countermeasures to guard against malware are highly developed today, and a properly configured computer system should be able to ward off most threats.

- One of the first lines of defense is the installation of an antivirus program designed to detect viruses, worms, Trojan horses, and other forms of malware.

- Software and/or hardware firewalls can be installed to add another layer of protection to a computer or network.

- The use of passwords to prevent unauthorized access to your computer and e-mail program is another important method in guarding against threats.

- When an antivirus program detects infected files, the user can direct the program to use one of three options for dealing with the files: cleaning, deleting, or quarantining.

- Antivirus programs usually employ three different methods to detect malware: signature scanning, heuristic scanning, and behavior blocking.

- Virus definition files must be updated frequently via download to maintain the antivirus program's ability to recognize virus signatures and defend against new threats.

- Microsoft has created security updates or patches to repair system vulnerabilities upon discovery.

- Criminals located around the world can gain access to people and information through the Internet.

- Because cyber crime often transcends local and national boundaries, law enforcement can be a nightmare because of unclear jurisdiction.

- Internet Explorer enables users to assign Web sites to different Web content security zones depending on how trusted the sites are.

- When you use e-mail to send messages across the Internet, it is possible for those messages to be intercepted and read by others without your knowledge.

- Encryption refers to the process of scrambling text or data into an unreadable format that cannot be unscrambled without the use of a key.

- A digital certificate provides a means of verifying that a public key belongs to the person who claims to own it.

- A digital signature uses encryption to help an Internet user confirm that a digitally signed message originates from the person claiming to have sent it, and that the contents of the message have not been altered.

- The Secure Sockets Layer (SSL) protocol ensures the security of financial transactions conducted over the Internet.

- Spam, spyware, adware, cookies, and inappropriate content all erode the privacy most people desire.

- Creators of shareware and freeware software programs often agree to include adware programs in exchange for a fee paid by the adware advertiser.

- Some adware includes a reporting function, making it a type of spyware.

- Adware and spyware are also controversial because the way they function can create problems that are just as serious as problems caused by malware.

- Working to reduce spam, spyware, adware, cookies, and inappropriate content to acceptable levels involves a combination of behavior modification and software control methods.

- A Web site can place a small text file called a cookie on a computer to help the Web site server recognize previous visitors and customize the viewing experience.

- There is no single standard for judging the appropriateness of Web page content, so individual users must form their own opinions about what is appropriate or inappropriate.

- Many Internet users unwittingly engage in activities that make it easy for spammers to gather their e-mail addresses for spam mailing lists.

- Internet Explorer 7 users can adjust the browser's custom privacy settings to enable different levels of cookie management.

- Windows Vista's Parental Control settings enable parents to control the Internet content that their children can access to prevent the children from viewing inappropriate content.

Key Terms

Numbers indicate the pages where terms are first cited in the chapter. An alphabetized list of key terms with definitions can be found on the Encore CD that accompanies this book. In addition, these terms and definitions are included in the end-of-book glossary.

antivirus program, *69*

authentication, *79*

behavior blocking, *71*

biometric authentication, *83*

brute force attack, *77*

cookie, *86*

denial-of-service (DoS) attack, *76*

digital certificate, *81*

digital signature, *82*

distributed denial-of-service (DDoS) attack, *77*

encryption, *79*

hashing, *82*

heuristic scanning, *71*

malware, *66*

parental control software, *90*

payload, *67*

phishing, *75*

proxy server, *72*

Secure Sockets Layer (SSL), *83*

spam, *85*

spoofing, *75*

spyware, *85*

Trojan horse, *68*

virus, *67*

virus definitions, *71*

virus signature, *70*

worm, *67*

Additional quiz questions are available on the Encore CD that accompanies this book as well as on the Internet Resource Center for this title at www.emcp.net/Internet2e.

Multiple Choice

Indicate the correct answer for each question or statement.

1. A _____ cookie remains on a computer after a session is over.
   a. residual
   b. temporary
   c. persistent
   d. permanent

2. Viruses, worms, and Trojan horses are types of
   a. spyware.
   b. adware.
   c. malware.
   d. shareware.

3. Cookies are
   a. small text files.
   b. small HTML files.
   c. large text files.
   d. a type of virus.

4. Fingerprint readers are an example of
   a. biometric authentication.
   b. aural authentication.
   c. second-tier authentication.
   d. secondary screener.

5. The URL for a secure SSL connection begins with
   a. http.
   b. ftp.
   c. https.
   d. hmtl.

6. Web site certificates are also known as
   a. personal certificates.
   b. personal identification.
   c. SSL certificates.
   d. personal security certificates.

7. Message digests are created using a mathematical process known as
   a. logarithmic algorithms.
   b. hashing.
   c. message reduction.
   d. digital certification.

8. Digital certificates
   a. are a form of credential.
   b. are created using encryption.
   c. work with public key encryption.
   d. All of the above

9. Public key encryption uses
   a. paired public and private keys.
   b. pi to create a key.
   c. authentication.
   d. spoofing technology.

10. A brute force attack is a
    a. method used to crack passwords.
    b. type of virus attack.
    c. form of pulsing zombie.
    d. type of DoS attack.

True/False

Indicate whether each statement is true or false.

1. A virus signature is a string of binary code that is unique to a virus.
2. Third-party cookies are cookies that are placed on your computer by the Web site you are visiting.
3. To create a digital signature, the contents of a message are reduced to a few lines using a mathematical process known as hashing.
4. A zombie is a computer that operates independently of a server.
5. Adware and spyware are forms of malware.
6. Cookies are very small HTML files that Web sites place on a computer to help a Web site server recognize previous visitors.
7. A blended threat combines spyware with a virus.
8. A denial of service (DoS) attack paralyzes a computer network by bombarding it with traffic in the form of packets of useless information.

9. A digital certificate provides a means of verifying that a public key belongs to the person who claims to own it.

10. Encryption refers to the process of scrambling text or data into an unreadable format that cannot be unscrambled without the use of a key.

Virtual Perspectives

1. What are some of the common sense things that Internet users can do in order to avoid being a victim of cyber crime?

2. Some members of the hacker community say that their goal is to expose security flaws rather than to cause damage, and refer to hackers that deliberately cause damage as crackers. Do you think that this is a valid distinction? Are there more constructive methods they could use to expose security flaws?

3. Protecting a computer or computer system usually involves a trade-off between security and convenience. What methods do you take, or would you take, to protect your computer against malware and cyber crime? Discuss the positive and negative aspects of each method.

4. Would you use parental control software, such as Vista's Parental Controls, to control your children's Internet use? What types of activities or material would you want to guard against? Do you think that using such software will help or hurt in the development of a trusting relationship between parent and child?

Internet Lab Projects

Project 1
Enable the Windows Vista Firewall

(Note: Ask your instructor if you are permitted to make these changes.)
1. Click Start and then click Control Panel.
2. Click Security, Turn *Windows Firewall* on or off.
3. If prompted by Window's User Account Control, choose Continue.
4. Click the *On* option in the Windows Firewall dialog box to enable the Firewall.
5. Click the Advanced tab in the Windows Firewall dialog box. Make sure that there is a check mark in the check box next to the name of the Internet connection method you are using.
6. Click the Windows Firewall OK button when you are finished.

Project 2
Create or Change Vista User Account Password

1. Click Start and then click Control Panel.
2. In the User Accounts and Family Safety category, click *Add or remove user accounts.*
3. Click your user name or the name of the account you are using.
4. Click the Create a password or Change the password hyperlinks to create a password or change an existing password. *(Note: Be sure to write down your password and store it in a safe place.)*
5. When creating a password, you will need to type it in one text box, and then retype it in another for confirmation. You may also create a hint that can be used

in the event you forget your password, though the password hint is optional. When you are finished click the Create Password or Change Password button.

6. Close all open windows and return to your desktop.
7. Restart your computer and log on using your new password.

Internet Research Activities

Activity 1
Discover More about Encryption

Use the Internet to research and write short paragraph answers to the following questions:

1. What is PGP?
2. What is RSA, and how does its algorithm work?
3. Why does the United States government forbid the export of powerful encryption tools?
4. What is the FBI's Carnivore program?

Activity 2
Research the Department of Homeland Security's National Cyber Security Division (NCSD)

In the aftermath of the 9/11 attacks the United States government created the Department of Homeland Security. In 2002, the Department created the National Cyber Security Division (NCSD). Use the Internet to learn more about the NCSD and then write or type a short paper describing the NCSD and the role it plays in ensuring U.S. security.

Activity 3
Net Challenge

A digital certificate is required in order to encrypt or digitally sign e-mail messages. Log on to a Certification Authority (CA) Web site such as www.thawte.com or www.cacert.org and complete the personal security certificate application process. When you receive your certificate, install it in Internet Explorer. Practice exchanging encrypted and digitally signed e-mails with your classmates. Ask your instructor for instructions on how to verify that you have successfully completed this challenge activity.

UNIT 1

Emerging Trends

Digital Divide

The digital divide refers to the unequal access to digital technology that exists among communities, particularly as it relates to computers and the Internet. At the global level, the digital divide sees wealthy nations on the "have" side of the divide and poor nations on the "have not" side. The World Bank recently released welcome news that the global digital divide is shrinking rapidly, as the speed with which developing nations are gaining access to needed digital technology is increasing at rates far faster than just a few years ago. To close the divide even more rapidly, an African initiative undertook the establishment of a Digital Solidarity Fund in early 2005. The fund is designed to end the digital divide by seeking money that will be used to provide access for disadvantaged areas that do not attract private-sector interest. Exactly how long it will take to bridge the divide is unknown, but if current trends continue, the divide will be just a memory in the not-too-distant future.

Sources: "Global digital divide 'narrowing.'" http://news.bbc.co.uk/1/hi/technology/4296919.stm, "Digital Divide Narrowing Fast, World Bank Says." www.bizreport.com/print/8700

Fat Links and Physical Hypertext

Now that browsers such as Mozilla Firefox and Netscape Navigator support tabbed browsing, Jakob Nielsen, the "Web Usability Guru," foresees the appearance of fat links, hyperlinks that can point to more than one document at a time. Each document would open in a different tab in browsers that support that feature. Nielsen also envisions physical hypertext that would allow users to retrieve Web pages by manipulating physical objects.

FAT LINKS

Source: www.useit.com/alertbox/20050103.html

Internet Explorer 7

Microsoft officially released Internet Explorer 7 in late 2006, marking the first major upgrade of the browser in five years. It features enhanced protection against phishing and malware, tabbed browsing, automatic pop-up blocking, changing of zoom level, and print resizing. It also features built-in parental controls for users of Microsoft Vista.

Sources: "Next IE will ship before Longhorn." http://news.zdnet.co.uk/software/windows/0,39020396,39188053,00.htm, "Microsoft Plans New IE Browser, Better Security." http://news.yahoo.com/news?tmpl=story&u=/nm/20050216/ts_nm/tech_microsoft_browser_dc_9

Fraud Threat

The director of the United States Secret Service has pointed out that increasingly sophisticated criminals could potentially disrupt the American economy with just a few key strokes. One disturbing trend is that criminal organizations are enlisting the services of Internet hackers to perpetrate fraud through online scams such as phishing, the use of spyware, and other methods. Shortly before the director raised the issue, an example of the kind of threat he was referring to was provided by ChoicePoint, the leading identification and credential verification service in the United States. ChoicePoint had the unenviable task of notifying thousands of American consumers that they were vulnerable to identity theft after unauthorized parties gained access to confidential data gathered by ChoicePoint. While there is no need to panic, the Secret Service warning should remind both business owners and individuals that they need to be vigilant if they do not want to fall victim to cyber crime.

Source: "Secret Service: Fraud Threatens Economy." www.bizreport.com/news/8691

Fiber to the Home (FTTH)

Once dismissed as prohibitively costly, the use of fiber optic cable to replace the copper wires used in the last-mile connections from telephone company central offices to homes will soon offer some American consumers a faster alternative to cable and DSL Internet connections. The typical DSL and cable Internet service offers download speeds of up to 2 Mbps, but fiber has the potential to provide the much higher speeds that will be necessary to support future bandwidth-intensive applications such as high definition television (HDTV). While Verizon Communications plans to roll out a 30 Mbps service to homes in selected areas, the bandwidth potential for Fiber to the Home (FTTH) is even higher. More and more upscale housing developments are featuring FTTH as developers try to entice buyers and stay competitive. As the prices of the technology continues to fall, American consumers may increasingly find their high-speed Internet needs being met by FTTH.

Source: "Has Your Broadband Had Its Fiber?" www.pcworld.com/news/article/0,aid,117684,00.asp, "Fiber Hits Home." www.builderonline.com/industry-news.asp?sectionID=13&articleID=92180

Discussion Questions

1. What is the economic and social impact of the digital divide? If it is not equalized, what do you speculate the impact is for the future?

2. Jakob Nielsen and others have envisioned physical hypertext that allows users to retrieve Web pages by manipulating physical objects. Think of this and then try to envision one or two future applications of this concept.

3. Do you think enough is being done to prevent Internet-based fraud? If not, what measures would you recommend be put in place? If identity theft occurs, what measures would solve the problem sooner?

UNIT 2

Accessing Information on the Web

- Using a Web Browser
- Accessing Information Resources
- Downloading and Storing Information

Chapter
Using a Web Browser

4

Learning Objectives

- Define the role and function of Web browsers.

- Identify the different Internet Explorer elements.

- Differentiate between the different buttons on the Standard Buttons toolbar.

- Explain how to use the Favorites Center to store and retrieve Web pages.

- Contrast the different ways to save Web pages and print Web pages and Web page content.

- Examine how to configure Internet Explorer.

- Utilize the Internet Explorer Help feature.

- Open and use multiple browser tabs.

Living on the Net

Bob has been using the Internet for a number of years and considers himself to be an expert at using a Web browser. His skills improved greatly after he took a short course on using Web browsers offered at his workplace a few years back. Bob had been reluctant to take the course because he thought he already knew all there was to know about using a Web browser. To his surprise, he found that he had been unaware of a number of different ways to make using a Web browser easier.

One of the most important things he learned was that the browsers usually offered more than one way to execute a command, and to his chagrin Bob realized that he had often been using the slowest method. He grimaced when he thought of all the paper he had wasted before he realized it was possible to print a selection of a Web page rather than the entire page. After the course was over, Bob immediately put what he had learned to work. Once he understood all the different command possibilities and features, his productivity when using the Web improved significantly. The majority of Internet users start using a Web browser

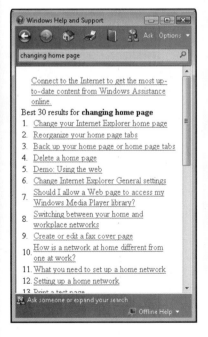

without much instruction, slowly learning more about using the browser through trial and error or from friends. The Internet Explorer Help function provides answers to questions. Search engines provide another excellent way to learn more about using browsers, especially finding tips and tricks that can help make life easier. Whatever the source of information, spending a little time learning how to use a browser is time well spent.

Browser Basics

Tech Demo 4-1
Web Browsers

browser a software program that enables the user to view the different materials available on the portion of the Internet known as the World Wide Web

Address bar browser bar that displays the IP or URL address of the currently displayed Web page and enables the user to browse to other URLs

A **browser** software program enables the user to access and view the different materials available on the portion of the Internet known as the World Wide Web. Popular Web browsers such as Internet Explorer or Mozilla Firefox use point-and-click technology. It is possible to navigate the Web using only mouse clicks, although you must use a keyboard to enter data such as URLs.

When the user clicks a document hyperlink or types a URL in the browser **Address bar**, the browser seeks and retrieves the document located at the address represented by the hyperlink or URL. Material at an address may be located on a user's computer or on a server located thousands of miles away. Browsers interpret and display HTML documents and images, and with the help of add-on programs known as plug-ins, can display other types of media such as PDF files, Flash movies, and so on. Browsers come with built-in plug-ins for most popular media types, but users can add plug-ins to a browser, if required. Plug-ins will be further discussed in Chapter 10, *Experiencing Multimedia*.

Until recently, the various versions of the Internet Explorer Web browser enjoyed almost 95 percent of the browser market share, with the remaining segment shared by Netscape Navigator, Opera, and Mozilla. The various security vulnerabilities inherent in Internet Explorer have led some users to abandon it for other browsers that are more secure, to the point that Internet Explorer's market share has slipped below 90 percent for the first time in years. It is too early to tell whether the various security improvements made to Internet Explorer 7 will persuade former users to use it again.

All the main browsers offer similar interfaces, and a user familiar with one browser will be able to quickly learn how to use another browser because of the similarities in formats and commands. Figure 4.1 shows the menu and toolbar areas for Internet Explorer, Netscape Navigator, and Mozilla Firefox. While they share many features, buttons are often in different locations and sometimes labeled differently. For example, the function that allows users to store Web page URLs for easy retrieval is known as Favorites in Internet Explorer and Bookmarks in Netscape Navigator and Mozilla Firefox.

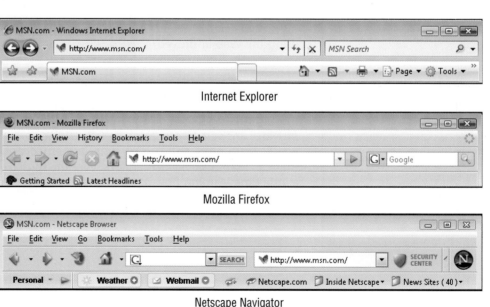

Internet Explorer

Mozilla Firefox

Netscape Navigator

Figure 4.1 Internet Explorer, Mozilla Firefox, and Netscape Navigator Toolbar Areas

Concept
Review 1 Browser Basics

1. What is a Web browser?
2. Why has Internet Explorer lost market share recently and why might it experience resurgence in its popularity?
3. How difficult is it to switch between different browsers?

Skill
Review 1 Compare Web Browsers

1. Open the Google search engine Web site (www.google.com).
2. Use Google to find the home page URLs for the Internet Explorer, Mozilla Firefox, and Netscape browsers. *(Note: Substitute another browser for Netscape if needed.)*
3. Visit each browser home page and follow the links to learn more about each browser.
4. Conduct additional research to find more information about each browser, particularly comparisons or reviews.
5. Use the information you gather to write or type a short essay (one to two double-spaced pages) describing which browser you would choose to install on your computer. Support your choice with at least five different reasons.

The Browser Wars Reignited

When Microsoft won the so-called browser wars in the late nineties, most observers thought the war was over for good. Microsoft's ability to bundle Internet Explorer with Windows provided a marketing advantage that Netscape and other competitors could not match. To the surprise of many, the official launch of the open-source Mozilla Firefox Web browser in late 2004 has reignited the browser wars. Within four months of its November 2004 debut Firefox had pushed Internet Explorer's share of the market from over 95 percent down to barely 90 percent.

The rapid uptake of Firefox has in large part been due to the perception of Internet Explorer as being riddled with security vulnerabilities, though Microsoft has improved this substantially with the release of Internet Explorer 7. Unlike Internet Explorer, Firefox is not integrated into Windows, so a security flaw in Firefox does not necessarily offer a backdoor into a computer's operating system. Firefox also does not load ActiveX scripts, which have been exploited by hackers. Firefox users report only infrequent problems loading Web pages that use ActiveX scripts.

Firefox and the new Internet Explorer 7 come loaded with a number of desirable features, including built-in pop-up blocking, an RSS reader, an integrated customizable search facility (called the **Instant Search Box** in Internet Explorer 7), and, perhaps most important of all, tabbing. Tabbing enables each **browser window** to hold multiple open Web pages, indicated by a tab that appears at the top of the window. Users can shift between pages simply by clicking a tab. Internet Explorer 7 goes one step further and allows users to view a page of thumbnails representing each open tab, making it very easy and intuitive to click any thumbnail and return to the page loaded within that tab.

browser window the area of a Web browser where Web page content appears

 **Tech Demo 4-2 Different Browsers**

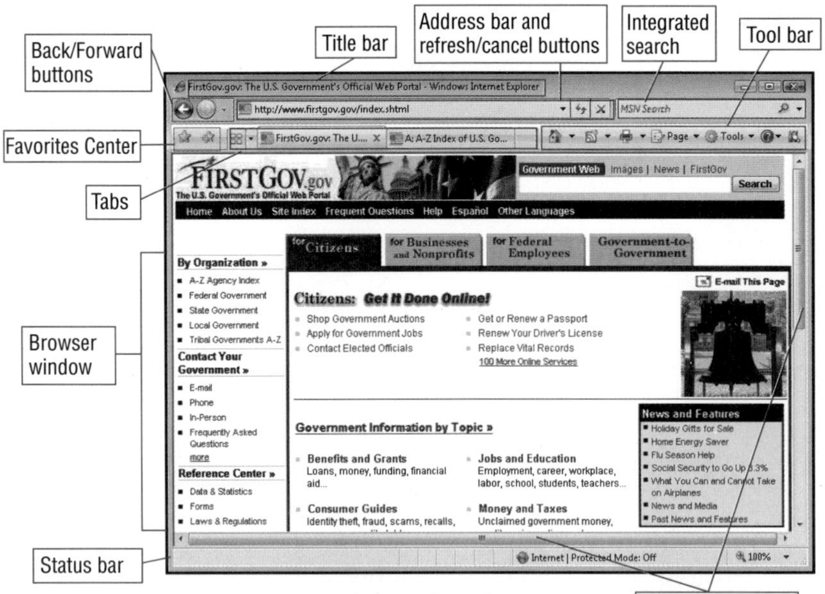

The figure at top shows "Figure 4.2 Internet Explorer Basic Elements" with labels:

- Back/Forward buttons
- Favorites Center
- Tabs
- Browser window
- Status bar
- Title bar
- Address bar and refresh/cancel buttons
- Integrated search
- Tool bar
- Horizontal and Vertical scroll bars

Figure 4.2 Internet Explorer Basic Elements

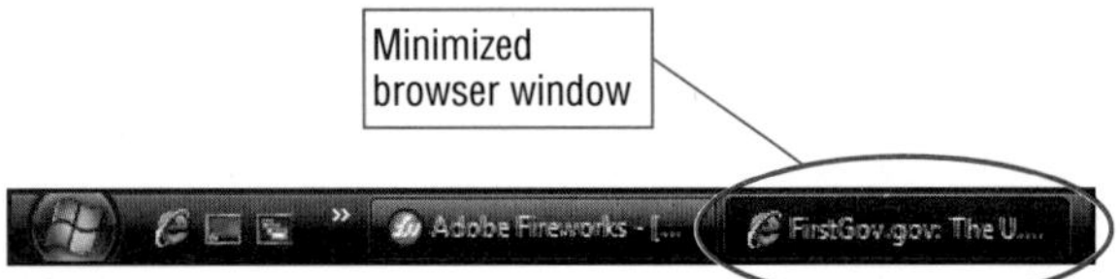

Figure 4.3 Taskbar Button

Minimized browser window

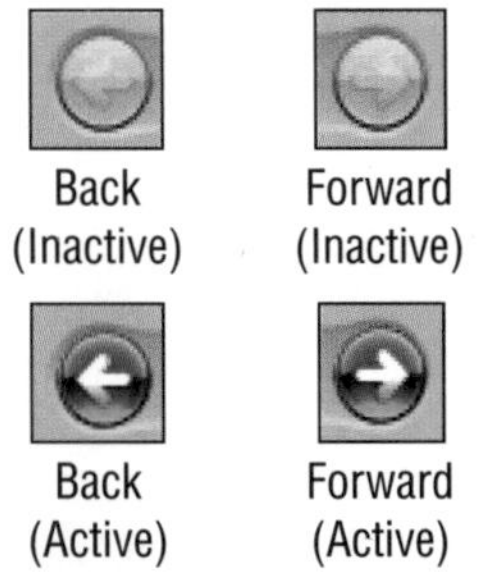

Back (Inactive)   Forward (Inactive)

Back (Active)   Forward (Active)

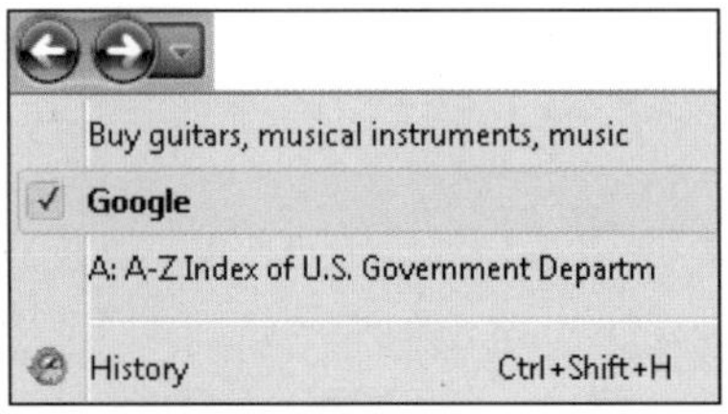

Buy guitars, musical instruments, music
✓ **Google**
A: A-Z Index of U.S. Government Departm
History   Ctrl+Shift+H

Recent Pages menu arrow

Internet Explorer Elements

The main elements of the Internet Explorer screen include the title bar, toolbar, Address bar, tabs, browser window and scroll bars, and the status bar as shown in Figure 4.2.

Title Bar

The *title bar* displays the name of the Web page that is open in the browser window along with the name of the browser. The title bar in Figure 4.2 shows that the Web page displayed in the browser window is the default Internet Explorer home page, www.msn.com. The default browser home page displays when the user first starts the program. The right side of the title bar contains the Minimize, Restore Down, and Close buttons. Placing the mouse pointer on any of the buttons displays a ToolTip describing the button function. Clicking the Minimize button collapses the window into a taskbar button as shown in Figure 4.3. Clicking a taskbar button restores the browser window to its previous size. When a browser window is displayed in full size (maximized), clicking the Restore Down button reduces the window size by approximately 50 percent. With the window at that size, pointing to the Restore Down button displays a ToolTip identifying its new name *Maximize*. Clicking the Maximize button restores the browser window to full screen size.

Back and Forward Buttons

The *Back* and *Forward* buttons can be used to navigate backwards and forwards between previously visited Web pages. When you first start Internet Explorer, these buttons appear dimmed because at that point only the browser home page has been visited; there are no other previously visited pages to move to. If you browse to another Web page, the Back button will become active, and clicking it returns the browser to the previously visited home page. At that point, the Forward button becomes active because there are now two previously-viewed Web pages to move between. Returning to the first Web page viewed deactivates the Back button, and returning to the final Web page viewed deactivates the Forward button. To the immediate right of these buttons you will find the Recent Pages menu arrow which, when clicked, displays a list of up to nine previously visited pages. Clicking a listing displays that page.

Address Bar

When the user clicks a hyperlink, the URL appears automatically in the *Address bar* once the requested document is retrieved and displayed in the browser window. The user also can enter a URL or IP address in the Address bar to browse to the specified location. To go to a URL using the Address bar, click the current address to select it, type the URL, and then press Enter. To save time, you do not need to retype an entire URL. Instead, select the current URL by clicking it once and then drag over the text you wish to replace to select it. For example, if the URL displayed in the Address bar is http://www.cnn.com, you could select *cnn* so that you only need to type **msn** if you wish to visit the MSN Web page.

Internet Explorer does not require the user to enter the full URL. For example, rather than entering http://www.cnn.com, the user can type **www.cnn.com** in the Address bar to locate and display the CNN Web page in the browser window. You can also copy and paste URLs into the Address bar.

Click the down-pointing arrow located to the right of the Address bar to display a list of previously entered URLs. Click a URL from the list to place that URL in the Address bar as shown in Figure 4.4.

Figure 4.4 Address Bar URL History List

When the browser makes a connection to a secure server, a closed padlock icon appears on the right side of the address bar as shown in Figure 4.4. Clicking the padlock icon displays information about the certificate for the server hosting the Web page.

Refresh Button

The ***Refresh button*** refreshes the browser window display by submitting a new Web page download request. Use this button when a message informs you that a Web page cannot be displayed. Clicking the Refresh button resubmits the request to make another attempt to open the page.

The Refresh button can also be used to make sure that the Web page displays the most current information. To speed up page loading, Internet Explorer caches or saves Web pages in an Internet Temporary Files folder. Clicking the Refresh button ensures that you are viewing the very latest Web page version available rather than a cached version. Pressing the [F5] key activates the Refresh button.

Refresh

Refresh Button button on the Internet Explorer Standard Buttons toolbar that refreshes the browser window display by submitting a new Web page request when clicked

Stop button button on the Internet Explorer Standard Buttons toolbar that stops a URL request when clicked

Instant Search Box search box to the right of the address bar allowing instant searches of Internet search engines

Stop Button

The ***Stop button*** stops a Web page from downloading. Click this button if a Web page is taking too long to open or if you change your mind about the page you wish to view. Pressing the [ESC] key activates the Stop button.

Stop

Instant Search Box

Typing a word or phrase in the ***Instant Search Box*** and clicking the magnifying glass icon or tapping [ENTER] displays search results from MSN Search, the default search provider. This saves you the time of navigating to your preferred search engine before performing a search. No matter what web site you are on, you always have quick access to Internet searches via the Instant Search Box. Clicking the associated arrow menu allows you to search for text on the current page or change your preferences to use another search provider, which is described in the "Configuring Internet Explorer" section of this chapter.

Instant Search Box

Figure 4.5 Internet Explorer Favorites Center

Favorites Center
and Add to Favorites

Standard Buttons toolbar a toolbar of Internet Explorer command buttons

Favorites Center button button under the back/forward buttons that opens the Favorites Center to display Favorites, Feeds, and History

Favorites list list of saved URLs that can be organized for the quick retrieval of frequently visited Web pages

History button button on the Internet Explorer Standard Buttons toolbar that the user can click to display a list of previously visited Web sites in the Explorer bar

Quick Tab visible only when multiple tabs are open; displays thumbnails of pages open on tabs

Tab list visible only when multiple tabs are open; displays a list of all open tabs

Tab displays a web page in the browser window; multiple tabs can be open at once

Figure 4.6 RSS Feeds List

Figure 4.7 History List

Favorites Center and Add to Favorites Buttons

Clicking the *Favorites Center button* opens the Favorites Center as shown in Figure 4.5. You can access favorite pages, RSS feeds, and your browsing history from the Favorites Center. You can add a frequently visited Web page to the *Favorites list* so you can easily access it when needed. Clicking a Web page included in the Favorites list opens the page in the browser window.

Clicking the Feeds button in the Favorites Center displays a list of your subscribed RSS feeds as shown in Figure 4.6. RSS feeds alert you to new content on certain Web pages so you can always keep up to date with the latest information. Let's say there are five Web sites you frequently visit, but you don't want to constantly browse to the sites wondering if there is new content. By subscribing to the sites' RSS feeds (if the sites offer them), you can check your Favorites Center where your subscribed feeds alert you to new content. Clicking a feed displays the new content and saves you the trip to the actual Web site.

Clicking the *History button* in the Favorites Center displays a list of previously visited Web sites in the History bar as shown in Figure 4.7. Clicking the down-pointing arrow at the right of the History button displays a drop-down list that enables you to change the list sort order.

The section called "Storing and Retrieving Web Pages" later in the chapter explains how to work the Favorites Center.

Tabs Bar

The Tabs Bar allows you to switch between tabs holding open Web pages. When you initially launch Internet Explorer 7, only the tab for the current page and the New Tab tabs are visible. Clicking the New Tab tab opens a new tab with instructions on using the tab feature. From here, you can type a web address in the address bar or select a site from your favorites to load a page. If more than one web page is open, the *Quick Tabs* and *Tab List* tabs appear. Clicking Quick Tabs displays thumbnails of every open page while clicking Tab List displays a text list of current tabs. Clicking a thumbnail or item in the list will cause Internet Explorer to switch to that tab and display your selected page. Figure 4.8 shows the Tabs Bar with the Quick Tabs page displaying thumbnails of the current tabs. When a tab is active, it will display an X which you can click to close the tab. You can also force a link to open in a new tab by pressing the [CTRL] key as you click the hyperlink.

Standard Buttons Toolbar

The *toolbar* shown in Figure 4.9 offers quick access to commonly used commands. Some buttons are dual function and perform a task when the icon is clicked, but display a menu of additional commands when its associated arrow is clicked. Other buttons perform common tasks but do not officially reside in the toolbar area. These include the Back, Forward, refresh, and cancel buttons found on either side of the address bar.

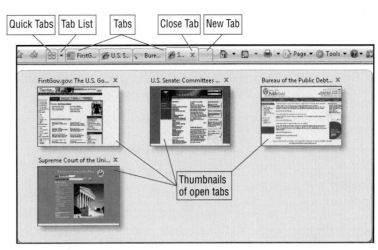

Figure 4.8 Tabs

Home Button

Clicking the *Home button* opens the home page or pages specified in Internet Explorer. See the section called "Configuring Internet Explorer" later in this chapter to learn how to specify home pages.

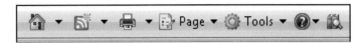

Figure 4.9 Standard Buttons Toolbar

Home

Home button button on the Internet Explorer Standard Buttons toolbar that displays the default browser home page in the browser window when clicked

Feeds Button

Clicking the Feeds button displays RSS feeds on the current page and allows you to subscribe to feeds. Subscribed feeds are listed in the Favorites Center where you are notified of new content. The section called "Storing and Retrieving Web Pages" later in the chapter explains how to work with RSS feeds.

Feeds

Print Button

Clicking the *Print button* prints a copy of the page displayed in the browser window. The "Printing Web Pages" section later in the chapter describes other printing options available in the associated arrow menu in more detail.

Print

Print button button on the Internet Explorer Standard Buttons toolbar that prints the current Web page using the current print settings

Page Button

The *Page button* grants access to many commands. From here you can launch a new window complete with its own tabs. You can also elect to email the current web page, or the current URL, to someone provided your computer is configured for email. Perhaps the most helpful commands under the Page button are Zoom, which lets you zoom in and out of the page, and Text Size, which allows you to enlarge or reduce the size of text on the current page.

Page

Page button grants access to many commands such as copy, paste, save as, and zoom

Tools Button

The *Tools button* offers commands to configure simple security and privacy settings, such as deleting your browsing history and configure settings for the built-in popup blocker and phishing filter. It also allows you to turn on and off certain toolbars, customize the standard toolbar, and access advanced Internet options.

Tools

Tools button offers commands to configure simple security and privacy settings

Help

Research

Figure 4.10 Research Task Pane

Help Button

The *Help* button is your portal to the Internet Explorer 7 user manual and tour. If you are new to Internet Explorer, the Internet Explorer Tour option is an excellent place to learn about all the features of Microsoft's newest browser. The Help button also provides links to the Microsoft support and feedback Web pages.

Research Button

Clicking the Research button displays the Research task pane in the left side of the browser window as shown in Figure 4.10. Typing a search term in the *Search for* text box will search a number of different online research services including reference books, research sites, business and financial Web sites, and so on. The resources that will be searched can be displayed by clicking the down-pointing arrow next to *All Reference Books*. Additional research services can be added to or removed from the list by clicking the <u>Research options</u> hyperlink at the bottom of the Research task pane and then using the Research Options dialog box to select additional options or remove existing options. If the research function is used offline, only the thesaurus and translation functions will be active. Clicking the <u>Get services on Office Marketplace</u> hyperlink will display a list of fee-based third-party research services in the browser window. Clicking a service provider hyperlink will open their home page.

Browser Window and Scroll Bars

Web content appears in the browser window. *Scroll bars* will appear if a Web page is wider or longer than your browser window as shown in Figure 4.11. A horizontal scroll bar appears at the bottom of the screen if a page is too wide, and a vertical scroll bar appears if a page is too long. Click on a scroll button or drag a scroll box to scroll a page up or down or left to right. With a wheel mouse, move the mouse pointer over the page and then turn the wheel to scroll. The scroll box position also indicates how much of a page is located above or below the portion of the page currently visible in the browser window.

Status Bar

The *status bar* appears at the bottom of the browser window. When a Web page loads, the status bar shows the URL for the Web page and provides a graphic progress bar representing the loading status, as shown in Figure 4.12. When the page finishes loading, the word *Done* appears at the left end of the status bar. When you place the mouse pointer over a hyperlink on a web page, the hyperlink path or URL appears in the status bar, enabling you to determine where the hyperlink leads before clicking on it. Double-click

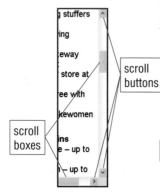

Figure 4.11 Scroll Bars

Figure 4.12 Status Bar

the small globe followed by the word Internet at the right end of the status bar to open the Internet Security Properties dialog box. This dialog box displays the settings for the current security zone.

Concept
Review 2 Internet Explorer Elements

1. Describe four aspects of the Tabs bar in Internet Explorer.
2. What is the Favorites Center used for?
3. How can you find Web pages that you have previously visited?

Skill
Review 2 Start and Use Internet Explorer

1. Click the Start button and then click Internet, or click the *Internet Explorer* icon on the desktop to open the browser.
2. Click the URL in the Address bar to select it and then type **www.cnn.com**.

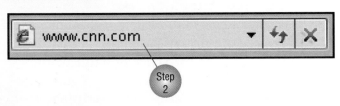

Step 2

3. Press Enter to open the CNN.com Web page.
4. Use the vertical scroll bar to scroll to the bottom of the CNN.com home page.
5. Click any of the hyperlinks on the CNN.com home page to display another CNN page in the browser window.
6. Click the Back button to return to the CNN.com home page.
7. Click the Forward button to return to the previous CNN.com page.
8. Click the Favorites Center button, then click the History button and the Today icon to view the History bar.
9. Click any page listed in the History list.
10. Click the Print button to print the page displayed in the browser.
11. Click the Close button in the upper-right corner of the browser window to close Internet Explorer.

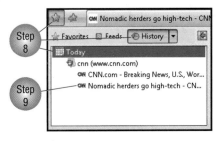

Storing and Retrieving Web Pages

Several methods enable you to save the URLs of previously viewed Web pages so that you can retrieve and view them again. The Internet Explorer Favorites list lets users save URLs and organize them in folders. The Feeds list lets the user store RSS feeds and offers notification of new content. Finally, the History list automatically maintains a record of previously visited Web pages for a user-designated time period. All three lists are available in the Favorites Center.

Figure 4.13 Add a Favorite Dialog Box

Favorites Center

The Favorites Center, as shown previously in Figure 4.5, is used to manage your lists of favorites, RSS feeds, and browser history. Click the Favorites Center button to the left of the Tabs, then click the button for Favorites, Feeds, or History to view your lists. The Favorites Center can be pinned to the left side of the browser window so that it stays visible all the time. To do this, click the Favorites Center button, then click the green Pin The Favorites Center button in the top right corner of the Favorites Center panel. The panel will become a permanent fixture to the Internet Explorer window and the Pin The Favorites Center button will be replaced by a Close button. Click the Close button to unpin and close the Favorites Center.

Favorites List

To add the URL for the currently displayed Web page to the Favorites list, use any of the following methods to start the process:

- Click the Add To Favorites button to the left of the Tabs.
- Press [CTRL]+[D] to add the current page to your favorites.
- Right-click in the Web page and then click Add to Favorites.

The Add a Favorite dialog box will appear as shown in Figure 4.14. The *Name* text box displays the title of the Web page. If the title does not clearly identify the Web page, you can modify or create a new name for the Web page by selecting the text in the *Name* text box and typing a new name. To add the page to your favorites, click Add or select a folder from the Create In menu to organize your new favorite. To create subfolders for organization, click the New Folder button, type a name for your new folder, and select a destination for your folder from the Create In menu. For example, to add the CNN Web site to your list of favorites, you may wish to organize it inside subfolders. As CNN is a news organization, it makes sense to store this favorite in a folder called News. You will do this in the next Skill Review activity. You click a folder in the Favorites Center to expand it and see the favorites stored inside.

Shortcut keys can be assigned to favorites for easy launch. For example, you may assign the key combination [CTRL]+[ALT]+[T] to launch the Tommy Shannon favorite. If you create that shortcut, whenever that key combination is pressed Internet Explorer will launch and load the Tommy Shannon web site. To configure shortcut keys, click the Favorites Center button, navigate to your favorite, right-click it and choose Properties. In the Shortcut Key box on the Web Document tab, enter the desired key combination and click OK.

Favorites can be organized by clicking the Add to Favorites button and then clicking the Organize Favorites menu option. This opens the Organize Favorites dialog box shown in Figure 4.15. The dialog box can be used to create, rename, or delete folders, and to move favorites to new folders. You can move a favorite or folder in the list at the top of the dialog box by dragging the favorite or folder to a new

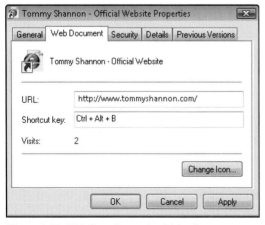

Figure 4.14 Web Page Properties Dialog Box

position in the list. As you drag, a black line will appear to indicate where the favorite or folder will be placed when the mouse button is released. The Organize Favorites dialog box can be closed by clicking the Close button.

Favorites can be sorted alphabetically by name. To do so, click the Favorites Center button, right-click any Favorite, and then click Sort by Name. Sort the favorites within a folder by right-clicking the folder and then clicking Sort by Name on the submenu that appears.

Figure 4.15 Organize Favorites Dialog Box

RSS Feeds

RSS (Really Simple Syndication) Feeds offer an easy way to stay current with the content of your favorite Web sites, provided the site offers an RSS feed. Navigate to your favorite Web site and if the RSS Feed button in the Internet Explorer turns orange, an RSS feed is available. If the button is gray and inactive, no RSS feeds are available. Once you find a site that offers an RSS feed, clicking the orange Feeds button displays the first available feed. Clicking the associated menu arrow to the right of the Feeds button displays a list of all available feeds allowing you to select the one you want. Once you click the Feeds button or make a selection from the menu arrow, you will have the opportunity to subscribe to the feed. Subscribing is as complicated as clicking the Subscribe To This Feed link at the top of the page. Doing so opens the Subscribe To This Feed dialog box which is almost identical to the Add To Favorites dialog box and functions exactly the same way.

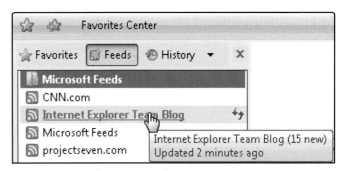

Figure 4.16 RSS Feed with New Content

RSS Feeds list List of subscribed RSS Feeds available from the Favorites Center

Once you have subscribed to a feed, open the Favorites Center and click the Feeds button. If new content has been added to the feed, the feed name will be in bold. Point to any subscribed feed to view a small pop-up box with information about the feed, including when the last content update was, as shown in Figure 4.16. Click the feed in the Favorites Center to load a Web page where you can read the new content. To remove a subscribed feed, right-click it in the Favorites Center and choose Delete from the pop-up menu.

History List

The ***History list*** displays Web pages that have been viewed within a user-specified time frame. Clicking a Web page in the History list opens the Web page in the browser window. The History list is useful for retrieving Web pages that may not be stored as Favorites, or to retrieve a Web page that was inadvertently closed.

You can change the length of time URLs remain in the History folder by clicking Tools on the menu bar, clicking Internet Options, then clicking the Settings button in the Browser History section to open the Temporary Internet Files and History Settings dialog box shown in Figure 4.17. You can change the *Days to keep pages*

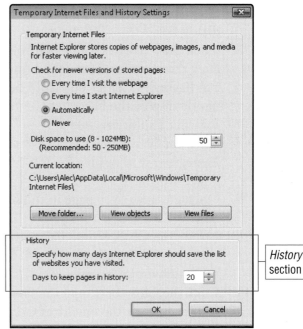

Figure 4.17 Temporary Internet Files and History Settings Options

in history option in the *History* section as desired using the up- and down-pointing arrows or by typing a number in the text box. Clicking the Tools button on the toolbar, selecting Internet Options, then clicking the Delete button in the Browsing History section empties the History folder. A quicker way to do this is to simply click the Tools button, then click the first menu option to Delete Browsing History. Some people do not like the fact that the History folder contains a record of the Web sites they have visited so they set the number of days to keep the pages at zero, or frequently clear the browsing history manually to remove that information. Clearing the History folder will also affect the Address bar, which will no longer list any URLs when the user clicks the down-pointing arrow located at the right of the Address bar.

Concept *Review 3* Storing and Retrieving Web Pages

1. What are the similarities and differences between the Favorites, Feeds and History features?
2. How can a Web page be saved to the Favorites list?
3. IIow can the History cache be cleared?

Skill *Review 3* Save a Web Page Favorite

1. Start Internet Explorer and open the CNN.com Web page (www.cnn.com).
2. Click the Add To Favorites button to the left of the Tabs and select Add To Favorites from the submenu.
3. Change the favorite name by typing **CNN Home Page** over the text in the *Name* text box.
4. Click the New Folder button to open the Create A Folder dialog box.
5. Type **News** in the *Folder Name* text box at the Create A Folder dialog box and then click Create.
6. Click Add to close the Add a Favorite dialog box.
7. Click the Favorites Center button then click the Favorites button and finally the Pin Favorites Center button to permanently display the Favorites Center in the Internet Explorer window.
8. Click the News folder you just created in the Favorites list to display the CNN Home Page favorite.
9. Open any new Web page in the browser window.
10. Locate the CNN Home Page favorite and click it to display the CNN.com home page in the browser window.
11. Click the Close button in the Favorites Center to close the Favorites Center panel.

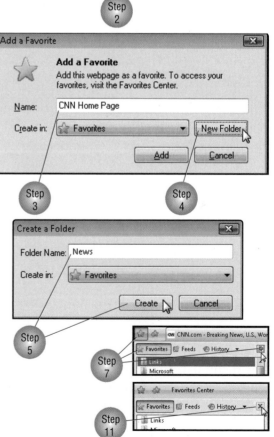

Saving Web Pages

Sometimes a Web page viewer may want to save a copy of a Web page in order to preserve a snapshot of the page for later reference or use. There are a number of different options for saving Web pages and the component files that make up a Web page, such as HTML files, images, and so on. The Save Webpage dialog box offers four different choices for saving a Web page, and there are other options for saving Web pages and Web page content that do not involve using the Save Webpage dialog box.

Save Webpage Dialog Box

To save the Web page displayed in the browser window, start by clicking the Page button on the toolbar and then clicking Save As. This opens the Save Webpage dialog box, shown in Figure 4.18. To specify a name for the saved Web page, select and type

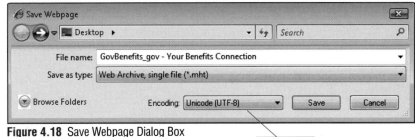

Figure 4.18 Save Webpage Dialog Box

Save format options

over the file name in the File name text box. Open the *Save as type* drop-down list to see save format options: saving the page as a complete HTML file, as a Web archive file, as an HTML only file, or as a text file.

Choosing *Webpage, complete (*.htm, *.html)* saves the Web page and all its component files in their original formats. The HTML portion of the Web page will be saved as a separate HTML file, and a folder will be created to contain all the other files used to create the Web page, such as CSS files, image files, and so on. You can modify and reuse the HTML file and the component file material once it is saved. Before you modify or reuse any Web pages, you should make sure you understand any plagiarism and copyright issues that may be involved. You will learn more about these issues in Chapter 5, *Finding Information*.

If you choose the *Web Archive, single file (*.mht)* option, the Web page and all its components will be saved in a single file as a MIME (Multipurpose Internet Mail Extension) HTML document with a .mht extension. A Web archive file is like a snapshot of a Web page, so the individual components that make up the Web page cannot be modified or reused as they can when a Web page is saved using the *Web page, complete (*.htm, *.html)* option. However, each Web archive file is a single file that is easier to work with and send via e-mail. You can view Web archive files using Internet Explorer v.5 or subsequent versions by pressing [CTRL]+[O], and then use the Open dialog box to locate and open the Web archive file in the browser window.

Choosing the *Webpage, HTML only (*.htm, *.html)* option will save the HTML code in a Web page but without the component parts of the page such as images, CSS style sheets, and so on. When you open this type of HTML file in a browser window, the Web page will appear with any non-HTML material missing, so areas with images will appear blank as shown in Figure 4.19.

Choosing the *Text File (*.txt)* option saves only the text displayed in the Web page. Save in this format if you plan to copy and use large portions of text. You can open a text file using a browser or any text or word processing program

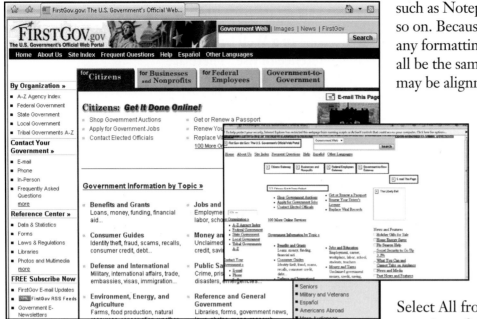

such as Notepad, WordPad, Word, and so on. Because text files do not contain any formatting information, the text will all be the same size and style and there may be alignment problems.

Other Methods for Saving Web Pages

The material displayed in a Web page can be copied by selecting and copying it. To select the entire page for copying, right-click a blank spot on the page and choose Select All from the submenu. To select a section of the page, drag over the desired material. Copy the selected material by right-clicking the selection and clicking Copy in the shortcut menu. Once the material has been copied, it can be pasted in a document by whatever paste method the application supports.

Figure 4.19 Web Page Complete and HTML-Only File Displayed

The HTML code for a Web page can be viewed and saved by clicking the Page button on the toolbar and selecting View Source, or by right-clicking a text portion of the page and then clicking View Source in the shortcut menu. Notepad will open and display the HTML code as shown in Figure 4.20. The file can then be named and saved. Viewing the HTML code behind a page can help you learn more about HTML coding.

Figure 4.20 HTML Code Displayed in Notepad

Concept Review 4 · Saving Web Pages

1. What is the difference between using the *Web Page, complete* and *Web Archive, single file* file formats to save a Web page?
2. How can you save the HTML code for a Web page?
3. What is the benefit of saving a page in the .mht file format?

Skill Review 4 · Save and View a Web Page Offline

1. Open a Web page that you want to save.
2. Click the Page button on the toolbar and then click Save As to open the Save Webpage dialog box.
3. Type a new name for the Web page you are saving in the dialog box *File name* text box and set the Save As Type menu to Webpage Complete.
4. If necessary, click the Browse Folders button in the bottom left corner of the Save Webpage dialog box to display the Vista folder list on the left side.
5. If necessary, click the Desktop option to navigate to your desktop. (You will save the Web page to your desktop so it is easy to find.)
6. Click the Save button to save the Web page to your desktop.
7. Close Internet Explorer and any other programs you have running and return to your desktop.
8. Locate the saved file on your desktop and note there is a folder with the same name. The file is the HTML file while the folder stores all the images and other components used on the page.
9. Double-click the file (not the folder) to open the page in Internet Explorer.
10. Notice the address bar displays a local path to the file on your hard drive, not a fully qualified URL. This file is now available for viewing without an Internet connection because it has been saved to your hard drive.

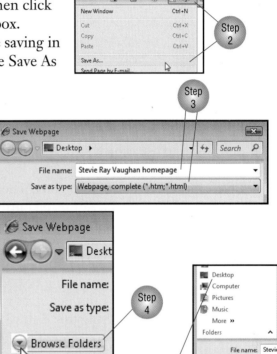

Printing Web Pages

Clicking the Print button on the Standard Buttons toolbar will print a Web page using the current printer settings, unless the print function has been disabled by the Web page publisher in order to protect the page content. You can change printer settings before printing a Web page by clicking arrow menu associated with the Print button on the toolbar and then clicking Print. The Print dialog box will open. In the Print dialog box, specify which printer

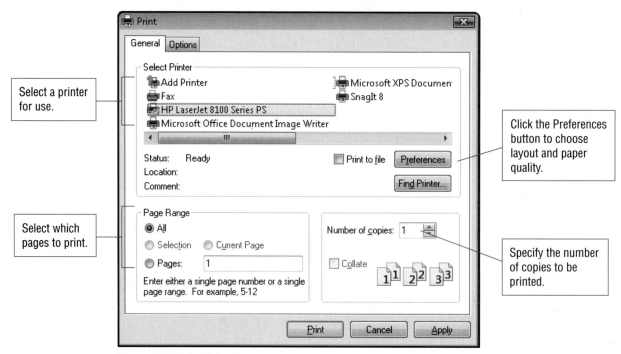

Figure 4.21 Print Dialog Box

to use, which pages to print, the number of copies to be printed, and so on as shown in Figure 4.21. Clicking the Preferences button opens the Printing Preferences dialog box, where you can choose layout and paper quality. Clicking the Advanced button at the Printing Preferences dialog box displays additional settings that can be modified. The options available in the Print dialog box will vary depending on the selected printer.

To print only a portion of a Web page, select the desired material and then open the Print dialog box. Click the Selection option in the Page Range section of the Print dialog box and then click Print to print only the selected material. Using this feature can save a lot of paper and ink if you need to print only a portion of a Web page.

Internet Explorer 7 offers the ability to scale the document being printed to fit on a single sheet of paper. This is an option you will have to configure manually. While it may save paper, too much content shrunk to fit on a single page may be difficult to read.

Concept Review 5 Printing Web Pages

1. Describe the different methods that can be used to print a Web page.
2. How can a user change the default printer settings?
3. How can a user print a portion of a Web page?

Skill Review 5 Print a Web Page

1. Choose a Web page to print and open it in your browser.
2. Click the arrow menu to the right of the Print button on the toolbar and select Print Preview to open the Print Preview dialog box.

3. Locate the page count at the bottom of the Print Preview window and note how many pages it will take to print your document.

4. Experiment with the various options in the Shrink To Fit menu. As you change the percentages, see how it affects the page count by checking the bottom of the Print Preview window.

5. Experiment dragging the Left/Right/Top/Bottom margin controls to change the margins of the printed document. Again, see how this affects the page count.

6. When you are through experimenting, click the Print Document button at the top of the Print Preview window.

7. If necessary, select a printer other than the default printer. *(Note: You may need to ask your instructor which printer to choose.)*

8. The Page Range defaults to All and the Number Of Copies defaults to 1. Click the Print button at the bottom of the dialog box to print your document.

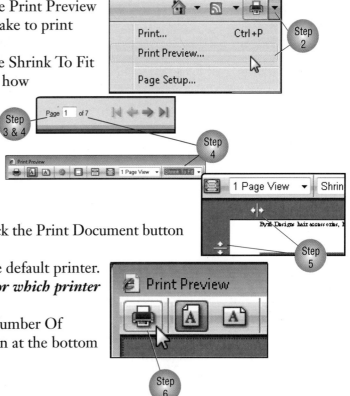

Configuring Internet Explorer

Internet Explorer includes a number of features that users can configure to customize the browser and tailor it to their needs. You can open or close toolbars, change their layout, and add or remove buttons. You can modify Web page text size, set the default browser home pages and search engine, and enable the AutoComplete feature to make filling out forms easier.

Toolbars

Clicking the Tools button and pointing to Toolbars opens a submenu of toolbar commands, shown in Figure 4.22. The Status Bar is displayed (checked) by default, but the Links bar may not be displayed in some versions of Internet Explorer. Clicking a toolbar name in the submenu will toggle the toolbar on or off. The Toolbars submenu may list additional third party toolbars if those toolbars have been downloaded and installed on your computer.

You can lock and unlock toolbar positions right-clicking the toolbar using the Lock the Toolbars command from the pop-up menu. When toolbars are unlocked, you can drag a toolbar to a new location using the handle (dotted vertical line) located at the left side of the toolbar as shown in Figure 4.22. You can drag a toolbar's handle to the left to expand it or to the right to contract it. You also can double-click the handle to resize the toolbar quickly. It is quite easy to inadvertently move a toolbar, so once you have toolbars located where you want them, it is a good idea to select the Lock the Toolbars command from the pop-up menu to protect them against being modified or moved.

Figure 4.22 Toolbar Options

Add-On Toolbars

You can download and install free add-on toolbars to add new capabilities to your Web browser. Google offers one of the best known add-on toolbars. The Google toolbar looks just like a normal Internet Explorer toolbar, but contains a built-in Google search box, pop-up blocker, link to the Google news service, translation service, and more. Not to be outdone, the popular Internet portal Yahoo! offers a toolbar that includes similar features as well as an anti-spyware program. To make writing easier, Dictionary.com offers a toolbar that includes a dictionary, thesaurus, and Word of the Day vocabulary-building feature.

Before installing an add-on toolbar you should do research to make sure that the toolbar is not a thinly disguised adware or spyware program. Doing a keyword search using the toolbar name and *spyware* will usually let you know if a toolbar is associated with adware or spyware activity.

Toolbars can be customized by clicking the Tools button, pointing to Toolbars, and then clicking Customize. This opens the Customize Toolbar dialog box that can be used to add or remove toolbar buttons, change button text location, or change button size.

Text Size

The default Web page text size can be changed by clicking the Page button on the toolbar, pointing to Text Size, and then clicking the desired relative text size. The ability to display a default text size is dependent on how text fonts are specified in a Web page, so some Web page text may not be affected by a change to the Text Size setting. Figure 4.23 shows the difference in a Web page viewed with the smallest and largest text settings.

Figure 4.23 Web Page Displayed with Smallest and Largest Text Sizes

Default Internet Explorer Home Pages

The default Internet Explorer home page can be changed by opening the desired new home Web page in the browser window, clicking the arrow menu associated with the Home button on the toolbar, and then choosing Add or Change Home Page. In the Add Or Change Home Page dialog box, shown in Figure 4.24, you can choose to make the current page your only home page or add it to the list of Home Tabs. When you add Web pages to your list of Home Tabs, clicking the Home button on the toolbar opens all your home pages—each in their own tab. This is a convenient way to specify multiple home pages that open in individual tabs when Internet Explorer is launched.

If you have already opened several tabs, clicking the Add Or Change Home Page option

Figure 4.24 Add or Change Home Page Dialog Box

offers a third option as shown in Figure 4.25—to make the currently open tabs your home page tab set. Home pages can be removed by clicking the arrow menu associated with the Home button on the toolbar, pointing to Remove, and clicking the page you want removed from your Home Tabs set.

AutoComplete

The *AutoComplete* feature stores previously entered Web addresses, form field

Figure 4.25 Add or Change Home Page Dialog Box with Additional Option

information, user names, and passwords. As soon as a user begins typing text in a field, AutoComplete compares what is being typed to the stored items and then provides suggestions in the form of a list of possible matches. The user can ignore a suggestion and keep typing, or click a suggestion in the list to complete the field using that particular suggestion. Enabling AutoComplete can speed up repetitious tasks such as filling out forms and typing long URLs in the Address bar. One drawback is that AutoComplete also stores user names and passwords, so if someone gains access to your computer, the AutoComplete feature could enable that person to access personal accounts and other information. Fortunately, you can specify that AutoComplete not provide suggestions for user names and passwords, or turn off AutoComplete altogether.

AutoComplete Internet Explorer feature that stores previously entered information so it can be matched against text being entered in form fields in order to speed up the data entry process

To configure AutoComplete, click the Tools button on the toolbar and then click Internet Options. At the Internet Options dialog box, click the Content tab and then click the Settings button in the AutoComplete section to open the AutoComplete Settings dialog box as shown in Figure 4.26. Check (enable) or uncheck (disable) AutoComplete options as desired. Form data and password histories as well as Web address history can be cleared by clicking the Tools button on the toolbar and selecting Delete Browsing History, then

Start Page Hijacking

Browser start or home pages can be hijacked by adware, spyware, or malware programs attempting to redirect users to other Web pages. This redirection may have any number of purposes. The more benign hijackers redirect users to their own Web pages to inflate page hits and increase advertising revenue. Sinister hijackers may redirect users to Web pages with a criminal purpose in mind. In either case, hijacking is annoying at best and dangerous at worst. Hijackers can gain a foothold through a visit to a Web site or by downloading and installing a program containing adware or spyware. In many cases, you can use the Add or Change Home Page dialog box to restore the previous home page, but sometimes a hijacker will continue to reset the start page every time Internet Explorer is opened. Correcting more serious hijacking cases may require making changes to a computer's registry—something you should not attempt unless you know what you are doing. Many spyware removal programs can undo a hijacking, but the best protection is to make sure that your browser security settings are up-to-date and set high so that you are notified whenever attempts are made to change your computer's settings.

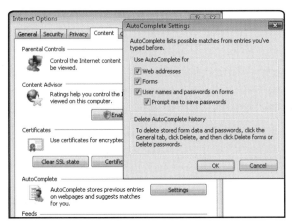

Figure 4.26 AutoComplete Settings Dialog Box

Figure 4.27 Delete Browsing History Dialog Box

clicking the appropriate Delete button for the content you wish to clear as in Figure 4.27.

Screen Resolution

Changing your computer's screen resolution can change the size of the content appearing in your browser. In Windows Vista, the screen resolution can be changed using the Display Settings dialog box, which can be opened by right-clicking in the desktop and then clicking Personalize, then choosing Display Settings. Drag the Resolution slider to the desired screen resolution and then click the Apply button as shown in Figure 4.28. The screen will go dark for a few seconds and then reappear using the new screen resolution. If the Monitor Settings dialog box appears asking if you want to keep these settings, click Yes. Click the OK button to close the Display Settings dialog box. If you are using a computer at your school, check with your instructor before changing your screen resolution.

Figure 4.28 Screen Resolution Settings

Concept Review 6 Configuring Internet Explorer

1. What is the difference between a Home Page and a Home Tab set?
2. How can a user change the default Web page text size?
3. What is the AutoComplete feature's purpose, and how can a user change its defaults?

Skill Review 6 Configure Home Tabs

1. Make sure only one tab is open, then type www.microsoft.com in the Address bar and press Enter.
2. Click the arrow menu associated with the Home button and select Add Or Change Home Page.
3. Select the option *Use this webpage as your only home page* and click Yes.
4. Type **www.apple.com** in the address bar and press Enter. The Apple web site loads.

5. To return to your new home page, click the Home button in the toolbar. The Microsoft site (your home page) returns.
6. In the Address bar, type **www.cnn.com** and press Enter.
7. Click the arrow menu associated with the Home button, select Add Or Change Home Page, select the option for *Add this webpage to your home page tabs*, and click Yes.

Step 7

8. In the address bar, type **www.apple.com** and press Enter to return to the Apple Web site.
9. Click the Home button on the toolbar. As you have created a home page tab set, both of your home pages open in separate tabs.

Step 9

Other Internet Explorer Features

Once you become comfortable using Internet Explorer, you can begin exploring some of the many specialized features that can make using the browser even more convenient. Learn about these by using the Internet Explorer Help function, discover them by yourself, or learn about them from friends. Some of the more useful features are described below, but this text is by no means an exhaustive description of the different features you can use in Internet Explorer.

Internet Explorer provides **keyboard shortcuts** for common commands. To view the keyboard shortcut list, click Help on the Internet Explorer menu bar and then Contents and Index. Type **internet explorer keyboard shortcuts** in the *Search Help* text box and then press the Enter key. A Topics Found dialog box will appear. Finally, select *Internet Explorer keyboard shortcuts*. Click the Viewing and exploring Web pages link to display the list of keyboard shortcuts.

keyboard shortcut a quick command input method that enables a user to press a function key such as F1 to choose a command

Full Screen an expanded browser view that hides toolbars and menus

Using Help

Internet Explorer comes with a very complete Help system accessible by clicking the Help button on the toolbar and then clicking Contents and Index. Clicking the Browse Help icon as in Figure 4.29 displays a list of instructional categories. To view help on a certain topic, simply click a category.

Full Screen View

The Internet Explorer browser window shrinks to accommodate any toolbars that are displayed. Opening all the toolbars and placing them on separate rows can lead to a drastic reduction in the amount of space available in the browser window. Clicking the Tools button on the toolbar and then clicking **Full Screen** provides an alternative to closing toolbars to free up browser window space. Alternatively, you can tap the [F11] key. Full Screen view enlarges the browser display to

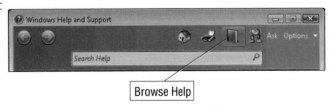

Browse Help

Figure 4.29 Internet Explorer Help Window

fill the screen, while removing the toolbars, address bar, and tabs from view. Moving the mouse pointer up to the top of the browser window will cause these elements to drop into view. Once the toolbar has dropped back into view, click the Tools button and select Full Screen or press F11 to restore the previous browser view.

Links Bar

Links bar an Internet Explorer toolbar that provides a quick method for accessing frequently viewed Web pages

The ***Links bar*** provides a quick method for accessing frequently viewed Web pages. To display the Links bar, if needed, click the Tools button on the toolbar, point to Toolbars, and then click Links. The Links bar will appear under the Address bar. Clicking a button on the Links bar opens a Web page. Figure 4.30 shows an example of the Links bar.

There are four different methods that can be used to add links to the Links bar:

- Drag the Explorer icon at the left end of the URL displayed in the Address bar to a position on the Links bar as shown in Figure 4.30.
- Drag a hyperlink from a Web page to a position on the Links bar.
- Drag a Favorites listing to a position on the Links bar.
- Add a URL to the Links folder in the Favorites list.

To remove a link, right-click it on the Links bar and then click Delete in the shortcut menu that appears. Drag links into the desired position on the Links bar as needed. When the Links bar contains more links than it can display, a double arrow button appears at its right end. Click the double arrow button to display additional links.

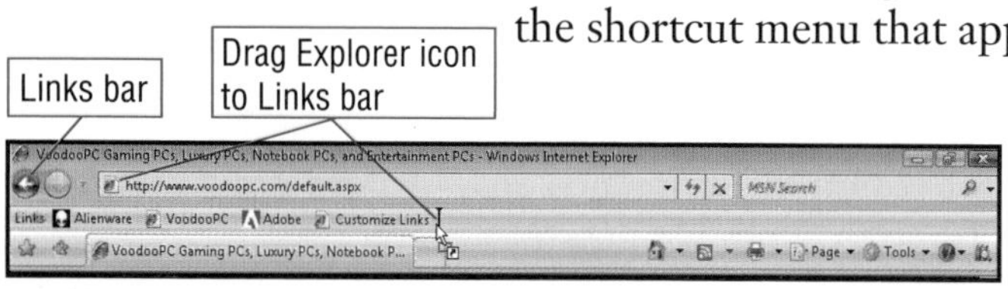

Figure 4.30 Links Bar

Search Engine

The search engine that the Instant Search Box next to the Address bar uses defaults to MSN Search, but can be changed by clicking the arrow menu associated with the Instant Search Box and clicking the Change Search Defaults hyperlink and then clicking the Find More Providers link. A Web page will open allowing you to change the search engine used by the Instant Search Box. You will do this in the next Skill Review activity.

Concept Review 7 Other Internet Explorer Features

1. How can a user enable the Full Screen view feature?
2. List three keyboard shortcuts you can use with Internet Explorer. Be sure to state the keys you need to press and the task they perform.
3. How does the Links bar work?

Skill Review 7 Configure the Default Search Engine

1. Click the arrow to the right of the Instant Search Box and choose Change Search Defaults. ***(Note: The default search engine is MSN Search, but may have been changed by your instructor.)***

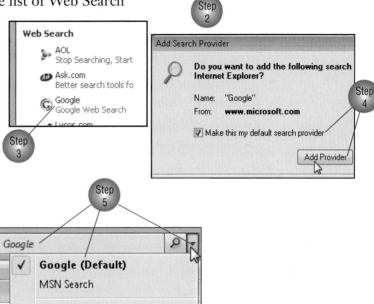

2. In the Change Search Default dialog box, click the Find More Providers hyperlink. A web page opens allowing you to change your search provider.

3. Click the Google hyperlink from the list of Web Search providers on the left of the page.

4. In the Add Search Provider dialog box, check the box to make Google the default search provider, then click Add Provider.

5. Notice the Instant Search Box now lists Google as the default provider. Either type in a search term and press Enter to search Google, or type your search term, click the arrow menu, and select MSN Search to search with MSN.

Web Search

AOL
Stop Searching, Start

Ask.com
Better search tools fo

Google
Google Web Search

Lycos.com

Step 3

Step 5

Chapter Summary

- When the user clicks a document hyperlink or types a URL in a browser Address bar and then presses Enter, the browser seeks and retrieves the document located at the address represented by the hyperlink or URL. When the browser connects to a secure server, the closed padlock icon appears at the right end of the Address bar.

- Material located at an IP or URL address may be located on a user's computer or on a server located thousands of miles away.

- Browsers interpret and display HTML documents and images. With the help of add-on programs known as plug-ins, browsers can display other types of media.

- The various security vulnerabilities inherent in Internet Explorer 6 have led some users to abandon it for other browsers that are more secure.

- Microsoft has addressed many of the security concerns and has added more features with Internet Explorer 7, leading many users back to the Microsoft browser.

- Internet Explorer provides several different methods for inputting commands, including the Standard Buttons toolbar, shortcut menus displayed by right-clicking an onscreen object, and keyboard shortcuts.

- The Internet Explorer Standard Buttons toolbar is the main place to find commands for performing common tasks.

- The Favorites Center offers a convenient place to access your favorites, subscribes RSS feeds, and offers browser history.

- The Favorites list enables users to store and organize URLs for easy access when needed.

- The Feeds list displays subscribed RSS feeds and alerts the user to new content.

- The History list displays a list of previously visited Web sites in the History bar.

- It is not necessary to enter the protocol portion of the URL for Web pages.

- Clicking the down-pointing arrow located at the right end of the Address bar displays a list of previously entered URLs.

- Web page content appears in the browser window. Scroll bars will appear if a Web page is wider or longer than the browser window display at its current size.

- The Internet Explorer status bar displays the URL for the current Web page and provides a graphic progress bar representing page-loading status.

- Organize favorites by opening the Add To Favorites button and then clicking the Organize Favorites option.

- The Delete Browsing History option under the Tools button displays a dialog box where you can clear your browsing history, stored data from forms, and other items.

- Some people do not like the fact that the History folder contains a record of the Web sites they have visited, so they set the number of days to keep the pages at zero or frequently use the Delete Browsing History option to remove that information.

- Clearing the Browsing history also affects the Address bar, which will no longer show any URLs when the user clicks the down-pointing arrow at the right end of the Address bar.

- The Save Webpage dialog box offers four different formats for saving a Web page, and there are other options for saving Web pages and Web page content that do not involve using the Save Webpage dialog box.

- To view the HTML code for a Web page, right-click a text portion of a Web page and then click View Source in the shortcut menu that appears.

- Clicking the Print button on the Standard Buttons toolbar will print a Web page using current print settings unless the print function has been disabled by the Web page publisher in order to protect the page contents.

- The user can specify print settings by clicking the arrow menu associated with the Print button and then clicking Print to open the Print dialog box.

- The user can configure a number of different Internet Explorer features to customize the browser and tailor it to their needs.

- The Links bar may not be displayed in some versions of Internet Explorer as it is not shown by default.

- When toolbars are in unlocked mode, you can drag a toolbar to a new location using its handle (the dotted vertical line located on the left end of each toolbar).

- It is quite easy to inadvertently move a toolbar, so once you have toolbars located where you want them, it is a good idea to select the Lock the Toolbars command.

- Customize the Standard Buttons toolbar by clicking the Tools button, pointing to Toolbars, and then clicking Customize. This opens the Customize Toolbar dialog box, with options for adding or removing toolbar buttons, changing button text location, or changing button size.

- The default Internet Explorer home page can be changed by opening the desired home page in the browser window, clicking the arrow associated with the Home button, and choosing Add Or Change Home Pages.

- For easier access to Google, download the Google toolbar from the Google Web site. Once installed, the Google toolbar can be used to conduct searches when required. Alternatively, change the default search provider to Google or the search engine of your choice from the Instant Search Box's Change Search Defaults option.

- The AutoComplete feature stores previously entered Web addresses, form field information, user names, and passwords. One drawback to AutoComplete is that it can remember user names and passwords, so if someone gains access to your computer, the AutoComplete feature could facilitate that person accessing accounts and private information.

- Changing your computer's screen resolution can change the size of the content appearing in your browser.

- Internet Explorer includes a very complete Help function that the user can access via the Help button on the toolbar.

- Full Screen view enlarges the browser main window display so that it fills the screen while removing the address bar, tabs, and toolbars from view.

- Using multiple browser tabs can save time by enabling the user to read one Web page while another downloads. A user also can move back and forth between multiple tabs to compare information.

- The Links bar provides a quick method for accessing frequently viewed Web pages.

Key Terms

Numbers indicate the pages where terms are first cited in the chapter. An alphabetized list of key terms with definitions can be found on the Encore CD that accompanies this book. In addition, these terms and definitions are included in the end-of-book glossary.

Address bar, *104*

AutoComplete, *121*

Back button, *106*

Browser, *104*

Browser window, *105*

Favorites Center button, *108*

Favorites list, *108*

Forward button, *106*

Full screen view, *123*

Help, *110*

History list, *113*

History button, *108*

Home button, *109*

Instant Search Box, *107*

Keyboard shortcut, *123*

Links bar, *124*

Page button, *109*

Print button, *109*

Quick Tab, *108*

Refresh button, *107*

RSS Feeds list, *113*

Scroll bars, *110*

Standard Buttons toolbar, *108*

Status bar, *110*

Stop button, *107*

Tab, *108*

Tab list, *108*

Title bar, *106*

Tools button, *109*

Additional quiz questions are available on the Encore CD that accompanies this book as well as on the Internet Resource Center for this title at www.emcp.net/Internet2e.

Multiple Choice

Indicate the correct answer for each question or statement.

1. Add-on programs that enable browsers to display content such as pdf files, Flash movies, and so on are known as
   a. GUI programs.
   b. plug-ins.
   c. Favorites.
   d. HTML.

2. A list of keyboard shortcuts can be found in the Internet Explorer
   a. Help feature.
   b. History list.
   c. Favorites list.
   d. Search Companion.

3. This Internet Explorer bar displays the URL or path for a document open in the browser window.
   a. title bar
   b. Favorites Center
   c. status bar
   d. Address bar

4. When the user hovers the mouse pointer over a hyperlink, the path or URL for the link will appear in the _____ bar.
   a. status
   b. Address
   c. menu
   d. History

5. The History list displays
   a. a list of favorite Web sites.
   b. URLs of historical interest.
   c. a list of previously visited Web sites.
   d. a history of previous browser users.

6. To save a Web page so that its component parts are saved in their original format you would use which of the following file formats?
   a. Web Page, complete (*.htm, *.html)
   b. Web Archive, single file (*.mht.)
   c. Web Page only (*.htm, *.html)
   d. Text File (*.txt)

7. The Toolbars command is found under which of the following buttons?
   a. Tools
   b. Help
   c. Reference
   d. Home

8. A toolbar can be dragged by its
   a. toolbar button or command.
   b. handle (the vertical dotted line at the left end of an unlocked toolbar).
   c. top edge.
   d. top or bottom edge.

9. The search engine used by the Instant Search Box can be changed by
   a. clicking the Instant Search Box menu arrow and then clicking the Change Search Defaults option.
   b. clicking the Tools button on the toolbar, pointing to Internet Options, and then clicking the Search option.
   c. The search feature can only be customized by making changes to a computer's registry.
   d. clicking the Search button on the toolbar, clicking the Change Preferences hyperlink, clicking the Change Internet search behavior hyperlink, selecting a new search engine from the list, and then clicking the OK button.

10. The AutoComplete feature can automatically complete
    a. Address bar, form, user name, and password entries.
    b. file name entries.
    c. table entries.
    d. documents.

True/False

Indicate whether each statement is true or false.

1. Browsers can only display material located on other servers.
2. The browser window title bar displays the title of the current Web page.
3. The Refresh button can be used to open a new browser window.
4. The Print button opens the Print dialog box.
5. The length of time that a URL will remain in the History list cannot be changed.
6. The toolbar enables users to execute various commands using familiar button icons.
7. Choosing the Web Page, complete (*.htm,*.html) format when saving a Web page saves it as a single file.
8. IP addresses cannot be typed in the Address bar.
9. Default browser text size can be changed by users.
10. The HTML code for a Web page can be viewed by right-clicking a text portion of a Web page and then clicking View Source from the shortcut menu.

Virtual Perspectives

1. Discuss the five browser features you use the most and the five you use the least. Are your least-used features least used because you have no need for them, or because they are difficult to understand or use?
2. What features would you like to see added to the Web browser you use? Explain why you would like to see those features added to your browser. Are the features you would like available on other browsers, or are they things you would like to see developed? Would you switch browsers if you saw one that contained one or more of the features you would like to see?
3. What do you think is the best default home or start page for a browser? Have you specified the default home page for the browser you use? If yes, discuss your reasons for choosing that page.

Internet Lab Projects

Project 1
Change the Internet Explorer Home Page

1. Surf the Web to find a Web page that you would like to be your browser home page.
2. With the Web page you want open in the browser window, open the Add Or Change Home Page dialog box and select the appropriate option to make the current page the home page. Be sure to create a single home page and not a home tab set.

Project 2
Change the Default Search Companion Search Engine

1. Click the Instant Search Box arrow menu and select the appropriate option to add a new search provider.
2. Configure Yahoo as your default search engine.
3. Use the Instant Search Box to conduct a search using the search engine you selected.
4. Use the Instant Search Box to conduct a search using a search engine other than your default.

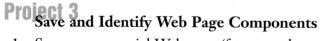

Project 3
Save and Identify Web Page Components

1. Save a commercial Web page (for example, a news or catalog Web site) as a complete Web page.
2. Open Windows Explorer or a similar file manager, and view the files and folders that make up the Web page. Use the file manager to find answers to the following questions:
   a. How many different files does the Web page contain?
   b. What is the size of the Web page in kilobytes (KB)?
   c. What are the different file types that make up the Web page?

Internet Research Activities

Activity 1
Explore Browser History

Mosaic was one of the first graphical user interface (GUI) Web browsers. Most of the Web browsers in use today can trace their ancestry back to the Mosaic browser, including Internet Explorer. This common ancestry in part explains the similar layout and appearance of most Web browsers. Research the history of Web browsers and write or type a short paper tracing the history of the first GUI Web browsers up to those currently available.

Activity 2
Research Internet Explorer 7 Tips and Tricks

Internet Explorer 7 contains a number of little-known ways to make using it easier and more convenient to use. Search the Web to find information about tips and tricks for using Internet Explorer 7. Write step-by-step instructions for three tips or tricks that were not covered in this chapter.

Activity 3
Net Challenge

Millions of people have visual, hearing, physical, or neurological disabilities that might impair their ability to access Web page content using traditional Web browsers. To address these needs, a variety of alternative browsers are available for disabled Internet users. Research this topic and write or type a paper describing some of the issues of accessibility. Profile at least two browsers that are designed for people with disabilities and describe how they work.

Chapter 5

Accessing Information Resources

Living on the Net

Bob recently read that the Google search engine averaged more than 250 million queries per day. He thought to himself that he must account for a good portion of those requests, reflecting on how much he depends on the Internet in both his personal and professional lives. Bob has used search engines and subject directories to find information since he started using the Internet and has been impressed with the continual improvement in their capabilities.

Bob depended solely on search engines to find the things he wanted when he first started surfing the Web. Soon afterwards, he discovered subject directories that organized information in categories and subcategories. He found the Yahoo! directory helpful when he needed general topical information rather than an answer to a specific question.

One of the most interesting things Bob learned about the Web was that search engines and subject directories index only a very small percentage of the information available. He was surprised to learn that there was an entire world of information that he was missing simply because he did not know about the tools and strategies needed to access that information.

Over the years, Bob learned the importance of clearly identifying the information he was looking for and then developing a search strategy to find that information. He also realized that an understanding of how search engines work and the proper use of keywords, operators, and search conventions yield better search results.

Information Resources on the Web

The size of the Web and the amount of information it contains is staggering. In 2003, the University of California (Berkeley) School of Information Management and Systems estimated that the size of the Web, excluding e-mail and instant messaging, was 92,017 terabytes. A terabyte is 1,024 gigabytes, or approximately one trillion bytes. The fact that the average Web page is approximately 50 kilobytes provides an idea of the Web's massive size.

The variety of the information available on the Web is equally astounding. With a few mouse clicks, a user can access news reports, commentary, scholarly papers, weather information, radio and television broadcasts, statistics, encyclopedia and dictionary entries—there is almost no limit to the content available. In addition to the typical Web page HTML files, the Web's resources include image, audio, and movie files, as well as documents in proprietary formats such as Microsoft Word or Excel.

No central controlling authority governs the Internet or the Web, so anyone with a computer and Internet access can add more information. Because of this structure, the information on the Web is not organized or presented in a systematic manner. To find the disparate information available through the Web, a user must use special tools such as search engines and subject directories.

While these are two of the most popular search tools available, they access only a very small percentage of the information available on what is known as the *surface Web*; the portion of the Web that search engines and subject directories can index. The remainder of the Web that generally lies beyond the reach of search engines and subject directories is known as the deep, or invisible, Web. The previously cited University of California study found that the size of the surface Web was 167 terabytes as compared to 91,850 terabytes for the *deep Web*, making the deep Web approximately 550 times larger than the surface Web.

Typical deep Web resources include searchable databases that generate dynamic Web pages, non-HTML files, sites that require passwords or registration, archives, library catalogs, and information located behind firewalls. Although these resources lie beyond the reach of search engines and subject directories, they are often accessible by other means, such as using databases and deep Web directories.

> **surface Web** the portion of the Web that can be indexed by search engines and subject directories
>
> **deep Web** the portion of the Web that is generally beyond the reach of search engine spiders

Concept Review 1 Information Resources on the Web

1. What is the difference between the deep Web and the surface Web?
2. Which contains more information, the deep Web or the surface Web?

Skill Review 1 Research Web Statistics

1. Open the Google search engine Web site (www.google.com).
2. Use Google to find the following information:
   a. What is the most recent estimate of the size of the Web that you can find?
   b. What is the most recent Web growth rate statistic that you can find?
   c. Find at least one Web growth rate projection.

3. For each of your answers, provide a description of the Web page containing the information and its URL. *(Hint: If you are typing your answers for this exercise, you can copy URLs by selecting a URL in the Internet Explorer Address bar, right-clicking, and then clicking Copy in the shortcut menu that appears. You can then paste the URL in a Word document by clicking Edit on the menu bar and then Paste, or by right-clicking within a document and clicking Paste in the shortcut menu.)*

Search Engines

Search engines are Web sites that use software tools to index the contents of the Web so that information can be located and retrieved. A search engine user types a *query* into a search text box and then presses the Enter key or clicks a command button as shown in Figure 5.1 to enable a search engine to search its database to retrieve information related to the query. Queries consist of one or more keywords, important or significant words likely to be found in the information being sought. Information relevant to the query is presented

query a request for information typed in a search engine search text box

 **Tech Demo 5-1**
Search Engines

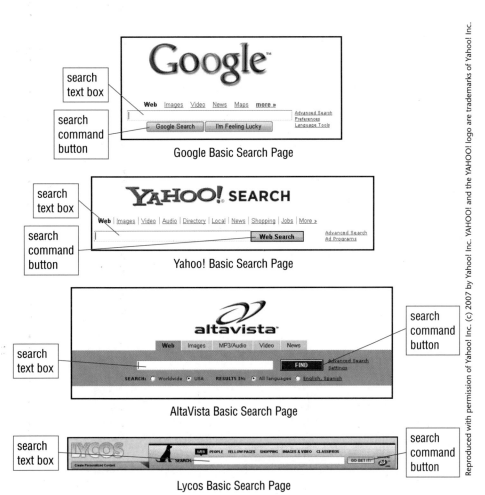

Google Basic Search Page

Yahoo! Basic Search Page

AltaVista Basic Search Page

Lycos Basic Search Page

Figure 5.1 Search Engine Search Text Boxes and Search Command Buttons

Reproduced with permission of Yahoo! Inc. (c) 2007 by Yahoo! Inc. YAHOO! and the YAHOO! logo are trademarks of Yahoo! Inc.

Figure 5.2 Google Search Results Page

as a series of listings known as search hits displayed on a Web page known as a results page as shown in Figure 5.2. Clicking a hit hyperlink opens the Web page indexed by the hit.

Most search engines offer their services for free, but some search engines aimed at businesses and information professionals charge fees for specialized or custom services. Rather than charging search fees, free search engines make money from advertising and sponsored links, from paid inclusion, and from licensing unique search technologies for use by others. Most search engines list sponsored links separately as shown in Figure 5.2 so that users realize that those links are a form of advertising.

Search Engine Information Gathering and Storage

Because of its huge size it would be impossible to directly search the Web in real time, so a search engine typically searches its own database containing information that was gathered using robotic programs known as *spiders*. Spiders search the Web for documents to index by crawling from link to link. A spider starts with a Web site's home page and then follows the page's links wherever they lead. When the spider encounters a new page, it stores information about the page or the page itself in the search engine database, depending on the search engine. A program known as an *indexer* sorts the words contained in or related to the Web page and organizes them in a database. When a user enters a search query, a query processor compares the content of the query to the contents of the search engine index to produce a list of relevant documents.

spider automated program used by search engines to "crawl" the Internet looking for Web pages and other documents

indexer search engine program that sorts the words contained in or related to the Web page and organizes them in a database

Spiders also remove Web pages from the search engine database when those pages no longer exist on the Web. Because of the constantly changing nature of the Web, spiders cannot always keep pace, so sometimes clicking a results page hit displays a message that the Web page found at that URL cannot be displayed as shown in Figure 5.3. Some search engines such as Google and Yahoo! Search have a cache feature that enables users to view the cached or saved Web pages in its database as shown in Figure 5.4. Clicking the Cached hyperlink displays the most

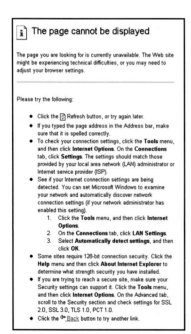

Figure 5.3 Page Cannot Be Displayed Message

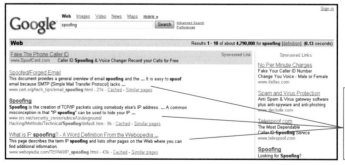

Figure 5.4 Google Cache Feature

Click a Cached link to view the most recently indexed version of a page.

recently indexed version of a page if the search engine cannot display the current version for any reason.

Search engines also index Web pages submitted by Web site owners. It can take weeks or even months for a search engine's spiders to get around to checking out and indexing a new Web site. Some search engines accept paid submissions from Web site owners in a hurry to have their sites included in search results.

Search engines differ greatly in the way they gather and store information located on the Web. Some, like Google and Yahoo! Search, use full-text indexing, which means those search engines store the entire content of the Web pages indexed in their databases. This approach enables those search engines to cache Web pages, as previously described. Other search engines only store basic information about each indexed Web page, such as its title, ***meta tags***, and some of the text on a page. Meta tags are HTML tags added into the header section of a Web page by its creator to better identify the Web page and do not appear as page content in a browser window. Figure 5.5 shows description and keywords meta tags from the HTML code for a newspaper home page. Some search engines, such as Google, completely ignore meta tags, while other search engines recognize them to varying degrees.

```
<meta name="description" content="startribune.com,
website of Star Tribune, newspaper of the Twin Cities">

<meta name="keywords"
content="Minneapolis,St.Paul,Minnesota,newspaper,Star
Tribune,news,weather,sports,business,entertainment,
jobs,employment">
```

Figure 5.5 HTML Description and Keywords Meta Tags

meta tags HTML tags, located in the header section of a Web page's HTML document, that contain title, description, keywords, and other document-related information

Search Results

Most search engines rank the hits on a results page, listing the most relevant results first. The methods search engines use for ranking pages differ, but most generally rank pages by their relevance to a query. Google pioneered factoring in the number of links to a page from other pages as a page ranking determinant. A search engine may penalize a page that contains content designed to unfairly affect page ranking, such as excessive keyword use. Almost all search engines ignore meta tag keywords when ranking pages to prevent Web page creators from manipulating page rankings. In determining page ranking, search engines examine the frequency with which keywords appear on a page and keyword location in a document. But even then, search engines use proprietary methods to detect nonrelevant stuffing of keywords throughout a page intended to move the page up the ranking ladder.

A particular query entered in different search engines will almost always produce different search results because each search engine uses different methods to search for and index Web information. Figure 5.6 shows

Google Search Results

Alta Vista Search Results

Figure 5.6 Search Results Comparison

Google Tips and Tricks

Google is currently the most popular search engine, but many Google users may be unaware of some little-known Google special features that can make life easier. For a start, Google can be used as a calculator. Type a mathematical equation in the Google search text box and then press Enter to view the answer at the top of the results page. Type a name, city, and state in the search text box and then press Enter. Any telephone numbers matching those parameters will appear. Typing a street address in the search text box and pressing Enter will return a map link the user can click to display a map for the address. The map page includes links the user can click to create driving instructions to the address from any other address.

Typing **define** followed by a word and then pressing Enter will display a results page that will be headed by a link to a list of any definitions Google finds. If no definitions are available a normal search results page will be returned. Another little known method for obtaining a definition is to click any of the hyperlinked search query keywords found in the shaded band at the top of a results page. Clicking a keyword hyperlink will display a dictionary definition for the keyword. To get a stock market quote, type **stock:** followed by a ticker symbol and then press Enter.

Google also provides spell checker capabilities. Type a word in the search text box, press Enter, and if the word is misspelled Google will display *Did you mean:* followed by the correct spelling of the misspelled word. The purpose of the I'm Feeling Lucky button located next to the Google Search button on the Google home page may be the best "secret" Google feature. Clicking the I'm Feeling Lucky button will display only the Web page containing the

most relevant match for any query. A user should employ the I'm Feeling Lucky button only if he or she has confidence that the query is so specific and unique that the top-ranked result will provide the relevant information.

search results for an identical query entered in two different search engines; none of the hits listed come from the same Web site. For this reason, it is always a good idea to try another search engine when one does not return the information being sought.

Sometimes the keywords from a search query can be difficult to find in a Web page as they may be located deep within the page or displayed throughout a document. Several methods can help the user find relevant text on a Web page. Search within a Web page by pressing Ctrl+F to open the Find dialog box shown in Figure 5.7. Type the keyword in the *Find what* text box and then click the Find Next button to highlight the first instance of the keyword on the page as shown in Figure 5.7. Click the Find Next button again to find any subsequent occurrences of the keyword. The Find dialog box also includes options for searching up and down the page.

Viewing a cached version of a Web document (from a search engine that offers this feature) also can help the user find keywords in the document. When

Figure 5.7 Find Dialog Box

search engines display a cached page, any of the keywords contained in the search query appear highlighted. In some cases, search engines highlight the matches for each keyword in a different color as shown in Figure 5.8.

Specialized Search Engines

Specialized search engines offer features that can complement regular search engines like Google and Yahoo! Search. Subject-specific search engines may be the best tools when the user knows or

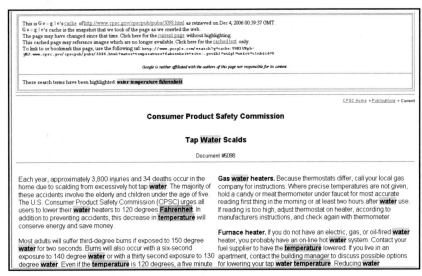

Figure 5.8 Cached Web Page Showing Highlighted Keywords

suspects that an answer lies within a specific subject area. Another tool, a meta search engine, offers a quick way to search a number of different search engines and compare results—which are not always the same. Finally, internal search engines enable users to quickly search the contents of a Web site for desired information. Table 5.1 contains a list of different search and meta search engines.

subject-specific search engine
search engine that narrows the focus of the Web content they index by dealing with a single subject or field

Subject-Specific Search Engines

A *subject-specific search engine* narrows the focus of the Web content it indexes by dealing with a single subject or field. A subject-specific search engine often can offer greater information about a topic because of the search engine's narrow focus and specialization. A good example of a subject-specific search engine is the Health On the Net Foundation Web page shown in Figure 5.9.

Table 5.1 Search and Meta Search Engines

Search Engines	
Name	**URL**
Ask	www.ask.com
Google	www.google.com
Lycos	www.lycos.com
Windows Live Search	www.live.com
WiseNut	www.wisenut.com
Yahoo! Search	www.search.yahoo.com
Meta Search Engines	
Name	**URL**
Accumo	www.accumo.com
Dogpile	www.dogpile.com
Metacrawler	www.metacrawler.com
Vivisimo	www.vivisimo.com

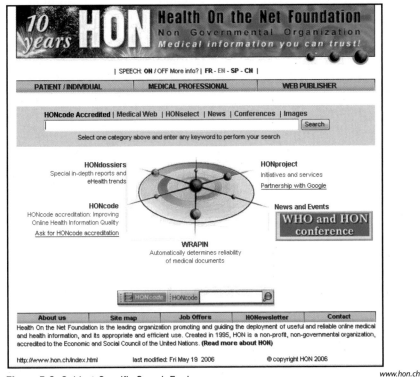

www.hon.ch

Figure 5.9 Subject-Specific Search Engine

Health On the Net specializes in helping both consumers and medical professionals find answers to their medical questions.

Meta Search Engines

Because search engines usually provide different results for the same queries, it is often worthwhile to submit a query to more than one search engine. A *meta search engine* simplifies this task by submitting a search query to a number of different search engines at the same time and then displaying the most relevant hits from each search engine in a single results page with duplicate results removed from the list.

Dogpile is one of the best known meta search engines. Dogpile simultaneously submits each search query to the Google, Yahoo! Search, MSN, Ask.com, About, MIVA, and LookSmart search engines and directories. The user can sort Dogpile results by relevance or by search engine as shown in Figure 5.10. Meta search engines display only the most relevant search results for each search engine, so a user should query other search engines individually if he or she wants to view more extensive search results.

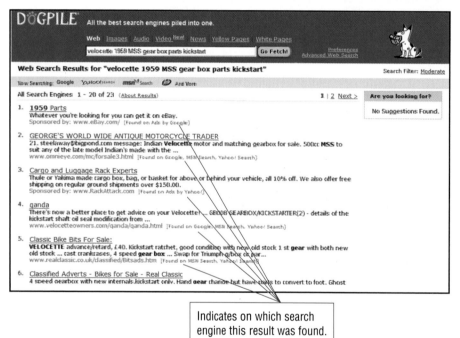

Indicates on which search engine this result was found.

Figure 5.10 Dogpile Meta Search Engine Results

search result clusters

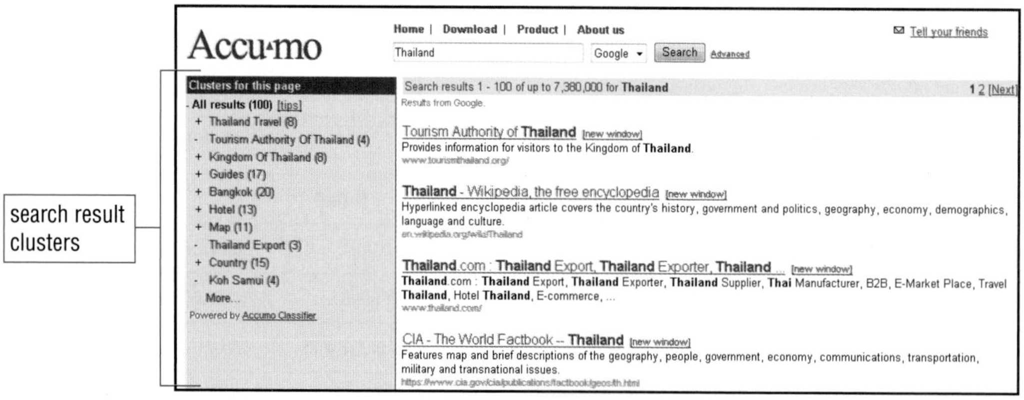

Figure 5.11 Clustered Search Results

Some meta search engines, such as Accumo and Vivisimo, cluster or group results by topic as shown in Figure 5.11. Clicking a cluster on the left side of the Accumo page will display the cluster hits on the right side of the page. Each cluster is numbered to show how many hits it contains. Clustered results can help the user sort through a long list of search results by making it easier to discern whether a cluster might contain the desired information.

Internal Search Engines

A Web site might feature its own *internal search engine* that restricts searches to the contents of the site. An internal search engine typically uses search technology provided by a search engine company such as

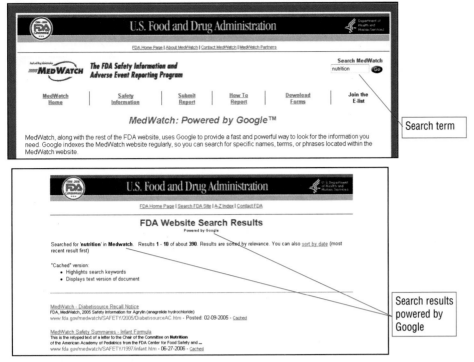

Figure 5.12 Amazon.com Internal and External Search Engines

Google, as shown in Figure 5.12. Providing technology for internal search engines provides an income source for some search engine companies.

Concept Review 2 Search Engines

1. How do search engines index information?
2. How are page results ranked?
3. What are clustered search results?
4. What are meta search engines?

Skill Review 2 Conduct a Search

1. Open the Google search engine (www.google.com) Web site.
2. Type **camping catalogs** in the search text box and then press Enter or click the Google Search button.
3. Look at the results list and read the descriptions to see if there are any hits that are not directly related to camping catalogs.
4. Scroll to the bottom of the page and then click the last Result Page link number to go to that page.
5. Check the search results on the last page to see how many are directly related to camping catalogs and compare your finding to the results on the first page.

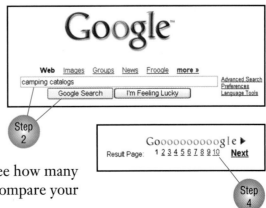

6. Go back to the first search results page. Click one of the links in the results list to view the Web page.

7. Press Ctrl + F to open the Find dialog box.

8. Type **camping** in the Find dialog box *Find* text box. Continue pressing Enter or clicking the Next button and note the number of hits for camping. When you are finished searching the document, close the Find dialog box.

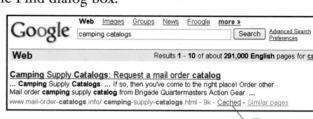

9. Return to the first results page and click the Cached hyperlink for the first hit on the list. Note the number of hits for camping. *(Note: Search results change over time, so the results you see displayed here may differ from the ones you see.)*

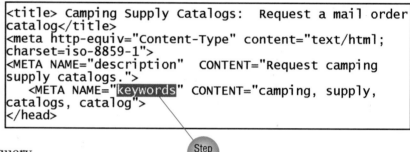

10. Right-click on the page and then click View Source to view the HTML code for the page. Maximize the Notepad window and then click Edit and then Find to open the Find dialog box. Type **keywords** in the *Find what* text box and then press Enter to find the keywords information in the head section of the document. Examine the keywords and note whether they relate to the keywords you used in your keyword query.

```
<title> Camping Supply Catalogs:  Request a mail order
catalog</title>
<meta http-equiv="Content-Type" content="text/html;
charset=iso-8859-1">
<META NAME="description"  CONTENT="Request camping
supply catalogs.">
    <META NAME="keywords" CONTENT="camping, supply,
catalogs, catalog">
</head>
```

Subject Directories

subject directory a search tool that contains links to Web sites and pages organized in hierarchically arranged subject categories

A *subject directory* contains links to Web sites and pages organized in hierarchically arranged subject categories. For example, to use the Yahoo! Directory at http://dir.yahoo.com to find movie reviews, the user would start by clicking the Movies subcategory located under the Entertainment main category. A page listing the subcategories under Movies, one of which is Reviews, appears. Clicking Reviews opens a new page with a number of movie review options linking to movie reviews as shown in Figure 5.13. Each subject directory uses its own system for subject categorization, so it can sometimes be difficult to know how a topic might be classified. Many directories cross-reference information

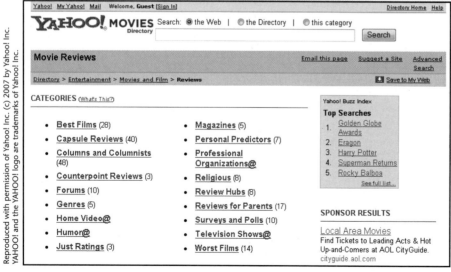

Figure 5.13 Yahoo! Directory Movie Review Subcategory

Figure 5.14 Google Directory Home Page

http://directory.google.com

under more than one subject heading, so there can be more than one path leading to a Web site or page.

Some subject directories use human experts to gather and categorize information, some use computer technology, and others use a combination of both human experts and computers. Subject directory entries often contain helpful annotations written by subject experts that provide a capsule description of the kind of information that can be found on a categorized Web site or page.

Subject directories typically index only a Web site's home page rather than all the pages contained on the site. While search engines index far more information than subject directories, the way in which subject directories organize the information and prescreen the information for relevance make subject directories valuable resources, especially for general topic research.

The Yahoo! Directory was one of the first subject directories and remains one of the most popular, but it now has many competitors, including the Google Directory shown in Figure 5.14. Some subject directories such as About.com identify their experts. Each About.com expert, known as a Guide, has his or her own page containing links to Web pages with more information about their particular area of expertise as shown in Figure 5.15. A user can contact an About.com Guide by e-mail to ask additional questions or make suggestions.

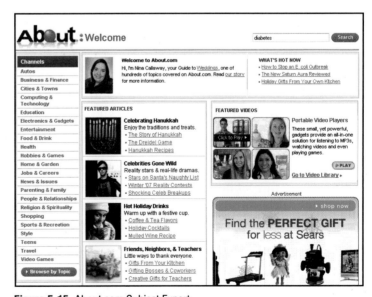

Figure 5.15 About.com Subject Expert

Table 5.2 Subject Directories and Portals

Directories	
Name	**URL**
About.com	http://about.com
Google Directory	http://directory.google.com
LookSmart	http://search.looksmart.com
Open Directory Project	http://dmoz.org
Yahoo! Directory	http://dir.yahoo.com
Portals	
Name	**URL**
Excite	www.excite.com
Go.com	www.go.com
Yahoo!	www.yahoo.com

As subject directories have evolved over the years, many have added search engines. In such an instance, the user can use the search engine to search among the directory categories or to search the Web. A search tool combining a search engine and a subject directory is known as a hybrid search engine. Subject directories or hybrid search engines that combine other features such as e-mail, online shopping, and so on are sometimes referred to as Web portals because they serve as gateways to the Web. Table 5.2 contains a list of different subject directories and portals.

Concept Review 3 Subject Directories

1. How do subject directories differ from search engines?
2. What are subject experts and what do they do?
3. What is a hybrid search engine?

Skill Review 3 Use a Subject Directory to Find Information

1. Pick a travel destination in a foreign country, such as Cabo San Lucas in Mexico. In your search you will be looking for a place to stay in the city you choose. *(Note: Your instructor may provide you with another search topic.)*

2. Open the Yahoo! Directory (http://dir.yahoo.com/) Web site.

3. Look at the Yahoo! Directory categories and choose the one that you think may lead to information about your travel destination. Follow the topic links until you find information about places to stay at your travel destination city.

4. Look at the top of the directory for the hyperlink path you took to find the information. Select the path and copy and paste it into a blank Word document, or write the path down. *(Note: When selecting, click before or after the hyperlinks in order to avoid activating them.)*

5. Return to the directory home page and try to find another path to the information you just found. *(Note: There are at least two different routes to finding information about places to stay at a travel destination.)* Use the same method you used in Step 4 to record the path that took you to the page with information about places to stay. Compare the two paths to see if one was more efficient than the other. Go back to the directory home page to see if you can find an even quicker path through the categories to reach the information you found.

6. Use the Yahoo! Directory Search text box to find information on places to stay at your travel destination. Type your keywords into the Search text box, click the *the Directory* option button to confine your search to the Yahoo! Directory, and then click the Search button. Compare the results with the results of your previous category searches to identify differences in the quality and quantity of the information you found.

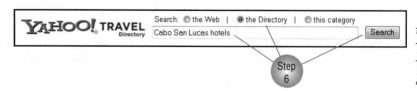

The Deep Web

The deep Web contains Web resources that lie below the surface Web—the portion of the Web indexed by search engines and subject directories. The bulk of this information remains hidden because it resides in searchable databases that present several obstacles to search engine spiders. First, searchable databases generate Web pages in response to queries, and traditional spiders cannot generate queries. Second, because the Web pages created in response to a query are often assembled "on the fly" from information contained in a database, those Web pages are usually not saved anywhere as HTML files, unlike the pages found and indexed on the surface Web.

Sites or databases requiring registration and logon with a password present another obstacle to search engines. Because spiders cannot generate passwords or fill out forms, the information contained in such sites cannot be indexed unless the site owners deliberately choose to make the content accessible. Online newspaper and magazine sites increasingly require registration and even subscription payments, so more and more news stories lie beyond the reach of search engines.

Because the content of the deep Web may be beyond the reach of search engines, users need other means to find information there. Accessing the deep Web is known as **drilling down**. Drilling down involves connecting directly to the databases or other types of content not indexed by search engines. To start drilling down, the user can include the word *database* in the list of keywords in a query. The search engine may then return hits containing links to databases relevant to the query. Users also can take advantage of one or more deep Web directories that contain links to databases and other resources not indexed by search engines, such as the one at www.completeplanet.com, shown in Figure 5.16. The CompletePlanet deep Web directory indexes searchable databases by topic. Clicking a link takes the user directly to the database where a query can be entered in the database's search text box.

drilling down connecting directly to the databases and other types of content not indexed by search engines in order to access the deep Web

Not all deep Web material is accessible. Web sites that require fee payments and sites protected for security or proprietary reasons will remain out of reach. Some material on the Internet may not be linked by other pages, and these dead end or orphan pages are almost impossible to find except by chance discovery.

As search engines evolve, their ability to access the information stored in the deep Web increases. Google can now index Web pages stored in PDF format by first converting those pages into HTML documents. Users then have the option of opening the original PDF format file or an HTML copy of the file as shown in Figure 5.17. The major search engines and some prospective search engine companies are currently working on spiders that can emulate human behavior so that they

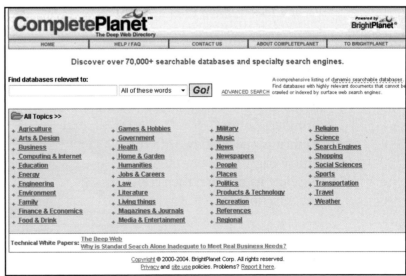

Figure 5.16 CompletePlanet Deep Web Directory

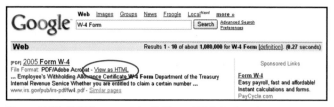

Figure 5.17 PDF Document Available as HTML in Google

Table 5.3 Deep Web Directories

Name	URL
CompletePlanet	http://aip.completeplanet.com
Direct Search	www.freepint.com/gary/direct.htm
Invisible Web Directory	www.invisible-web.net

can fill out forms and submit queries to penetrate deep Web databases. Table 5.3 contains a list of deep Web directories.

Concept Review 4 The Deep Web

1. What prevents search engines and search directories from indexing the deep Web?
2. What is drilling down?
3. What kinds of deep Web information may be inaccessible?

Skill Review 4 Find Deep Web Information

1. Open the CompletePlanet deep Web directory (www.completeplanet.com) Web site.
2. Click the <u>Newspapers</u> subcategory hyperlink located under the *All Topics* category.
3. Click a state from the sub-category list containing state names.
4. Click a small town or local newspaper hyperlink to open its home page.

5. Look for the newspaper's internal search engine and conduct a search using the keywords *school board*. **(Note: Most local papers carry news about school board meetings or local school-related issues. If your search does not return any results, ask your instructor for another topic.)**
6. Click any of the article hits from the results page that is returned.
7. Open a new browser window by pressing Ctrl + N. Browse to the Google search engine (www.google.com) in the new browser window.
8. Return to the window with the article page. Use your mouse to select its title and then copy the selection.

9. Return to the Google page, paste the copied title into the Google search text box, and then press Enter.

10. Check the results page to see if you can find a hit for the article at the same URL. If you can, that means that the newspaper you chose has made its database contents openly available.

11. If you did find the article via Google, repeat Steps 1 through 10 using another newspaper and topic to see if you can find an article that is not indexed on Google.

Defining a Search Question

As a first step in conducting any Web search, the user should make sure to clearly define his or her search question in order to focus their search. A search question is not the same as a query. A search question is a question that clearly states what information is being sought. The search question can then be used to derive key terms that can be used in a search query. A clearly stated and focused search question increases the chances that the search will yield information related to the desired topic and reduces the amount of time spent wading through irrelevant material. The nature of the search question will also help determine the type of search tool to use. Search questions fall into two categories: specific search questions that seek facts or details, and general search questions that seek contextual or background information. The user can refine the results generated by a general search question by using specific search questions.

The user should create a specific search question when he or she already knows something about a topic and is looking for more details or facts related to the topic. An example of a specific search question would be, "What is the capital of North Dakota?" When posing a specific question, the task is to zero in on the answer in the minimum amount of time, so the best search tool to use would be a search engine. Typing in a search query using the keywords *North Dakota capital* would produce an answer on the first results page hit since this is a very specific question about a well-known subject.

General questions serve as a starting point for learning more about a subject. Using a search engine to find answers to general questions will almost always yield too many results, so a subject directory is often the best starting point. The subject or topical organization of a subject directory enables the user to start out using a broad category and then gradually narrow the focus of a question by proceeding through related subcategories. For example, if a student were assigned to write a paper on a subject related to the United States, he or she could begin the search process with the Yahoo! Directory by clicking the Countries subcategory hyperlink located under the *Regional* category. The student could then click United States in the list of country subcategories. The directory would then display a page with additional subcategories, such as Arts and Humanities, Education, Government, and so on. Proceeding in this way leads the student from the general to the specific, and somewhere in this search journey he or she is likely to find a United States-related topic for the paper. If anywhere along the way the student needs an answer to a specific question, he or she can use a search engine to find an answer. Most subject directories include search engines that can search within the directory or the entire Web.

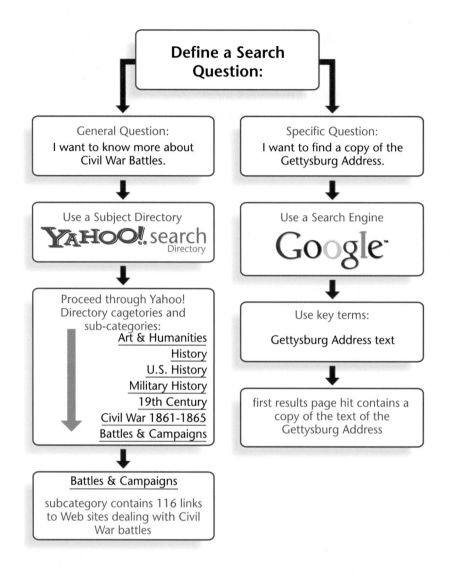

Figure 5.18 Search Question Flow Chart

Figure 5.18 contains a flow chart illustrating how formulating a search question determines the best type of search tool to use. A search question uses everyday or natural language, such as the search questions shown near the top of Figure 5.18. While some search engines such as Ask (www.ask.com) can deal with natural language questions, most search engines work by matching keywords in a query to words contained in documents. The next section of this chapter discusses choosing keywords (based on a search question) and methods to use to make a search as efficient and productive as possible.

Concept Review 5 Defining a Search Question

1. What is the difference between a specific search question and a general search question?
2. How can formulating a search question help determine the type of search tool that should be used?
3. What is the difference between a search question and a search query?

Skill *Review 5* **Define Search Questions**

1. Create three specific search questions and three general search questions. Form the questions as full sentences, as in *What year was the Kodak Brownie camera invented?* or *What was the War of 1812 about?*

2. Write or type your questions under Specific and General headings. Leave some space between each question.

3. Underline the keywords you would use to find answers for your specific question.

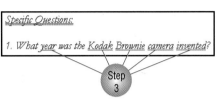

4. Browse to Google (www.google.com) or another search engine, and use the keywords in your search questions to conduct a search. Check the results page hits to see if they contain the answers to your questions.

5. Browse to the Yahoo! Directory (http://dir.yahoo.com). Look at the major categories and then write down which major category you think would be the best start for each of your general questions.

6. Use the Yahoo! Directory to search for information about your general questions and to see whether or not you chose the best initial category to find the information you are looking for.

7. Keep the list of questions you created for use in the next exercise.

Formulating Search Queries

Once the user has developed a search question, he or she must next create a search query that will return the desired information. Search queries can consist of keywords, phrases, or a combination of phrases and keywords. Determining which keywords will produce the best results is an important factor in any search query, but it is almost as important to know the logic and search syntax conventions used by a search engine in processing a query. Each search engine uses different logical methods, known as search logic, when processing search queries. The search logic used by a search engine affects the search results produced by a query. Some general rules known as syntax conventions determine how a search engine processes keywords.

Keyword Queries

As discussed earlier in the chapter, keywords used in a search query enable the search engine to find information relevant to the search question. When a search engine processes a query, it works to match the search query keywords to words found in the documents indexed in the search engine database. Most search queries contain a string of two or more keywords because a query containing a single keyword would return too many search result hits.

Most search engines ignore certain words known as stop or filter words. Stop words include extremely common words and characters such as *the*, *in*, *for*, *to*, *#*, *&*, and so on. Search engines ignore stop words to keep search results hits to a manageable level and to increase the speed of any search, so there is usually no need to include them in a keyword query. If a particular stop word is important in a keyword query, most search engines will recognize the word if it is preceded by a plus sign (+) or if it is included in a phrase search as described later in this section.

To determine what keywords to use in a search query, users should try to imagine the keywords likely to appear in an answer to the question being posed. For example, if the user wants to know the freezing point of water in degrees Fahrenheit, any answer will almost certainly contain the keywords *water*, *freezing point*, and *Fahrenheit*.

Phrase Queries

Phrase queries involve visualizing phrases likely to appear on a Web page containing the desired information. For example, Web pages containing information about the freezing point of water are likely to contain the phrase, "The freezing point of water is." Almost all search engines will search for the exact combination and order of words enclosed in paired quotation marks ("… "), called a **phrase search**. Typing the keywords *the freezing temperature of water is* without surrounding those keywords with quotation marks will return search results hits for pages that contains all those words, even if the words appear in different parts of a document. Using quotation marks around those words indicates to the search engine that the keywords compose a phrase, so the search engine will return only hits for pages containing that exact phrase, including any stop words that would normally be ignored. A phrase query can be combined with a keyword search by including keywords outside of the phrase quotation marks. Using the previous example, if a user wanted to know the freezing temperature of water in Celsius instead of Fahrenheit they could enter *Celsius* as a keyword outside of the phrase to ensure any results included that term. Use phrase searching to find quotations, poetry, articles, and so on.

Refining Keyword Queries

phrase search a search for an exact combination and order of words in a search engine, conducted by placing quotation marks around a phrase or word combination

Using a single keyword for a keyword query will result in too many search result hits, many of which will have nothing to do with the user's original question. On the other hand, using too many keywords will reduce the number of hits, which may cause the search engine to ignore a page with the answer if that page does not contain at least one instance of every one of the keywords in the keyword query. A middle approach works best. Use two or three keywords in a query and then gradually add more keywords if the search engine does not produce the desired information. The process of modifying a search query to obtain better results is known as refining a search. Figure 5.19 shows how using additional keywords can help narrow the number of hits generated to a manageable list containing relevant information.

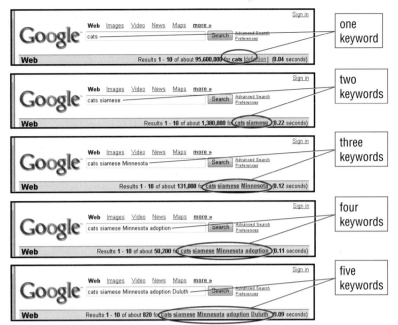

Figure 5.19 Using Multiple Keywords to Refine a Search

Concept Review 6 Formulating Search Queries

1. What is a keyword?
2. What are stop words?
3. Name and describe two different types of search queries.

Skill Review 6 Refine a Search Query

1. Go to Google (www.google.com) using your Web browser.
2. Use the keywords you selected for one of the specific search questions you created in Skill Review 5 to create a search query. Press Enter, or click the Search Google button to begin the search.
3. Look at the search results to see if you can find the answer to your question in the first three hits. If you can, proceed to Step 4. If you cannot, proceed to Step 5.
4. If you found your answer in the first three hits, try removing one keyword from your query and then conducting a new search to see how the results change. Continue experimenting until you find the minimum number of keywords needed to produce the information you need within the first three hits.
5. If your search did not produce an answer within the first three hits, refine the search by adding a keyword that you think will increase the chances of finding an answer. You can also change the keywords you used if you think other keywords may produce better results. Continue experimenting until you can find the information you want within the first three hits.
6. Try different phrase searches to see if you can find an answer to a question. Remember to enclose the phrase in quotation marks.

Search Logic and Syntax Conventions

All search engines use search logic and employ syntax conventions to search for and retrieve the information indexed in their databases. Logic refers to the reasoning or judgmental processes a search engine uses to determine whether indexed information is relevant to the keywords in a search query. The majority of search engines use Boolean logic. Search engine syntax conventions refer to the individual ways that search engines interpret or accept logical processes.

Boolean Logic

Boolean logic a type of algebraic logic that employs expressions using operators

Boolean logic is a type of algebraic logic that employs expressions using operators. A Boolean expression produces a true/false result that can be used to define the relationship between different values. When used with search engines, the Boolean logic defines the relationship between keywords by using Boolean operators. Boolean operators consist of single words, usually capitalized, with the most common Boolean operators used by search engines being AND, OR, and NOT. Search engine policies for the use of Boolean operators in queries differ, so it is always a good idea to consult a search engine comparison table like the one shown in Figure 5.20 or a search engine's Help, Search Tips, or Advanced Search pages.

Using the Boolean operator AND between two keywords tells the search engine to return hits containing both words. A search query containing the keywords *apples AND oranges* would return results page hits containing both the words *apples* and *oranges*, but would not return hits for pages containing only one of the words. The default Boolean operator for almost all search engines is AND, meaning the user need not type this operator in a query; the search engine assumes the AND is included.

The Boolean operator OR used between two keywords returns hits for pages containing at least one of the two words. The OR operator is helpful when searching for similar or synonymous words or concepts such as *railroad* and *railway*. If a query uses the keyword string *railroad OR railway*, the search engine would return some hits containing *railroad*, some hits containing *railway*, and some hits containing both keywords.

The Boolean operator NOT can be used to exclude words from search query results. For example, the word *bass* can be a musical term or refer to a type of fish. If the user were to include *bass* as a keyword, the search results page would contain hits relating to both definitions. However, if the user were to add a NOT operator to exclude a keyword from the search, such as *bass NOT fish*, the results

Selected Internet Search Engines				
Search Engine	**Database**	**Boolean**	**Other search options**	**Miscellaneous**
<u>Google</u> **google.com** <u>Advanced Search</u>. Ranks based on popularity (#of pages linked from).	Full text of web pages, .pdf, .doc, .xls, .ps, .wpd, <u>others</u> (Huge, probably largest web search engine). **Plus:** <u>News</u> (4500 sources); <u>Images</u>; <u>Groups</u> (*Usenet posts 1981)-*, <u>Local</u> (yellow pages+maps), <u>Froogle</u> and <u>Catalogs</u> (shopping), <u>Scholar</u> (articles), <u>Book Search</u>, <u>Video Search</u>, and <u>more</u>	AND *(default)* OR *(capitalized)* - to remove words or phrases. + to include common words	* wildcard to replace word(s) (e.g., **to * or * * *)** No truncation. Quotes for phrase. Stems some words (+ to turn off). **Fields:** intitle:, site:, inurl:, filetype: , <u>more</u>. <u>Uncle Sam</u> (.gov & .mil) **Similar pages** - *finds related sites.*	Spell checker. **Cache** - *great for finding 404s* 50+ languages. <u>Translates</u> to/from some European and 3 Asian languages and Arabic. <u>International Searches</u>. ~ searches synonyms (~**food**) define: finds definitions **Tools:** <u>math/equivalents</u> <u>calculator</u>, <u>phone book</u>, <u>maps</u>, <u>stocks</u>.- <u>more</u>
<u>Yahoo! search</u> **search.yahoo.com** <u>Advanced Search</u>. <u>Yahoo! Directory</u>. Ranks based on relevancy (occurrence of terms).	Full text of web pages (Also huge), .pdf, .ps, flash, and others. **Plus:** <u>News</u> (7000 sources), <u>Images</u>, <u>Maps</u>, <u>People</u>, <u>Local</u>, <u>Travel</u>, <u>Shopping</u>, <u>Video</u>, <u>Audio</u>, <u>Podcasts</u>, and <u>more</u>	AND *(default)* *Accepts:* AND, OR, AND NOT, NOT and **( )** for nesting. Operators must be capitalized. - to remove words or phrases if not using Boolean. + to include common words	No truncation. Quotes for phrase. Limit by date, language, domain, file type, and country in Adv Srch. **Fields:** intitle:, inurl:, link:, site:, url:, hostname:	Spell checker. **Caches** - *great for finding 404s* <u>Translates</u> similar to Google. **Shortcuts** give quick access to dictionary, synonyms, ISBNs, patents, traffic, stocks, encyclopedia, & <u>more</u>.
<u>Ask.com</u> **www.ask.com** <u>Advanced Search</u>	Ask.com searches the Teoma database of web pages.	AND *(default)*. OR *(capitalized)*.	No truncation. Quotes for phrase. **Fields:** intitle:, inurl:,	Spell checker. **Ask.com** suggests Narrower and Broader

www.infopeople.org/search/chart.html

Figure 5.20 Search Engine Comparison Table Web Page

the results page would not contain any hits containing the words *bass* and *fish*, increasing the likelihood that these results will be relevant to a search related to the musical definition of *bass*. A few search engines require that AND be combined with NOT, as in *bass AND NOT fish*. Figure 5.21 contains a graphical representation of the results returned using the AND, OR, and NOT Boolean operators.

Some search engines allow the nesting of Boolean search operators using parentheses to ensure that the logical operations are evaluated in the intended sequence, with the operation contained inside the parentheses being performed first. For example, a **nested search query** such as *steam AND (railways OR railroads)* will first find pages containing the words *railways*, *railroads*, or both *railways* and *railroads* and then perform the AND operation to find pages that also contain the word *steam*. Nesting can be combined to build even more complex search queries, such as *(locomotive OR engine) AND (railway OR railroad)*. This nested search query would produce results that contained the words *locomotive* and/or *engine* and *railway* and/or *railroad*.

nested search query a search query containing some Boolean operators in parentheses to indicate the order in which Boolean expressions should be evaluated

Syntax Conventions

A user can employ a number of search syntax conventions to create more effective searches. Syntax conventions include the use of paired parentheses to indicate a phrase (described above), the use of the plus sign (+) before a stop word to make sure it is not ignored, the use of the minus sign (-) before a word to exclude it, and capitalizing Boolean operators. Several more common

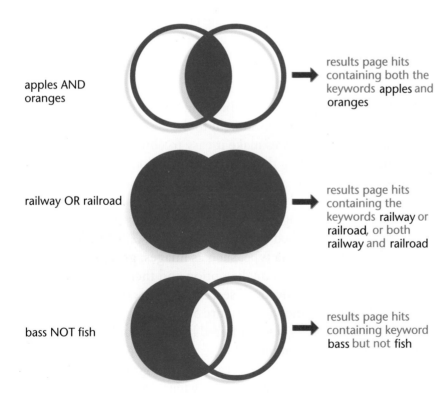

Figure 5.21 Results from Boolean Operators

syntax conventions are worth knowing, including conventions related to case sensitivity, stemming, and truncation.

Case Sensitivity

In the past, some search engines were case sensitive, meaning that they would take into account whether or not a query keyword was capitalized. Currently, all major search engines ignore capitalization, so search results will be the same whether or not the user capitalizes a keyword. Boolean operators should be capitalized, however, because most search engines will treat lowercase operators as stop words.

Stemming

Stemming, sometimes referred to as truncation, refers to the ability of some search engines to search for root words or partial form of keywords as well as the keywords themselves. Stemming happens automatically in some search engines such as Google, while other search engines require that the user include wildcard symbols such as *?* or *** to find stem or partial forms of a keyword. For example, to find pages containing any form of the word *diet*, including *dietary*, *dietician*, and so on, the user would include the asterisk wild card with the stem form *diet* resulting in a keyword entry of *diet**. Some search engines allow the user to insert wildcard symbols inside a word to return results containing both singular and plural forms of a word, such as using *wom*n* to find results containing both *women* and *woman*. Some users may wish to see only results containing a keyword exactly as typed, so they would not want their results to be stemmed. Stemming can be disabled in Google by placing a plus sign (+) in front of the keyword. Google will then turn off its automatic stemming feature for that word and only return results containing the entire word.

Advanced Search Options

All of the popular search engines offer advanced search pages that feature a number of different search options combined in a single user-friendly interface. Many experienced Internet users go straight to the advanced search page because the advanced search page features make it easy to conduct complex searches that increase the odds of finding the desired information. Typically, clicking an <u>Advanced Search</u> hyperlink located on the search engine start page, as shown in Figure 5.22, displays the advanced search page.

Search engines such as Google and Yahoo! Search now enable users to specify the media type to be searched as shown in Figure 5.22. This option lets the user search for a specified media type, such as images, groups, news, and so on. The user should first select a media option and then click the <u>Advanced Search</u> hyperlink to open an advanced search page specific to the specified media type such as the one shown in Figure 5.23.

While the advanced search options offered by the major search engines overlap considerably, each search engine typically includes some advanced features unique to that search engine. For that reason, it is a good idea to experiment using different advanced search pages to see what options are available and to learn how they work. The following sections describe some of the advanced search options common to most search engines.

---

stemming the ability of some search engines to search for the root words or partial form of keywords, as well as the keywords themselves

filtering the process of including or excluding certain information to create a complex search

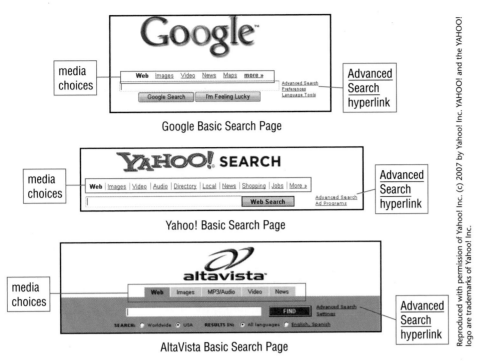

Google Basic Search Page

Yahoo! Basic Search Page

AltaVista Basic Search Page

Figure 5.22 Search Page Advanced Search Hyperlinks

Word Filter Search Options

Filtering simplifies the search process by enabling the user to include or exclude words to create complex searches. Google lets users input keywords into text boxes as shown in Figure 5.23. In the *Find results* section of the Google advanced search page the phrase "with **all** of the words" is equivalent to using the Boolean AND operator, "with **at least one** of the words" is equivalent to using the Boolean OR operator, and "**without** the words" is equivalent to using the Boolean NOT operator. "With the **exact phrase**" is the equivalent of placing quotation marks around a phrase. Other search engines use very similar language to create equivalent phrases for Boolean operators.

Field Search Options

Most advanced search engines enable the user to specify the fields that will be searched in a query. Commonly available choices include options to search the body, title, and URL of a Web page, as well as the URLs of referring links. Some advanced search pages such as Yahoo! Search enable the user to opt to exclude as well as include fields in any search. In most advanced search pages, field search options appear in the section dealing with filtering, but in Google this option is included in the *Occurrences* drop-down list as

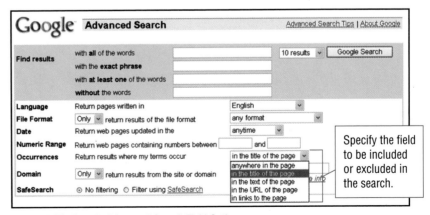

Figure 5.23 Google Advanced Search Field Options

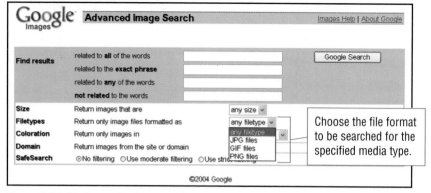

Figure 5.24 Media-specific Advanced Search Page

shown in Figure 5.23. The drop-down list enables the user to specify the field to be included or excluded in a search.

Media and File Format Search Options

Most advanced search engine pages enable the user to specify the type of documents to search, based on media type or file format. As noted earlier, the Google and Yahoo! Search standard search pages enable the user to choose a media type and then choose to view the advanced search page for the specified media type, if desired. The advanced search page usually includes a file format option that lets users choose the file format that will be searched for the specified media type as shown in Figure 5.24. The available file formats will vary.

Domain/Site Restriction Options

Domain or site restriction can be used to restrict a search to a top-level domain, such as .org or .com, or to a Web site, such as amazon.com. The domain/site restriction feature can also be used to exclude a domain or site from a search.

Date Search Options

When conducting research, it is important to know whether information is current. One way to determine the currency of a Web page is to check when the document was last updated. To facilitate that process, most advanced search pages provide an option for restricting a search to a specified update time frame as shown in Figure 5.25.

Language Options

The Web includes a vast store of information contained in Web pages written in languages other than English. Most advanced search pages enable a user to tap these foreign language resources by choosing a language for search result documents as shown in Figure 5.26. To obtain the best results, the keywords used in any search query should be in the specified language. Both Google and Yahoo! Search offer automatic page translation, as shown in Figure 5.27, so it is not necessary to be able to read a language if the specified document language is able to be translated by the search engine. Clicking the Translate this page hyperlink will translate the page into English and

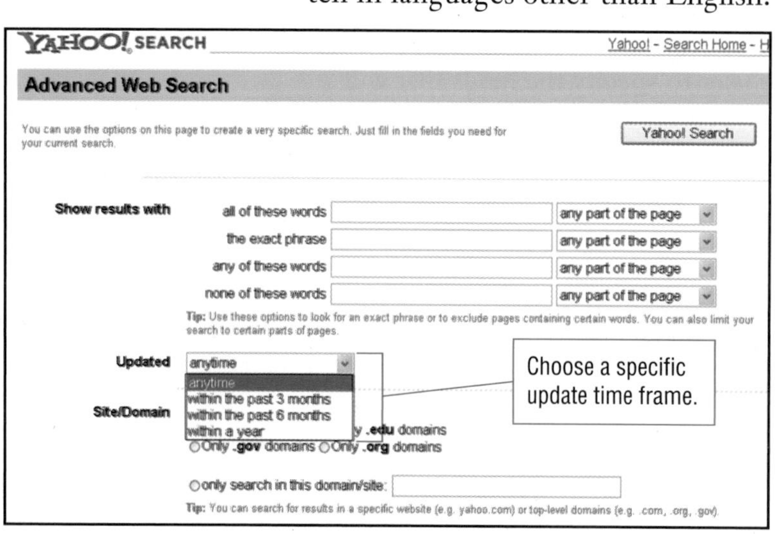

Figure 5.25 Last Update Search Options

open the translated version in the browser window. Because automatic page translation is still being perfected, most translated pages are only good enough to allow readers to understand the gist of what was written, and the translated pages often contain errors, confusing passages, or untranslated words.

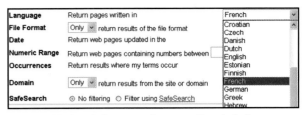

Figure 5.26 Google Document Language Search Options

Numeric Range

Google offers a *Numeric Range* advanced search option that can be used to specify a number range, such as 1920 to 1930, $50 to $100, or 100 lbs to 200 lbs. A unit of measure should be included whenever possible in order to ensure that the numerical range hits represent the desired type of numerical range.

Offensive Content Blocking

Most of the popular advanced search pages enable the user to specify a level of protection against offensive content. Offensive content blockers work by blocking material containing explicit language in keywords, URLs, file names, page content, and so on. Three options are usually offered: strict filtering, moderate filtering, or no filtering. Google offers a *SafeSearch filtering* option, but the Google SafeSearch filtering level options must be set using the Google Preferences page shown in Figure 5.28. The Preferences page can be opened by clicking the <u>Preferences</u> hyperlink on the Google start page.

Offensive content blocking is a useful feature for families with children and for those who do not wish to view material containing adult content. None of these services is perfect, so some offensive material may sneak by even with the filtering option set to the highest level. In addition, some nonoffensive material may be blocked when the strictest filtering option is selected.

Figure 5.27 Google Results Page Translation Hyperlink

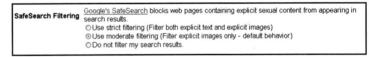

Figure 5.28 Google SafeSearch Preferences

Concept Review 7 Search Logic and Syntax Conventions

1. Describe the common Boolean search operators and explain how they work.
2. What does nesting Boolean operators do?
3. Describe some common advanced search engine features.

Skill Review 7 Use an Advanced Search Engine Page

1. Use an advanced search engine page to exclude a word from a search by completing the following steps:
   a. Open the Google search engine (www.google.com).

b. Click the <u>Advanced Search</u> hyperlink located to the right of the search text box.

c. Create a search query using any keyword with more than one definition, such as *bear* (*polar bear* or *bear a load*) or *lead* (*lead a parade* or *a lead mine*). Press Enter to start the search and then view the results.

d. Use the ***without*** *the words* text box to obtain results for one definition for your keyword while excluding the other by typing a word related to the meaning you do not want in the text box. Start the search and view the results. Note the results should only show hits related to the definition you wanted.

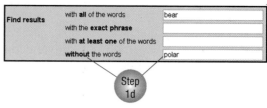

2. Use an advanced search engine page to find an exact phrase by completing the following steps:

a. Think of a one sentence phrase from a song you like and then type it in the *with the* ***exact phrase*** text box. Press Enter or click the Search Google button to see if you get hits that return the lyrics to the song.

b. Click the browser Back button and try the same search again, but this time type the keyword *lyrics* in the *with* ***all*** *of the words* text box. Check the results page hits to see whether or not that produced better results. ***(Hint: If you still cannot find the lyrics you are looking for, try adding the name of the band or composer in the*** **with the exact phrase** ***text box.)***

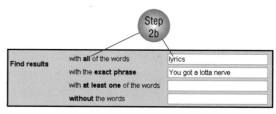

3. Use an advanced search engine page to conduct a numeric search by completing the following steps:

a. Type **digital camera** in the *with* ***all*** *of the words* text box.

b. Scroll down to the *Numeric Range* section and type **$150** in the first text box and **$250** in the second text box. Press Enter to start the search. Examine the search results to see if they contain information about digital cameras in the specified price range.

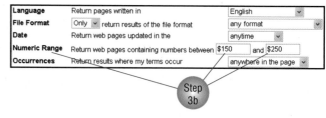

Evaluating and Using Internet Resources

Users should carefully evaluate any information found on the Web before relying on it for any purpose. Before using any information obtained from the Internet, the user should understand plagiarism, and know how to properly cite any Web material whenever appropriate. The user should also understand intellectual property concepts such as copyrights and trademarks, and understand what is meant by the fair use of copyrighted material to avoid any problems related to that issue. Table 5.4 describes traditional methods for evaluating information resources, along with their Web-specific counterparts.

Table 5.4 Traditional and Web-Specific Information Evaluation Methods

	Traditional Methods	Web Methods
Source: *Identify the source of any information so that the source can be cited when the information is used. Anonymous material should not be used because its validity and accuracy cannot be verified.*	• Is the publisher or source of the material identifiable, that is, not anonymous? • Is any contact information provided? • Does the source contain any stated goals or objectives?	• Look for <u>About Us</u>, <u>Info</u>, or similar hyperlinks to find more about a site or page. • Look for address and e-mail contact information. • Check that the top-level domain matches the content; for example, an educational Web site will usually use an .edu top-level domain.
Source Type: *Not all information sources have the same reputation for honesty and accuracy.*	• Is the information contained in a peer-reviewed scholarly publication, a newspaper, a personal Web site, or other known and credible source?	• Use a search engine to learn more about the publisher or Web site.
Authorship: *It is important to know the identity of an author in order to know whether the author is knowledgeable about the subject in question, and whether the author is known to have any ideological bias that might slant his or her interpretation.*	• Is the author or source of the information identified? • What are the author's credentials and experience, and are they relevant to the information?	• Look for biographical or background information for the author on the page or available through a hyperlink. • Use a search engine to find more information about the author. Check any claims made in a biography or résumé.
Currency: *Whenever appropriate it is important to have the latest and most up-to-date material. You also need to know the date of publication in order to properly cite it in any scholarly work.*	• How current or up-to-date is the information?	• Many pages will display last update or modification information. If a page does not contain any update information: **Internet Explorer users**: Type **javascript:alert(document.lastModified)** in the *Address* text box and then press Enter to open a dialog box displaying the date the page was last modified. **Note:** Pages with dynamic content will display the current date and time.
Content: *Examining the content of a document can reveal the perspective of the author and how well the subject was covered.*	• How objective does the information appear to be? • Are opposing viewpoints mentioned or described? • How complete is the coverage?	• Look for similar or related information and compare it to what you have found to get a feel for how objective the source material is and whether the author did a good job of covering the subject material.
Documentation: *Factual claims, quotations, and so on should all be documented so that the source of any claims or quotations can be verified.*	• Are any factual claims, statements, or quotations documented using footnotes or endnotes?	• Follow any link-based footnotes or endnotes to see if they support the citation. Evaluate the cited material in the same way you would evaluate the referring document.
Links: *A good information source will make liberal use of footnotes and endnote links and contain links to related content. Referring or incoming links can also reveal a lot about a Web page or site.*	• Does the source contain linked footnotes and/or endnotes? • Does the source contain links to related content?	• Do links work, and do they link to the appropriate pages or sites? • Check to see what kind of pages are linking to the source page by using Google to do a link search. Type **link:** and then the URL in the Address bar. The number of pages linking to the source URL will be displayed along with results page hits. Look to see if any subject directories link to the source because they usually evaluate sites before linking to them.

Evaluating Internet Resources

Most people already use a variety of different techniques to evaluate the accuracy and reliability of the information they encounter in their everyday lives. Few of us would attach the same amount of credibility to an article appearing in a tabloid journal as we would to an article appearing in our local newspaper because experience teaches us that tabloids often exaggerate or even make up stories in order to sell more copies. A person would also tend to be skeptical of any information from anonymous sources, due to the impossibility of checking the source of the information. The unique nature of the Web requires the use of additional evaluation techniques specific to this new form of communication.

Plagiarism

Plagiarism involves representing someone else's words, writings, or findings as your own, and is a form of theft. Plagiarizing other people's work is a serious ethical violation that can result in expulsion from many academic institutions as well as legal penalties if the violation involves commercial activity. This does not mean that you can never use other people's ideas, writings, statements, and so on in your work; you must provide proper attribution to acknowledge the use and make it clear that the material is not your own. You can use other people's sayings and their writings by attributing the material to the speaker or writer or by placing quoted material between quotation marks as in the following two examples:

> *Will Rogers once said that he never met a man he didn't like.*
>
> *Churchill wrote, "History will be kind to me for I intend to write it."*

Consult a style manual to learn more about creating footnotes and endnotes for any sources you use in your work. (Most academic institutions require students to follow a particular style manual, so consult the course instructor if you are ever in doubt about which style manual to follow.) Even if you paraphrase other work by putting it in your own words, you should still provide attribution so that the reader will know that the paraphrased material is your interpretation of another person's work.

Intellectual Property

Intellectual property refers to creative ideas and expressions afforded specific legal protection. Two forms of intellectual property that you need to be concerned with when using the Internet are *copyrights* and *trademarks*.

The copyright provisions of United States law give the owner of copyrighted material exclusive control over its use and distribution. A wide variety of material can be copyrighted, including literary and artistic works. To establish copyright, the copyright owner must be the original author or creator of the copyrighted material, except in cases where copyright ownership has been transferred. In the United States, any copyrighted material created after January 1, 1978, is protected for the duration of the copyright holder's life plus 70 years. It is no longer necessary to go through any formal process to copyright material. Material is considered copyrighted once it is created in tangible form, and remains copyrighted until the expiry of the copyright, or until the copyright material is placed in the public domain. Although not required, standard copyright information includes the copyright symbol (©) followed by a date and the copyright holder's name, such as © 2005 John M. Baker. You should consider all material you encounter on the Internet copyrighted, unless you have specific information stating that it is now in the public domain. Copyrighted material cannot be used in your own work unless you have received express written permission from the copyright holder.

There are exceptions to the prohibition against using copyrighted material without permission that fall under the *fair use* provisions of U.S. copyright law. Fair use allows the use of copyrighted material for criticism, commentary, news, parody, personal use, and so on, but even then only a limited amount of a copyrighted work can be used. The guidelines for the fair use of copyrighted material are somewhat murky, so if in doubt you should err on the side of caution and use as little copyrighted material as possible.

Trademarks, another form of intellectual property, also enjoy legal protection. A trademark is a legally registered name, slogan, or symbol used to identify a product or service in order to distinguish it from competitors and to create recognition. If you want to use a trademark, you need to request permission from the trademark owner to do so.

copyright legal protection afforded to creative ideas and expressions

trademark a legally registered name, slogan, or symbol used to identify a product or service in order to distinguish it from competitors and to create recognition

fair use refers to provisions of U.S. copyright law that permit the use of some copyrighted material for criticism, commentary, news, parody, personal use, and so on

Proper Citation

When you are researching information you should always note the URL for material you might use so that you can cite it later if needed. Because URLs tend to be lengthy, the easiest way of recording a URL is to select it in the Address bar, right-click, click Copy, and then paste the copied URL into a document that you can save or print. If you print a copy of a Web page, its URL will usually print automatically at the bottom of the document. It is also a good idea to save a referenced Web page as a Favorite so that you can refer to the page later to verify information.

The citation methods used for material found on the Internet differ from those used for traditional print material. All the popular style manuals such as the *Publication Manual of the American Psychological Association* and the *MLA Style Manual and Guide to Scholarly Publishing* now provide guidance on correctly citing electronic or Web-based material. There also are a number of

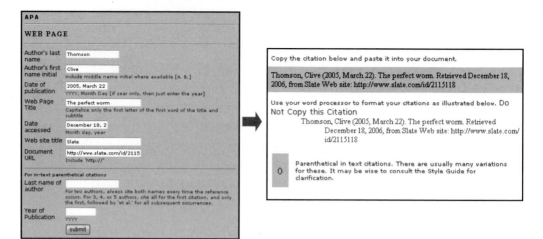

Figure 5.29 Web Bibliographic Citations

Web sites that will automatically create citations from user input, such as the Citation Machine (www.citationmachine.net). Figure 5.29 shows the Citation machine input form and the resulting citation styles. You should check with your instructor before writing anything that may require citation in order to find out what style you should use.

Concept Review 8 Evaluating and Using Internet Resources

1. Describe some of the methods that can be used to evaluate information found on the Internet.
2. What is plagiarism?
3. How does fair use relate to copyrighted material?

Skill Review 8 Evaluate and Use Information Found on the Internet

1. Use a search engine to find three short biographies about George Boole, the founder of Boolean algebra. Save the biographies as Favorites so you can refer to them again when necessary.
2. Use the bold headings in the left-hand column of Table 5.4 to develop an evaluation checklist. Create three empty columns next to each heading.
3. Use the checklist to evaluate each biography using both traditional and Internet-specific methods. Write, type, or paste the URL for each article at the top of the three blank columns. For each biography, write or type a number from 0 to 2 next to each heading, with 2 representing an excellent score, 1 representing an average score, and 0 a poor score. Total up the score for each biography when you are finished and then divide it by the number of headings to create an average score.
4. Ask your instructor for guidance on which style manual you should use for creating a bibliographic citation for each biography. Create a citation for the top-rated biography and then write a short paragraph describing it followed by the score it received. Repeat this step for the second-rated and third-rated biographies.

Chapter Summary

Check your knowledge of chapter concepts by using the flash cards available on the Encore CD that accompanies this book as well as on the Internet Resource Center for this title at www.emcp.net/Internet2e.

- Because the information on the Internet is not organized in a systematic manner, users need to employ search tools such as search engines and subject directories to find desired information.

- Search engines and subject directories access a very small percentage of the information available on what is known as the surface Web. The portion of the Web that is generally beyond the reach of search engines is known as the deep or invisible Web.

- Search engines send out spiders to search the Internet automatically, looking for documents to index by crawling from link to link.

- An indexer sorts the words contained in or related to the documents found by spiders and organizes the words and documents in a huge database.

- When a search engine receives a query, a query processor compares the content of the query to the contents of the search engine index to produce a list of relevant documents.

- Most search engines rank the hits on a results page with the most relevant results listed first. The Web pages represented by a results page hit can be opened by clicking the hit's hyperlinked title.

- Subject directories contain links to Web sites and pages presented in a hierarchical organization.

- Some subject directories use human experts to gather and categorize information, some use computer technology, and others use a combination of both human experts and computers.

- The first step in conducting any Internet search is to make sure that your search question is clearly defined.

- Search questions can be divided into two categories: specific search questions that seek facts or details and general search questions that seek general or background information.

- While some search engines such as Ask are designed to deal with natural language questions, most search engines work by matching keywords in a query to words contained in documents.

- Once the user has developed a search question, the next step is to create a search query that will produce the desired information, which typically answers the search question.

- Determining which keywords will produce the best results is an important factor in any search query, but it is almost as important to know the logic and syntax conventions used by a search engine when it processes a query.

- Each search engine uses different logical methods, known as search logic, when processing search queries. The search logic used by a search engine will affect the search results produced by a query.

- When a search engine processes a query, the search engine works to match the search query keywords to keywords found in the documents indexed in its database.

- Using a single keyword for a keyword query will result in too many search result hits, many of which will have nothing to do with the question to be answered.

- Boolean logic is a type of algebraic logic that employs operators that evaluate to a true/false result. The result then can be used to define the relationship between different values.

- All of the popular search engines offer advanced search pages featuring a number of different search options combined in a single user-friendly interface.

- Plagiarizing other people's work is a serious ethical violation that can result in expulsion from many academic institutions and legal penalties if the violation involves commercial activity.

- You should consult a style manual to learn more about creating footnotes and endnotes for any sources you use in your work.

- The provisions of U.S. copyright law give the owner of copyrighted material exclusive control over its use and distribution.

- There are exceptions to the prohibition against using copyrighted material without permission that fall under the fair use provisions of U.S. copyright law.

- Trademarks are another form of intellectual property that enjoy legal protection.

Key Terms

Numbers indicate the pages where terms are first cited in the chapter. An alphabetized list of key terms with definitions can be found on the Encore CD that accompanies this book. In addition, these terms and definitions are included in the end-of-book glossary.

Boolean logic, *152*

copyright, *161*

deep Web, *134*

drilling down, *145*

fair use, *161*

filtering, *154*

indexer, *136*

internal search engine, *140*

meta search engines, *140*

meta tags, *137*

nested search query, *153*

phrase search, *150*

query, *135*

spider, *136*

stemming, *154*

subject directory, *142*

subject-specific search engine, *139*

surface Web, *134*

trademark, *161*

Multiple Choice

Indicate the correct answer for each question or statement.

1. Which of the following is not a typical deep Web resource?
   a. dynamic databases
   b. sites requiring a password or registration
   c. documents located behind firewalls
   d. personal home pages

2. Search queries consist of one or more
   a. negative statements.
   b. hits.
   c. keywords.
   d. natural language operators.

3. Search engines use this type of program to locate information on the Internet.
   a. indexers
   b. spiders
   c. Webfinders
   d. document cachers

4. Subject directories
   a. are best used for specific search questions.
   b. categorize information.
   c. cluster search results.
   d. are not indexed by search engines.

5. Natural language
   a. refers to the language used to communicate with computers.
   b. refers to the language used to formulate keyword search queries.
   c. is the language used in everyday conversation.
   d. cannot be understood by any search engines.

6. Stop words are
   a. used to exclude keywords from a search.
   b. keywords used to terminate a search.
   c. used to filter searches.
   d. words that are ignored by search engines.

7. Most search engines recognize phrase searches if they are enclosed by
   a. parentheses.
   b. brackets.
   c. quotation marks.
   d. commas.

8. A search engine that searches multiple search engines to produce search results is known as a(n)
   a. multitasker.
   b. subject directory.
   c. meta search engine.
   d. internal search engine.

9. Boolean operators
   a. are a type of algebraic logic.
   b. are a form of geometry.
   c. are rarely used by search engines.
   d. only work in Google.

10. Nested search queries contain Boolean operators enclosed by parentheses to
    a. exclude those operators from the search function.
    b. perform the operations in the desired sequence.
    c. make them a subset of another operator.
    d. Parentheses are never used with Boolean operators.

True/False

Indicate whether each statement is true or false.

1. The deep Web contains more information than the surface Web.
2. Search engines and subject directories are synonymous terms.
3. Some plagiarism is allowed under the fair use provisions of copyright law.
4. The best search queries contain only one keyword.
5. Search engines use robotic programs known as spiders to crawl the Internet looking for documents to index.
6. Cached documents are documents that have been saved by a search engine.
7. Most search engines consider keywords when ranking Web pages.
8. A subject directory is the best type of search tool to use for a specific search question.
9. Boolean search operators are multi-word terms that are never capitalized.
10. Almost all popular search engines can process natural language search queries.

Virtual Perspectives

1. Many search engines accept paid listings on the search results page. The methods used to distinguish paid listings differ between search engines. Have you had any trouble distinguishing between a paid listing and a nonpaid listing? What do you think of this practice? Conduct Internet research on this topic before discussing.

2. What is your favorite search engine or subject directory? State the reasons why you think your choice is better than the other search engines or subject directories. Offer examples to back up your reasons whenever possible.

3. What do you think is the best strategy for finding the information you are looking for on the Internet? Discuss any tips or tricks you have discovered or learned elsewhere that you feel are worth sharing.

4. Discuss your understanding of plagiarism, fair use, and intellectual property. Have you run into any situations related to these issues where you have not been sure what use is allowed or not allowed? Are there any references or guidelines that you can consult for advice on these issues?

Internet Lab Projects

Project 1
Compare Natural Language and Keyword Searching

1. Think of a specific search question that you will use for this exercise.
2. Start the Ask natural language search engine (www.ask.com) and type your search question in the search text box as a complete sentence. Phrase the question just as you would if you were asking it of a person. Click the Search button and then check the first three result hits to see if they contain an answer to your question.
3. Formulate keywords for your search question and use the keywords as a query in a traditional keyword search engine, such as Google or Windows Live Search. Check the first three results to see if they contain an answer to your question.
4. Repeat Steps 1-3 three more times using either specific or general questions.

5. Compare your results and write a short paragraph answering the following questions:
   a. Which type of search engine produced better results?
   b. Are there any circumstances in which you would use a natural language search engine like Ask? If so, describe them.

Project 2
Use Google to Find a Map and Driving Instructions for Your School

1. Print out a map of your school by completing the following steps:
   a. Open the Google search engine (www.google.com) Web site.
   b. Type the address for your school in the search text box and press Enter or click the Search Google button.
   c. Click the hyperlink that begins with <u>Map for,</u> followed by your school's address.
   d. Once the map appears in your browser window, click the uppermost Zoom button to obtain the most detailed map.
   e. Print a copy of the map by clicking the <u>Print</u> hyperlink at the top of the map.
   f. When the printable map page is displayed click the <u>Send to Printer</u> hyperlink at the top of the page to open the Print dialog box. Use the Print dialog to print a copy of the map.
2. Print out driving instructions from your house to your school by completing the following steps:
   a. Use your browser's Back button to return to the first map page.
   b. Type your address in the appropriate text boxes located below the map. Make sure that the *To* option is selected in the *Get directions* box. Click the Get Direction button when you are finished.
   c. Repeat Steps 1e and 1f to print a copy of the driving instructions.

Project 3
Find Government Documents with FirstGov.gov

1. Open the FirstGov (www.firstgov.gov) Web site.
2. Use FirstGov to find the following information. Print a copy of the first page of each item.
   a. Border wait times for entering the United States
   b. A copy of the Form 1040 income tax form
   c. Information about the National Air and Space Museum

(Hint: Find FirstGov subject categories by scrolling down the site home page. You also can use the FirstGov search text box located at the top of the home page.)

Internet Research Activities

Activity 1
Examine Plagiarism and Intellectual Property Laws

Use the Web to find documents containing information that you can use to understand more about the issues below. Print a copy of the most informative document you found for each topic.
1. plagiarism
2. copyright law
3. fair use provision of U.S. copyright law
4. trademarks

Activity 2 Research the Controversy over Efforts to Strengthen Copyright Protection for Database Information

In 2004, controversial legislation that would strengthen the copyright protection afforded to databases was proposed. The Database and Collections of Information Misappropriation Act met with strong opposition from people and organizations in a number of different sectors, especially those in the Internet community who feared that it would have a drastic impact on the ability of search engines to index and make available factual data that to date has been exempt from copyright protection. Research this issue and write a short paper outlining the issues involved. Include information on the current status of the act and the status of any other similar legislation.

Activity 3 Net Challenge

Familiarize yourself with the advanced search pages of three different search engines. Once you understand the different advanced search options, create a table that will allow readers to compare the features offered. Each advanced search option should include a short description in the left-hand column of the table, as shown in the sample table layout below. Include special remarks in the search engine table cells wherever those remarks would help clarify a description.

Search Engine Advanced Search Comparison			
Feature	Search Engine 1	Search Engine 2	Search Engine 3
Filtered Search (description)	Yes	Yes	Yes
File Format (description)	No	Yes (.doc, .pdf, .ppt,.ps, .rtf, .xls)	No
Country (description)	Yes	Yes (By region)	No

Chapter

Downloading and Storing Information

6

Learning Objectives

- Define the role and function of File Transfer Protocol (FTP).

- Explain how to use command-line and GUI FTP client programs.

- Demonstrate how file compression works and how to use file compression programs to compress and decompress files.

- Describe how software download sites work and how to download programs from software download sites.

- Compare and contrast shareware and freeware.

- Explain online storage and how to create an online storage account.

Living on the Net

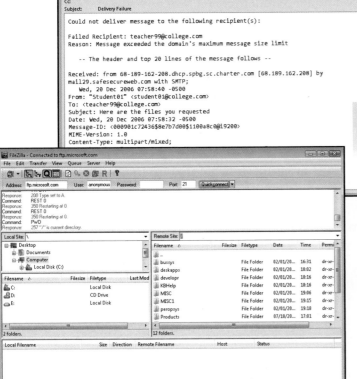

Carolyn writes for a publishing company located in a city over a thousand miles from where she lives. When she first started writing for the company, she would submit manuscripts as attachments to e-mail messages. She soon ran into problems with messages being rejected because the attachments were too large. Either her ISP's e-mail server or the company's e-mail server was always having trouble with attachments. Carolyn could avoid the problem by splitting documents into smaller sections and then sending them separately, but this was time consuming and confusing. She was relieved when her publishers set up an FTP server that would enable her to transfer documents using File Transfer Protocol (FTP).

The new FTP site immediately made life easier for both the publisher and Carolyn. At first Carolyn uploaded and downloaded documents using the command-line FTP client program that came with her computer's operating system. Soon after, she discovered that Internet Explorer included built-in FTP capabilities, so she began using Internet Explorer to transfer files. She enjoyed using a graphical user interface because the ability to drag and drop documents was convenient.

Currently, Carolyn uses a dedicated (stand-alone) FTP client program rather than Internet Explorer for most of her document transfer needs. She made the switch because the program she now uses offers numerous convenient file transfer features such as a split-screen view and easier file and folder management. When Carolyn looks back to the time when she started working for the publisher, she is amazed to think of the amount of time wasted doing something that now takes only a few moments to accomplish.

File Transfer Protocol (FTP)

Tech Demo 6-1
File Transfer Protocol

As described in Chapter 1, File Transfer Protocol (FTP) was developed to enable users to transfer files between networked computers. Although users can send and receive files as e-mail attachments, e-mail servers often place limits on the size or type of files allowed as attachments. Mailboxes also have size limits and can fill up quickly with large attachments. FTP avoids these problems by allowing any size or type of file to be uploaded or downloaded. FTP also enables communication between computers using varying operating systems, as long as the systems use the TCP/IP network protocol.

To enable FTP communication, a host or remote computer must run ***FTP server software*** that allows client computers access to files in specified folders, also known as directories, within the host machine. Client machines or computers are also known as local machines. Once a client computer establishes an FTP connection, the client computer can then download and upload files to and from the host computer, as long as the client has permission to do so. In FTP terminology, uploading a file is known as putting a file, while downloading a file is known as getting a file.

The administrators of any FTP site can control the folders accessible to users, as well as the actions users can perform on folder content. FTP servers restrict access by requiring user names and passwords, but ***anonymous FTP servers*** are open to the public. If a user name is required by the anonymous server, the user can usually try entering *anonymous*, *guest*, or *ftp*. If a password is not required, a user should enter his or her e-mail address as a courtesy to let the FTP server administrators know who is using the service.

Anonymous FTP servers typically only allow users to download files. Restricted folders may be visible, but access will be denied if a user tries to download or upload documents to a restricted folder. Files available to the public can usually be found under a folder named *pub*.

To access another computer via FTP three items are required: FTP client software, the FTP host address, and any user name and password required by the host FTP server. Several different types of FTP client software provide the capability to transfer files using FTP. ***Command-line FTP client programs*** feature an interface in which the user types simple commands such as *get*, *put*, and so on. Windows Vista contains a command-line FTP client program that can be accessed by clicking the Start button, typing **ftp** in the Instant Search box, and pressing Enter. Typing an FTP address in the Internet Explorer Address bar will open the FTP site using Internet Explorer. Both these methods will be discussed later in this chapter.

Graphical user interface (GUI) FTP client programs like the one shown in Figure 6.1 provide a point-and-click interface that enables the user to choose actions via buttons or menus, or by dragging and dropping files. Most Web browsers now incorporate GUI FTP capabilities, as do some file managers such as Windows Explorer. GUI FTP client programs are also available as stand-alone or dedicated programs, such as WS_FTP or CoffeeCup. Dedicated FTP client programs offer a wider range of features than command-line and browser-based FTP client programs.

The user needs to know the host address to connect to an FTP server and start an FTP session. The address can be in the form of a URL such as

FTP server software software that enables a computer to act as an FTP server

anonymous FTP server an FTP server open to the public, usually allowing log on using anonymous, guest, or ftp as the user name and a user's e-mail address as a password

command-line FTP client programs FTP client programs that feature an interface in which the user types simple commands such as get, put, and so on

graphical user interface (GUI) FTP client programs FTP client programs that provide a point-and-click interface that lets users input commands via buttons or menus, or by dragging and dropping files

ftp.wsftp.com, or an equivalent IP address such as 156.21.4.25. The FTP client program used determines how the user should enter the host address.

You should only download material from trusted sites because of the danger posed by malware. Once a file has been downloaded, you should use virus scanning software to check the file for any viruses. The exercises in this chapter deal primarily with using FTP to download files.

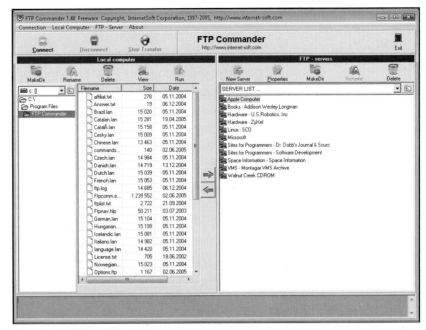

Figure 6.1 GUI FTP Client Program

Concept
Review 1 File Transfer Protocol (FTP)

1. What advantages does FTP offer compared to transferring files through e-mail?
2. What three items are necessary to transfer files to and from another computer via FTP?
3. What passwords do anonymous FTP sites usually accept?

Skill
Review 1 Research File Transfer Protocol

Use the Web to conduct research that will help you write short answers for the following:
1. What ports does FTP usually run on?
2. What do you need to run an FTP server on your computer?
3. Find five different public FTP sites and list their addresses. Describe the type of content they hold.

Command-Line FTP Client Program

The Windows Vista command-line FTP client program can be started by clicking Start, typing **ftp** in the Instant Search box, and pressing Enter. Figure 6.2 shows the Vista FTP client program currently connected to an FTP server. Clicking the Maximize button expands the program window, or the user can drag any window border to resize the window. An FTP session can generate many lines of code, so the

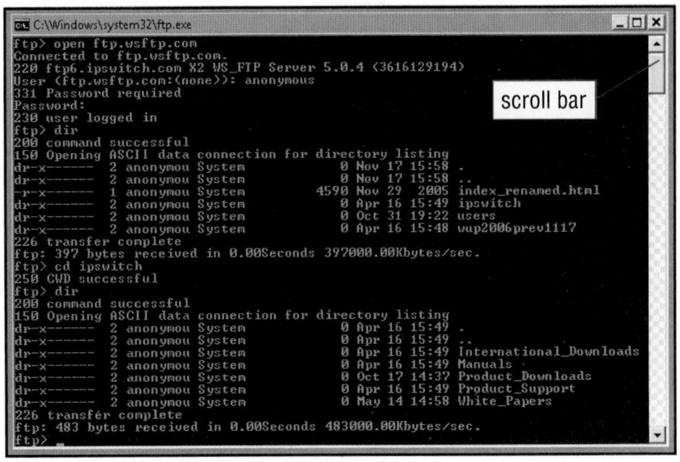

Figure 6.2 Command-Line FTP Session

window contains a scroll bar on the right which can be used to scroll up and down to review the session activity.

To enter a command, type the command and any necessary arguments at the ftp prompt and then press Enter. Commands should always be typed in lowercase and include a space between the command and any text typed after it, such as a folder or file name. Typing **help** or the question mark symbol (?) after the ftp prompt and then pressing Enter will display a list of the available FTP commands as shown in Figure 6.3. Typing **help** or ? followed by a command will display a definition for the command as shown in Figure 6.3. As shown in the first command line list in Figure 6.3, commands can be abbreviated, such as using *op* for *open*. The available commands and command names vary somewhat from program to program, but Table 6.1 describes some of the most commonly used FTP commands and their functions.

To begin a command-line FTP session type **open** followed by the FTP host's URL or IP address and then press Enter. A message stating you are connected to the server will appear

command list request

command definition request

command definition

command list

Figure 6.3 Windows Vista Command-Line FTP Client Program Help

Table 6.1 Command-Line FTP Client Program Commands

Command	Description
ascii	specifies ASCII transfer for text files
bell	sounds a beep when command is completed
binary	specifies binary transfer for nontext files
bye	terminates the FTP session and exits the program
cd	changes the host (remote) folder
close	terminates the FTP session but does not exit the program (same as disconnect)
dir	lists the contents of the remote folder (same as ls)
disconnect	terminates the FTP session but does not exit the program (same as close)
get	downloads a file
hash	creates a series of hash marks to show downloaded buffers
help	displays a list of commands (typing **help** followed by a command defines command)
lcd	changes the client (local) folder
ls	lists the contents of remote folder (same as dir)
mget	receives multiple files
mput	puts (uploads) multiple files
open	begins session with remote FTP server
prompt	enables or disables prompt for multiple commands such as mget and mput
put	uploads a file (same as send)
send	puts (uploads) a file (same as put)

followed by a User command prompt. If the FTP server requires an account and password, you would type your user name and then press Enter. A Password prompt then appears. You should type your password and then press Enter. As a security measure, the password does not appear on the screen as it is typed. (If you are using an anonymous FTP server, you should type **anonymous** or **ftp** at the User prompt, and then type your e-mail address at the Password prompt.) The FTP client notifies you of a successful log on and displays the ftp prompt as shown in Figure 6.4.

request to establish connection with ftp server

connection established

successful log on

password (invisible)

user name for anonymous ftp

Figure 6.4 Windows Vista Command-Line FTP Client Program Log On

Typing the *lcd* command and pressing Enter displays the current local folder on your computer, which is the location on your computer or network where the FTP client will save any downloaded files. Typing **lcd** followed by a local computer or network drive and folder name (for example **lcd c:/downloads**) and then pressing Enter changes the local folder. Typing **dir** displays the contents of the current remote or host folder on the FTP server. Typing **cd** followed by a remote folder name changes the current remote folder. Each time a folder is changed, you will need to execute the *dir* command again to view the current folder's contents. In

local (client) directory

remote directory (begins with d)

remote file (begins with -)

Figure 6.5 Command-Line FTP Client Folder and File Listings

the content listing, each line listing a remote folder begins with d and each line listing a remote file begins with a dash (-) as shown in Figure 6.5.

FTP can use two different transfer modes: *ASCII mode* for text files and *binary mode* for all other files. Most command-line FTP clients use ASCII mode by default, so to download a text or HTML file, you do not need to change the mode. To download any other type of file, you should type **binary** at the ftp prompt and then press Enter to enable binary transfer.

ASCII mode FTP transfer mode used for text files

binary mode FTP transfer mode for nontext files

If a download takes a long time, it can be difficult to tell if the program is working or not, so using the hash command will display a hash mark (#) each time blocks of memory known as buffers are transferred. Type **hash** at the ftp prompt and press Enter to toggle the hash marks on. Type **hash** again and press Enter to toggle them off.

file name

Typing **get** followed by the file name and then pressing Enter begins the download process. File and folder names must be typed exactly as they appear on the screen. Figure 6.6 shows a completed download with a series of hash marks representing each downloaded buffer.

The *mget* command can be used to download multiple files at the same time.

successful download notification

hash marks represent downloaded buffers

Figure 6.6 Command-Line FTP Program File Download

Each file name should be separated by a space before the file name. Once the command is entered, a prompt to confirm each file to download will appear. Typing **y** confirms a download and typing **n** rejects it.

Typing **disconnect** or **close** and then pressing Enter terminates a session but leaves the program open so that you can start another FTP session, if desired. Typing **bye** and pressing Enter will close the session and the program as well.

Concept Review 2 Command-Line FTP Client Program

1. What does the *mget* command enable the user to do?
2. What command is used in a command-line FTP client to start an FTP session?
3. What are the two different transfer modes, and what type of files is each used for?

Skill Review 2 Use a Command-Line FTP Client Program to Download a File from an FTP Server

(Note: Ask your instructor if you have permission to download and save files to your computer or network location. If you do have permission, ask your instructor where you should save the file you download for this exercise.)

1. Start the command-line FTP client by clicking Start, All Programs, Accessories, Run to open the Run dialog box.
2. Type **ftp** in the *Open* text box of the Run dialog box and then click OK to open the Windows Vista FTP client program window.

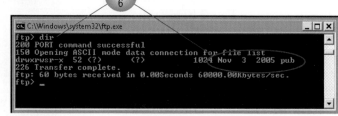

3. Type **open** at the ftp prompt in the FTP client program window. Press the spacebar and then type **ftp.irs.gov**. Press Enter to execute the command. *(Hint: Be sure to type .gov and not .com.)*
4. Type **anonymous** at the User prompt that appears once the FTP client connects to the IRS server and then press Enter.
5. Type your e-mail address at the Password prompt and then press Enter. *(Note: For security reasons your password will not be displayed.)*

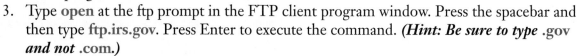

6. Type **dir** at the ftp prompt and then press Enter to view the available folders. *(Hint: pub should be the only folder displayed.)*

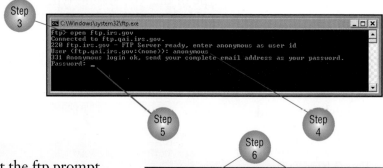

7. Type **cd pub** and then press Enter to make pub the current folder.

8. Type **dir** and then press Enter to display the contents of the pub folder.
9. Type **cd irs-pdf** and then press Enter to make irs-pdf the current folder.
10. Type **dir** and then press Enter to see the files in the irs-pdf folder.
11. The list of IRS forms is so long that when the list of files in the irs-pdf folder finishes downloading, you may not be able to scroll all the way to the top of the list. Since the IRS forms are prefaced with an *f* followed by the form number, to find the 1040 form you can narrow down the list by typing **dir f10*.pdf** at the ftp prompt. The asterisk is a wildcard, so this command will return a more manageable list of all pdf documents beginning with *f10.*

12. Scroll up and locate the f1040.pdf file. This is an Adobe® Acrobat® version of the IRS Form 1040. Once you have located the file press Enter to automatically scroll down to the bottom of the list to the ftp prompt.
13. At the ftp prompt type **lcd**, press the spacebar, and then type the location of the folder on your computer or network where you want to download the form, such as **c:\downloads** or **d:\ downloads\irsforms**. Press Enter to execute the command. *(Hint:*
    Be sure to type a colon and a back slash after the drive letter. Each folder should be separated by a back slash.)

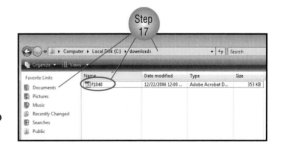

14. Scroll down to the ftp prompt and type **binary** to indicate binary transfer for a nontext file. Press Enter to execute the command.
15. At the ftp prompt, type **hash** and then press Enter to show hash marks during the download process.
16. At the ftp prompt, type **get f1040.pdf** and then press Enter to download the file.
17. When the download is complete, open Windows Explorer and locate the f1040.pdf file in the local folder you saved it in.
18. Return to the command-line FTP client window. Type **bye** at the ftp prompt and then press Enter to end the FTP session and close the program.

Web Browser FTP Use

All the major Web browsers—including Internet Explorer, Netscape Navigator, Mozilla Firefox, and Opera—contain built-in FTP capabilities, providing an easy-to-use graphical interface for transferring files. After the user browses to an FTP host using Internet Explorer, files can be copied and pasted or dragged and dropped between the browser window and a local computer or network location. Users can choose commands via the menu bar or by shortcut menus.

To start an FTP session in Internet Explorer, type the FTP host address in the browser Address bar and then press Enter. For example, to start a session with the IRS FTP site, the user would type **ftp.irs.gov** in the Address bar.

Figure 6.7 Log On As Dialog Box

If an FTP server requires a username and password, the Log On As dialog box will appear as shown in Figure 6.7. Enter the appropriate user name and password in the *User name* and *Password* text boxes.

The dialog box contains a checkbox that can be used to enable automatic anonymous log on. Click the Log On button to complete the log-on process once a user name and password have been entered.

Once connected to an FTP site, you may click the Page button in the Standard Toolbar and click Open FTP Site In Windows Explorer to open the FTP site in a Windows Explorer window. You will again be prompted for your username and password, but the dialog box will provide an additional checkbox option for you to save your password.

Clicking the Folders button opens a folder tree view in the Explorer bar at the left side of the browser as shown in Figure 6.8. The folder tree shows the files and folders on both the local computer or network and on the remote host. The top folder in an FTP site is known as a ***root folder***. The folder tree displays other folders under the root folder in a descending hierarchy as shown in Figure 6.8. The user can adjust the size of the Explorer bar by dragging its right border.

root folder the top folder (directory) on an FTP server

When a folder in the Explorer bar is clicked, the folder's contents will appear in the main (right) pane of the browser window. If a file or folder is clicked for which access is forbidden, the FTP Folder Error message box shown in Figure 6.9 will appear.

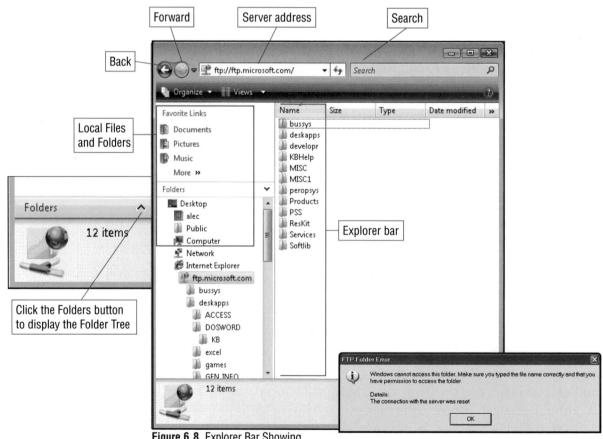

Figure 6.8 Explorer Bar Showing Folder Tree

Figure 6.9 FTP Folder Error Message Box

The user can click the Views button to change the way the main browser pane lists folders and files. As in the Windows Explorer file manager, the available views include Tiles, Icons, List, and so on.

The easiest way to download files from the FTP site is by dragging and dropping between Internet Explorer and a separate Computer window. The Computer window can be opened by clicking Start and then Computer. Once the target folder is located and opened, the Computer window can be minimized by clicking the Down button on the right side of the title bar. The window can be further resized by clicking and dragging any of the window borders. The Computer window can be moved to any location on the screen by clicking inside its title bar and dragging it to a new position. Files and folders can then be dragged from Internet Explorer to the open folder in the Computer window. Multiple files can be selected by holding down the Ctrl key when making selections. When the user releases the mouse button, the file transfer will begin.

Figure 6.10 Copying Message Box

Uploading works in a similar fashion. The user locates the file or folder to be uploaded in the My Computer window and then drags it to the desired FTP folder in Internet Explorer. When any file transfer begins, a Copying message box appears and shows the transfer status as shown in Figure 6.10. Unlike command-line FTP clients, Web browser and GUI FTP clients automatically switch between ASCII and binary transfer mode, so users do not have to specify a transfer mode.

Instead of dragging and dropping, files can also be downloaded from an FTP server by right-clicking the desired file in the browser window and then clicking Copy to Folder in the shortcut menu that appears. Choosing the Copy to Folder command opens the Browse For Folder dialog box shown in Figure 6.11. The dialog box can be used to browse and locate the folder to which the downloaded file will be saved.

Figure 6.11 Browse For Folder Dialog Box

Standard file management tasks such as renaming, deleting, cutting, and pasting are available when accessing an FTP site with Internet Explorer. Whether or not the FTP server permits these functions is determined by the server administrator. A warning message or symbol mouse pointer will appear if a user attempts to execute a forbidden activity. For example, attempting to move folders in an FTP server will typically cause the mouse pointer to change to a forbidden symbol as shown in Figure 6.12.

forbidden activity symbol indicating prohibited file movement

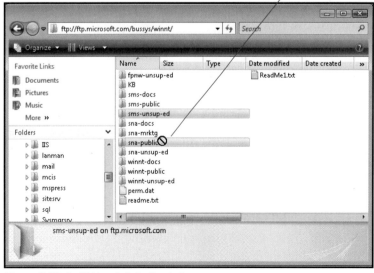

Figure 6.12 Forbidden Activity Symbol

1. How can you start an FTP session using Internet Explorer?
2. What happens if a user attempts to execute a forbidden activity?
3. What techniques can you use to transfer files from an FTP server accessed via Internet Explorer?

Skill
Review 3 **Use a Web Browser to Connect to an FTP Site**

(Note: Ask your instructor if you have permission to download and save files to your computer or network location. If you do have permission, ask your instructor where you should save the file you download for this exercise.)

1. Start Internet Explorer.
2. Click the URL in the Address bar to select the URL, type ftp.microsoft.com, and then press Enter to start the FTP session. *(Note: If the Log On As dialog appears, type anonymous in the User name textbox and your e-mail address in the Password text box and then click the Log On button.)*
3. Click the Page button in the Standard Toolbar and click Open FTP Site In Windows Explorer. *(Note: If a security warning dialog box appears asking to open web content, click Allow.)*

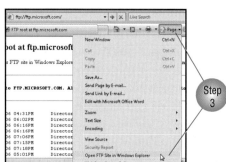

4. Click the Views button and then click Details to show file details in the main browser window.
5. Double-click the Softlib subfolder located under the **ftp.microsoft.com** root folder to display the subfolder's contents.
6. Click Start and then Computer to open the Computer window.
7. Locate and open the target folder that will contain the file you wish to download.
8. If necessary, click the Restore Down button on the Computer title bar.
9. Drag the Computer window to a location that allows you to see the README.TXT file in Internet Explorer. If necessary, further shrink the Computer window by dragging any of the borders inward.
10. Click the README.TXT file and drag it to the open folder area in the Computer window. When you release the mouse button, the Copying dialog box will appear to let you monitor the progress of the download.

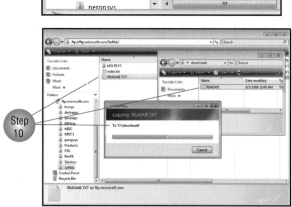

11. Use the Computer window to check to see that a copy of README.TXT has been downloaded to the target folder you selected in Step 7.
12. Close Internet Explorer and the Computer window.

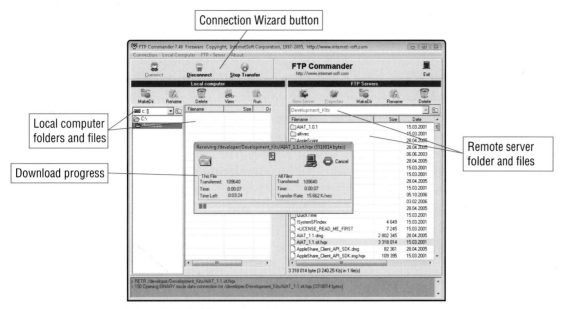

Figure 6.13 FTP Commander Interface

Dedicated FTP Client Programs

While Internet Explorer and other Web browsers offer basic FTP capability, stand-alone or **dedicated GUI FTP client programs** offer additional features that make them even more convenient to use. Most dedicated GUI FTP clients feature a split-view interface that displays local folders and files in the left pane of the window and remote server folders and files in the right pane, as in the FTP Commander interface shown in Figure 6.13. Files and folders can be uploaded or downloaded using several different methods, including dragging and dropping, using the shortcut menu, or by selecting a file or folder and then clicking the appropriate download or upload arrow as shown in Figure 6.13. Dedicated GUI FTP clients offer a number of custom features, including the ability to save FTP addresses and log-on information, connection wizards, automatic binary or ASCII file transfer assignment, customizable file and folder views, and so on.

Dedicated GUI FTP client programs can be located by searching the download sites that you will learn about later in this chapter, or direct from the developer's Web site. Many of the programs are shareware, but there also are some freeware FTP GUI clients available, such as Filezilla, which is an open-source GUI FTP client that can be downloaded and installed free of charge from the developer's Web site (http://filezilla.sourceforge.net), although donations are encouraged.

dedicated GUI FTP client program a stand-alone GUI FTP client program that is not part of another program

Concept Review 4 Dedicated FTP Client Programs

1. What do the panes in a split-view GUI FTP client interface show?
2. How can files and folders be transferred using GUI FTP clients?

Skill Review 4 Install and Use FTP Navigator 7.50

(Note: Ask your instructor if you have permission to install programs on your computer or network location. If you do have permission, ask your instructor where you should install the program for this exercise. Installation instructions can change. Follow the instructions in the installation screens or dialog boxes if they conflict with the instructions below. FTP Navigator 7.50 is a shareware program with a 30-day free trial offer.)

1. Download and Install FTP Navigator 7.50 by completing the following steps:

   a. Start Internet Explorer.

   b. Type **www.softwarea.com** in the Address bar and then press Enter.

   c. Click the FTP Navigator hyperlink on the left side of the page.

   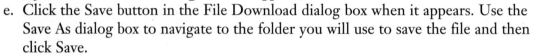

   d. Click the Download hyperlink. *(Note: If the Windows Vista Firewall is enabled on your computer, you may need to click the information bar that appears in order to accept the download before the Download dialog box will appear.)*

   e. Click the Save button in the File Download dialog box when it appears. Use the Save As dialog box to navigate to the folder you will use to save the file and then click Save.

   f. If necessary, Click the Close button when the Download Complete dialog box appears then close Internet Explorer.

   g. If you have permission to install the program, open Windows Explorer, find the ftpnavigator.exe file, and double-click it to begin the installation process. If the Open File Security Warning dialog box appears, click Run.

   h. If the User Account Control dialog box appears, click Allow. Click the *I agree with the above terms and conditions* option and then click Next.

   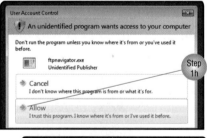

   i. If the destination folder is correct, click the Start button to begin installing the program. *(Note: If you want to install it in another folder, click the Browse button to use the Browse for Folder dialog box to browse and locate the folder. Click the Start button when you are finished.)*

   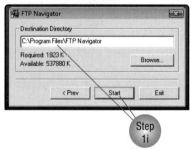

   j. When the installation is complete, make sure the *Run Installed Application* check box is selected and then click OK to run FTP Navigator 7.50. *(Note: You can open the program in the future by clicking Start, pointing to All Programs, and clicking FTP Navigator.)*

2. Use FTP Navigator 7.50 to download a program by completing the following steps:

   a. Click FTP–Server on the menu bar and then click Connect to New Server to open the FTP–Server Properties dialog box.

   b. Type **WinZip** in the *Name* text box.

c. Type **ftp.winzip.com** in the *FTP Server* text box.

d. Type **anonymous** in the *User ID* text box.

e. Type your e-mail address in the *Password* text box. **(Note: This is usually optional, but it is a courtesy to the FTP site administrators.)**

f. Click the Save button in the upper right corner of the dialog box to save the connection profile information you just entered. Select the WinZIP profile at the bottom of the Server List, then click the Connect button at the top of the window to connect to the WinZIP FTP server. **(Note: If the Windows Vista firewall dialog box appears, click Unblock.)**

g. Click the winzip110.exe file in the right-hand pane.

h. Use the left-hand pane to navigate to and select the folder on your local computer that will be used to save winzip110.exe.

i. Click the left-pointing purple arrow to begin the download.

j. Click Connection on the menu bar and then Exit to close the session and shut down the program. Click Yes at the Attention dialog box to confirm that you want to quit the program. **(Note: You have just downloaded a 20-day evaluation copy of a file compression program named WinZip 11.0. You will install and use this program in the next exercise.)**

File Compression Utilities

File compression utilities are programs that use algorithms to compact the data in a file. The resulting new file is smaller than the original. Compressing files economizes the amount of space that they occupy when saved on a disk, as well as reducing FTP and e-mail transfer times.

Text files contain a lot of repeated information, and a compression program can reduce the file size of a text document by 50 percent or more. After compressing a file, most compression programs will display the percentage reduction achieved as shown in Figure 6.14. Many image formats such as JPEG, GIF, and PNG are already stored in compressed form, so compressing image files or documents containing a lot of images will not result in a significant file size reduction. When a file is decompressed and restored to its original size, no data is lost. This type of compression is known as lossless compression. In Chapter 10, *Experiencing Multimedia*, you will learn about other compression methods that use lossy technologies, which discard some original data that will not be missed by the human eye or ear.

A number of different file compression utilities can be used to compress and decompress files, with WinZip being one of the most popular. The most popular compression utilities create compressed files

Tech Demo 6-2
File Compression

file compression utilities programs that use algorithms to reduce the amount of redundant or repeated data in a file

zip file an archive that contains one or more compressed files

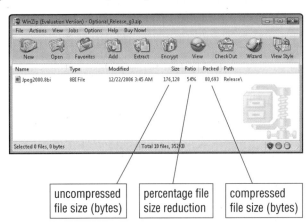

uncompressed file size (bytes) | percentage file size reduction | compressed file size (bytes)

Figure 6.14 WinZip Classic Interface Showing Compression Statistics

FTP and Security

The Windows command-line FTP client and some GUI FTP client programs transmit user names and passwords in plain text. This means that these important items could be intercepted by third parties. If a third party gains access to a user name and password while someone is uploading or downloading files to an FTP site, that third-party could then log on to the site and hack it by maliciously altering its contents.

Two different methods are used to guard against FTP data interception: secure FTP (FTPS) and secure shell FTP (SFTP). FTPS uses the Secure Sockets Layer (SSL) technology that is used to protect Internet transactions in combination with FTP to provide secure FTP connections, while SFTP provides security using SSH, a command interface and protocol.

Glub Tech Secure FTP

FTP software publishers frequently offer a basic program version providing limited security, and a full-featured version that includes enhanced security. The popular Ipswitch FTP client programs are an example, with WS_FTP Pro offering security options not available to WS_FTP Home users. Some freeware FTP client programs also feature enhanced security, such as Glub Tech Inc.'s Secure FTP freeware that is available in both command-line and GUI versions.

Figure 6.15 WinZip Wizard

with a .zip file name extension, creating a compressed file type known as a **zip file**. Compressing a file is also referred to as zipping a file, and decompressing a file as unzipping or extracting a file.

WinZip files are known as archives, and an archive can contain one or more compressed files. When using the WinZip Wizard, files can be added to an archive by clicking the Add Files button, or by dragging files from the Windows Explorer window into the WinZip Wizard window. An archive can be attached to an e-mail or transferred using FTP as a single zip archive file. The archive recipient can decompress the archive, expanding the separate files contained in the archive back to their original sizes.

WinZip 11.0 can be configured to display the WinZip Wizard on start-up as shown in Figure 6.15, or the WinZip Classic interface as shown in Figure 6.14. The WinZip Wizard guides the user through all the steps necessary to zip or unzip a file. The Wizard also contains a WinZip Classic button the user can click to display WinZip 11.0 in a traditional interface for those who do not want to use the Wizard. The user can change back to the WinZip Classic interface by clicking File on the menu bar and then Wizard.

WinZip can be started by using the Start menu or by clicking a desktop icon. The program can also be started by right-clicking a file in Windows Explorer, pointing to WinZip, and then clicking Add to Zip File to compress a file or Extract to extract a zipped file. Double-clicking a zipped file in Windows Explorer also launches WinZip.

Concept Review 5 File Compression Utilities

1. How do compression utilities work?
2. What is an archive?
3. What file types will not result in a smaller file size when compressed using a lossless compression technology?

Skill Review 5 Install and Use a File Compression Utility

(Note: Ask your instructor if you have permission to download and install programs on your computer or network location. If you do have permission, ask your instructor where you should install the program you use for this exercise. Installation instructions can change. Follow the instructions in the installation screens or dialog boxes if they conflict with the instructions below.)

1. Install WinZip 11.0 by completing the following steps:
    a. Close any programs that are running on your computer.
    b. Open Windows Explorer and navigate through your local folders until you find the copy of winzip110.exe you downloaded in Skill Review 4. *(Note: Depending on how your computer is configured, you may not see the .exe file extension.)*

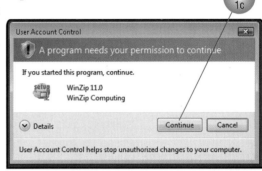

    c. Double-click the winzip110.exe file to begin the installation process. If the User Account Control dialog box appears asking for permission to continue, click Continue.
    d. Click the Setup button when the Setup dialog box appears.

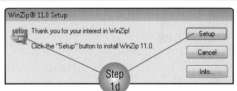

    e. The WinZip Setup dialog box will display the folder location where the program will be installed. Click OK to confirm this selection, or click Browse to browse and locate a different folder. *(Note: Ask your instructor where the program should be installed.)*

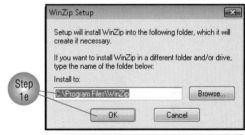

    f. If the Google Tools dialog box appears offering to install additional software, uncheck all checkboxes before clicking Continue.
    g. Another dialog box will appear thanking you for installing the program and listing program features. Click Next to continue to the next dialog box.
    h. Click Yes to accept the License Agreement and Warranty Disclaimer. *(Note: You may want to click View License Agreement to read the agreement before agreeing to it.)*

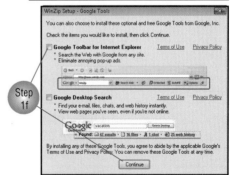

    i. The next dialog box offers an option to view or print the Quick Start guide. Click Next to continue to the next dialog box. *(Note: You can print a copy of the Quick Start guide for later reference if your instructor gives permission to do so.)*
    j. Select the *Start with WinZip Wizard* option when the next dialog box appears, then click Next.
    k. Select the *Quick Search (faster)* option, then click Next.

l. The next dialog box tells you how many folders were added to your Favorite Zip Folders. Click Next to continue.

m. The next dialog box will associate WinZip with different archive file types. Click Next to continue.

n. When the message appears indicating the WinZip Wizard Setup is complete, click Next to start the WinZip Wizard. *(Note: If you click the Close button, you can start the program by clicking Start, All Programs, WinZip. When a newly installed version of WinZip starts, you will see a welcome screen with three choices: Use Evaluation Version, Buy Now, or Enter Registration Code. Click the Use Evaluation option unless you wish to purchase the program.)*

2. Use WinZip 11.0 to compress (zip) a file by completing the following steps:

a. Start Windows Explorer and use it to create two new folders named WinZip Zipped Docs and WinZip Unzipped Docs. Minimize Windows Explorer when you are finished. *(Note: Ask your instructor where these folders should be created.)*

b. If the WinZip Wizard dialog box is still on your screen from the previous exercise, skip this step and jump ahead to step 2C. Otherwise, start WinZip by clicking Start, All Programs, WinZip. If necessary, click Use Evaluation Version. Click Next.

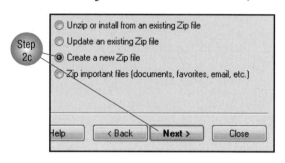

c. Select *Create A New Zip File* and then click Next.

d. Click the Browse button to use the New Archive dialog box to locate and select the WinZip Zipped Docs folder you created. Create a name for the archive you will create by typing *Zip Test* in the File Name box and then clicking OK.

e. Click Next.

f. Click the Add Files button and then use the Add Files dialog box to navigate to any Word document located on your computer or network. Double-click the file, or select it and click OK, to add the file to the WinZip Wizard. *(Note: Ask your instructor if there is a specific file you should use.)*

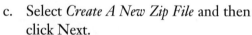

g. Click the Zip Now button to compress the file you selected.

h. Click Finish to close the program.

i. Maximize Windows Explorer and use it to navigate to your WinZip Zipped Docs folder to look at the Zip Test compressed file you just created. Note the file size in kilobytes. Use Windows Explorer to browse to the original copy of the file you compressed and note its size in kilobytes. You should notice a considerable reduction in file size for the compressed file when you compare file sizes.

3. Use WinZip 11.0 to decompress (unzip or extract) a compressed file by completing the following steps:

a. Use Windows Explorer to navigate to the location of the Zip Test archive located in the WinZip Zipped Docs folder.

b. Double-click the archive.

c. Click the Use Evaluation Version button to start the WinZip Wizard.

d. Click Next. *(Note: If a message appears asking if you want to add D:\WinZip Zipped Docs to your Favorite Zip Folders, click Yes.)*

e. If necessary, select the *Unzip or install from "Zip Test.zip"* option and then click Next.

f. The next dialog box confirms your selection. Click Next.

g. The WinZip Wizard displays WinZip's default folder for the content's unzipped archives. To locate the WinZip Unzipped Docs folder you created, click the Select different folder button and use the Select Folder dialog box to locate and select the WinZip Unzipped Docs folder. Click OK when you are finished and then click the Unzip Now button.

h. WinZip 11.0 will minimize and Windows Explorer will display your decompressed document. It should be the exact same file size as the original document.

i. Click on the WinZip Wizard icon in the Taskbar to display it and then click Finish to close the program.

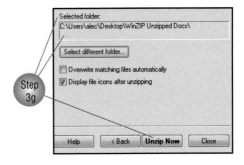

Software Download Sites

Software download Web sites such as the tucows.com site shown in Figure 6.16 offer freeware and shareware software programs for download and installation. The terms *freeware* and *shareware* refer to whether a program's user compensates the program's developer.

Freeware is copyrighted software that its developer makes available for free distribution and use. Freeware developers forgo compensation but typically require that the software cannot be modified or sold. Freeware is not the same as public domain software because a software program is automatically considered copyrighted unless its author or authors specifically state that it is in the public domain. While many freeware products work without problem, they can sometimes contain more bugs or errors than commercial programs that have already gone through extensive testing.

Shareware can be released as trial ware or demo software. Initially available at no cost, shareware programs typically require registration and a modest purchase payment after a limited trial period—usually 30 days. At the end of the trial period the software may be disabled, or pop-up windows may periodically appear to remind the user to register and pay.

freeware software that developers make available for free distribution and use

shareware software made available at no cost but requiring registration and payment at the end

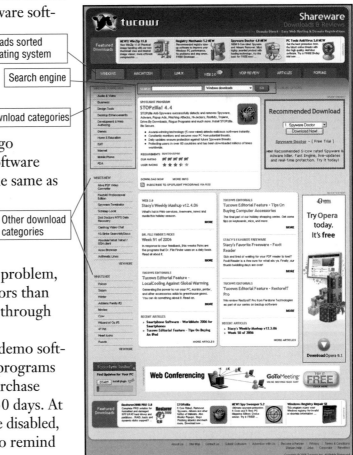

Figure 6.16 Tucows Software Download Site Home Page

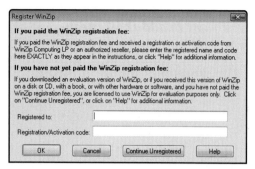

Figure 6.17 Shareware Product Registration Screen

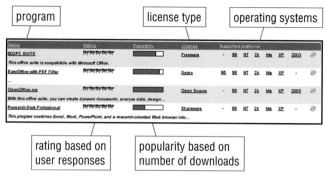

Figure 6.18 Download Site Program Descriptions

When a user pays for the program, he or she will receive a registration code or key to enter in a dialog box like the one shown in Figure 6.17, to terminate the trial period and continue using the program as a fully licensed version. Some limited edition software programs, stripped-down versions of regular software programs, will enable previously inaccessible or inactive features and tools once the user registers the product. Some graphics editing programs will imprint a watermark reading *unregistered* or *unregistered copy* on any images manipulated with an unregistered version of the software.

There are a number of different software download sites on the Web, with tucows.com and download.com currently being among the most popular sites. Software download sites, such as the tucows site shown in Figure 6.16, offer users a wide selection of freeware and shareware programs categorized by type and operating system. Users can also use the download site's internal search engine to search for a particular type of program.

Tucows, Download.com, and other sites offer product ratings and other information as shown in Figure 6.18 that users can evaluate before selecting and downloading a product. A user can click one of the hyperlinks to find further information and then can begin the download process if desired.

mirror site a server that duplicates the content of another server to help take some of the load off the more heavily trafficked Web sites

Many download sites make use of mirror sites in locations around the world to speed up the download process as shown in Figure 6.19. A ***mirror site*** server duplicates the contents of another server in order to help take some of the load off the busier server. Periodic updates ensure that mirror sites, reflect any changes made to the original site. Tucows shows the number of daily updates as shown in Figure 6.19.

When you download a file from a download site, you may see a warning dialog box as shown in Figure 6.20. The Save button can be clicked to save a download to a folder where it can be checked using an antivirus program before installing the program.

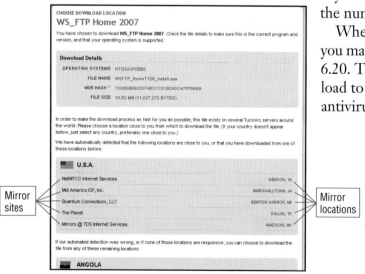

Figure 6.19 Download Mirror Site Selection

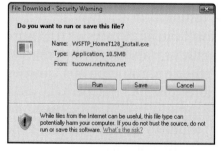

Figure 6.20 File Download Dialog Box

Concept Review 6 **Software Download Sites**

1. What is a software download site?
2. What is the difference between freeware and shareware?
3. What are mirror sites?

Skill Review 6 **Download a Program from a Software Download Site**

(Note: Ask your instructor if you have permission to download and save files on your computer or network location. If you do have permission, ask your instructor where you should save the file you download for this exercise.)

1. Start Internet Explorer, **type www.tucows.com** in the Address bar, and then press Enter.

2. Click the **Business** category hyperlink in Windows Downloads.

3. Click the **Calculators** subcategory under Business.

4. Click the **Unit Conversion** subcategory under Calculators.

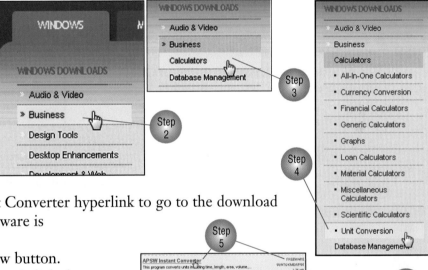

5. Click the APSW Instant Converter hyperlink to go to the download page. Note that this software is **freeware.**

6. Click the Download Now button.

7. Scroll through the page and click the hyperlink for the mirror closest to your location.

8. Click the Save button in the File Download dialog box when it appears. Use the Save As dialog box to navigate to the folder you will use to save the file and then click Save.

9. If necessary, click the Close button when the Download Complete dialog box appears.

10. If you have permission to install the program, open Windows Explorer, find the file, and double-click it to begin the installation process.

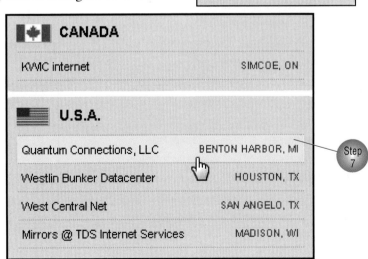

Online Storage

Online storage services provide remote storage space on their servers that can be accessed online. Once a user establishes an account, he or she can log on with a user name and password to use his or her designated storage space. File download and upload methods vary by provider, but include using an FTP client program, a Web browser, an interface provided by the online storage provider, or a combination of these methods. Because online storage space exists remotely from the user's local system, the online storage provides an ideal site for storing backup files. Online storage users can specify the parties that will have access to stored materials, providing an alternative to using e-mail or FTP to share files. Table 6.2 contains a list of online storage providers.

Table 6.2 Online Storage Providers

Provider	URL
bigVault	www.bigvault.com
box.net	www.box.net
Files Anywhere	www.filesanywhere.com
IBackup	www.ibackup.com
iStorage	www.iomega.com/istorage
Xdrive	www.xdrive.com
Yahoo! Briefcase	http://briefcase.yahoo.com

Many online storage providers offer limited storage space for a free trial period as shown in Figure 6.21. After the trial period, the user can pay a monthly or annual fee based on the needed amount of storage space. Some online storage providers, such as Yahoo! Briefcase, offer permanent free storage and make additional space available for a fee as shown in Figure 6.22.

An online storage service is only as good as the provider. Most providers back up the storage service contents on a regular basis to protect against data loss, but if a provider goes out of business, users could lose

The History of Shareware

Shareware has its origins in the hundreds of small computer applications created by enthusiasts in the early days of personal computing. These applications were distributed through bulletin board services and on diskettes because their authors either wanted to share what they had created for altruistic reasons or felt that their creations did not have any commercial value. That situation changed in the early 1980s when two programmers independently developed the shareware model, although neither called it shareware at the time.

The birth of the idea that was to become shareware occurred when Jim Knopf (also known as Jim Button) and Andrew Fluegleman both hit upon the idea of including a request for donations with their software asking users to help defray the costs involved in improving the product. Knopf called his marketing method user-supported software, while Fluegleman called his Freeware, a term he trademarked. Both men were pleasantly surprised at the response they received, which demonstrated that people were willing to pay for software after using it on a trial basis. Knopf's program, PC-File, became so popular that he eventually quit his job with IBM to handle sales and eventually went on to create a multimillion dollar software company.

Knopf's user-supported software and Fluegleman's Freeware soon became known as shareware, and shareware revenues today are in the hundreds of millions of dollars. Fluegleman did not pursue his Freeware trademark, and today freeware refers to software made available without a requirement for registration and payment. Shareware methods differ; some programs operate on an honor system, some programs provide limited editions that can be upgraded upon registration and payment, while others disable reminder messages known as nagware once a product has been paid for.

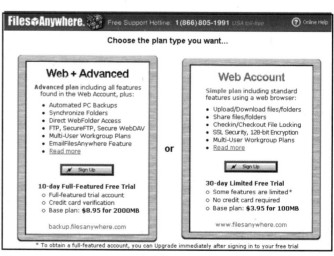

Figure 6.21 Online Storage Trial Offer

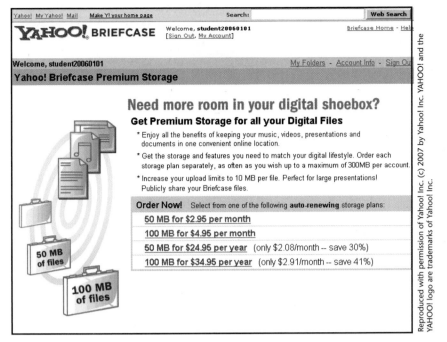

Figure 6.22 Yahoo! Briefcase Additional Storage Space Offers

data forever. For that reason, users should still maintain copies of anything stored on an online storage service and should back up critical data on two different storage services to provide an extra safety margin.

Concept Review 7 Online Storage

1. What are some of the methods that can be used to upload and download files to or from an online storage service?
2. What can an online storage service be used for?

Skill Review 7 Use an Online Storage Provider

1. Sign up for an online storage account by completing the following steps:
   a. Start Internet Explorer, type **briefcase.yahoo.com** in the Address bar, and then press Enter. *(Note: The briefcase address does not contain **www**.)*
   b. If you are already registered with Yahoo!, click the Sign In hyperlink to log in. Go to Step 2a once you are logged on. If you are not yet registered click the Sign Up hyperlink.
   c. Follow the instructions to apply for your Yahoo! ID.
   d. Once your Yahoo! account is activated, type your Yahoo! ID and password in the appropriate text boxes on the Yahoo! Briefcase page and then click the Login button. *(Note: If you see a Security Alert dialog box warning you that you are about to view a page over a secure connection, click the OK button to close it.)*
2. Create your Yahoo! Briefcase account and add a file by completing the following steps:
   a. Leave the default folder and view settings as they are and type

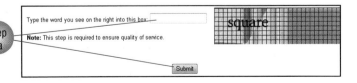

the confirmation code in the text box at the bottom of the screen and then click Submit.

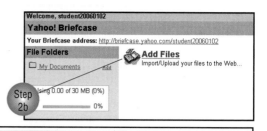

Step 2b

b. Click the <u>Add Files</u> hyperlink to add a file to your briefcase.

c. Click the *My Documents* option to select it and then click the uppermost Select button.

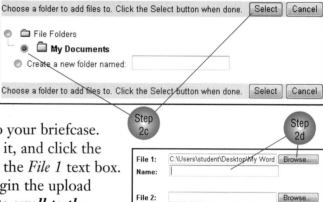

Step 2c

Step 2d

d. Click the Browse button beside the *File 1* text box, and use the Choose file dialog box to browse and locate a file you want to add to your briefcase. Double-click the file, or select it, and click the Open button to add the file to the *File 1* text box.

e. Click the Upload button to begin the upload process. ***(Note: You will need to scroll to the bottom of the page to find the Upload button.)***

f. Click the Back to Folder button when the upload finishes. The name and file details of the document you uploaded will now appear under the My Documents folder.

Step 2f

3. Download a file from your Yahoo! Briefcase account by completing the following steps:

a. Click the hyperlink for the file you just uploaded.

b. A File Download dialog box will appear, asking you if you want to open or save the document. Click the Save button. ***(Note: Some document formats such as image files and text documents may open automatically. To save an image to your computer, right-click the image and then click Save Picture As. Use the Save Picture As dialog box to browse and locate the folder on your computer that you want to save the picture in. Other documents may open in their native environment, such as Notepad. You can click File and then Save from the menu bar to save the document.)***

Step 3b

c. Use the Save As dialog box to browse and locate the folder to save the file on your local computer or network. Click the Save button to save the file to the folder you indicated.

d. If necessary, click the Close button when the Download Complete dialog box appears.

e. Use Windows Explorer to verify that the file was saved to the folder you indicated.

f. Return to Yahoo! Briefcase and click the <u>Sign Out</u> hyperlink to sign out of your account and then close the browser window.

Step 3f

WebDAV

When Tim Berners-Lee first conceptualized the World Wide Web, he envisioned a collaborative environment with documents that could be read and edited even when located on remote servers. As the Web developed, the latter vision was not fulfilled, so while users could read documents on remote servers, the users could not edit the documents unless first downloading them to a local computer.

The need for people to work on documents collaboratively without transferring the documents back and forth led a group of developers to seek a way to enable collaborative Web editing. The result was Web-Based Distributed Authoring and Versioning (WebDAV). WebDAV is a set of extensions to the HTTP/1.1 protocol used to send and receive Web pages over the Internet. With WebDAV, geographically dispersed groups can work together on a document even though the document remains on a remote server.

In addition to the benefits of being able to work collaboratively, WebDAV offers several advantages over FTP. Because of its close relationship to HTTP, it has fewer problems with firewalls and offers a more secure environment for transferring and working on documents. The fact that WebDAV consists of

extensions to HTTP also eases the ability of developers to make Web-related products supporting WebDAV.

WebDAV includes a number of key features: locking, properties, name space management, and collections. Locking, or concurrency control, prevents authors from writing to the same document at the same time. Properties enable authors to create, remove, or edit document information that will be stored in the document. Name space management enables users to copy and move documents, while collections enables users to create and display file system folders.

Microsoft Windows 95 and above feature a built-in WebDAV client known as WebFolders. WebFolders are shortcuts to a remote online storage service, network location, or FTP site, but appear and work just like any other local folder even though they are actually located on a remote server. Double-clicking a document from such a folder opens the document in its native environment, such as Word or Excel. WebFolders function just like regular folders, so the standard cut-and-paste and drag-and-drop features can be used to work with WebFolder documents and files.

Chapter Summary

Check your knowledge of chapter concepts by using the flash cards available on the Encore CD that accompanies this book as well as on the Internet Resource Center for this title at www.emcp.net/Internet2e.

- File Transfer Protocol (FTP) enables file transfers between networked computers.

- FTP servers can restrict access by requiring user names and passwords, but anonymous FTP servers are open to the public.

- Accessing another computer via FTP requires three items: FTP client software, the host server FTP address, and the user name and password for the host FTP server if required.

- Command-line FTP client programs feature an interface in which a user types simple commands such as *get*, *put*, and so on.

- Graphical user interface (GUI) FTP client programs provide a point-and-click interface that enables a user to choose commands via buttons or menus, or by dragging and dropping files.

- Most browsers now incorporate built-in FTP capabilities, as do some file managers such as *My Computer* and *Windows Explorer*.

- Because of the danger posed by malware, users should only download material from trusted sites.

- If using an anonymous FTP server, you should use *anonymous* or sometimes *ftp* as the user name and your e-mail address for the password.

- There are two different transfer modes used with FTP: ASCII mode for text files and binary mode for all other files.

- All the major Web browsers such as Internet Explorer, Netscape Navigator, Mozilla Firefox, and Opera contain built-in FTP functionality that provides an easy-to-use graphical interface for transferring files.

- The top folder in an FTP site is known as a root folder. Other folders appear under the root folder in a descending hierarchy (tree).

- Many image formats such as JPEG, GIF, and PNG are already stored in compressed form, so compressing image files or documents containing a lot of images will not result in a significant file size reduction.

- Software download sites are Web sites that offer software programs for downloading and installation.

- A mirror site server duplicates the content of another server to take some of the load off of the more heavily trafficked Web site.

- Online storage services provide remote storage space on servers that can be accessed online.

- Online storage users can specify the parties who will have access to stored materials, providing an alternative to using e-mail or FTP to share files.

- It is a good idea to maintain copies of anything stored on an online storage service, and critical data should be backed up on two different storage services to provide an extra safety margin.

Key Terms

Numbers indicate the pages where terms are first cited in the chapter. An alphabetized list of key terms with definitions can be found on the Encore CD that accompanies this book. In addition, these terms and definitions are included in the end-of-book glossary.

anonymous FTP server, *172*

ASCII mode, *175*

binary mode, *175*

command-line FTP client programs, *172*

dedicated GUI FTP client program, *181*

file compression utilities, *183*

freeware, *187*

FTP server software, *172*

graphical user interface (GUI) FTP client programs, *172*

mirror site, *188*

online storage services, *190*

root folder, *178*

shareware, *187*

zip file, *183*

Net Check

Additional quiz questions are available on the Encore CD that accompanies this book as well as on the Internet Resource Center for this title at www.emcp.net/Internet2e.

Multiple Choice

Indicate the correct answer for each question or statement.

1. Anonymous FTP servers usually let users log on using the following as a user name?
   a. anonymous or user
   b. anonymous, guest, or ftp
   c. ftp or user
   d. user or client

2. FTP client programs featuring a point-and-click interface are known as _____ client programs.
   a. command-line FTP
   b. Windows FTP
   c. Mouse command FTP
   d. GUI FTP

3. The FTP Commander Home window displays
   a. local folders and files in the right pane.

b. remote folders and files in the left pane.

c. WS_FTP home page information in the right pane.

d. local folders and files in the left pane.

4. _____ files are already compressed and will not benefit from further compression.

    a. HTML

    b. Text

    c. Excel

    d. Image

5. Files compressed using the most popular compression utilities usually have this file extension.

    a. .txt

    b. .zip

    c. .html

    d. .gif

6. Commands used with a command-line FTP program should be typed

    a. in uppercase.

    b. in lowercase.

    c. using italics.

    d. with spaces between each letter.

7. This command is used to start an FTP session in a command-line FTP client program.

    a. start

    b. get

    c. open

    d. mget

8. The two transfer modes used by FTP are

    a. ASCII and binary.

    b. ASCII and primary.

    c. SFTP and FTPS.

    d. SSH and SSL.

9. To enable FTP communication, a host or remote computer must run FTP _____ software.

    a. client

    b. server

    c. binary

    d. ASCII

10. Downloading a file is also known as _____ a file.

    a. putting

    b. logging

    c. getting

    d. extracting

True/False

Indicate whether each statement is true or false.

1. An anonymous FTP server does not allow access to the general public.

2. Binary mode is used in FTP file transfers for transferring text files.

3. Standard file management tasks such as renaming, deleting, cutting, and pasting are not available when accessing an FTP site with Internet Explorer.

4. File compression utilities use algorithms to reduce the amount of redundant or repeated data in a file.

5. You should indicate whether or not ASCII or binary transfer mode should be used before beginning a file download with a command-line FTP client program.

6. The FTP site administrator has no control over the folders that users can access.

7. A password is usually optional for an anonymous server log on, but the user's e-mail address should be used as a courtesy to the FTP server administrators.

8. The FTP Commander window displays the remote host folder in the right pane.

9. Multiple files can be uploaded or downloaded when using a GUI FTP client program by holding down the ALT key when selecting files.

10. Internet Explorer contains built-in FTP capabilities.

Virtual Perspectives

1. The majority of computer users prefer using programs with a GUI software interface, but a minority still like to use command-line programs for certain activities, such as FTP. Use your personal experience and information gathered from Internet research to discuss the pros and cons of command-line and GUI software programs.

2. Shareware programs are often much cheaper than commercial software packages. Discuss the pros and cons of using shareware versus commercial software. If you have ever registered and paid for a shareware program, discuss your experience and whether you feel you received value for your money.

3. A number of different software download sites enable users to download shareware and freeware programs. Many include features such as reviews, links to the software developer's home page, ratings, and so on. Discuss your favorite software download site and state the reasons why you prefer it to other sites.

Internet Lab Projects

Project 1
Access WinZip from My Computer

1. Click Start > Computer.
2. Navigate to any Word document.
3. Right-click the document, point to WinZip on the shortcut menu, and click Add to Zip file.
4. Click the *Use Evaluation Version* option when WinZip opens.
5. Click the New button in the Add dialog box to open the New Archive dialog box. Use the dialog box to browse and locate the WinZip Zipped Docs folder you created in Skill Review 5 and place it in the dialog box *Save in* text box. Type **Word Doc** in the *File name* text box and then click OK to create an archive named *Word Doc*.
6. Click the Add button in the Add dialog box to add the file to the archive you created in the previous step.
7. Close WinZip and return to Computer.
8. Use Computer to navigate to the WinZip Zipped Docs folder. Open the folder, right-click the Word Doc folder, and then click Extract at the shortcut menu.
9. Click the *Use Evaluation Version* option when WinZip opens.
10. Use the WinZip Extract dialog box to browse to and select the WinZip Unzipped Docs folder you created in Skill Review 5.
11. Click the Extract button.
12. Use Computer to locate the WinZip Unzipped Docs folder and open it. The document you extracted should appear there.

Project 2
Share One of Your Yahoo! Briefcase Folders with a Friend

1. Ask your friend or partner for their Yahoo! User ID. *(**Note: You only need their user ID, not their password.**)*
2. Log on to your Yahoo! Briefcase account.
3. Click the <u>Share With Friends</u> hyperlink on your Yahoo! Briefcase front page.

4. Select the folder you wish to share by clicking the folder option and then pressing the Select button.
5. Click the *Friends* option to select it.
6. Type your friend's Yahoo! user ID in the text box located below the *Friends* option and press the Save button when you are finished.
7. Click the <u>Sign Out</u> hyperlink to sign out of your Yahoo! Briefcase account.
8. Have your friend enter the URL for your Yahoo! Briefcase in the Internet Explorer Address bar in this format: http://briefcase.yahoo.com/[your user ID]. After pressing Enter or clicking the Go button your friend should have access to the folder you designated.

Internet Research Activities

Activity 1
Explore Freeware and Shareware FTP Client Programs

Use the Internet to research the different shareware and freeware FTP client programs available and then create a table comparing at least four different programs. Your table should include a list of features as well as information about the cost of the programs, if any.

Activity 2
Compare Online Storage Services

Use the Internet to research the different online storage services available and then create a table comparing at least four of these services. Your table should include a list of features as well as information on service packages and costs.

Activity 3
Net Challenge

Conduct Internet research and use Microsoft Help to find out more about Windows WebFolders. Use what you learn to create a WebFolder on your local machine that you can use to store documents on an online storage service. When you are finished, write a set of step-by-step instructions describing how to create and use WebFolders with Windows Vista.

UNIT 2

Emerging Trends

The Form of the Future

Anyone who has signed up for anything on the Web has used a Web-page based form. Current HTML forms use scripting languages to perform many processing tasks, and the resulting code can be quite complicated. XForms is the next generation XML-based form standard supported by the W3C. XForms promise a number of advantages, including a reduction in the need for scripting languages, multi-step processing capability, and the ability to perform calculations and other activities without requiring a trip to a server. The W3C also promises that XForms will make authoring forms easier. Currently no major browsers support XForms, but the Mozilla Foundation recently announced the release of a beta version of an XForms plug-in for the Firefox and Mozilla browsers. Within the next few years expect XForms support to be standard on all major browsers.

W3C® XForms

Source: Jonathan Bennett, "Mozilla tries out next-generation Web forms." http://news.zdnet.co.uk/internet/0,39020369,39188193,00.htm
"XForms 1.0 Frequently Asked Questions." www.w3.org/MarkUp/Forms/2003/xforms-faq.html#advantages

Scholarly Assistance

Google Scholar is a new search service that provides specialized literature search capabilities. To increase the amount of available literature, Google has worked with publishers to make content available that was previously inaccessible except to those with subscriptions. As a result, Google has persuaded many publishers to allow access by spiders, and to provide abstracts of articles so that those using Google Scholar can determine whether or not a document meets their criteria. Google Scholar uses special algorithms to perform citation analysis that allows it to place the most frequently cited papers at the top of any ranking. Google Scholar can also provide information about papers that its spiders have only heard about but not seen.

> [CITATION] **Return of the Luddites**.
> E Niou, PC Ordeshook - Cited by 8 - Web Search
> International Security, 1999

When one of these results is returned, a search link will appear nearby so that users can search for the document. Google Scholar is still available only as a beta version, but very shortly is likely to be available as a regular release.

Source: Danny Sullivan, "Google Scholar Offers Access To Academic Information." http://searchenginewatch.com/searchday/article.php/3437471

Should the Web Smell?

Scent-Dome

Trisenx copyright 2004   Design: Tingbin Tang

The Scent Dome is a small device developed by TriSenxthat can be attached to computers to provide an additional level of sensory perception to the Web. It is well known that smells can trigger memories and emotions, and the Scent Dome is equipped to do just that. Each Scent Dome contains a number of aroma cartridges containing fragrances and food aromas. Web sites can feature fragrance files that can trigger the Scent Dome, or the files can be included in e-mail messages as attachments. Currently in beta testing, the Scent Dome offers 60 smells, but the manufacturers say that future models may offer as many as 2,000 different smells. Whether or not the market is ready for the Scent Dome is an open question. A similar capability offered by a company called Digiscents failed to attract much interest and closed its doors in 2001. TriSenx is well-funded, and intends to succeed where their competitors failed.

Visual Search Results

Most Web users are familiar with the static search results lists generated by search and meta search engines. What they may not be aware of is the fact that there is a visual alternative. A meta search engine named Kartoo.com presents search results using utilizing interactive Flash-based maps that show the relationship between different search results. The size of a document displayed in a map is related to its relevance to the search query, and placing the pointer in the map area displays a list of keywords on the left side of the screen. Clicking a keyword will further refine a search and display a new map, while holding the pointer over a document displays a site description on the left side of the browser window. The interactive maps can be saved for future reference, and Kartoo offers

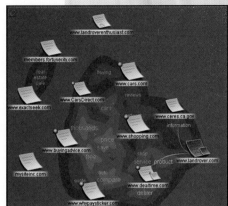

searching in a number of different languages. Kartoo will probably never be a threat to Google, but its intuitive visual interface appeals to a growing niche market.

High Speed Downloading with BitTorrent

A relatively new peer-to-peer file sharing protocol known as BitTorrent offers a high-speed alternative to using FTP to download files. In normal peer-to-peer file sharing networks, one party uploads a file that is then downloaded by another party. Uploading speeds are almost always slower than downloading speeds, but BitTorrent works around the uploading bottleneck by simultaneously uploading bits of a file from a number of different BitTorrent users, in a technique referred to as swarming. The ability of BitTorrent to download large files quickly has led some users to use it to illegally download movies and other copyrighted materials. Despite those concerns, many see a bright future for BitTorrent as a method for making large files rapidly available.

Discussion Questions

1. Many Web users complain that just as they get comfortable with one technology, another one comes along to replace it. Their reaction is sometimes summed up by the old saying, "If it ain't broke, don't fix it." What do you think about this? Are some changes made only for change's sake, rather than to meet a real need? Can or should anything be done to control the pace of technological changes? Can you provide any examples of Internet-related technological changes you could have done without?

2. You have just read about Web pages that feature smells, and there have been other attempts to improve the Web browser experience, such as 3-D browsers. So far these ideas have failed to catch on with the majority of Web users. Undoubtedly there will be other attempts to enhance the browsing experience, some of which may succeed where others have failed. Think of some of the things you would like to see in a Web browser. Describe how you think these new features might work, and why they would be useful.

3. Currently Google is far and away the most popular search engine. Although Google has a number of competitors, so far none have been able to catch up to Google's lead. Why do you think that is? Do you think this is a temporary phenomenon, or will Google remain the most popular search engine for some time to come? Discuss any events that might lead to Google losing its lead to a competitor.

UNIT 3

Communications Technology

- Experiencing Multimedia
- Using E-mail
- Asynchronous Communications
- Synchronous Communications

Chapter 7
Experiencing Multimedia

Learning Objectives

- Explain the role of plug-ins and helper applications in supporting multimedia on the Web.

- Demonstrate how to download and install plug-ins.

- Explain how images are supported by HTML.

- Examine and evaluate the different image formats suitable for Web use.

- Summarize how Internet audio and streaming audio and video works.

- Explain peer-to-peer file sharing networks.

- Differentiate between the various methods used to create animated content on the Web.

- Demonstrate how to use the Windows Media Player.

Living on the Net

Since Bob and Carolyn first began using the Internet, they have seen it develop from a text-based communication method to one that more and more frequently incorporates multimedia. The history of the Web site of the company Bob works for provides a good example of this change. Bob has witnessed the Web pages on the company site evolve from text pages with a few static images to Web pages with Flash movies that now provide customers with tours of the company's facilities and detailed product presentations.

In their personal lives, Bob and Carolyn now enjoy multimedia over the Internet in a number of different ways. The formerly text-only instant messaging they use to keep in touch with friends and family now includes video provided by inexpensive webcams. Like many of their friends, Bob and Carolyn have purchased portable media players so they can listen to their favorite music wherever they are. They both enjoy visiting online music stores to purchase and download songs and albums. They can then download songs to their media players, which seem to have almost limitless storage capacity. Being somewhat of a language buff, Carolyn now watches television webcasts from Germany in her browser window on weekends, and Bob has been listening to Internet radio since it first became available.

Bob and Carolyn both notice one drawback to the huge increase in multimedia—the constant improvement in computer speed and memory required to keep up with multimedia applications means that a computer seems outmoded almost from the time it is first plugged in. They find that buying the highest performance computer they can afford makes better sense than buying a lower performance model and increases the time before they feel the need to buy a new computer.

Browsers and Multimedia

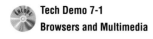
Tech Demo 7-1
Browsers and Multimedia

In the context of the Web, the term *multimedia* refers to the use of more than one type of media on a Web page, including text, graphics, animated graphics, video, audio, or even hypertext. Used wisely, multimedia in Web pages enhances the viewer's experience. Web page viewing can even become an interactive experience, with Flash, Shockwave, or Java applets enabling browsers to accept user input to control the viewing experience. Users can control games, calculators, animations, or any number of other different interactive activities online.

In the early days of the Web, technical considerations constrained the use of multimedia in Web pages, but as capabilities improve, more and more Web pages include multimedia. Web browsers still vary widely in the ability to display Web pages integrating multimedia, so Web page designers need to consider whether or not potential viewers will be able to take advantage of multimedia. Anyone designing Web pages should carefully consider why multimedia is being used, and whether it will enhance the viewer experience or needlessly complicate it.

Web browsers are HTML interpreters, and they must look for help in displaying any type of media beyond text and images. Programs embedded in Web pages such as JavaScript or Java applets enable a browser to display different media. **Browser extensions** are programs that extend the function of a browser, and can take the form of **helper applications**—stand-alone programs such as Microsoft Word or Excel that can be opened to display content downloaded by a browser, or **plug-ins**—small programs or program modules that work within a browser.

browser extensions programs that extend the function of a browser

helper application stand-alone program, such as Microsoft Word or Excel, that can open to display content downloaded by a browser

plug-ins small programs or program modules that work within a browser

Helper Applications

Helper applications are stand-alone programs that a browser can call on to display different media content once the browser downloads the content. Whenever a browser encounters a file, it looks at its file extension to determine its MIME (Multipurpose Internet Mail Extension) type. Table 7.1 shows some of the more commonly encountered MIME types and their extensions. Browsers use the MIME type to determine how to display or handle a file. If a file contains an extension that the browser can handle, such as .htm or .gif, then the browser has no problem displaying the file content. However, if a file uses a MIME type that the browser cannot display on its own, it must look for a helper application to use in order to display the file content. For example, if the browser is asked to display a Microsoft Word file with a .doc extension, the browser will look for a copy of the Word program on the computer and will open that program to display the file. A browser also must use a helper application to display an Adobe PDF file. Whenever a browser encounters a file with a .pdf extension, it looks for a copy of the Adobe Acrobat Reader application, and opens the program to display the file as shown in Figure 7.1. If multiple

Table 7.1   Common Media MIME Types and File Name Extensions

MIME Type	File Extension
Audio MPEG (Moving Pictures Experts Group)	.mp2, .mp3
Audio Video Interleave	.avi
Flash	.swf
Musical Instrument Digital Interface	.mid, .midi
QuickTime	.mov
RealAudio	.ra, .ram, .rm
Shockwave	.dcr
Video MPEG (Moving Pictures Experts Group)	.mpe, .mpg, .mpeg
Waveform Sound	.wav

helper applications for a particular MIME type are installed on a computer, a dialog box may prompt the user to choose a program as the default association for a MIME type. The user can typically prevent such dialog boxes from reappearing by checking an option in the dialog box as shown in Figure 7.2.

Plug-ins and ActiveX Controls

Plug-ins are small programs that extend the capability of browsers in dealing with different types of media. Plug-ins differ from helper applications in that they are not stand-alone programs like MS Word or Adobe® Acrobat.® Instead, the sole purpose of a plug-in is to enable a browser to deal with a specific type of Web page content. In addition, plug-ins do not require content to be downloaded before it can be displayed.

Figure 7.1 Adobe PDF File Displayed in Acrobat Reader®

Plug-ins reside in a browser's plug-ins folder located inside the browser's application folder as shown in Figure 7.3. For example, when a browser encounters a file with an extension such as .swf (used by Flash content), it looks for and opens the Flash player plug-in located in its plug-ins folder. It is difficult to predict exactly how a browser might deal with a given media type because even the same browser versions can be configured to handle plug-ins differently. Browsers come with some plug-ins already installed, and the user can download and install new plug-ins to the plug-ins folder when needed.

The two most common browser plug-in types are *Netscape-style plug-ins* and *ActiveX controls*. Netscape originally developed the browser plug-in concept for its Navigator browser, and Microsoft later developed ActiveX controls for use in its Internet Explorer browser. Two key differences between these two types of plug-ins are the type of tag they use to insert media into Web pages, and the scripting language used for communication between the browser and the plug-in or ActiveX control. Netscape-style plug-ins use the embed tag (<embed>) to insert media and JavaScript for communication, while ActiveX controls use the object tag (<object>) and VBScript for communication.

Netscape-style plug-in a plug-in developed by Netscape

ActiveX control a set of Microsoft programming/scripting language technologies that expand Internet Explorer capabilities; ActiveX controls are often referred to as a type of plug-in

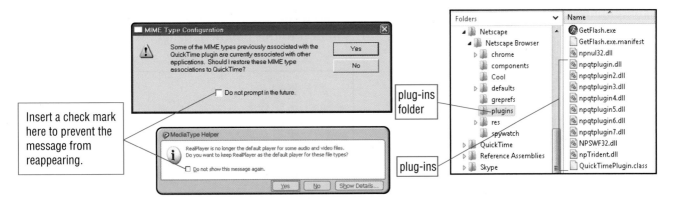

Insert a check mark here to prevent the message from reappearing.

Figure 7.2 MIME Type Configuration Dialog Boxes

Figure 7.3 Browser Plug-ins Folder

Online Gaming

Online computer games take advantage of all the multimedia capabilities supported by today's computers by letting game players play games using an Internet-connected PC or a game console such as the Sony PlayStation 2 or the Microsoft Xbox. Each connection method has its advantages and disadvantages. PCs offer better graphics, access to more game titles, and downloadable upgrades, but cost more than console systems, lack portability, and do not come equipped with a handheld controller. Computer-savvy individuals will not find any problems using their PC to play online games, but for the less technically adept the simplicity of a console may be more appealing. The type of game being played may also determine whether or not a PC or console is best. Role-playing games require more keyboard input and are thus more suited to PC play, while action games may be better played using handheld controllers.

Playing a game over the Internet allows players to expand their horizons beyond their own neighborhood and compete with other players located anywhere in the world. Playing online games against other opponents or competitors is known as multiplayer gaming. Some virtual reality games may have thousands of players online simultaneously and are known as MMOGs (Massive Multiplayer Online Games).

A profusion of game titles are available over the Web, and there are a number of Internet portals such as Yahoo! Games that allow visitors to choose and play games individually or against other players. Some games can only be played online, while others are available in downloadable versions as well. Game developers often offer free game versions and charge for versions offering more features.

One subset of the online gaming world causing concern is online gambling. Online gambling is illegal in many countries, but that has not stopped it from experiencing rapid growth. In the United States, the Wired Communications Act prevents U.S. citizens from paying for bets using U.S.-issued credit cards, but gamblers and online casinos have found a number of ways to circumvent any prohibitions.

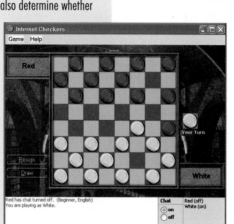

http://games.yahoo.com

Before the advent of ActiveX controls, Internet Explorer supported Netscape-style plug-ins. Not long after ActiveX controls came into being, Internet Explorer dropped the Netscape-style plug-in support. What this means is that when Internet Explorer encounters an embed tag, it looks for an ActiveX control to handle the content indicated by the tag. If the browser cannot find an ActiveX control to handle the content, the content is not displayed.

The use of media requiring a plug-in can cause problems if a user does not have a required plug-in installed in the browser he or she is using. If a browser cannot find the correct plug-in, the viewer will be looking at a blank screen, a static placeholder image, or a message advising the user that the needed plug-in cannot be found as shown in Figure 7.4. One way to avoid that possibility is for the Web page author to include HTML code for the page that specifies a URL where a copy of the needed plug-in can be found. If the browser cannot find the called-for plug-in, it will automatically go to the URL, offering the user the option of downloading and installing the needed plug-in, a one-time process.

Almost all plug-ins or extensions are available for free in order to support the use of particular multimedia content. On the other hand, the authoring programs used to develop that content usually require payment. For example, the Adobe Flash Player that comes preinstalled in most browsers is also available as a free download, but Flash 8, the program used to develop Flash content, must be purchased.

While ActiveX controls help expand Internet Explorer capabilities, they also can let spyware, adware, and other programs install themselves without the knowledge of a computer user. One solution to this potential danger is to disable

Figure 7.4 Missing Plug-in Message

ActiveX controls. Once this is done, Web sites trying to install ActiveX controls on a computer will cause a message to appear letting users know that their security settings do not allow the installation of new ActiveX controls. If the new controls are wanted disabled ActiveX settings will have to be re-enabled. ActiveX controls can be disabled using Internet Explorer by completing the following steps:

1. Click the Tools button on the Internet Explorer standard toolbar and then click Internet Options.
2. Click the Security tab in the Internet Options dialog box, make sure *Internet* is selected as the content zone, and then click the Custom Level button in the *Security level for this zone* section.
3. In the Security Settings dialog box, click all the Disable option buttons in the *ActiveX controls and plug-ins* category, with the exception of the *Binary and script behaviors* and *Run ActiveX controls and plug-ins* options. Click the OK button when you are finished.
4. Click Apply in the Internet Options dialog box to change the settings and then click OK to close the dialog box.

Concept Review 1 Browsers and Multimedia

1. What is the difference between a helper application and a plug-in?
2. What are MIME types, and what role do they play in browser functionality?
3. Why do some computer users disable ActiveX controls?

Skill Review 1 Download, Install, and Use a Plug-in

(Note: Ask your instructor if you have permission to download and save files to your computer or network location. If you do not have permission, ask your instructor where you should save the file you download for this exercise.)

1. In Internet Explorer, type www.adobe.com/shockwave/download/alternates/#sp in the Address bar and then press Enter.
2. Scroll down the Macromedia Web Players page until you reach the *Shockwave Player* section.
3. Click the Full Installer Windows Shockwave Player hyperlink under the Internet Explorer/AOL heading. *(Note: If you are using another browser, click the appropriate Shockwave Player hyperlink.)*

Shockwave Player			
			(System Requirements)
Windows 98/2000/XP	**Internet Explorer/AOL**	**Netscape**	
Full Installer	Shockwave Player 10	Shockwave Player 10	
Slim Installer	Shockwave Player 10	Shockwave Player 10	
Uninstaller	Shockwave Player Uninstaller		

Step 2
Step 3

4. Click the Download Now button on the Shockwave Player Download Center Web page.
5. Click the Run button in the File Download-Security Warning dialog box.
6. If the User Account Control dialog box appears asking for permission to continue, click the Continue button.

7. If a dialog box appears asking to install the Google toolbar, uncheck the install box and click Next.

8. When installation is complete, the Installing Shockwave Player dialog box will reappear. Click Finish to close the dialog box.

9. When the Register for Games and Entertainment dialog box appears, click the appropriate radio button for your age and click Next.

10. Enter the information on the next screen and click Next.

11. Shockwave will automatically open a browser window to the Adobe Shockwave Player Installation Complete Web page. *(Note: You will use the Shockwave Player later in this chapter to play Shockwave movies.)*

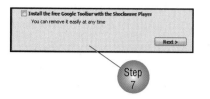

Step 7

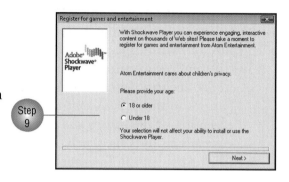

Step 9

Images

Images in Web pages are not saved as part of the Web page document. Instead, they exist as separate files. An HTML image tag (`<img>`) and source attribute (SRC) in an HTML document direct the browser to load an image file from a specified location and display the image as part of a Web page as shown in Figure 7.5. Because a Web page with images requires multiple files, the browser will typically require more time to retrieve all of the necessary elements to display the complete page; the load time will vary depending on the size of the various files involved.

When a Web page designer creates a Web page, it is important that the designer selects image files with relatively small sizes to ensure that a Web page does not take too long to load. Many experts recommend that a single Web page be no larger than 100 KB (kilobytes) in size, with smaller sizes being preferable. Thus, the file size of an HTML page plus all of its images added together should be less than 100 KB whenever possible. Avoiding the excessive use of images on a page should also keep down the cumulative file size. The exception to this rule occurs if the same image is repeated on a page. That does not increase loading time because the browser loads the actual image file only once.

HTML document with image tag and SRC

image file

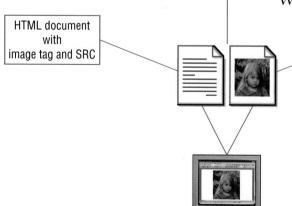

Figure 7.5 How Images Are Displayed

Image Formats

Digital images are saved as *bitmap* or raster files, meaning that image information is stored as a grid composed of tiny picture elements known as *pixels*. When viewed from any distance, the pixels blend together to compose the image. Bitmap images are resolution dependent, so image quality will be adversely affected if an image is enlarged or reduced. Figure 7.6 shows a bitmap image and an inset containing a portion of the image that has been enlarged to the point that individual pixels are visible. Uncompressed bitmap file formats produce file sizes that are too large for Web use. The ideal Web image formats supported by most browsers use compression techniques to produce small file sizes. The three image formats ideal for Web pages include GIF (Graphics Interchange Format), JPEG (Joint Photographic Experts Group), and PNG (Portable Network Graphics).

pixel

Figure 7.6 Bitmap Image Showing Pixel Detail

GIF images are the most commonly used on the Web and are the result of a lossless technology that shrinks an image's file size without sacrificing any of the original data. Because the GIF format supports only 256 colors it is not suitable for all images, and it is therefore often used for drawings or illustrations. The GIF format has two variations: GIF87a and GIF89a. The original GIF87a format is for simple images, while the later GIF89a format allows interlacing, transparency, and simple animation. *Interlacing* allows the Web browser to display an image gradually as the image downloads, somewhat like a picture slowly coming into focus as shown in Figure 7.7. Transparency allows the Web page background color to show through a selected portion of an image as shown in

bitmap an image file type that stores image information as a grid composed of tiny picture elements, known as pixels

pixel the smallest unit of information contained in a bitmap image

GIF image lossless image format that is the most commonly used image format on the Web

interlacing enables an image to display gradually as it downloads into a Web page

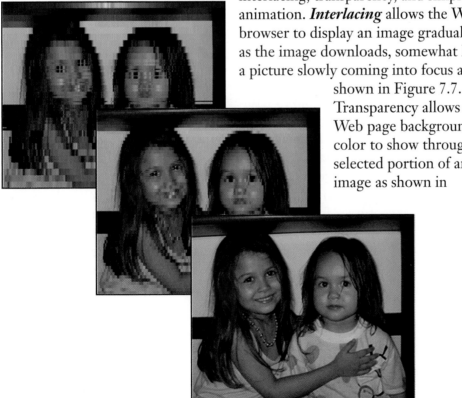

Figure 7.7 Interlaced GIF Image Loading

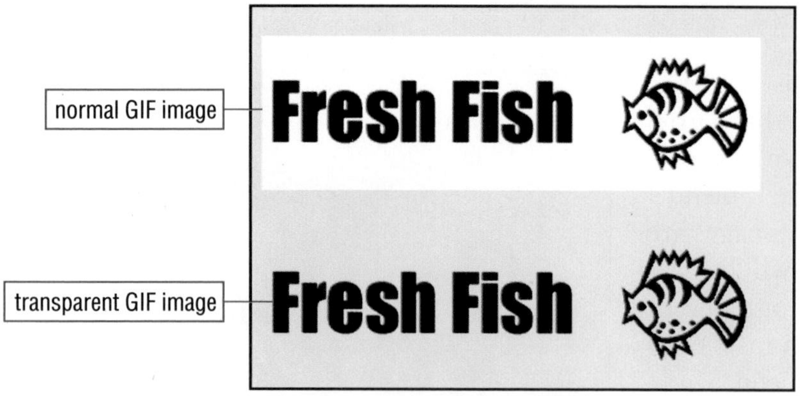

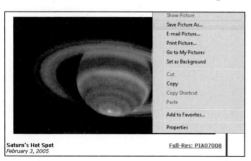

normal GIF image

transparent GIF image

Figure 7.8 Normal and Transparent GIF Images

Figure 7.8. **Animated GIFs** create an illusion of motion by instructing a browser to load two or more images in succession.

JPEG images use a lossy image compression technology that supports more than 16 million colors and is the best Web image format for photographs. Lossy technologies discard some data during the compression process, so saving an image as a JPEG file causes some of the original data to be lost. When used to display large images, a JPEG file will be smaller than a comparable GIF file.

A third type of image format, PNG, offers interlacing and transparency, and produces smaller file sizes than the GIF or JPEG formats. Because *PNG images* are supported only by browser versions 4.x and above, they should not be used on Web pages likely to be viewed by people using older browsers.

Using Web Images

Using images found on a Web page without permission may violate copyright law. If a Web page does not contain a copyright statement, that does not necessarily mean that users are free to download and use any images found on the page. If there is any doubt about copyright status, the user should contact the Web site owner to inquire about permission to use an image. There are exceptions for the fair use of copyrighted material under certain circumstances, as described in Chapter 5, but before using any material under this exception, the user should be certain that his or her intended use falls under fair use provisions.

Copying Web Images

A user can copy and download an image from a Web page by right-clicking the image and then clicking Save Picture As as shown in Figure 7.9. This opens the Save Picture dialog box, which can be used to browse to and select a folder in which to store the image. This option may not be available on some Web pages that contain scripting to disable the right-click function.

The user also can use screen capture software to capture images, even images on Web pages that contain scripting that prevents them from being downloaded. Screen capture software works by taking a snapshot of a computer screen or portion of the screen. The user can even crop the screen capture to save a portion of any screen, as shown in Figure 7.10, which illustrates a screen shot being saved and cropped using the SnagIt screen capture software.

Finding Images

Several search engines, including Google and Yahoo!, allow users to search for images on the Web by clicking a hyperlink or button that enables image-only searching. Figure 7.11

Figure 7.9 Saving a Picture

animated GIF a type of GIF image file that creates an illusion of motion by instructing a browser to load two or more images in succession

JPEG image lossy image format that supports more than 16 million colors and is the best Web image format for photographs

PNG image image format that offers interlacing and transparency and produces smaller file sizes than the GIF or JPEG formats

shows the Yahoo! Image results page for a search using the key term *flowers*. Each thumbnail displays the full URL for an image. Clicking an image thumbnail will open a new Web page that shows the image in its original context, including a thumbnail the user can click to display a full-size copy of the image.

Many Web sites created and maintained by U.S. government agencies contain images that can be freely used for private and commercial purposes. Before using any images from these sites, the user

Figure 7.10 Cropping a Screen Capture

should carefully read any terms of use information. For example, the NASA Web site contains reproduction guidelines covering the use of any images and emblems found on the www.nasa.gov Web site as shown in Figure 7.12. The NASA reproduction guidelines are similar to the guidelines issued by other government agencies, with the main restriction being that images should not be used in any way that implies NASA's endorsement of a product or service.

Figure 7.11 Yahoo! Image Search Results

Figure 7.12 Reproduction Guidelines for Use of NASA Images and Emblems

iband.com

Figure 7.13 Stock Image Web Site

A number of Web sites offer copyright-free, royalty-free, or public domain images and clip art that can be used on Web pages you create, such as the iBand site shown in Figure 7.13. Some of these sources provide images free of charge, while others let users download images during a fixed subscription period. Some sites offering free images require that a hyperlink to the image source URL be placed beside or below an image, or that a general credit line regarding the image source be placed at the bottom of the Web page. Terms, conditions, and restrictions differ from site to site, so it is very important to read any legal or copyright information before using an image from one of these sites.

Concept Review 2 Images

1. What are the three principal image formats used in Web pages?
2. Which of the three image formats uses lossy compression?
3. Which image format supports interlacing, transparency, and animation?
4. How can an image be saved from a Web page?

Skill Review 2 Use a Free Image Web Site to Find and Download Images

(Note: Ask your instructor if you have permission to download and save files to your computer or network location. If you do not have permission, ask your instructor where you should save the file you download for this exercise.)

1. In Internet Explorer, type **www.freeimages.co.uk** in the Address bar and then press Enter.
2. Click the Terms hyperlink located on the left side of the page and read the terms for using the images on the site.
3. Click the Help Centre hyperlink when you are finished reading the Terms page. Read the page to learn about downloading images from the site.
4. Click the Images hyperlink to return to the Images page.
5. Choose a gallery hyperlink and click it. *(Note: Gallery choices will vary depending on user selections. Some galleries may be restricted to members. Membership application information can be accessed by clicking the About Us hyperlink.)*

6. If necessary, click additional subgallery hyperlinks until you arrive at a page displaying thumbnail images.

7. View a full-size copy of an image and download it by clicking an image thumbnail. When the larger image fully loads in the browser, right-click inside the image and then click Save Picture As. Use the Save Picture dialog box to locate and select a folder in which you will save the picture. Click the Save button when you are finished. *(Note: It may take some time for the image to fully download. Step 9 describes a quicker method that can be used to download images.)*

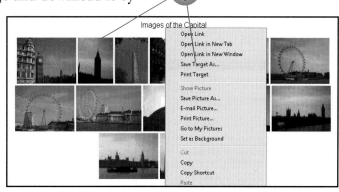

8. Click the Internet Explorer Back button to return to the image page.

9. Download another image by right-clicking inside a thumbnail and then clicking Save Target As. Use the Save As dialog box to locate and select a folder that you will save the picture to. Click the Save button when you are finished. *(Note: This image downloading method is quicker than the one described in Step 7 because the image is downloaded directly to a folder without being displayed in the browser.)*

10. Use either of the image downloading methods you learned in Steps 7 and 9 to download three more images.

Audio

While it was possible to download and listen to music and other audio from the very start of the Internet, the state of Internet and computer technology at that time limited its popularity. Although early audio file formats were able to offer high-fidelity sound, they did so at the cost of huge file sizes—a three-minute song recorded using the uncompressed ***WAV audio file format*** could result in a 30 megabyte file. Audio files had to be downloaded before they could be played back on a computer, and the combination of large files and low-bandwidth Internet connections meant that downloading even a short song could take hours. The storage capacity of personal computers was also many times smaller than it is today, and a handful of songs recorded using the audio file formats available at the time could fill up a hard drive very quickly. Two developments in audio technology emerged to change this scenario: compressed audio file formats that offered satisfactory sound quality coupled with small file sizes and streaming audio that eliminated the need for downloading by delivering audio content on a continuous just-in-time basis.

WAV audio file format uncompressed digital audio file format developed by Microsoft

Compressed Audio Formats

In Chapter 6 you learned about the file compression technologies used to compress file data to create smaller file sizes. Compression technologies can be divided into two broad categories: lossless and lossy. As the name implies, lossless technologies compress without any loss of the original data, while lossy technologies compress by sacrificing some original data.

Table 7.2 Popular Compressed Audio File Formats

Format	File Extension	Codec
Advanced Audio Coding	.aac, .m4a	lossy
Apple Lossless Encoding	.ale	lossless
ATRAC 3	.oma, .omg	lossy
AU	.au	lossless
Audio Interchange File Format	.aiff	lossless
Free Lossless Audio Codec	.flac	lossless
MPEG Audio Layer 3 (MP3)	.mp3	lossy
Vorbis	.ogg	lossy
Windows Media Audio	.wma	lossy

codec a compression technology used to compress and decompress audio files

sampling rate measures how frequently samples of an audio waveform are recorded per second

bit rate the number of bits used per second to record samples

The compression technologies used to compress and decompress audio files are often referred to as *codecs*, derived from the terms *compression* and *decompression*. Lossy codecs remove irrelevant or redundant data from audio files, such as sounds that humans cannot hear or sounds that are masked by other sounds. As a result, the average person will not notice any difference in the sound quality between an uncompressed and compressed audio file. Table 7.2 shows some of the most commonly encountered audio compressed file formats; the lossy formats are the ones most commonly exchanged over the Internet because of the smaller file sizes they produce. As the availability of broadband Internet connections increases and the cost per gigabyte of hard drives decreases, lossless formats are becoming increasingly popular and may some day overtake the lossy formats. Audio files saved for archival purposes use lossless compression formats or uncompressed formats since those methods maintain all of the original audio data.

Two important factors determine the quality and size of digital audio encoding. The *sampling rate* measures how frequently samples of an audio waveform are recorded per second as shown in Figure 7.14. Higher sampling rates produce better audio quality. Sampling rates are expressed in kilohertz (kHz), with 44.1kHz being the rate used for CD-quality recordings. A 44.1 kHz sampling rate records 44,100 samples per second.

The second important factor is the *bit rate* used during the encoding process. A *bit*, a term derived from binary digit, is the smallest unit of computer data

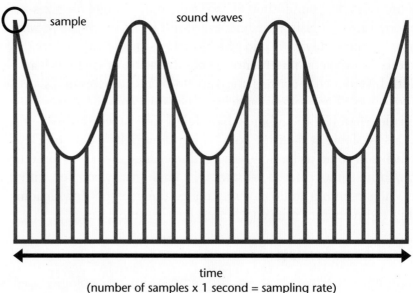

time
(number of samples x 1 second = sampling rate)

Figure 7.14 Sampling

and is represented using a 1 or a 0 in the binary system used by computers. The bit rate is the number of bits used per second to record samples. The higher the bit rate, the more information recorded over a given time period, which produces higher quality sound but also larger file sizes. *Variable bit rate encoding (VBR)* features a continuously changing bit rate that increases or decreases depending on the complexity of the content being encoded.

MP3 Audio File Format

The *MP3 audio file format* is far and away the most popular audio file format in use on the Internet today. MP3 is short for MPEG Audio Layer 3, and was developed to comply with standards created by the Moving Picture Experts Group (MPEG). MP3 can be used to produce CD-quality audio using only a fraction of the space required by uncompressed audio file formats, resulting in dramatically smaller files. A typical MP3 file may be 10 percent of the size of a corresponding uncompressed WAV file. This means that a three-minute song that might result in a 30 megabyte WAV file can be converted to an MP3 file under 3 megabytes in size.

The high audio quality and tremendous reduction in file sizes offered by the MP3 format meant that it became practical to download and share audio files over the Internet. Songs were extracted from audio compact discs (CDs) and converted to the MP3 format and shared with others, a process that became known as ripping. MP3 files could then be burned (copied) onto CD-Rs (writeable CDs) by users and played back in CD players, or played directly from a hard drive using an MP3 software interface known as an MP3 player. The appearance of portable hardware MP3 players allowed users to download MP3 files from the computer to the player's storage media for later playback.

Software and hardware MP3 players now handle a number of different audio file formats and are often referred to as media players. The Nullsoft Winamp media player pictured in Figure 7.15 is an example of a popular freeware media player, but there are a number of other popular software media players in current use, including the Windows Media Player that comes bundled with Vista,

variable bit rate encoding (VBR) digital recording technology that features a continuously changing bit rate that increases or decreases depending on the complexity of the content being encoded

MP3 audio file format short for MPEG Audio Layer 3, the most popular audio file format in use on the Internet today

Tech Demo 7-2 MP3 Technology

Figure 7.15 Nullsoft Winamp Media Player Interface

Figure 7.16 Apple iPod Portable Media Player

RealPlayer, and Apple's iTunes. The Apple iPod shown in Figure 7.16 is an example of a portable media player. Current versions of the iPod can store up to 80 GB of audio files, and play AAC, MP3, MP3 VBR, ALE, WAV, and AIFF audio formats. Media players are not restricted to playing songs, and are often used to play spoken book, magazine, and newspaper content. Web sites such as Audible.com offer a wide variety of books and other print material in audio formats.

File Sharing

The ease with which MP3 songs could be shared took a tremendous leap with the appearance of peer-to-peer (P2P) file sharing programs like the original Napster. In a typical network arrangement, client computers connect to servers in what is known as a client/server system or model. Clients can download files stored on the servers as needed. In P2P systems, each client computer (peer) acts as a miniserver and can share files directly with other peers, vastly increasing the number of files potentially available for sharing. Napster, the first widely used P2P file sharing system, became immensely popular by allowing Internet users around the world to share MP3 song files with each other.

Unfortunately for Napster, it was not a true P2P system in that it used servers to maintain a searchable index of the songs available for sharing on client computers, as shown in Figure 7.17, and that proved to be its downfall. Napster's success immediately attracted the attention of song copyright

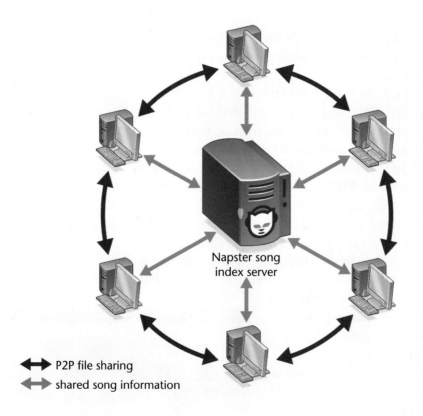

Figure 7.17 Napster's Semi-P2P File Sharing Arrangement

holders, resulting in legal challenges raised by the Recording Industry Association of America (RIAA). Napster argued in court that the service it provided was no different than friends sharing songs, but it eventually lost that argument when a court found that the failure to ensure that the songs indexed under its control did not contain copyrighted works made Napster a party to copyright violation. The Napster brand and logos were subsequently acquired by Roxio, Inc. and Napster currently operates as a legitimate online music store similar to Apple iTunes.

Around the time of the dismantling of the original Napster, true P2P file sharing systems such as Gnutella appeared. These P2P systems eliminated the need for a file index server. The lack of a central server and therefore a central authority that could be sued makes it difficult, if not impossible, for legal authorities to shut these systems down. To counteract illegal file sharing on these P2P networks, the RIAA now files lawsuits against the users of such systems who download copyrighted material in the hope that others will be discouraged from downloading copyrighted files. Whether or not this strategy will prove effective remains to be seen.

Although the RIAA was ultimately successful in shutting down the original Napster, the experience forced the music industry to come to terms with the reality of the Internet and its capabilities, and there are now a number of different companies that let users legally purchase and download songs over the Internet. One of the most successful examples of an online music store, Apple iTunes, has over 3.5 million songs in its catalog as shown in Figure 7.18. To buy songs from the iTunes store, the user must first

Figure 7.18 Apple iTunes Online Music Store

Podcasting

Podcasting, a term derived by combining Apple's *iPod* media player and *broadcasting,* is a method of distributing audio content through the Internet on a subscription basis, allowing subscribers to listen to programs whenever they want. Although an iPod is a popular means for playing podcasts, any media player that can handle MP3 files can be used. Podcasting is the brainchild of former MTV VJ and Internet visionary Adam Curry, who wondered if the RSS XML format used to automatically distribute text-based content to subscribers could be adapted to distribute MP3 files. Curry mentioned his idea to RSS developer Dave Winer, who soon developed enclosure elements for RSS that contain a URL pointing to a file location. It was now possible to use RSS to deliver MP3 files, but Curry wanted to automate the download process, so he taught himself AppleScript. With the help of a number of other developers, he created the iPodder, a media aggregator that automatically downloads podcasts and stores them on a media player for playback. The rest is history—iPodding has taken the Internet by storm. Podosphere members can now visit pod portals to find podcasts they like and subscribe to them by adding a feed URL to their aggregator. The aggregator can then be scheduled to periodically check for and download new podcasts, which can be played on a computer-based media player or downloaded to a portable media player. Creating podcasts is relatively simple and inexpensive, and the number of different homemade or professionally produced podcast programs is increasing rapidly. Podcasting is now attracting the attention of commercial enterprises, and many terrestrial and Internet radio stations are offering podcast content for their listeners.

download the iTunes program. The iTunes program can then be used to organize and play songs on a computer, copy songs from a computer to an iPod portable media player, or connect to the iTunes online music store to buy and download songs.

Streaming Audio

Streaming audio is another method used to deliver audio over the Internet. Streaming works by transmitting portions of audio (and more recently video) data that can be played as soon as it is received, avoiding the necessity of downloading an entire file before it can be played. Streaming audio became popular in 1995 with the debut of Progressive Network's (now RealNetworks) RealAudio streaming codec, which created streaming audio content that could be played using the company's RealAudio Player software. There are now a number of different streaming audio and video technologies in use, and a wide variety of different Web-based media players that can be used to play streaming media. The two most frequently encountered streaming formats are those offered by RealNetwork and Microsoft, so many webcasters offer streaming programs in both formats.

Streaming broadcasts employ a technique known as *buffering* to avoid broadcast interruptions due to bandwidth fluctuations. The initial portion of the broadcast downloads before the broadcast starts playing, creating a buffer or store that can be drawn on to compensate for differences between transmission and playback rates. If the difference becomes too great, the buffer will be exhausted and the broadcast will stop until the buffer can refill with data, a process known as rebuffering.

Many radio stations were quick to offer streaming Internet broadcasts, now popularly referred to as webcasts. Thousands of different radio stations offer streaming broadcasts from around the world over the Internet. Figure 7.19 shows a small portion of Apple's iTunes media player radio station listing. In addition to the webcasting of conventional terrestrial radio broadcasts, a number of sources now offer webcasts available via the Internet only. Setting up a Web-based Internet radio station is not very complicated, and the number of Internet-only stations may soon outnumber the number of terrestrial radio stations.

Streaming media may be delivered via one of two different methods: live and on-demand. *Live streaming* makes the broadcast available only during a certain time period, such as the time frame concurrent with a live radio broadcast, whereas *on-demand streaming* makes a broadcast available on user request. Many streaming radio broadcasts are first available as a live stream and then later archived for on-demand use. Figure 7.20 shows an on-demand listing for a previous live broadcast of a National Public Radio's "All Things Considered" radio show. Users can listen to

Figure 7.19 Internet Radio Station Listing

the entire broadcast at their convenience, or click any of the story hyperlinks to listen to shorter story segments.

Embedded Audio

Audio files can also be embedded in Web pages to create background music. Various browsers' ability to handle audio varies greatly and depends on a number of different variables, including the plug-ins installed in the browser, whether the computer is equipped with a soundcard and the type of soundcard installed, whether sound settings are enabled, whether the system has speakers, and so on. The huge number of variables creates a high likelihood that some viewers will not be able to enjoy embedded audio on a Web page.

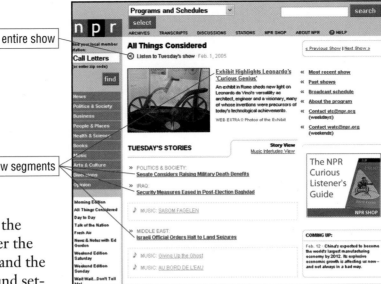

Figure 7.20 On-Demand Program Listing

Musical Instrument Digital Interface (MIDI) audio file format digital audio format that contains musical instructions rather than an actual sound recording

The ***Musical Instrument Digital Interface (MIDI) audio file format*** is often used for embedding background music on Web pages because MIDI files are usually very small. Their compact size is due to the fact that MIDI files contain musical instructions rather than an actual sound recording. For that reason, the MIDI format cannot be used to record nonmusical sound, such as voice. Many people find background audio intrusive, so it should be used only in the appropriate circumstances. In most cases, it is preferable to add a link to an audio file so that viewers can determine whether they want to hear the audio or not.

Concept Review 3 Audio

1. What is a codec?
2. What is a sampling rate?
3. What is streaming audio?

Skill Review 3 Download and Listen to a Music File

(Note: Ask your instructor if you have permission to download and save files to your computer or network location. If you do not have permission, ask your instructor where you should save the file you download for this exercise. In order to listen to audio files your computer must be equipped with a sound card and speakers or earphones.)

1. Download an audio file by completing the following steps:
   a. In Internet Explorer, type **www.mididb.com** in the Address bar and then press Enter.

b. Click the <u>Rock</u> hyperlink at the top of the page to open the Rock category of MIDI songs. *(Note: When you are finished with this exercise you can return to this page and pick any category you want to download additional songs.)*

Step 1b

c. Scroll down the Rock page and click the <u>Ace</u> hyperlink.

d. Right-click the <u>How Long.mid</u> hyperlink and then click Save Target As.

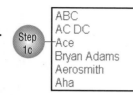

Step 1c

Step 1d

e. Use the Save As dialog box to browse to and select a folder in which to save the MIDI file. Click the Save button after selecting a folder. *(Note: Be sure to remember or write down the folder location so that you can find it again in Step 2.)*

f. If necessary, click the Close button when the Download complete dialog box appears.

2. Use the Windows Media Player to play the song you just downloaded by completing the following steps:

a. Click Start, click All Programs, and then click Windows Media Player to open it.

b. Press Ctrl+O to launch the Open dialog box.

c. Use the Open dialog box to browse to the MIDI file you downloaded in Step 1. Click the MIDI file name so that it appears in the *File name* text box and then click the Open button.

Stop | Play/Pause

Step 2d

d. The song should begin playing. You can stop the song by clicking the Stop button, and start it again by clicking the Play button. When the Play button is enabled, clicking it again will pause a song. *(Note: If another program opens to play the song, follow the instructions in Step 3 to make Windows Media Player the default player for your media files. If Windows Media Player opens but you cannot hear anything, try the troubleshooting steps in Step 4.)*

3. a. Make sure Windows Media Player is closed.

b. Click Start, then click Control Panel.

c. In the Control Panel window, click the Control Panel Home hyperlink, then click the Programs option. *(Note: Be careful to click the large word Programs and not the smaller phrases underneath.)*

d. In the Default Programs category, click the Set Your Default Programs hyperlink.

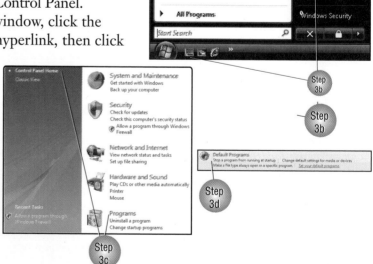

Step 3b

Step 3b

Step 3d

Step 3c

e. Select Windows Media Player from the list of programs, click Set This Program As Default, and click OK.

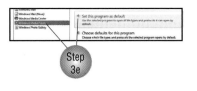

Step 3e

f. Close the Control Panel window, navigate to the folder containing the file you wish to play, and double-click the file to launch Windows Media Player and automatically play the file.

4. Try the following steps if you experience a problem listening to the song:

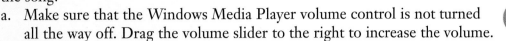

Step 4b   Step 4a

a. Make sure that the Windows Media Player volume control is not turned all the way off. Drag the volume slider to the right to increase the volume.

b. Make sure the volume has not been muted by checking the mute button. If the button appears with a small red circle the sound is muted. Click the button to un-mute.

c. Make sure that your speakers or headphones are plugged in.

d. If your speakers or earphones have an on/off control, and/or a volume control, make sure that they are turned on and that the volume is loud enough for you to hear.

e. Check to see if the computer you are using has a sound card by clicking Start, and clicking All Programs, clicking Accessories, clicking System Tools, and then clicking System Information. When the System Information window appears, click the Components plus sign (+) to expand it and then click *Sound Device*. If a sound card is installed, details will appear on the right side of the window.

Step 4e

f. Close the Windows Media Player and the System Information window when you are finished.

Animated Content

The process used to create the impression of animation or motion on a Web page is the same process used to produce the motion effect seen in film or video. Images with slight changes rapidly display one after the other, and the slight changes in each image or change in image location trick the human eye into thinking that it is viewing a single image, producing the illusion of motion. Figure 7.21 illustrates a bouncing ball animation created by using twelve separate frames. Each frame displays an image of the ball in a slightly different location than the previous frame. For Web animation, the most frequently used frame speed is 12 frames per second (fps). Using the 12 fps frame rate would show the ball in Figure 7.21 moving across the screen from point A to point B in one second. Higher fps rates, such as those used in video and film, create more lifelike animation but produce larger file sizes.

Web developers can use a number of different technologies to implement animation effects on Web pages, including JavaScript, Java Applets, animated GIF images, Flash and Shockwave movies, and the different video formats. How a browser handles animated content depends on a number of different factors, including the browser version, the plug-ins installed, the browser configuration settings for dealing with animated multimedia content, and the different helper applications installed on the computer. Figure 7.22 shows the

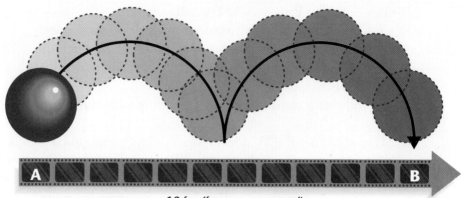

12 fps (frames per second)

Figure 7.21 Bouncing Ball Animation Effect

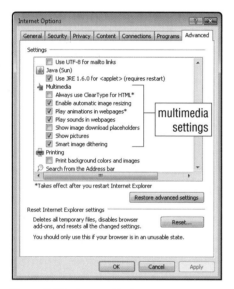

Figure 7.22 Internet Explorer Multimedia Options

multimedia settings in Internet Explorer on the Advanced tab of the Internet Options dialog box. Because of all the variables and different configuration possibilities, a movie may play inside a browser on one computer and play inside a helper application using another computer. If the appropriate plug-ins or helper applications are unavailable, animated multimedia may not play at all. As mentioned earlier, if the appropriate plug-in is unavailable the user may be prompted to visit a Web site to download and install the missing plug-in.

JavaScript

JavaScript is a scripted programming language that resides within an HTML document. The use of JavaScript enables a browser to change page content dynamically in response to viewer input. Mouse-over events/actions and form validation are two examples of the types of interactive functions that JavaScript can enable. Mouse-over events trigger actions when certain events take place, such as rolling the mouse over a button. Form validation checks forms and prompts users for any information that is lacking or incorrectly filled out. More recently, JavaScript has been combined with HTML and CSS-P (Cascading Style Sheets-Positioning) to create dynamic HTML (DHTML). Rollover images and navigation bars on Web pages are examples of DHTML that you may already be familiar with. DHTML-enabled images and navigation bars change their appearance when they are clicked or when the cursor is rolled over them. The Web developer places JavaScript between script tags (`<script>`) in the header region (and sometimes body section) of an HTML document, as shown in Figure 7.23.

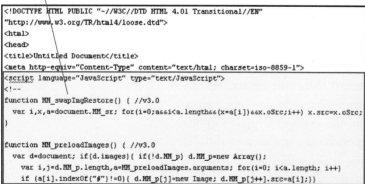

Figure 7.23 Rollover JavaScript

JavaScript is supported by most browsers, but DHTML is supported only by the latest browser versions (versions 4.x and up).

Java Applets

Java applets are small applications (programs) created using the Java programming language. Java applet code embedded in Web pages provides interactivity, which can include audio and video. Java applets can be used to create calculators, games, and other interactive tools for Web sites, as well as any number of interesting animation and audio effects. Although programming Java applets is fairly complicated, installing and using them is not. Java applets are available through a number of sites on the Internet for free or for a small license fee, as shown in Figure 7.24, and installation is often as simple as copying and pasting the applet code into a HTML document.

Java applet small application (program) created using the Java programming language

Animated GIF Files

Animated GIF files can be created using the GIF89a image format. A software program known as GIF animator is used to stitch together a series of GIF images as shown in Figure 7.25. The software saves the final product as a single GIF image file. The animated GIF contains instructions for browsers, including information about the frame rate to be used for displaying the images stored in the animated GIF, whether the image loops (replays automatically), and so on. GIF animations are usually of fairly short duration because the more images used in creating a GIF animation, the larger the file size. Web developers usually create longer animations using vector-based animation tools, such as Flash or Shockwave. GIF animations do not contain sound and are not interactive.

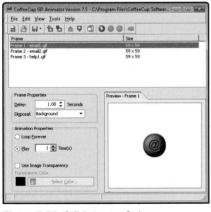

Figure 7.25 GIF Animator Software Program Showing Animated GIF Component Images

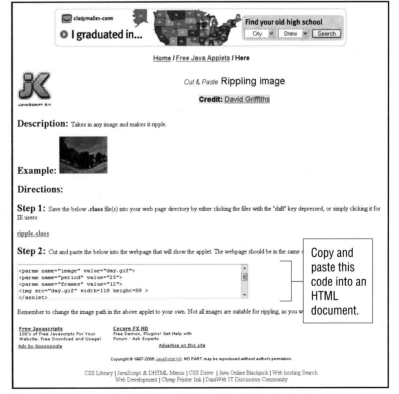

Figure 7.24 Free Java Applet Source Code and Installation Instructions

Internet Protocol Television (IPTV)

Expectations are high for a new alternative to the cable television transmission into homes. An emerging technology called Internet Protocol Television (IPTV) can deliver television programming over conventional copper telephone wires using broadband xDSL technology, allowing telephone companies to compete head-to-head with cable TV companies for viewers. Microsoft is supporting these efforts with their Microsoft® TV Internet Protocol Television (IPTV) Edition software platform. To take advantage of the Microsoft IPTV service, viewers need to install a set-top box running Windows CE, the Windows operating system designed for consumer electronics devices. An external 80 GB hard drive attached to the set-top box can be used to save up to 150 hours of programming. A router connects to a telephone line and sends signals to the set-top box through either a wired or a wireless connection. Unlike cable TV, IPTV only transmits one channel at a time, so telephone lines do not require the massive bandwidth capacity available with coaxial cable. While a cable TV cable delivers numerous channels simultaneously to a set-top box, IPTV only delivers one channel at a time. IPTV viewers will not notice any difference when channel surfing because the lag between the time they select a station and the time it is transmitted from a programming data center is only 200 milliseconds. IPTV offers the potential for a number of software-driven features, including interactivity. One potential drawback to wider acceptance of IPTV is that the increasingly popular High Definition Television (HDTV) requires vast amounts of bandwidth not available through conventional ADSL connections. Supporters of IPTV do not see this as a long-term problem because newer xDSL technologies such as ADSL+ promise speeds many times faster than conventional xDSL and will therefore support HDTV. Cable companies plan to fight the threat posed by IPTV by offering Internet telephony over their cable networks. Both cable companies and telephone service providers are seeking to increase revenues by being able to provide consumers with what in telecom industry terms is known as the "triple-play": voice, data, and video. IPTV certainly provides a cheaper alternative to building cable networks in new areas, and if the technology meets with consumer approval, it may one day rival and even surpass cable TV as a means of delivering television programming into homes.

Sources: "Interactive TV poised for rollout." www.cnn.com/2005/TECH/02/14/interactive.tv.ap/index.html
"The Battle For Broadband." www.spectrum.ieee.org/WEBONLY/publicfeature/jan05/0105wbro.html
"IPTV News Net." www.iptvnews.net. "Microsoft TV IPTV Edition." www.microsoft.com/tv/content/Solutions/IPTV/mstv_IPTV_Overview.mspx

Adobe Flash® and Shockwave® Players

vector-based animation animation method that uses mathematical values to describe images instead of saving them in individual frames

keyframes important reference-point frames used in Flash animations

tween frames the frames located between keyframes in Flash (and other) animations

scalable when an image can be enlarged or reduced without suffering a loss in quality

Flash and Shockwave are two very popular *vector-based animation* applications used to create Web page animation. Vector-based animations use mathematical values to describe images instead of saving them in individual frames. For example, the ball animation shown in Figure 7.22 could be created in Flash or Shockwave using vector-based beginning and ending *keyframes*. The software would create the intermediate frames between the keyframes, known as *tween frames*, by describing any changes to the ball and the ball location that occur between the first keyframe and the last keyframe. The end result would be an identical animation, but the Flash file would be much smaller than a corresponding animation created using bitmap images. Another advantage of vector-based animations is that they are *scalable*, meaning that they can be enlarged or reduced without suffering a loss of image quality.

A Flash or Shockwave file plays inside a browser window and can be streamed so that the animation begins playing before the entire file downloads. Flash and Shockwave animations will often feature an introductory animation known as a preloader that informs viewers that content is downloading before it begins playing as shown in Figure 7.26. Flash and Shockwave can also incorporate

Figure 7.26 Flash Preloader Animation

bitmap images and video and audio content, and can be used to create interactive animations.

More browsers support Flash, with Adobe claiming that more than 98 percent of browsers in current use feature the Flash plug-in necessary to play Flash animations. All current mainstream browsers come with the Flash plug-in installed. Shockwave is not as well supported as Flash, with about 52 percent of browsers having the Shockwave plug-in installed. Flash animations are authored using the Adobe Flash program and feature the .swf extension, while Shockwave animations are created using Adobe Director with files containing .dcr extensions. Shockwave is in some ways more full featured than Flash and is often used for creating more complex animations.

Macromedia, the company that originally developed Flash and Shockwave technologies and a multitude of software applications including Dreamweaver and Director, was acquired by Adobe in late 2006. You may see these technologies and software programs referred to as Macromedia or Abode products for example, Macromedia Flash or Adobe Flash.

Video

Digital video is the digital equivalent of the motion picture film used to record real-life motion pictures. Digital video movies use a variety of different video file formats. Table 7.3 lists the most commonly encountered digital video formats on the Internet. As with digital audio programs, users can download and view video movies, or stream them from live events or archived video. When played, video may appear within a browser window or in the screen of a helper application such as the Windows Media Player, RealNetwork's RealPlayer, or Apple's QuickTime Player. Streaming video employs a buffer, and bandwidth fluctuations may cause interruptions if transmission rate cannot keep up with the playback rate. When that happens, a buffering message or icon like the one from Windows Media Player shown in Figure 7.27 will appear. For that reason, a broadband connection is recommended for the best results in viewing streaming video broadcasts.

Table 7.3 Popular Digital Video Formats

Format	File Extension
Advanced Systems Format	.asf
AVI (Audio Video Interleave)	.avi
MPEG-1 (Moving Pictures Expert Group)	.mpg
QuickTime Format	.mov
RealVideo Format	.rm, .ram

Figure 7.27 Windows Media Buffering Icon

Concept Review 4 Animated Content

1. What is the best kind of Internet connection for viewing streaming video?
2. What can cause interruptions to a streaming video broadcast?

1. Play a game online by completing the following steps:

   a. In Internet Explorer, type **www.shockwave.com** in the Address bar and then press Enter.

   b. Click the <u>Jigsaws</u> hyperlink on the left side of the page.

   c. Click the Play Free Online button. If an Information Bar dialog box appears alerting you that a pop-up was blocked, click Close.

   d. When the puzzle pieces appear, right-click inside the Shockwave window to display a shortcut menu. Not all the commands will be active. Click the About Shockwave Player command to visit the Shockwave site in a new Web page. Visit the page to learn more about Shockwave. Close the page when you are finished and return to the puzzle. *(Some Shockwave movies will contain a longer list of active commands. The commands that are available are determined by the Shockwave content developer.)*

   e. The puzzle contains a number of different commands that allow you to customize the game. Experiment by using these commands to rearrange the puzzle pieces, change the number of pieces, preview the completed puzzle, change the background color, move a number of pieces at once, and so on.

   Step 1d

   f. Move puzzle pieces by dragging them to the desired location.

   g. Click the Close button on the title bar to close the puzzle.

   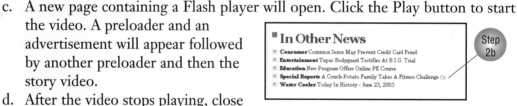

   Step 1e

2. View a streaming video by completing the following steps:

   a. In Internet Explorer, type **wcco.com/homepage** in the Address bar and then press Enter.

   b. Click the hyperlink for any story followed by a video camera icon.

   c. A new page containing a Flash player will open. Click the Play button to start the video. A preloader and an advertisement will appear followed by another preloader and then the story video.

   ■ **In Other News**
   - **Consumer** Common Sense May Prevent Credit Card Fraud
   - **Entertainment** Tupac Bodyguard Testifies At B.I.G. Trial
   - **Education** New Program Offers Online PE Course
   - **Special Reports** A Couch-Potato Family Takes A Fitness Challenge
   - **Water Cooler** Today In History - June 23, 2005

   Step 2b

   d. After the video stops playing, close Internet Explorer.

   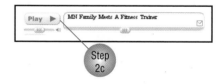

   Step 2c

Windows Media Player

Windows Media Player comes installed with Windows Vista and can be launched by clicking Start, clicking All Programs, and then clicking Windows Media Player. If Windows Media Player has been associated with a particular MIME type, it will automatically open to begin playing a media file once an associated file type has been double-clicked in the Computer window or in Windows Explorer. As a multifunctional media player, Windows Media Player can:

- Play music located on CDs, computer drives, or other media
- Play Internet radio programs
- View DVDs and VCDs (a DVD drive must be installed for DVD play)
- Play Internet video
- Rip songs from CDs, store them on your computer, and burn them to a CD-R
- Create playlists and organize media content
- Synchronize content to portable devices

Users with experience using previous versions of Windows Media Player will notice the menu bar does not display by default. To display the menu bar (which is hidden by default in Windows Media Player 1.1 which is installed with Vista), click the Library tab at the top of the Windows Media Player window, click the Layout Options menu, then click Show Classic Menus to turn on the old style menu bar. Media files can be opened in the media player by clicking File on the menu bar and then clicking Open or Open URL. The Now Playing tab at the top of the player can be used to view visualization and song information when playing songs as shown in Figure 7.28. The Library tab can be used to create song playlists and organize content. The Rip tab enables the user to copy tracks from an audio CD. Once the tracks are copied and stored on the computer, the user can then burn or copy the

tracks to a CD-R by clicking the Burn tab. The Sync tab enables the user to synchronize content to a portable media player. Moving the mouse cursor over any tab causes a small arrow to appear underneath the tab. Click the small arrow to display a submenu with various commands and options.

The button to the right of the Sync button changes to display the selected music store, the Windows Media Guide, or a list of online stores as shown in Figure 7.29. Click the small arrow under the tab to change between online stores and the Media Guide. Choosing the

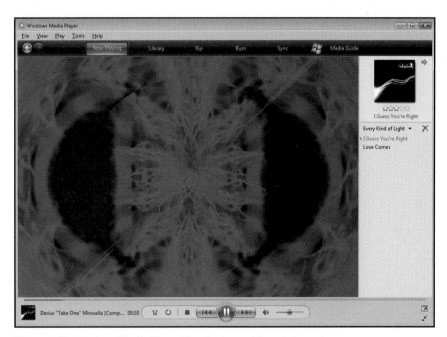

Figure 7.28 Windows Media Player Visualization and Song Information

Figure 7.29 Windows Media Player Online Store Submenu

Browse All Online Stores option displays a list of online music stores. Click one to visit the store and purchase music, as shown in Figure 7.30. While all online music store differ, conceptually they are similar in that clicking an album link will normally display more information about the artist as well as list album songs. Clicking a song will normally play a short clip. To purchase albums and individual songs by credit card, click the Buy or Add To Cart button.

Displaying the Media Guide and then clicking the Internet Radio link displays a list of radio stations sorted by genre as shown in Figure 7.31. Browse the categories, then click the name of a radio station to view the station options, which may include Add To My Stations, Visit Website, Visit Website To Play, or Play. Click Add To My Stations to add the station as a favorite, which Windows Media Players calls My Stations. Click Visit Website to open an Internet Explorer window and view the radio station's Web site. Click Play to play the radio station. Some stations play directly in Windows Media Player while others open an Internet Explorer window and play music from a Web page. Click the small arrow under the Media Guide tab and select Media Guide to return to the main Media Guide page where you can select other media types, such as cartoons, high definition, movies, and games, as shown in Figure 7.32. Just as with radio stations, some video content plays directly in the Media Player while others launch a Web page to play the content. When

Click a Buy button to purchase albums and individual songs.

Figure 7.30 MSN Music Store Viewed in Windows Media Player

viewing a video in Windows Player, click the View Full Screen icon at the bottom right corner of the player window to view the video in full screen mode. Press the Esc key to return to the previous screen size. The Media Guide view functions somewhat like a Web browser as clicking the Back and Forward buttons on the left side of the toolbar navigate through your previous views.

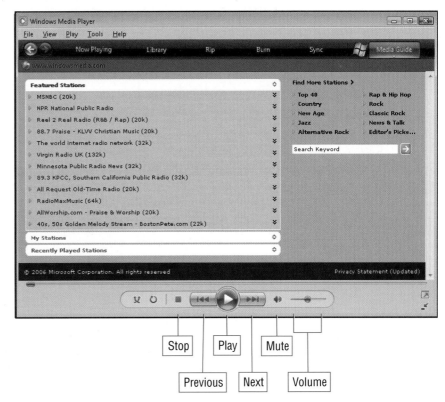

Figure 7.31 Windows Media Player Radio Mode

Figure 7.32 Radio Station Information

Concept Review 5 Windows Media Player

1. What can the Windows Media Player be used for?
2. How can an online store be changed?
3. How can a radio station be saved to the My Stations group?

Skill Review 5 Use Windows Media Player to Listen to Internet Radio Stations

(Note: This exercise is based on Windows Media Player version 11.)

1. Click Start, click All Programs, and then click Windows Media Player to open the Windows Media Player.
2. If necessary, click the small arrow under the far right tab and select Media Guide.

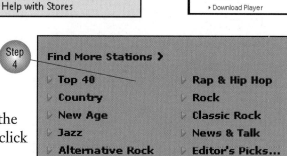

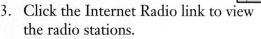

3. Click the Internet Radio link to view the radio stations.
4. Click any of the categories in the Find More Stations section to view station in that genre.

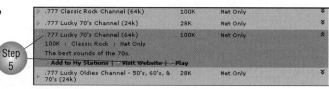

5. When you find a station you like click the station name to view the options, then click the Play button. There may be a short delay during the initial buffering process, noted at the bottom of the player, before playback begins. *(Note: If you have a problem hearing a station refer to Skill Review 3, Step 4 for troubleshooting steps.)*
6. If a dialog box appears asking permission to play the content, click Yes.
7. If a Web page opened to play the station, click the Windows Media Player taskbar icon to bring Windows Media Player back into view.
8. Click the Back button in the toolbar to return to the Internet Radio guide.
9. If necessary, click the station name to view the options. Add the station to your My Stations by clicking the Add To My Stations link under the station's name.

10. Return to the Internet Radio guide by repeating Steps 2 and 3.
11. Click My Stations to view the list of your favorite stations, which may consist entirely of the single station you added in Step 9.
12. Close Windows Media Player by clicking the Close button in the top right corner of the player window.

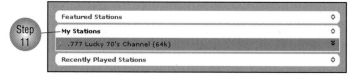

Chapter Summary

- In the Web context, the term *multimedia* refers to the use of more than one type of media on a Web page, such as any combination of text, graphics, animated graphics, video, audio, or even hypertext.

- Web-page viewing can become an interactive experience, with Flash, Shockwave, or Java applets letting browsers accept user input to control the viewing experience.

- Anyone designing Web pages should carefully consider why multimedia is being used, and whether it will enhance the viewer experience or needlessly complicate it.

- Web browsers are HTML interpreters, and they must look for help from plug-ins or helper applications in displaying any type of media beyond text and images.

- Web page images are not saved as part of a Web page document. Instead, they are located in separate files, with an HTML image tag (<img>) and source attribute (SRC) in the HTML document directing the browser to the image file location so that the browser can retrieve the file and display it as part of the Web page.

- When a Web page designer creates a Web page, it is important to keep image file sizes relatively small to ensure that Web pages do not take too long to load.

- The ideal image format for the Web uses compression techniques to produce small file sizes and is supported by most browsers.

- Animated GIFs create an illusion of motion by instructing a browser to load two or more images in succession.

- Using images on a Web page without permission may be a violation of copyright law.

- Several search engines, including Google and Yahoo!, enable users to search for images on the Web by clicking a hyperlink or button on the search engine that enables image-only searching.

- Many Web sites created and maintained by U.S. government agencies include images that can be freely used for private and commercial purposes.

- A number of Web sites offer copyright-free, royalty-free, or public domain images and clip art that can be used on Web pages you create.

- The compression technologies used to *compress* and *decompress* audio files are often referred to as codecs, derived from the terms compression and decompression.

- Lossy codecs remove irrelevant or redundant data from audio files in such a way that the average person will not notice any difference in the sound quality between an uncompressed and compressed audio file.

- Audio files saved for archival purposes use lossless compression formats or uncompressed formats since those methods maintain all of the original audio data.

- Two important factors determine the quality and size of digital audio encoding: the sampling rate measures how frequently samples of an audio waveform are recorded per second and the bit rate is the number of bits used per second to record samples.

- Variable bit rate encoding (VBR) features a continuously changing bit rate that increases or decreases depending on the complexity of the content being encoded.

- The MP3 audio file format is far and away the most popular audio file format in use on the Internet today.

- A typical MP3 file may be 10 percent of the size of a corresponding uncompressed WAV file.

- Software and portable (hardware) MP3 players now handle a number of different audio file formats and are often referred to as media players.

- In P2P systems, client computers (peers) acting as miniservers can share files directly with each other, vastly increase the number of files potentially available for sharing.

- Streaming works by transmitting audio (and more recently video) data so that it can be played as soon as it arrives, avoiding the necessity of downloading an entire file before it can be played.

- Many radio stations were quick to offer streaming Internet broadcasts, now popularly referred to as webcasts. It is now possible to listen to thousands of different radio stations from around the world over the Internet.

- Streaming media uses two different delivery methods: live and on-demand. Live streaming makes a broadcast available only during a certain time period, such as at the same time as a live radio broadcast, whereas on-demand streaming makes a broadcast available on user request.

- Audio files embedded in Web pages create background music, but many people find background audio intrusive, so it should be used only in the appropriate circumstances.

- A number of different technologies can be used to implement animation effects on Web pages including JavaScript, Java Applets, animated GIF images, Flash and Shockwave movies, and different video formats.

- Adobe Flash and Shockwave are two very popular vector-based animation applications used to create Web animation.

- Vector-based animations use mathematical values to describe images instead of saving them in individual frames.

- Flash and Shockwave files play inside a browser window and can be streamed so that they begin playing before the entire file downloads.

- Digital video is the digital equivalent of the motion picture film used to record real-life motion pictures. Digital video movies can be saved in one of numerous video file formats.

- If Windows Media Player has been associated with a particular MIME type, it will automatically open to begin playing a media file once an associated file type has been double-clicked in the My Computer window or in Windows Explorer.

Key Terms

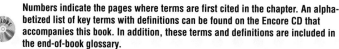

Numbers indicate the pages where terms are first cited in the chapter. An alphabetized list of key terms with definitions can be found on the Encore CD that accompanies this book. In addition, these terms and definitions are included in the end-of-book glossary.

ActiveX control, *205*

animated GIF, *210*

bitmap, *209*

bit rate, *214*

browser extensions, *204*

buffering, *218*

codec, *214*

GIF image, *209*

helper application, *204*

interlacing, *209*

Java applet, *223*

JPEG image, *210*

Additional quiz questions are available on the Encore CD that accompanies this book as well as on the Internet Resource Center for this title at www.emcp.net/Internet2e.

Multiple Choice

Indicate the correct answer for each question or statement.

1. Vector-based animation
   a. saves image data as a grid of picture elements.
   b. uses mathematical values to describe images.
   c. is not scalable.
   d. is not suitable for color animations.

2. Helper applications are
   a. the same as plug-ins.
   b. stand-alone programs that a browser can use to display content.
   c. a MIME type.
   d. only used by Internet Explorer.

3. The size of a Web page with images ideally should be no greater than
   a. 100 KB.
   b. 500 KB.
   c. 1 MB.
   d. 350 KB.

4. Image files that store image information as a grid composed of tiny picture elements are known as
   a. pixel images files.
   b. vector-based image files.
   c. bitmap files.
   d. Flash files.

5. The best type of Web image format for drawings or illustrations is
   a. GIF (.gif).
   b. JPEG (.jpeg).
   c. TIFF (.tif).
   d. PNG (.png).

6. The best type of Web image file format for photographs is
   a. GIF (.gif).
   b. JPEG (.jpeg).
   c. TIFF (.tif).
   d. PNG (.png).

7. The GIF format supports _____ colors.
   a. 256
   b. 512
   c. 16 million
   d. 1,024

8. JPEG images use a
   a. lossless image compression technology.
   b. lossy image compression technology.
   c. combination lossy/lossless image compression technology.
   d. None of the above

9. PNG images are only supported by browser versions
   a. 4.x and above.
   b. 5.x and above.
   c. 6.x and above.
   d. All browser versions support PNG images.

10. Which of the following is a lossless audio file format?
    a. Windows Media Audio (.wma)
    b. Vorbis (.ogg)
    c. MP3 (.mp3)
    d. WAV (.wav)

True/False

Indicate whether each statement is true or false.

1. Java applets are small applications (programs) created using the Java programming language.
2. Interlacing allows images to be combined.
3. Transparent images allow the background color of a Web page to show through a selected portion of an image.
4. Most browsers do not need any extensions in order to display multimedia content.
5. Browsers determine how to deal with a file by looking at its MIME type.
6. Almost all browsers come with the Flash plug-in installed.
7. GIF images use lossy compression.
8. The three different image formats most suitable for Web use are the GIF, JPEG, and PNG formats.
9. MP3 files can approximate CD-quality sound to the naked ear.
10. Copying tracks from an audio CD is known as ripping.

Virtual Perspectives

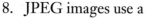

1. In a somewhat ironic role reversal, some cable TV providers are now providing telephony services over cable networks, while some telephone service providers are providing television service over telephone lines. The companies are doing this to achieve the lucrative goal of being a single-source provider of voice, data, and video services to consumers. Research this issue, and discuss your feelings on how this competition may play out. Will one winner take all, will they end up sharing these markets, or is there another scenario that you think might take place?

2. Some of the most recent peer-to-peer file sharing networks use what is known as BitTorrent protocol. BitTorrent is particularly suited to the exchange of large files, such as movies and software programs. Although there is nothing inherently illegal about this type of file sharing arrangement, it has become popular with those seeking to share illegal copies of movies and television programs. Research BitTorrent and then discuss the current status of efforts to prevent the misuse of this type of file sharing network. What do you think can, or should, be done?

Internet Lab Projects

Download and Modify an Image (Requires Microsoft Word 2007)

1. If necessary, connect to the Internet, start Internet Explorer, and visit a Web page containing images.
2. Right-click inside an image, click Save Picture As, and save the image to your computer. *(Note: You can rename the image if you like. Be sure to remember where you saved it so you can find it again.)*
3. Start Word and create a new blank document.
4. Click the Office button then click Save As. In the Save As dialog box, name the document **ch7_project_1** and change the Save As Type menu option to *Web Page (*.htm, *.html)*. Be sure to note the location to where you are saving your file.
5. Click the Insert tab, locate the Illustrations command group, then click Picture. Locate the file you saved in Step 2 and then click the Insert button to insert the image in your HTML document.
6. Place the insertion point to the right of the image and repeat Step 5 to insert another copy of the image next to the first picture. *(Note: You will modify the second copy of the image and leave the first copy as is so that your instructor can observe the changes you made.)*
7. Click inside the second copy of the image to display the Picture Tools contextual tab group, then click the Format tab.
8. Use the Format tab commands to make the following modifications to the second copy of the image:
   - Crop the picture in half
   - Increase the brightness
   - Change the color to grayscale
   - Rotate the image 90 degrees to the left

   If you want to cancel any changes, click the Reset Picture button in the Adjust command group of the Format tab. To learn more about using any of these options, click the Microsoft Office Word Help icon above the Ribbon on the right side of the screen. Search the Help function using key terms for any options, such as *cropping*, *picture brightness*, *picture contrast*, and so on.
9. When you are finished modifying the image, save the document and then close it.

E-mail a Web Page Image

1. If necessary, connect to the Internet, start Internet Explorer, and visit a Web page containing images.
2. Right-click inside an image and then click E-mail Picture from the shortcut menu that appears. If an Internet Explorer Security dialog appears asking permission to perform the operation, click Allow.
3. Choose the Smaller: 640×480 option from the Picture Size menu in the Attach Files dialog box, then click Attach.
4. If your email client is configured for an email account, proceed to the next step.
5. Enter your e-mail address in the e-mail message *To* text box.
6. Change the Subject line to read *Image Attachment*.
7. Type a short note to yourself in the message body and then click the Send button to send the message.

8. Wait a minute or two and then click the Send/Receive button. Look for the message you just sent and double-click it to open it in its own message window.

9. Right-click on the image file name in the *Attach* line and then click Save As. Use the Save Attachment As dialog box to save the attached image to your computer.

Project 3 — Download and View a Movie in the Windows Media Player

1. If necessary, connect to the Internet.
2. Start Internet Explorer.
3. Type **www1.jsc.nasa.gov/er/seh/movies.html** in the Address bar and then press Enter.
4. Scroll down the page until you come to the movie description area. Pick a movie you like and then download it by right-clicking on the (.avi) hyperlink and then clicking Save Target As. Use the Save As dialog box to locate a folder for the file. Click the Save button to begin the download process. *(Note: .avi is the file extension for Audio Video Interleave, a Microsoft movie format.)*
5. Start the Windows Media Player.
6. Press Ctrl+O and use the Open dialog box to locate and select the file you just downloaded. Click the Open button after selecting the file.
7. The movie should begin playing in the player. Use the Stop, Pause, and Play buttons at the bottom of the player to control the movie.
8. Close Windows Media Player.

Internet Research Activities

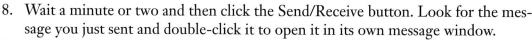

Activity 1 — Research More about IPTV

Write or type a short paper addressing the following:
1. Where is IPTV currently in use?
2. How many IPTV viewers are there worldwide?
3. How successful have IPTV trials been?
4. Describe any new technological breakthroughs for IPTV.

Activity 2 — Explore Podcasting

Write a short tutorial describing the process of creating a podcast, and another tutorial describing the process involved in listening to a podcast.

Activity 3 — Net Challenge

Obtain two or more music (audio) CDs. Use the Windows Media Player to rip the tracks from the CDs to your computer. Create a playlist of your favorite songs from the CDs you ripped, and then burn the playlist to a new recordable CD (CD-R or CD-RW). Label the new CD.

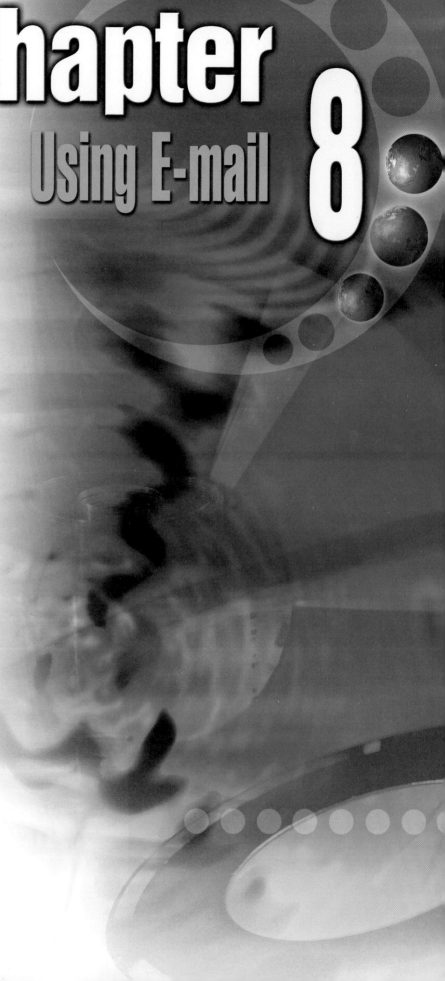

Chapter
Using E-mail 8

Learning Objectives

- Explain how e-mail works.

- Add or edit Windows Mail e-mail accounts and specify different Windows Mail options.

- Send and receive e-mail messages.

- Print and save e-mail messages.

- Differentiate between emoticons, acronyms, and text shortcuts.

- Manage Windows Mail folders.

- Explain how to use Windows Contacts.

- Find messages and contacts in Windows Mail.

- Use a Web-based e-mail service (webmail).

Living on the Net

Bob has been using e-mail since he first started using the Internet. In fact, e-mail was the reason he became interested in the Internet in the first place. The first e-mail client he used featured a command-line interface. It was not difficult to use, but he was happy to switch to a GUI e-mail client when it became available because he found point-and-click interfaces much easier to use.

Currently, Bob has four different e-mail accounts. He has one account through his office that he uses for any work-related correspondence. He is careful not to misuse the account, because his employer sometimes monitors messages. Bob also has an e-mail account provided by his ISP; he uses this ISP account for most of his personal correspondence needs. His third account is a free webmail account with Yahoo! Mail that he uses when he is traveling. Because it is Web-based, he can use the account wherever he has Internet access. Not only is this convenient, but it saves money because he does not have to dial a long-distance phone number to access his ISP account when he is out of town or overseas. Bob has another webmail account that he

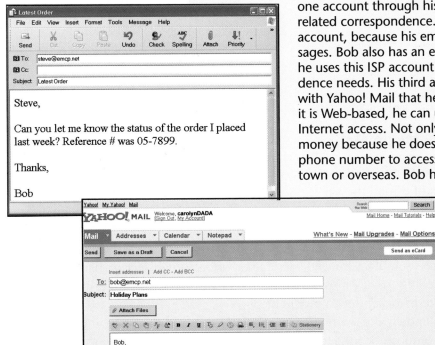

uses when he participates in discussion lists and newsgroups. He uses this address because he wants to keep the amount of spam that he receives in his ISP e-mail account inbox to a minimum. If he gets into a flame war or starts getting too much spam, he just starts a new webmail account and uses that address to resubscribe to any discussion lists or newsgroups.

The one big drawback to e-mail that irritates Bob is the amount of unsolicited messages, or spam, that he receives. He sometimes finds it hard to find legitimate messages among all the spam cluttering his inbox. Bob does what he can to minimize the amount of spam he receives, but hopes that some of the technological and legal efforts to defeat spam will soon make that job easier.

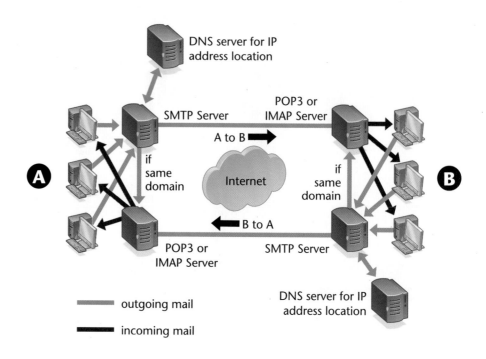

Figure 8.1 E-mail Message Routing

E-mail (Electronic Mail)

e-mail client a software program used to compose, send, and receive e-mail messages, such as Windows Mail or Eudora

Simple Mail Transfer Protocol (SMTP) the protocol used to send e-mail messages

Tech Demo 8-1
E-mail

E-mail, or electronic mail, is the most popular Internet application. Users send billions of e-mail messages every day, with those messages traveling from one computer to another through the Internet. E-mail messages are transmitted using packet switching technology that divides each e-mail message into packets that travel various routes to a destination where the packets are reassembled. Special servers known as e-mail servers handle e-mail traffic. Figure 8.1 shows a simplified diagram of the path e-mail messages take from sender to recipient.

Programs known as *e-mail clients*, popularly referred to as e-mail programs, are used to compose, send, and receive e-mail messages. Currently the most popular e-mail clients are Microsoft Outlook and Outlook Express, though Outlook Express has been replaced with Windows Mail in the Windows Vista operating system. There are a number of other popular e-mail clients in current use such as Eudora and Mozilla Thunderbird.

When an e-mail message is sent, the message travels to an e-mail server on the sender's domain. The e-mail server examines the e-mail address to determine where to forward the message. An e-mail address has a two-part construction separated by an @ sign (at sign) as shown in Figure 8.2. The user name or local part appears to the left of the @ sign, and the part to the right of the @ sign contains the domain name. The protocol used to send e-mail messages is known as *Simple Mail Transfer Protocol (SMTP)*. When a message is sent, the originating SMTP server examines the

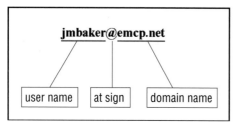

Figure 8.2 E-mail Address

e-mail address to determine the domain to which the message is addressed. If the SMTP server resides on the same domain as the message destination, the server will send the message to an incoming mail server for the domain. If the message is addressed to another domain, the SMTP server will contact a DNS server to find the IP address for the domain and route the message accordingly. Eventually, the incoming mail server on the destination domain will receive and reassemble the message packets.

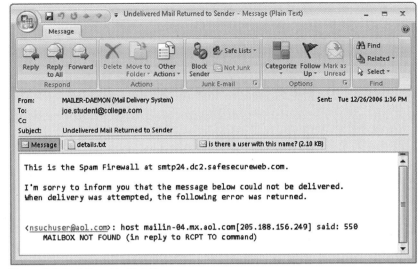

Figure 8.3 Undeliverable Mail Message

If the originating SMTP server cannot connect with the destination mail-server, the e-mail message will go into a queue or waiting list from which it is periodically resent. If attempts to send the message continue to fail, the sender will be sent a message letting them know there is a problem, usually after four hours. The originating server will continue to try to send the message for several days. If the message is still undeliverable after that time, the sender will receive a message informing them the message failed as shown in Figure 8.3.

Incoming e-mail servers generally handle messages using one of two different protocols: ***Post Office Protocol 3 (POP3)*** or ***Internet Message Access Protocol (IMAP)***. POP3 and IMAP differ in the way they handle incoming mail. With POP3, the e-mail client connects to the POP3 server and downloads the messages stored on the server to the user's local computer. After downloading the messages, the server usually erases the messages from its own storage unless the user's e-mail client has been configured to request that the messages remain on the server. With IMAP, the e-mail client enables the user to read and manipulate messages on the server without downloading the messages to a local machine. Unlike POP3 messages, IMAP messages remain on the IMAP server so users can access them from a variety of different computers. Most IMAP e-mail clients cache messages, so the user can view messages offline. Aside from POP3 and IMAP, some mail providers, such as Hotmail, let users receive mail through a standard e-mail client using the HTTP protocol.

Servers handle e-mail message attachments using the ***Multipurpose Internet Mail Extensions (MIME)*** protocol. The MIME protocol allows binary documents such as images, videos, and formatted text documents to be attached to an e-mail message. When the recipient opens the attachment, it will open in its native application if available on the recipient's machine.

Post Office Protocol 3 (POP3) an incoming mail protocol where the user's e-mail client connects to a POP3 server and downloads the messages stored on the server to the local computer

Internet Message Access Protocol (IMAP) an incoming mail protocol where e-mail messages are read and manipulated on the server without downloading them to a local machine

Multipurpose Internet Mail Extensions (MIME) protocol used to handle attachments to e-mail messages

Concept Review 1 E-mail (Electronic Mail)

1. Describe the process by which an e-mail message travels from sender to recipient.
2. Describe the difference in the way that POP3 and IMAP incoming mail servers work.
3. What happens if an SMTP server cannot find a destination POP3 or SMTP server right away?

1. Open the Google search engine Web site (www.google.com).
2. Use Google to find the home page URLs for the Eudora and Thunderbird e-mail clients. *(Note: You can substitute another e-mail client for either of these clients if your instructor suggests that you do so.)*
3. Visit each e-mail client's home page and follow the links to learn more about each client.
4. Conduct additional research to find more information about each client, particularly comparisons or reviews.
5. Use the information you gather to write a short essay (one to two double-spaced pages) describing which e-mail client you would choose to install on your computer if you decided not to use Windows Mail, the e-mail client included with the Windows Vista operating system. Support your choice with at least five different reasons.

Windows Mail

Tech Demo 8-2
Windows Mail

Microsoft includes the Windows Mail e-mail client as part of the default Windows Vista installation, replacing the older Outlook Express which was included with previous versions of Windows. Windows Mail includes several new features not present in Outlook Express, including spam and phishing filters. Windows Mail needs to be configured before it can be used to send and receive e-mail.

Windows Mail also offers a number of different preference settings users can choose, including font settings, the folder that the program will display on opening, how often the program will check the incoming mail server for new messages, whether or not the program plays a sound when new mail arrives, and so on.

Setting up a Windows Mail E-mail Account

The first time Windows Mail is started, a wizard will open to guide users along the set-up process. Before setting up Windows Mail for the first time, users should obtain the following information from their ISP:

- Account name and password

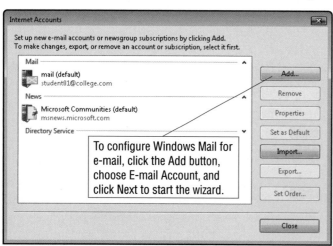

- Type of e-mail server (POP3, IMAP, HTTP)
- Name of the incoming and outgoing e-mail server to be used (not necessary for outgoing HTML)
- Whether or not their ISP requires Secure Password Authentication (SPA)

Once an e-mail account has been added to Windows Mail, new accounts can be added, or existing accounts changed, by clicking Tools on the menu bar and then clicking Accounts. This opens the Internet Accounts dialog box as shown in Figure 8.4.

Figure 8.4 Windows Mail Internet Accounts Dialog Box

To change Windows Mail e-mail account settings, click the Add button, click E-mail Account in the menu that appears, and click Next. This will launch a wizard which leads the reader step-by-step through the e-mail mail account set-up process as shown in Figure 8.5.

Once you have set up an e-mail account in Windows Mail, you can check the set up by selecting the account in the Mail category of the Internet Accounts dialog box and then clicking the Properties button. This opens the Properties dialog box, which contains a number of different tabs with different connection properties. The Servers tab in the Properties dialog box as shown in Figure 8.6 can also be used to set up an e-mail account in Windows Mail instead of using the wizard.

Figure 8.5 E-mail Account Wizard

Setting Windows Mail Options

Default Windows Mail options can be changed by clicking Tools on the menu bar and then clicking Options. This opens the Options dialog box as shown in Figure 8.7. The Options dialog box contains the following tabs: General, Read, Receipts, Send, Compose, Signatures, Spelling, Security, Connection, and Advanced, which you can choose from to set various options. Once the user chooses new options, clicking the Apply button confirms the changes and clicking OK closes the dialog box. Table 8.1 describes the options available under each tab.

The Windows Mail Window Layout Properties dialog box as shown in Figure 8.8, opened by choosing Layout from the View menu, can be used to change the default Windows Mail layout. This chapter assumes your Windows Mail layout is configured as shown in Figure 8.8.

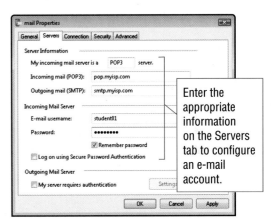

Figure 8.6 Windows Mail Properties Dialog Box with Servers Tab Selected

Figure 8.7 Windows Mail Options Dialog Box

Figure 8.8 Window Layout Properties Dialog Box

Table 8.1 Options Dialog Box Tab Options

Options Dialog Box Tab	Available Options
Advanced	Advanced options and maintenance button with access to settings for empty Deleted Items folder on exit, purge deleted messages when leaving IMAP folders, message clean up and compacting, and store file options
Compose	Font, stationery, and business card options
Connection	Dial-up and Internet connection options
General	New message notification, automatic display of folders with unread messages, message arrival sound, send and receive messages at startup, and message check interval options
Read	Mark message as read interval, automatic grouped message expansion, automatically download messages in Preview Pane, read all messages in plain text, show ToolTips for clipped items, highlight watched messages, and font and default coding options
Receipts	Request read receipts, never send return read receipts, always send return read receipts, notify for read receipt requests, and secure receipt options
Security	Virus protection, image download, encryption, and digital signature options
Send	Save sent messages to Sent Items folder, send messages immediately, automatically put reply addresses in Address Book, e-mail address auto-complete, include message in reply, reply to message in same format as sent, and HTML and plain text format options
Signatures	Add, create, and edit signature options
Spelling	Always check spelling, suggest replacement spelling, ignore uppercase words, ignore words with numbers, ignore original text in reply and forward messages, ignore Internet addresses, and language options

Concept
Review 2 Windows Mail ●

1. What information is needed to set up a Windows Mail e-mail account?
2. How can a Windows Mail e-mail account be added or changed?
3. How can Windows Mail default options be changed?

Skill
Review 2 Add a Windows Mail E-mail Account and Change Windows Mail Options

(Note: Before starting this exercise, ask your instructor to provide you with the account information you will need, such as your e-mail address, incoming server type, incoming and outgoing server addresses, and your e-mail account name and password.)

1. Set up an e-mail account in Windows Mail by completing the following steps:
   a. Start Windows Mail by clicking Start, clicking All Programs, and then clicking Windows Mail.
   b. Click Tools on the menu bar and then click Accounts to open the Internet Accounts dialog box.
   c. Click the Add button.

d. Select E-mail Account and click Next.

e. Type your name as you would like it to appear in the From field in an e-mail message in the Display Name text box and then click Next.

f. Type your e-mail address in the *E-mail address* text box and then click Next.

g. If necessary, click the down-pointing arrow and select the type of incoming mail server used by your ISP. Type your incoming and outgoing server addresses in the appropriate text boxes and then click Next. Check the Outgoing Server Requires Authentication checkbox if your instructor says it is necessary.

h. Type the account name and password provided by your ISP in the appropriate text boxes. Click the Remember password option to disable it if you are sharing a computer and then click Next.

i. Check the check box for Do Not Download My E-mail At This Time so Windows Mail will not immediately check for new mail when you click Finish. Click Finish to complete and close the wizard. The Internet Accounts dialog box will display your new account in the list on the Mail tab. *(Note: If more than one account is listed, select your new account and then click the Set as Default button to make it the default account.)*

j. Click the Close button to close the Internet Accounts dialog box.

2. Use the Windows Mail Options dialog box to add a signature to your e-mail messages by completing the following steps:

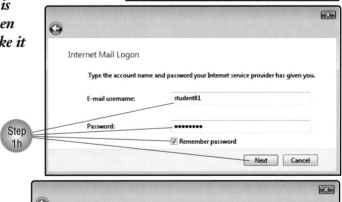

a. Click Tools on the menu bar and then click Options to open the Options dialog box.

b. Click the Signatures tab.

c. Click the New button.

d. Place a check mark in the *Add signatures to all outgoing messages* check box at the top of the window to enable that option.

e. Make sure the *Text* option is selected in the *Edit Signature* section.

f. Type your name in the Text box, press Enter to create a new line, and then type the city and state where you live. Click the OK button to close the dialog box. *(Note: When you create an e-mail message in the next exercise, the signature you just created will automatically appear below the body of the message.)*

Sending and Receiving E-mail

The Windows Mail menu bar and toolbar offer the commands necessary to send and receive e-mail messages, as well as those needed to perform related functions as shown in Figure 8.9. Right-clicking the mouse on messages and items onscreen will open a shortcut menu with applicable commands.

By default, Windows Mail opens with the Inbox selected in the Folders list. The message list displays mail that has been downloaded from the mail server. The chronological order used to display messages can be changed by clicking the Received column heading above the message list. Messages can be listed by sender in ascending (A-Z) or descending (Z-A) alphabetical order by clicking the From column heading. The preview pane displays the contents of the message selected in the message list.

Create and Send a Message

A new e-mail message can be created by clicking the Create Mail button, which opens a New Message window as shown in Figure 8.10. The New Message window can be expanded to fill the screen by clicking the Maximize button on the window title bar. The New Message window contains its own buttons and menu commands as shown in Figure 8.10.

The top portion of the New Message window enables the user to enter the message header information and contains the *To*, and *Cc* (carbon copy) text boxes, as well as the *Subject* text box. A *Bcc* (blind carbon copy) text box can be displayed by clicking View on the menu bar and then clicking All Headers. The message sender should type the applicable e-mail addresses in the *To*, *Cc*, and *Bcc* text boxes. A copy of the message will be sent to any e-mail address in the *Cc* and *Bcc* text boxes. The recipients of blind carbon copy messages (Bcc) will not be visible to other recipients. To send a message to more than one

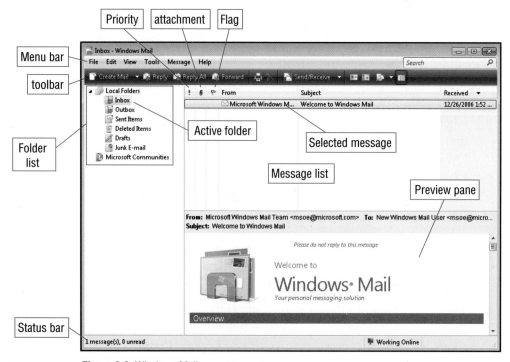

Figure 8.9 Windows Mail

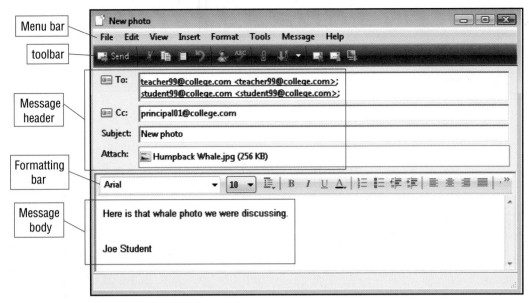

Figure 8.10 New Message Window

address, the user can separate each address using a comma (,) or a semicolon (;). Windows Mail will try to match any addresses in Windows Contacts to an address as it is being typed. Pressing the Enter button will confirm a proposed address. It is very important that e-mail addresses be entered without any errors because a single mistake will make it undeliverable.

The user can click on the *To*, *Cc*, or *Bcc* message header address text box labels (which are also buttons) to open the Select Recipients dialog box as shown in Figure 8.11. Selecting a recipient name and then clicking the To, Cc, or Bcc buttons places the selected e-mail address in the appropriate address text box. Because blind carbon copy addresses are not visible to other message recipients, placing a recipient's address in the *Bcc* text box protects the privacy of that recipient and also avoids a lengthy message header list of addresses.

The *Subject* text box can be used to enter a subject for the message you are about to create and send. A subject header is a courtesy that allows recipients to glance at their mailbox and know a message's topic before opening the message. If no subject header is created, Windows Mail will prompt users to enter a subject when the Send button is clicked.

Clicking the message window toolbar Set Priority button will add a High Priority notification to a message in the form of an exclamation point so the recipients will know that the message is important. Clicking the down-pointing arrow at the right of the Set Priority button displays a drop-down list offering three priority choices: High Priority, Normal Priority, and Low Priority. A low priority message will contain notification in the form of a down-pointing arrow.

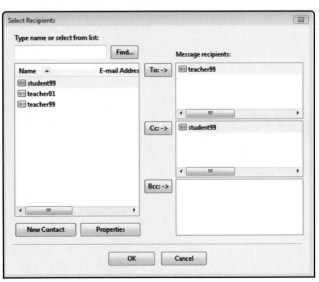

Figure 8.11 Select Recipients Dialog Box

Low Priority

High Priority

Figure 8.12 Message Priority Notification

Figure 8.13 Read Receipt Dialog Box

read receipt an automated receipt that lets an e-mail message sender know when a message was read by a recipient

signature a name and address or other personal information automatically appended to the end of an e-mail message

Figure 8.12 displays messages received with High and Low Priority notifications. A ***read receipt*** can be added to a message by clicking Tools on the message window menu bar and then clicking Request Read Receipt. Enabling this option means that the sender requests confirmation that the recipient received and read the message. When a recipient reads the message, a dialog box will prompt him or her to send a read receipt as shown in Figure 8.13. If the recipient clicks Yes, a return message will inform the sender of the date and time that the message was viewed. If the recipient clicks No, the sender will not receive a receipt notification.

If a user has already created a ***signature*** and specified that it should appear in new messages, the signature will be in the message body text box. If the message uses the HTML format, a formatting toolbar will become active, as shown in Figure 8.10, and can be used to format the message content. HTML or plain text message formats can be chosen by clicking Format on the menu bar and then clicking either Rich Text (HTML) or Plain Text.

The message window Cut, Copy, and Paste buttons can be used to move or copy information between the message body and other documents. Clicking the Spelling button performs a spell check on the message contents.

Once you are finished composing a message, clicking the Send button sends the message on its way and by default stores a copy in the Windows Mail Sent Items folder. To save a message before sending it, you can store the message in the Drafts folder by clicking File and then clicking Save. A dialog box informing you that the message will be saved in the Drafts folder will appear as shown in Figure 8.14. Messages saved in the Drafts folder can be opened by clicking the Local Folders button down-pointing arrow (in the Folders list of the Windows Mail window) and then clicking the Drafts folder. The contents of the Drafts folder will then appear in the message list. Double-clicking a saved message opens the message in its own window. Clicking File and then Save As in any message window enables the user to save the message, to a folder on the hard disk or local network in either the e-mail (.eml), text (.txt), or HTML (.htm) format.

Receiving Messages

A user can set up Windows Mail, using its Options dialog box, to check the mail server and download received messages at a regular time interval. Clicking the Send/Receive button tells Windows Mail to check the mail server in between the regularly scheduled

Figure 8.14 Draft Message Dialog Box

interval. When the Send/Receive button is clicked, any unsent mail in the Outbox folder will be sent as well. When a message is received it will be added to the Inbox folder message list.

Clicking a message listing will display the message contents in the preview pane as shown in Figure 8.9. The user can change the size of the preview pane by dragging the horizontal divider bar above the pane up or down. Double-clicking a message in the message list opens the message in its own window. Closing a message window does not delete the message.

Replying to and Forwarding Messages

A user can reply to a message by selecting the message in the Inbox message list and then clicking the Reply button, or by clicking the Reply button in a separate message window. Clicking the Reply button opens a reply message in a new window, with the sender's e-mail address now contained in the *To* text box and the recipient's e-mail address in the *From* text box. Clicking the Reply All button sends a response message to all the parties that received the original message, even those that received it via Cc or Bcc. The subject in a message sent using the Reply or Reply All functions will be prefixed with *Re:*, which means "in reference to" or "concerning."

When the Reply or Reply All buttons are clicked, the contents of the original message will still be contained in the message body, which the user can leave there or select and delete. A long vertical black stripe at the left edge of the text marks the original message contents as shown in Figure 8.15. It is often a good idea to leave the previous message contents, so both sender and recipients can reference that information. E-mail correspondence passed back and forth will then contain a complete record of any exchange.

A message can be forwarded to one or more parties by selecting the message in the message list and then clicking the Forward button, or by clicking the Forward button in an already opened message window. The message will appear with the *To* text box empty and the original message

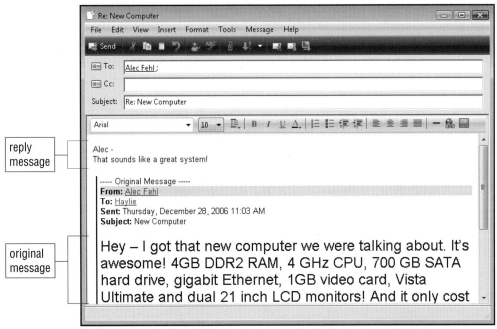

Figure 8.15 Reply Message

contents in the message body text box. A *Fw:* prefix appears before the subject. The message can be forwarded by entering e-mail addresses into the desired address text boxes and then clicking the Send button.

Deleting Messages

Messages can be deleted by selecting a message in the message list and then clicking the Delete button or choosing Delete from the Edit menu. If the message has been opened, it can be deleted by clicking the Delete button or choosing Delete Message from the File menu. Windows Mail stores deleted messages in the Deleted Items folder. The Deleted Items folder can be emptied by clicking Edit on the menu bar, and then Empty 'Deleted Items' Folder, or by right-clicking the folder and then clicking Empty 'Deleted Items' Folder from the shortcut menu that appears.

Printing Messages

A copy of a message can be printed by selecting the message listing, clicking File on the menu bar and then clicking Print to open the Print dialog box. An open e-mail message can be printed by clicking File on the message window menu bar and then clicking Print. Clicking the Print button in the Windows Mail window also opens the Print dialog box. The user can choose the desired print parameters in the Print dialog box and then print the message.

Adding Attachments

An attachment can be added to a new e-mail message by clicking Insert on the menu bar and then File Attachment, or by clicking the Attach button. Using either of these two options opens the Insert Attachment dialog box, in which the user can browse and locate the file(s) to attach to the message. After a document has been attached to an e-mail message, an *Attach* text box displaying the file name appears at the bottom of the message header area as shown in Figure 8.16. When the Reply or Reply All buttons are used to create a reply, any attachments that were contained in the original message will not be included, but attachments will be included when the Forward button is clicked to forward a message.

An attachment can be opened by double-clicking the file in the message *Attach* text box. When viewing a message in the preview pane, the user can click the paper clip icon at the right end of the message header and then click the file name to open the attachment.

Attachments can be saved by clicking File on the message menu bar and then Save Attachments. This opens the Save Attachments dialog box for saving the attachment file. The Save Attachments dialog box also can be opened by clicking the paper clip icon at the right end of the message header in the preview pane, and then clicking Save Attachments. The Save Attachment As

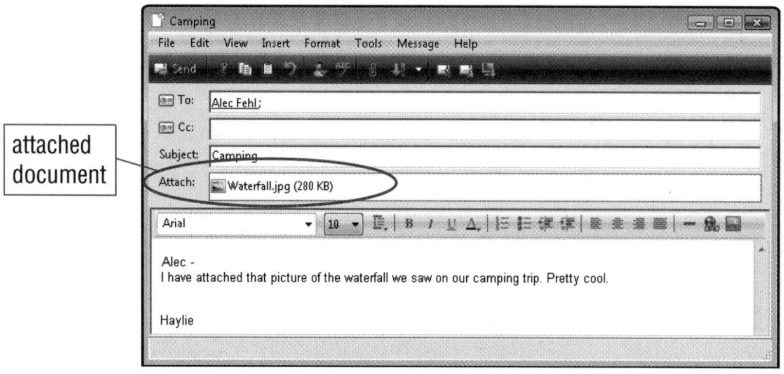

attached document

Figure 8.16 Message Attachment

dialog box can then be used to browse and locate a folder that can be used to save the attachment.

Attachments can contain viruses and other forms of malware, so antivirus software should always be used to check an attachment before it is opened. If an attachment is from an unknown sender or appears suspicious, the attachment and the message it is attached to should be deleted without opening either of them.

Netiquette

Etiquette refers to rules for good behavior in social situations. The rules for good behavior when communicating through the Internet are referred to as *netiquette*, a term created by combining *Internet* and *etiquette*. Users should be aware of a number of different netiquette rules, but first and foremost should always keep in mind that once an e-mail message has been sent, Windows Mail cannot retrieve it. For that reason, you should never send a message written in anger. If you have written an e-mail message when you are angry, you should save it and then review it once you have calmed down. More often than not you will be glad that you did not send it.

You should also be aware that you have no control over where a message may be forwarded once it has been sent, so you should never write anything that may embarrass you if it were made public. Although you may intend a message to be private, the person or people you send it to could forward it to someone else, and from that point it could travel anywhere. People have lost jobs and friends because an e-mail message they wrote fell into the wrong hands.

The following list contains additional e-mail netiquette you should be aware of:
- Do not write using uppercase letters because it is considered SHOUTING.
- Always write a short subject description in the *Subject* text box as a courtesy to the recipient(s) of your message.
- If you are copying a message to a large number of recipients, use the *Bcc* text box so that the message will not start with a long list of e-mail addresses that may be longer than the message.
- Ask permission before forwarding a message from someone else, particularly if the message contains any information that might be regarded as private.
- Do not forward chain letters.
- Check your messages for spelling errors and other mistakes so that readers will understand what you are trying to say and you will avoid making a poor impression.
- Before forwarding a warning about a virus or scam, verify the legitimacy of the warning by checking on a site like www.snopes.com. All too often virus warnings are hoaxes and sending these bogus warnings to friends, no matter how well intentioned, is considered spam.

Emoticons

When we communicate with people in person we use more than just words to convey what we are trying to say. A smile can indicate that something is meant to be humorous, while a frown shows displeasure. Because e-mail is not a face-to-face form of communication, it is easy for misunderstandings to occur. Something written in jest may not be perceived that way when read by

netiquette the rules for good behavior when communicating through the Internet; a term created by combining *Internet* and *etiquette*

emoticons keyboard character combinations used to communicate emotions and avoid misunderstandings in text communications

Table 8.2 Commonly Used Keyboard Emoticons

Emoticon	Meaning
:-)	Smiling, happy
:-(	Sad, frowning
:-D	Laughing
;-)	Winking
:-@	Screaming or shouting
: -O	Shock, surprise

Table 8.3 Commonly Used E-mail Acronyms

Acronym	Meaning
AFAIK	as far as I know
BTW	by the way
FYI	for your information
GIGO	garbage in, garbage out
IMHO	in my humble opinion
LOL	laughing out loud
ROTFL	rolling on the floor laughing
YMMV	your mileage may vary (used after expressing an opinion)

Table 8.4 Commonly Used Text Shortcuts

Text Shortcut	Meaning
ABT2	about to
B4	before
CU	see you
CUL8R	see you later
EZ	easy
FWD	forward
L8R	later
GR8	great
RU	are you
TNX	thanks
UR	your
ZZZ	tired or bored
4EVR	forever

someone else. To avoid misunderstandings many e-mail writers use **emoticons**, a term formed by combining *emotion* with *icon*. Emoticons are created using keyboard characters, such as :-) to represent a smile or :-(to represent a frown. Table 8.2 contains a list of some commonly used keyboard emoticons.

Acronyms

acronym a word formed from the first letter of each word in a phrase, such as LOL for "laughing out loud"

text shortcut letters or numbers used to imitate the sound of a phrase

An **acronym** is a word formed from the first letter of each word in a phrase, such as LOL for "laughing out loud." Acronyms are often used as a shortcut to typing a common phrase in full. Acronyms are suitable for informal e-mail messages and instant messages between friends or acquaintances, but may not be appropriate for more serious forms of communication such as business letters. Many e-mail users are unfamiliar with acronyms, so you should guard against using them too frequently unless you know the person you are corresponding with understands them. Table 8.3 contains a number of commonly used e-mail acronyms, but there are many more.

Text Shortcuts

Text shortcuts are similar to acronyms but are not created from the first letter of each word in a phrase. Instead, text shortcuts use letters and sometimes numbers to imitate the sound of a phrase, such as *CU* for *see you* or *L8R* for *later*. Table 8.4 contains a number of commonly used text shortcuts. A good way to learn more acronyms and text shortcuts is to consult an online dictionary such as www.netlingo.com.

Concept Review 3 Sending and Receiving E-mail

1. What does the header portion of an e-mail message window contain?
2. What is the difference between a carbon copy (Cc) and a blind carbon copy (Bcc)?
3. Describe some of the basic netiquette rules for e-mail.
4. What are emoticons, acronyms, and text shortcuts, and what are they used for?

Skill Review 3 Send and Receive E-mail Messages

(Note: Before starting this exercise, obtain e-mail addresses from at least three fellow students or use addresses provided by your instructor.)

1. Create and send an e-mail message by completing the following steps:

    a. Start Windows Mail by clicking Start, clicking to All Programs, and then clicking Windows Mail.

    b. Click the Create Mail button to open a New Message window.

    c. Type two student e-mail addresses in the *To* text box and one e-mail address in the *Cc* text box. *(Hint: Remember to separate e-mail addresses with a comma or semicolon.)*

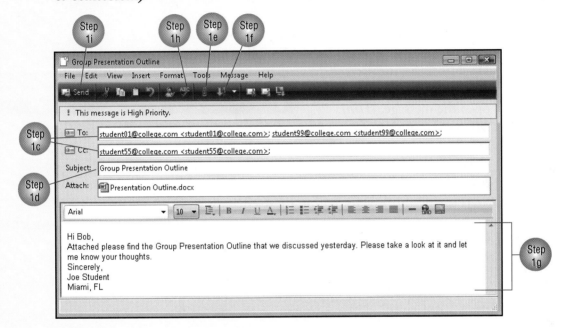

    d. Type **Group Presentation Outline** in the *Subject* text box.

    e. Click the Attach button and use the Insert Attachment dialog box to locate and select a file to attach to the e-mail message and then click the Attach button when you finish to close the dialog box and attach the selected file. *(Note: If you plan to add an attachment, it is a good idea to attach it before writing your message. If you wait until you are finished you might forget to add the attachment.)*

    f. Click the Priority button to make this a High Priority message.

    g. Place the insertion point above the signature in the message body, press Enter, and then type the following message:

    > **Hi Bob,**
    > **Attached please find the Group Presentation Outline that we discussed yesterday. Please take a look at it and let me know your thoughts.**
    > **Sincerely,**

    h. Click the Spelling button and use the Spelling dialog box to check the spelling in your message.

    i. Click the Send button to send the message.

2. Read, print, and reply to a message by completing the following steps:
   a. Click the Send/Receive button to check for new mail and then check your Inbox to see if you have any messages. *(Hint: If the Inbox is not the current folder, click Inbox in the Folders list to select it. Look for a message from one of your classmates containing the subject* **Group Presentation Outline**.*)*
   b. Double-click one of the messages you have received to open the message in its own window.
   c. Click File and then Print to open the Print dialog box. Use the Print dialog box to print a copy of the message.
   d. Click the Reply button to reply to the message.
   e. Type a short message at the top of the message body box in the reply message window.
   f. Click the Send button to send the reply.
3. Save an attachment by completing the following steps:

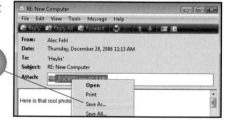

   a. Double-click a message containing an attachment to open the message. *(Hint: Messages containing attachments will contain a paper clip icon to the left of the message listing.)*
   b. Start saving the attachment by right-clicking it in the *Attach* text box.
   c. Click Save As to open the Save Attachment As dialog box. Use the dialog box to locate and select the folder in which the attachment will be saved. Click the Save button to complete the save.
   d. Start Windows Explorer and use it to locate and open the saved file.

Managing Folders

Windows Mail organizes e-mail messages in folders, and comes configured with Inbox, Outbox, Sent Items, Deleted Items, and Drafts folders as shown in Figure 8.17. These default folders cannot be deleted or renamed, but you can create additional folders. Folders that you create can be moved, renamed, or deleted using techniques similar to managing folders in Windows Explorer or any other file manager.

Windows Mail folders can be viewed in the upper left section of Windows Mail as shown in Figure 8.17. Clicking a hollow triangle next to a folder will expand the folder to display any subfolders located under that folder. Clicking a folder or subfolder will display its contents in the message list.

expanded folder (click – to collapse)

collapsed folder (click + to expand)

number of messages

Figure 8.17 Windows Mail Folders

A new folder can be created by clicking File on the menu bar, pointing to Folder, and then clicking New. This opens the Create Folder dialog box shown in Figure 8.18. You can specify the desired location and name for the folder and then click OK to close the Create Folder dialog box.

Nondefault folders can be deleted by selecting them in the Folders list, clicking File and then clicking Delete, or by right-clicking a folder and then clicking Delete in the shortcut menu. Folders can be renamed by following the same steps and then choosing Rename instead of Delete. This opens a Rename Folder dialog box that can be used to type a new name for the selected folder.

You can move messages into different folders by right-clicking them in the message list and then clicking Move to Folder or Copy to Folder in the shortcut menu, or by clicking Edit on the menu bar and then clicking Move to Folder or Copy to Folder. Selecting Move to Folder moves the message from the current folder to a new folder you select. Selecting Copy to Folder creates a copy of the current message and places the copy in the specified destination folder. Clicking the Move to Folder option opens the Move dialog box, while clicking the Copy to Folder option opens an identical Copy dialog box. Use either dialog box to select a target folder.

Message rules automate the process of directing incoming messages to specified folders and work only for POP3 mail server accounts. For example, the message rule shown in Figure 8.19 would direct any incoming messages

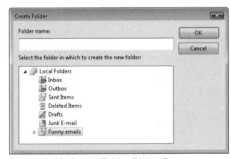

Figure 8.18 Create Folder Dialog Box

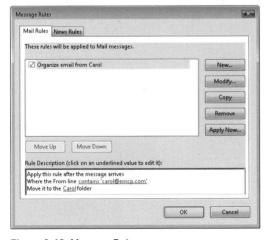

Figure 8.19 Message Rule

message rule rule created to automate e-mail processes for incoming e-mail, such as directing incoming messages to specified folders or blocking e-mail from specified e-mail addresses; works only with POP3 mail server accounts

Spam

Anyone who has ever used an e-mail account will be familiar with spam, the e-mail equivalent of junk mail that can quickly flood an inbox to the point that it becomes a nightmare. Some estimate that spam now accounts for 60 percent of all e-mail messages. Spam is not only a problem for e-mail users—it now affects instant messenger services, bloggers, newsgroups, and even mobile phones. Although users can do a number of things to reduce the amount of spam landing in an inbox, it is difficult to completely eliminate spam. Technological advances in the fight against spam provide only a temporary defense as spammers find alternative ways to get their messages past defenses and into inboxes.

News of the first jail sentence for a man thought to be one of the top ten spammers in the world cheered many when it was announced in late 2004. A court in Virginia handed down a nine-year sentence to the man for peddling a fraudulent FedEx refund processor scheme. Closer examination of the case reveals that the conviction was not for spamming, which is not a crime in Virginia, but for using stolen or fictitious IP addresses to disguise the origin of the spam. The extent of the problem posed by spam was revealed by the prosecutor when he said that America Online is the target of between 1.5 billion to 2.5 billion spam messages per day, and is only able to block 70 to 80 percent of the spam its servers receive. During the trial, it was claimed that the convicted man had made more than $24 million off various schemes, including luring over 12,000 people a month who were willing to part with $39.95 to learn about the bogus FedEx refund processor. While the conviction is certainly a step in the right direction, it seems unlikely that it will do much to stop spam, because the risk of prosecution and conviction is still low, and the potential to make huge sums of money with very little investment will continue to attract spammers.

from the e-mail address carol@emcp.net into a folder named Carol. Message rules can also automate a number of other tasks, including replying to messages, forwarding messages, creating copies of incoming messages and directing them to specified folders, and highlighting messages in specified font colors.

A message rule is created using the Message Rules dialog box, which can be opened by clicking Tools on the menu bar, pointing to Message Rules, and then clicking Mail.

Concept
Review 4 **Managing Folders** •

1. What are the default folders created in Windows Mail?
2. How can you create a new folder?
3. What can message rules be used for?

Skill
Review 4 **Add a New Folder and Create a Message Rule** • • • • • • • • • • • • •

1. Add a new folder in Windows Mail by completing the following steps:
   a. If necessary, start Windows Mail.
   b. If necessary, click the Inbox folder to display the Inbox message list.
   c. Click File on the menu bar, point to Folder, and then click New to open the Create Folder dialog box.
   d. Click *Local Folders* in the dialog box to select it and then type **Diverted Mail** in the *Folder name* text box. Click OK when you are finished.

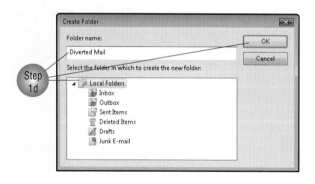 

   e. Look for the Diverted Mail folder you just created in the Windows Mail folder list.

2. Create a message rule by completing the following steps:

a. Click Tools on the menu bar, point to Message Rules, and then click Mail to open the New Mail Rule dialog box. *(Note: If message rules have already been created, the Message Rules dialog box will open. Click the New button at the Message Rules dialog box to open the New Mail Rule dialog box.)*

b. Click the *Where the From line contains people* check box in the *Select the Conditions for your rule* list to enable it.

c. Click the *Move it to the specified folder* check box in the *Select the Actions for your rule* list to enable it.

d. Click the <u>contains people</u> hyperlink in the *Rule Description* box.

e. Type a fellow classmate's e-mail address in the first text box of the Select People dialog box and then click the Add button. Click OK when you are finished. *(Note: You can also click the Contacts button and use the Rule Addresses dialog box to select an address and add it to the From text box.)*

f. Click the <u>specified</u> hyperlink in the *Rule Description* box.

g. If necessary, click the Diverted Mail folder you created to select it in the Move dialog box. Click OK to close the dialog box. *(Note: The Move dialog box contains a New Folder button that can be used to create folders.)*

h. Click OK at the New Mail Rule dialog box to close it.

i. Click OK at the Message Rules dialog box to close it.

j. Have the friend whose e-mail address you used in your message rule send you an e-mail message. The message should arrive in the Diverted Mail folder you created.

Windows Contacts

Windows Contacts, as shown in Figure 8.20, stores contact information, including e-mail addresses that can be used in Windows Mail messages. Windows Mail can automatically add a message sender's e-mail addresses to the Windows Contacts when the recipient replies to a message. If this automatic feature is not enabled, you can enable it by clicking Tools on the Windows Mail menu bar and then clicking Options to open the Options dialog box. You can then click the Send tab, check the *Automatically put people I reply to in my Contacts list* check box as

Figure 8.20 Windows Contacts

Google Gmail

Google raised eyebrows when it launched its Gmail e-mail service in April 2004. Available in an invitation-only beta version, demand for invitations to participate in the test was so high that they were being sold to the highest bidder on eBay. The reason for the interest was that Gmail offers a number of features that set it apart from competitors. By incorporating Google search technology, Gmail does away with the need to sort and store e-mail in folders by letting users instantly retrieve any e-mail message. A unique "conversations" feature displays e-mail in context, meaning that messages are displayed as a part of a back and forth exchange of e-mail messages.

Gmail also includes a Report Spam button that can be used to report spam to Google, which will then use the information gathered from Gmail users around the world to improve spam blocking. Other standard features include a spell checker, address book, autocomplete for addresses, and the ability to flag messages with labels according to sender or subject. To make Gmail even better, in November 2004 Google announced that it would begin providing free POP3 access. Mail will remain on the Gmail server, but users can download copies to e-mail clients (like Windows Mail) and mobile devices..

To many, the most attractive Gmail feature was that it offered 1 gigabyte (GB) of free storage. This is the equivalent of 500,000 e-mail pages! A year after its appearance, Gmail celebrated its first anniversary by upping free storage to 2 GB. Competitors such as Yahoo! Mail and Hotmail have been scrambling to keep up. Since Gmail made its first appearance Yahoo! Mail free storage capacity has been raised from 4 MB to 250 MB, and they recently announced that figure would be raised to 1 GB. Hotmail free storage has risen from 2MB to 250 MB and is likely to go higher in order to remain competitive.

Soon after it was launched, Gmail created some concern about privacy issues because it will scan e-mail messages to target advertising discretely featured on the right-hand side of the account holder's screen. The technology used is the same technology used by Google to target ads to the people who use its search engine. The scanning is done automatically, but Google promised that it would work with data protection authorities to help alleviate any privacy concerns.

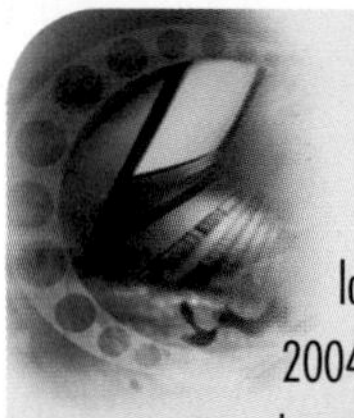

shown in Figure 8.21, and click OK. You can also manually add e-mail addresses to Windows Contacts by right-clicking a message in the message list and then clicking Add Sender to Contacts.

Windows Contacts stores a variety of different contact details, including phone numbers and addresses. Open Windows Contacts by clicking the Contacts button on the Windows Mail toolbar or by clicking Tools on the menu bar and then Windows Contacts. New contacts can be added to Windows Contacts by clicking the New Contact button in the Windows Contacts toolbar to open the Properties dialog box for a new contact as shown in Figure 8.22. Clicking a tab in the dialog box enables the user to enter the appropriate contact information. To modify a contact, double-click the contact in the Windows Contacts window to reopen the Properties dialog box for the contact.

Clicking the New Contact Group button in the Windows Contacts toolbar opens the Properties dialog box for creating a group as shown in Figure 8.23. A saved group identifies a collection of related e-mail addresses

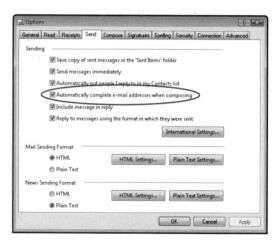

Figure 8.21 Windows Mail Contact List Automatic E-Mail Address Saving Option

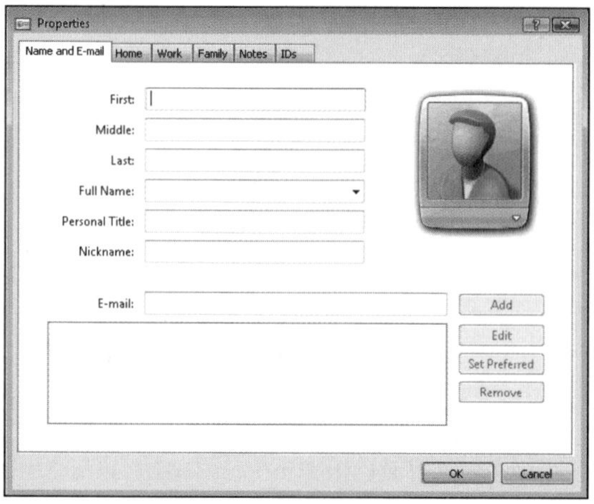

Figure 8.22 Properties Dialog Box for a Contact

that can save time when addressing e-mail messages. For example, if you regularly create e-mail messages that you send to your family members, you could create a Family group; then, to send a message to all the recipients included in the Family group, enter the Family group in the *To* text box instead of entering an e-mail address for each member of your family.

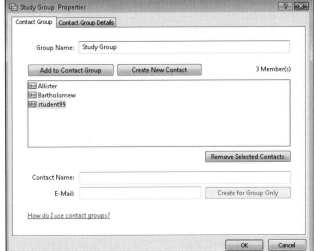

Figure 8.23 Properties Dialog Box for a Group

Print individual or group contact information by selecting the desired individual contact(s) or group(s) in the Windows Contacts window and then clicking the Print button. A consecutive block of contacts can be selected for printing by holding down the Shift key while selecting the first and last contacts, while nonconsecutive contact names can be selected by holding down the Ctrl key when selecting contacts. The Print dialog box contains *Memo*, *Business Card*, and *Phone List Print Style* options as shown in Figure 8.24. The *Memo* option will print all the Address Book information for a contact, the *Business Card* option will print business-related contact information, and the *Phone List* option will print contact phone numbers.

Choose an option for printing contact information.

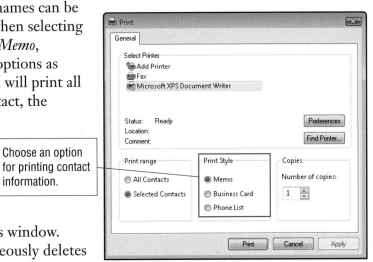

Figure 8.24 Print Dialog Box

Individual and group contacts can be deleted by clicking the Delete button in the Windows Contacts window. Deleting an individual contact simultaneously deletes it from any groups that it might be in. Deleting a group does not delete the individual contact addresses that comprise the group. An individual contact from a group can be deleted by double-clicking the group listing in the Windows Contacts window to open the Properties dialog box, selecting the contact to be removed in the *Group Members* section, clicking the Remove button, and then clicking OK.

Contacts in Windows Contacts can be sorted by clicking on a column heading. For example, clicking the *Name* column heading sorts the contacts by name. Clicking a column heading repeatedly switches the sort order from ascending to descending, such as from A to Z or Z to A.

Concept *Review 5* Windows Contacts ·

1. How can you save e-mail addresses to Windows Contacts?
2. What is a group contact?
3. What options are available for printing Windows Contacts contact and group information?

Skill Review 5 Work with Windows Contacts

(Note: Before starting this exercise obtain e-mail addresses, home addresses, and birthday information from at least four fellow students or use contact details provided by your instructor.)

1. Add an individual contact to Windows Contacts by completing the following steps:
   a. If necessary, start Windows Mail.
   b. Open Windows Contacts by clicking the Contacts button or by clicking Tools on the menu bar and then Contacts. *(Note: You may also start Windows Contacts without using Windows Mail by clicking Start > All Programs > Windows Contacts.)*
   c. Maximize the Windows Contacts window.
   d. Click the New Contact button to open the Properties dialog box.
   e. If necessary, click the Name And E-mail tab and then enter the contact information from one of your fellow students using the *First, Last*, and *E-Mail* text boxes. Note that as you type the first and last names, Windows Contacts automatically fills in the *Full Name* textbox. Click the Add button when you are finished.

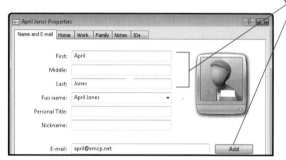

   f. Click the Home tab and then enter address and phone number contact details. *(Note: If you inadvertently click OK and close the Properties dialog box, reopen the dialog box by double-clicking the contact name you created in Step 1e.)*
   g. Click the Family tab and then click the *Birthday* check box to insert a check mark.
   h. Click the arrow at the right end of the *Birthday* text box to select the birth date. Click OK to close the Properties dialog box. *(Note: The Properties dialog box title bar now displays the name of the contact you created.)*
   i. Select the contact you have just created in the contact list in the Windows Contacts window and then click the Print button.
   j. If necessary, click the *Memo* option in the Print dialog box.
   k. Click the Print button to print a memo copy of the Windows Contacts contact you just created.
   l. Repeat Steps 1d through 1k to add contact information for the remaining three students.
   m. Close Windows Contacts by clicking the Close button on the Windows Contacts title bar.

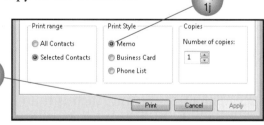

   n. Click the Windows Mail Create Mail button to open a New Message window.
   o. Click the To button to open the Select Recipients dialog box.
   p. Locate one of the contacts you just created, click to select it, and then click the To button to enter it in the *Message recipients* list. Click OK to close the dialog box.

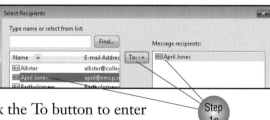

q. Type a subject for the new message in the *Subject* text box.

r. Write a short message letting your fellow student know that you have entered his or her contact details in your Windows Contacts.

s. Click the Send button to send the message when you are finished.

2. Add a group contact to Windows Contacts by completing the following steps:

a. Open and maximize Windows Contacts and click the New Contact Group button to open the Properties dialog box.

b. Type a name for the group you are about to create in the *Group Name* text box.

c. Add names and e-mail addresses to the group by clicking the Add To Contact Group button to open the Add Members To Contact Group dialog box.

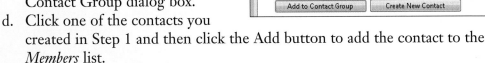

d. Click one of the contacts you created in Step 1 and then click the Add button to add the contact to the *Members* list.

e. Repeat Step 2d to add the remaining three student contacts to the group.

f. Click OK in the Properties dialog box to close it. *(Note: The Properties dialog box title bar now displays the name of the group you created.)*

g. Close Windows Contacts and then click the Create Mail button in Windows Mail to open a New Message window.

h. Click the message header To button to open the Select Recipients dialog box. Locate the group you just created, click it to select it, and then click the To button to enter it in the *To* text box. Click OK to close the dialog box.

i. Type a subject for the new message.

j. Write a short message letting your fellow students know that you have created a group with their names and contact details in your Windows Contacts.

k. Click the Send button to send the message when you are finished.

Finding Messages and Contact Information

Windows Mail includes a search function that offers a variety of different methods for finding e-mail messages and contacts. Clicking Edit on the menu bar, pointing to Find, and then clicking Message opens the Find Message window shown in Figure 8.25. The Find Message window can be used to search messages in the current folder, which will be displayed in the *Look in* line at the top of the window. The current folder can be changed by clicking the Browse button. This opens a dialog box that displays all the Windows Mail folders. Selecting a folder and then clicking OK makes it the current folder. The search results shown at the bottom of the Find Message box shown in Figure 8.25 will appear once the search is complete.

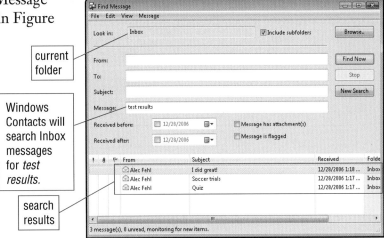

Figure 8.25 Find Message Window

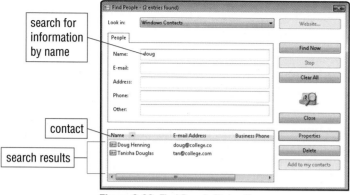

search for information by name

contact

search results

Figure 8.26 Find People Dialog Box

The Find Message window can be used to search for specified data located in the message header area and/or the message body. Specifying *Received before* and *Received after* dates finds messages in a particular time frame. Clicking the Find Now button begins the search. Search results appear in a message list at the bottom of the Find Message window as shown in Figure 8.25. Double-clicking a message listing opens it in a new window.

Windows Contacts can be searched by clicking Edit on the menu bar, pointing to Find, and then clicking People. This opens the Find People dialog box. After search data has been entered in any of the dialog box text boxes a search can be started by pressing the Find Now button. Search results will appear at the bottom of the dialog box as shown in Figure 8.26. Right-clicking a contact name, pointing to Action, and then clicking Send E-mail will open a New Message window addressed to the selected contact.

Concept Review 6 Find Messages and Contact Information

1. How do you open the Find Message window?
2. What parts of a message can Windows Mail search within?
3. How can a Find People dialog box search result listing be used to create a new e-mail message?

Skill Review 6 Find Messages and Contacts

1. Find a message by completing the following steps:
   a. If necessary, start Windows Mail.
   b. Click Edit on the menu bar, point to Find, and then click Message to open the Find Message window.
   c. Check to see that the Inbox is the current folder. If it is not, click the Browse button to open the Windows Mail dialog box, select the Inbox, and then click OK.
   d. Type a portion of the e-mail address for one of your fellow students in the *From* text box. *(Note: Use a partial e-mail address from one of the students who sent you a message in Skill Review 3.)*
   e. Click the Find Now button.

Find Message

File   Edit   View   Message

Look in: Inbox   ☑ Include subfolders   Browse..

Step 1c   Step 1c

f. Double-click the first message in the search results listing to open the message.

g. Close the Find Message window by clicking File on the menu bar and then Close or by clicking the Close button in the Find Message window title bar.

2. Find a contact by completing the following steps:

a. Click Edit on the menu bar, point to Find, and then click People to open the Find People dialog box. *(Note: If a dialog box asking you if you want to make Windows Contacts your default vCard viewer appears, click No to close it.)*

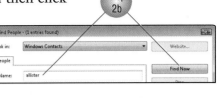

Step 2b

b. Type the name of one of the fellow students you entered as a Windows Contacts contact in the *Name* text box. Click the Find Now button.

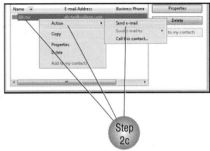

c. Right-click the contact name in the search results list, point to Action, and then click Send E-mail.

Step 2c

d. Use the New Message window to send an e-mail message to the found contact's e-mail address.

Webmail

Web-based e-mail, also known as *webmail*, provides e-mail accounts accessible through any Web browser. The contents of a webmail account usually remain on the webmail provider's server and are not downloaded to a local computer, accessible through any Web but some providers offer POP3 access that enables message downloading as well. When free webmail services first appeared, one of their drawbacks was that storage space was limited to a few megabytes, but currently the larger services such as Yahoo! Mail and Hotmail offer 250 MB of inbox storage, and Google's new Gmail webmail service offers 2.5 GB (2500 MB).

webmail Web-based e-mail that provides an e-mail account accessible through any Web browser

Webmail services underwrite free e-mail accounts through the advertising they carry, so users may have to put up with the annoyance of banner ads and pop-up windows. Some webmail services offer upgrade packages that eliminate advertising. Extra features offered by webmail accounts include message filtering, POP3 retrieval, message forwarding, spell checking, signatures, and antivirus and spam protection. Features vary by provider. Some features may be offered with free e-mail account packages, while others may be available in an upgrade package. Table 8.5 contains information about some of the most popular webmail providers offering free e-mail accounts.

Creating an account involves visiting the webmail provider's Web site and completing an online registration form. Once the provider issues a user name and password, the user can access his or her e-mail account through a URL provided by the

Table 8.5 Webmail Providers

Provider	URL	Maximum Message Size	Storage Limit
Excite mail	registration.excite.com	10 MB	125 MB
Gmail	gmail.google.com	10 MB	2.5 GB
Lycos mail	mail.lycos.com	unlimited	3 GB
Mail.com	www.mail.com	10 MB	100 MB
MSN Hotmail	login.live.com	10 MB	1 GB
myway	registration.myway.com	10 MB	125 MB
Yahoo! Mail	mail.yahoo.com	10 MB	1 GB

service. Webmail accounts offer the same features that can be found in standard e-mail clients, including mail folders, address books for storing contact information, the ability to create, reply to, and forward mail, and so on. Figure 8.27 shows the Google Gmail Inbox.

Because a webmail account is not tied to an ISP account or e-mail client, the user can access his or her webmail using a Web browser on any computer connected to the Web. While some people use a webmail account as their main account, others establish webmail accounts for privacy reasons, and still others use a webmail account when traveling because it can be accessed through any Web connection.

Most ISPs offer a webmail service to their regular e-mail customers so that each customer can access his or her e-mail when away from the home or office. A user typically accesses the ISP's webmail service through a hyperlink or button on the ISP's home page, like the example shown in Figure 8.28. Clicking the hyperlink or button opens a new Web page where the ISP customer can enter his or her regular e-mail user name and password to access e-mail.

Figure 8.27 Google Gmail Inbox

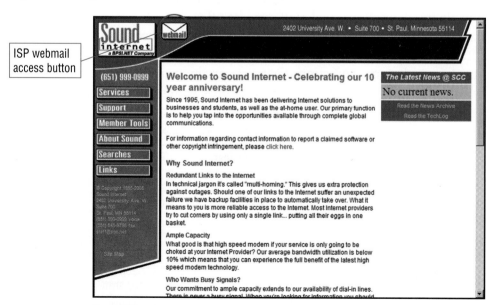

Figure 8.28 ISP Webmail Access Button

www.scc.net

Concept
Review 7 Webmail

1. What is webmail?
2. How can webmail providers offer free e-mail service?

Skill
Review 7 Create and Use a Yahoo! Mail Webmail Account

1. Create a free Yahoo! Mail webmail account by completing the following steps:
   a. If necessary, start Internet Explorer.
   b. Type **mail.yahoo.com** in the Address bar and then press Enter or click Go. *(Note: Do not type* **www.** *in the address.)*
   c. Click the Sign Up hyperlink at the bottom of the Yahoo! Mail home page.
   d. Enter the requested personal information in the registration form text boxes. Text boxes featuring an asterisk are mandatory and must be filled in. Be sure to verify your registration by entering the code in the *Enter the code shown* text box.
   e. Click the I Agree button to show that you agree with the terms of service and complete the registration process.

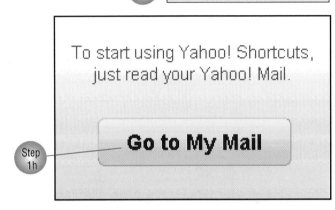

   f. Click the Continue Without Installing Yahoo! Toolbar button.
   g. If a page inviting you to try The All-New Yahoo! Mail Beta appears, click the *No Thanks, Remind Me Later* hyperlink to continue.
   h. Click the Go To My Mail button.
2. Use your Yahoo! Mail Account to send and receive e-mail messages by completing the following steps:
   a. Click the Compose button at the top of the page to compose an e-mail message.

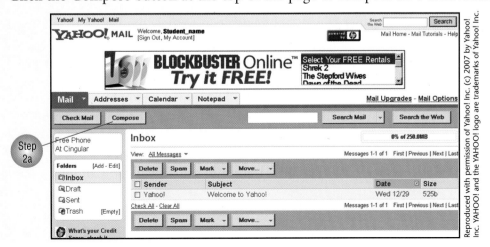

b. Type your Yahoo! Mail e-mail address in the *To* text box and a subject in the *Subject* text box. *(Note: You can use a fellow student's e-mail address instead of your own if you want.)*

c. Click the Attach Files button.

d. Click the first Browse file button to open the Choose file dialog box.

e. Use the Choose file dialog box to locate and select a file to attach to the e-mail message you are creating. Click the Open button when you are finished.

f. Click the Attach Files button when the selected file appears in the *File 1* text box. Yahoo! Mail will upload the attachment and scan it for viruses.

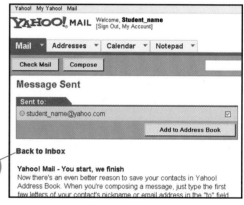

g. Click the Continue to Message button once the attachment process finishes.

h. Type a message in the message text box.

i. Click the Send button to send the message.

j. Click the Back to Inbox hyperlink in the Message Sent Web page.

k. Click the Subject column entry of the Inbox message listing for the message you just sent to open it.

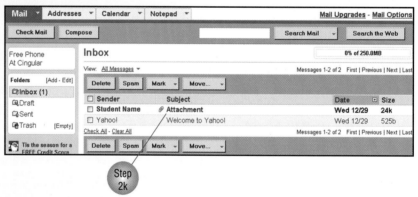

l. Click the paper clip (attachment) icon to view the list of attachments.

m. Click the Save to Computer hyperlink.

n. Click the Download Attachment button at the bottom of the Virus Scan results page.

o. Click the Save button in the File Download dialog box.

p. Use the Save As dialog box to select the folder on your computer or network location in which the attachment will be saved. Click the Save button to download and save the attachment.

q. If necessary, click the Close button in the Download Complete dialog box to close it.

r. Sign out of your Yahoo! Mail account by clicking the <u>Sign Out, My Account</u> hyperlink at the top of the page. *(Note: You can log on to your account again by clicking the <u>Return to Yahoo! Mail</u> hyperlink in the Web page that appears after you log out, or by opening the Yahoo! Mail home page at mail.yahoo.com.)*

Chapter Summary

Check your knowledge of chapter concepts by using the flash cards available on the Encore CD that accompanies this book as well as on the Internet Resource Center for this title at www.emcp.net/Internet2e.

- E-mail servers transmit e-mail messages using packet switching technology that divides an e-mail message into packets that travel various routes to a destination server, which reassembles the packets into the message.

- Programs known as e-mail clients, popularly referred to as e-mail programs, enable users to compose, send, and receive e-mail messages.

- When an e-mail message is sent it travels to an e-mail server on the sender's domain. The e-mail server examines the e-mail address to determine where to forward the message.

- E-mail addresses have a two-part construction separated by an @ sign (at sign). The first part contains the user name or local part, and the second part after the @ sign contains the domain name.

- The protocol used to send e-mail messages is known as Simple Mail Transfer Protocol (SMTP).

- If the originating SMTP server cannot connect with the destination mail server, the e-mail message will go into a queue or waiting list from which it is periodically resent.

- POP3 e-mail users connect to the POP3 server and download the messages stored on the server to their local computer.

- IMAP e-mail messages are read and manipulated on the server without downloading them to a local machine.

- Attachments to e-mail messages are handled using the Multipurpose Internet Mail Extension (MIME) protocol.

- A mail account must be set up in the Windows Mail e-mail client before it can be used to send and receive e-mail.

- The menus and toolbar in Windows Mail offer the commands necessary to send and receive e-mail messages, as well as those needed to perform related functions.

- The Windows Mail message list displays mail that has been downloaded from the mail server specified for the mail account.

- The preview pane displays the contents of the message currently selected in the message list.

- The top portion of the New Message window holds text boxes for entering the message header information, such as the *To* and *Cc* text boxes, as well as the *Subject* text box.

- A subject header is a courtesy that allows recipients to glance at the message list and know the topic of a message before opening it.

- Clicking the Priority button in the message window will add a High Priority notification to a message (in the form of an exclamation point), so the recipients will know that the message is important.

- The sender can add a read receipt request to a message to prompt the recipient to send an automated receipt message that informs the sender of the date and time that the message was read by the recipient.

- Windows Mail by default is set up to check the mail server and download messages at a regular time interval. The user can change the interval at which messages are checked in the General tab of the Options dialog box in Windows Mail.

- The user can click the Send/Receive button to have Windows Mail check the mail server in between the regularly scheduled interval.

- Reply to a message by selecting it in the Inbox message list and then clicking the Reply button, or by clicking the Reply button in an open message window.

- A message can be forwarded to one or more parties by selecting the message in the message list and then clicking the Forward button, or by clicking the Forward button in an open message window.

- To print a message, select the message in the message list, click File on the menu bar, and then click Print to open the Print dialog box. Choose the desired settings, and then click Print.

- Attachments can contain viruses and other forms of malware, so a user should always check an attachment with antivirus software before opening the attachment.

- The rules for good behavior when communicating through the Internet are referred to as netiquette.

- To avoid misunderstandings, many e-mail writers use emoticons, a term formed by combining *emotion* with *icon*. Emoticons are created using keyboard characters, such as :-) to represent a smile or :-(to represent a frown.

- Acronyms, such as LOL for "laughing out loud," are often used as a shortcut to typing a common phrase in full.

- Windows Mail saves e-mail messages in folders, and come with Inbox, Outbox, Sent Items, Deleted Items, and Drafts default folders.

- Message rules can be created to automate a number of tasks, including directing incoming messages to specified folders.

- Windows Contacts stores contact information including e-mail addresses that can be used to address Windows Mail messages.

- Windows Mail includes a search function that offers a variety of different methods for finding e-mail messages and contacts.

- Web-based e-mail, also known as webmail, provides e-mail accounts that can be accessed through any Web browser.

- Because a webmail account is not tied to an ISP account or e-mail client, the account holder can access the account using a Web browser on any computer that is connected to the Internet.

- Most ISPs offer a webmail service to their regular customers, so the customers can access their accounts when they are away from their regular computer.

Key Terms

Numbers indicate the pages where terms are first cited in the chapter. An alphabetized list of key terms with definitions can be found on the Encore CD that accompanies this book. In addition, these terms and definitions are included in the end-of-book glossary.

acronym, *252*

e-mail client, *240*

emoticons, *251*

Internet Message Access Protocol (IMAP), *241*

message rule, *255*

Multipurpose Internet Mail Extensions (MIME), *241*

netiquette, *251*

Post Office Protocol 3 (POP3), *241*

read receipt, *248*

signature, *248*

Simple Mail Transfer Protocol (SMTP), *240*

text shortcut, *252*

webmail, *263*

Net Check

Additional quiz questions are available on the Encore CD that accompanies this book as well as on the Internet Resource Center for this title at www.emcp.net/Internet2e.

Multiple Choice

Indicate the correct answer for each question or statement.

1. When you select a message in the Windows Mail message list, the message contents will appear in the
   a. preview pane.
   b. toolbar.
   c. status bar.
   d. message window.

2. Windows Mail message rules only work with this type of incoming mail protocol.
   a. IMAP
   b. SMTP
   c. HTTP
   d. POP3

3. The protocol used to send e-mail is
   a. POP3.
   b. HTTP.
   c. IMAP.
   d. SMTP.

4. The part of an e-mail address after the @ sign is the
   a. user name.
   b. local part.
   c. domain name.
   d. protocol part.

5. Software programs used to send and receive e-mail are known as
   a. e-mail sending units.
   b. e-mail clients.
   c. mail servers.
   d. SMTP servers.

6. If an SMTP server cannot connect with a destination mail server, a message will
   a. be discarded.
   b. go into a queue or waiting list where it will be periodically resent.
   c. be immediately returned to the sender.
   d. expire.

7. E-mail messages are transmitted using
   a. packet switching technology.
   b. connection wizards.
   c. electronic envelopes.
   d. mail folders.

8. Windows Mail automatically adds an e-mail address to Windows Contacts when
   a. messages are sent.
   b. a reply is sent.
   c. a message is forwarded.
   d. messages are saved.

9. LOL is an example of a(n)
   a. emoticon.
   b. acronym.
   c. instruction.
   d. shortcut phrase.

10. When a user's e-mail account uses this incoming mail protocol, messages are not downloaded to local machines.
    a. POP3
    b. HTTP
    c. HTML
    d. IMAP

True/False

Indicate whether each statement is true or false.

1. If you copy a message to a large number of people, you should use the *Cc* text box.

2. IMHO is an acronym that means "in my humble opinion."

3. Group contacts contain a number of different e-mail addresses under a single group name.

4. Windows Mail contains a search function that can search messages and Windows Contacts.

5. The protocol used for sending e-mail is known as SMTP.

6. Windows Mail users can click the Find button to check for mail in between the regularly scheduled interval.

7. POP3 and IMAP are two different protocols used for sending e-mail.

8. Clicking the Priority button in the message window will add a High Priority notification to an e-mail message.

9. The MIME protocol is used to handle e-mail attachments.

10. E-mail message addresses should be separated by colons.

Virtual Perspectives

1. Some people use an e-mail client for sending and receiving e-mail messages, others use Web-based e-mail accounts (webmail), and still others use both methods. Discuss the advantages and disadvantages of accessing e-mail through an e-mail client or through webmail. Discuss any circumstances where using one method might be preferable to using the other method.

2. It is easy for misunderstandings to develop when communicating by e-mail because the aural or visual cues present in other forms of communication are absent. Discuss any misunderstandings that you have experienced when using e-mail, and the steps that you take to ensure that the recipients of your e-mail messages understand them the way you intend them to be understood.

Internet Lab Projects

Block E-mail

1. Obtain an e-mail address from a fellow student.
2. Start Windows Mail.
3. Open the Message Rules dialog box and create a new rule.
4. In the Select The Conditions For Your Rule box, choose Where The From Line Contains People. In the Select The Actions For Your Rule box, select Delete It.
5. In the Rule Description box, click the hyperlink for Contains People, type an email address to block, click Add, then click OK. Click OK twice more to close the Message Rules dialog box and return to the main Windows mail window.
6. Have the sender of the e-mail address you blocked send you a message.
7. Click the Windows Mail Send/Receive button to download the latest e-mail messages from your mail server.
8. Check your Deleted Items folder to see if the message from the blocked sender was directed there.
9. Reopen the Message Rules dialog box and use it to remove the rule you just created.

E-mail Links and Web Pages

1. E-mail a Web page by completing the following steps:
   a. Start Internet Explorer.
   b. Open a Web page that you wish to send to a fellow student.
   c. Click the Page button on the standard toolbar and click Send Page By Email to open the Web page inside a new message window. *(Note: If an Internet Explorer Security dialog box appears, click Allow.)*
   d. Type or insert your fellow student's e-mail address in the *To* text box.
   e. Change the subject.
   f. Send the message. Check to see that it arrived and that the Web page is contained in the e-mail message.
2. E-mail a link to a Web page by completing the following steps:
   a. Open a Web page.
   b. Click the Page button on the standard toolbar and click Send Link By Email to open the Web page inside a new message window.
   c. Type or insert your fellow student's e-mail address in the *To* text box.
   d. Send the message. Check to see that it arrived and that the link works.

Change the New Mail Notification Sound

(Note: You will need a microphone to complete this exercise.)

1. Click Start, click All Programs, click Accessories, and then click Sound Recorder to open the Sound Recorder.
2. Click the Record button (with the red dot on it) and record a new mail message, such as "You have new mail." Click the Stop button (with the black rectangle on it) to stop Recording.
3. Click File on the Sound Recorder menu bar and then click Save. Save the sound file you created as a .wav file. Close the Sound Recorder when you are finished.
4. Click Start and then click Control Panel.

5. Click the Hardware And Sound icon, then click the Sound icon.
6. Click the Sounds tab at the Sound Properties dialog box.
7. Scroll down the *Program events* list, click *New Mail Notification*, and then click the Browse button to open the Browse for New Mail Notification sound dialog box. Use the dialog box to locate and select the sound file you created in Step 2. Click open to close the dialog box.
8. Click OK at the Sounds and Audio Devices Properties dialog box to close the dialog box.
9. Open Windows Mail and send an e-mail message addressed to yourself. Click the Send/Receive button to download the e-mail and hear the new mail sound you created.

Internet Research Activities

Activity 1
Compare Webmail Providers

Search the Web for more information about free webmail providers. Use the information you gather to create a table that compares the different features offered by at least four different webmail providers.

Activity 2
Explore Spam Blocking

Search the Internet to find out about the latest technological efforts to block spam. Use the information you gather to write a short paper describing at least four different current or planned spam-blocking technologies.

Activity 3
Net Challenge

Copy the e-mail addresses in your Windows Contacts to your Yahoo! Mail account. At the time of this writing, Yahoo! Mail cannot import contacts directly from Windows Contacts with Internet Explorer 7. To do this manually, click Start > All Programs > Windows Contacts. Click the Export button in the Windows Contacts toolbar and export your contacts in *vCards (folder of .vcf files)* format. Be sure to save the exported file to a location you remember, such as a folder on your Desktop. Start Yahoo! Mail, go to the Inbox page, and then click the Addresses tab. Click the *Import Your Contacts from Another Application* hyperlink at the bottom of the Welcome to Yahoo! Address Book page. At Step 1 of the Import Contacts page, choose *vCard (.VCF file)* from the drop-down menu and click the Continue button. At Step 2, click the Continue button. At Step 3, click the Browse button to open the Choose File dialog box. Navigate to the location of your exported .vcf files, select one of the Contacts, and click Open to close the Choose File dialog box, then click the Continue button. The Yahoo! Address Book displays your imported contact. Click the Addresses tab and repeat the process to add all of your contacts.

Chapter
Asynchronous Communications
9

Living on the Net

E-mail was the only Internet communication method Bob used when he first went online. He soon discovered e-mail mailing lists and eventually subscribed to a list for people interested in jazz. He enjoyed coming home from work and finding a digest full of interesting posts from jazz lovers around the world in his inbox.

Bob discovered newsgroups not too long after he subscribed to his first mailing list, and soon learned how to add a new account in Windows Mail so that he could use it to read newsgroups. While he still enjoys his mailing list, he finds that newsgroups have some features that mailing lists cannot match.

Bob also subscribes to a Web-based forum sponsored by a company that provided the Web editing software that he uses to create Web pages at work. The forum lets him post software questions that are often answered by other forum users. As Bob becomes proficient in using the software, he has begun to answer questions for other forum users.

Carolyn recently clued Bob into some interesting Internet discoveries she made. Not too long ago, her aunt worked with a voluntary group on a project in Central America for a few months, and while there she maintained a blog so that she could share her experience with friends and relatives, who could then leave comments on the blog for her to read.

Carolyn was also the one to let Bob know about wikis. Bob did not think that the strange-sounding wiki concept of letting anybody write on Web pages would ever work. But he became a believer when he tried using the Wikipedia online encyclopedia. Now he consults it frequently, and he has even contributed a few articles of his own.

What all these Internet communication methods have in common is that they are asynchronous. Asynchronous communication refers to communication that involves a time lag during any sender and recipient interaction. You have already learned about one asynchronous method of Internet communication—e-mail—and in this chapter you will learn more about the other asynchronous communication methods that Bob and Carolyn use every day.

asynchronous communication (sequential)

synchronous communication (simultaneous)

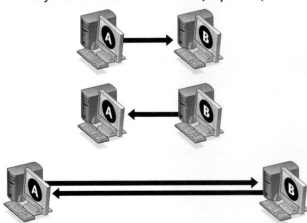

Electronic Mailing Lists

Electronic mailing lists, also known as e-mail discussion lists or groups, are e-mail based topic-focused discussion environments. Mailing lists are created using a number of popular mailing list software programs such as Majordomo, Mailman, and LISTSERV. Topics can concern almost any subject, such as a breed of dog (poodles), a hobby (quilting) or a vehicle (Ford Mustangs), and so on. E-mail messages sent to a mailing list are referred to as **posts**. Posts to a mailing list will be sent to all members of the mailing list.

Most mailing lists offer three reading options to members as shown in Figure 9.1; posts can arrive as individual e-mail messages, posts can arrive in a digest form that is a compilation of posts over a time period (usually daily) sent as one message, or posts can be viewed via a Web page. Many mailing lists generate a large number of posts every day and can rapidly flood an inbox so the digest form is

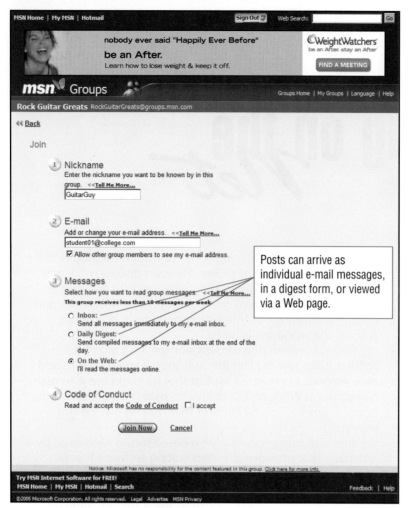

Posts can arrive as individual e-mail messages, in a digest form, or viewed via a Web page.

Figure 9.1 Mailing List Reading Options

post message sent to mailing lists, newsgroups, forums, and similar discussion areas

thread a series of posts on the same subject

often preferred. Some people like to read mailing lists on a Web page, if available, for ease of use and to avoid using an e-mail client.

Most mailing lists are archived so that members can view previous postings as shown in Figure 9.2. Archives often can be sorted by thread, subject, date, or author. A **thread** is a series of posts on the same subject. An archive sorted by thread shows the post that started the thread, followed by any subsequent posts (replies) in the same thread as shown in Figure 9.3.

Subscribing and Unsubscribing

The traditional method used to subscribe or unsubscribe from a mailing list is to send a command such as HELP or SUBSCRIBE in the subject or body of an e-mail message. The required command varies depending on the software used to run the mailing list, but a mailing list introductory message or Web page usually describes the proper

Figure 9.2 Mailing List Web Page Archive

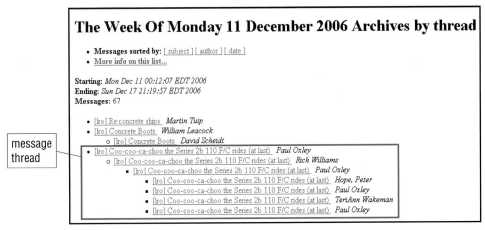

The Week Of Monday 11 December 2006 Archives by thread

- **Messages sorted by:** [subject] [author] [date]
- More info on this list...

Starting: *Mon Dec 11 00:12:07 EDT 2006*
Ending: *Sun Dec 17 21:19:57 EDT 2006*
Messages: 67

- [lro] Re:concrete ships *Martin Tuip*
- [lro] Concrete Boots *William Leacock*
  - [lro] Concrete Boots *David Scheidt*
- [lro] Coo-coo-ca-choo the Series 2b 110 F/C rides (at last) *Paul Oxley*
  - [lro] Coo-coo-ca-choo the Series 2b 110 F/C rides (at last) *Rich Williams*
    - [lro] Coo-coo-ca-choo the Series 2b 110 F/C rides (at last) *Paul Oxley*
      - [lro] Coo-coo-ca-choo the Series 2b 110 F/C rides (at last) *Hope, Peter*
      - [lro] Coo-coo-ca-choo the Series 2b 110 F/C rides (at last) *Paul Oxley*
      - [lro] Coo-coo-ca-choo the Series 2b 110 F/C rides (at last) *TeriAnn Wakeman*
      - [lro] Coo-coo-ca-choo the Series 2b 110 F/C rides (at last) *Paul Oxley*

message thread

Figure 9.3 Mailing List Archive Sorted by Thread

procedure as shown in Figure 9.4. The commands used for most mailing list software programs are not case sensitive, with the exception of passwords. A subscription request will usually be followed by a confirmation or welcome e-mail message letting you know that your subscription was successful as shown in Figure 9.5. The confirmation message may contain

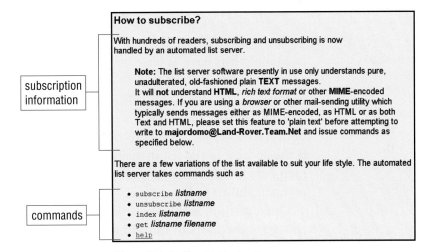

How to subscribe?

With hundreds of readers, subscribing and unsubscribing is now handled by an automated list server.

Note: The list server software presently in use only understands pure, unadulterated, old-fashioned plain **TEXT** messages.
It will **not** understand **HTML**, *rich text format* or other **MIME**-encoded messages. If you are using a *browser* or other mail-sending utility which typically sends messages either as MIME-encoded, as HTML or as both Text and HTML, please set this feature to 'plain text' before attempting to write to **majordomo@Land-Rover.Team.Net** and issue commands as specified below.

There are a few variations of the list available to suit your life style. The automated list server takes commands such as

- subscribe *listname*
- unsubscribe *listname*
- index *listname*
- get *listname filename*
- help

subscription information

commands

Figure 9.4 Mailing List Instructions

information about using the list and links to other information. It is a good idea to print out a copy of a confirmation e-mail and keep it in a safe place for future reference.

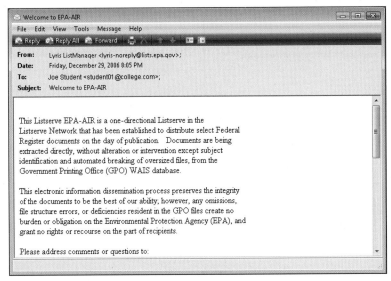

Figure 9.5 Mailing List Subscription Confirmation Message

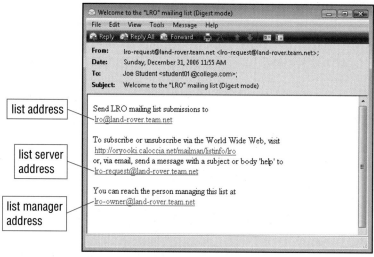

Figure 9.6 Mailing List E-mail Addresses

Tech Demo 9-1
Mailing Lists

Mailing lists have at least two and sometimes three different mailing addresses that are used to perform different list functions as shown in Figure 9.6. The list server address is the address that commands should be sent to. The list address is the e-mail address that posts are sent to for distribution to other list members. Some lists contain a third e-mail address, which is the address of the list manager or administrator. Many mailing lists allow members to subscribe through a Web page as well as by e-mail message command as shown in Figure 9.7.

Open mailing lists allow anyone to subscribe, while closed mailing lists can restrict subscribers to those meeting certain requirements, such as a university alumni list being restricted to alumni, or a nursing list being restricted to nurses. Some closed lists restrict membership to keep the list size manageable.

Moderated and Unmoderated Lists

A moderated list has a list moderator who reviews the posts to a mailing list before they are forwarded to other members. The moderator checks the posts for relevance to the list topic and for compliance with any rules of conduct, such as avoiding rude language. Moderating a list is time-consuming, so most lists are unmoderated. In some cases, an unmoderated list owner or administrator may step in to deal with a problem called to his or her attention.

Figure 9.7 Mailing List Subscription Web Page

Basic Communication Rules

Before posting messages to a mailing list, newsgroup, or similar discussion area you should look for any Frequently Asked Questions (FAQs) or any similar document that discusses guidelines or rules for posting. Rules are sometimes contained in a mailing list confirmation message or a list-related Web page as shown in Figure 9.8. Violating expected behavior may result in other list members flaming the offender. A *flame* is an abusive e-mail message or post. Most users wisely ignore flames because responding to a flame can ignite a flame war that can just make things worse. Violating list rules in a moderated list can result in warnings or even blacklisting. *Lurking*—reading mailing list posts without actively participating by making posts—can familiarize a beginner with acceptable list behavior. In addition to following mailing list rules, mailing list and newsgroup users should observe normal netiquette. The following are some common mailing list and newsgroup rules:

- Keep posts related to the mailing list topic. Posts that are not related to the list topic are known as off-topic posts.
- Do not *top-post*. Top posting is typing a response above what was written in a previous post rather than below it. Top posting forces readers to scroll down to see the original post to understand the reply.
- Do not post in HTML. Not all e-mail clients can handle HTML messages and it can cause problems with mailing lists. By default, Windows Mail creates messages in HTML format. To change the message format to plain text, click Tools and then Options, click the Send tab in the Options dialog box, click the *Plain Text* option in the *Mail Sending Format* area, and then click OK.
- Trim replies. You do not need to include the entirety of a previous post you are responding to. Areas where information was trimmed should be indicated by typing **snip**. Snipping should not be used as a means of distorting someone's comments.
- Use subject headers that appropriately describe the topic of any new post.
- Do not post attachments.
- Do not post advertising material or spam.
- Keep signatures short, usually no more than four lines.
- Do not write directly to any list members unless he or she has specifically requested it.
- Respect copyright rules.

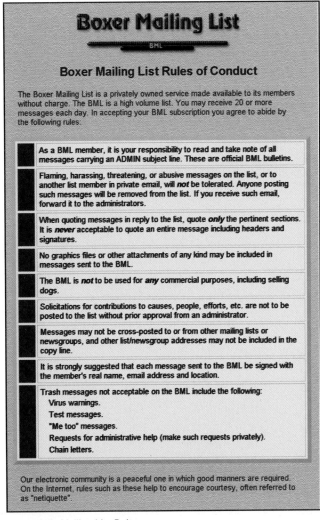

Figure 9.8 Mailing List Rules

Finding Mailing Lists

A number of Web sites and databases catalog mailing lists. L-Soft maintains a searchable database called the Catalist (www.lsoft.com/catalist.html) for mailing lists created using LISTSERV software as shown in Figure 9.9. Yahoo! Groups offers comprehensive mailing list descriptions that allow users to learn more about particular mailing lists they are interested in. Yahoo! Groups allows subscribers to use traditional e-mail commands or subscribe through the Web as shown in Figure 9.10. Mailing lists with Web-based access often offer additional features such as the ability to post photos and links, create polls, and so on.

Users also can find a mailing list using a search engine. Typing a query containing the desired mailing list

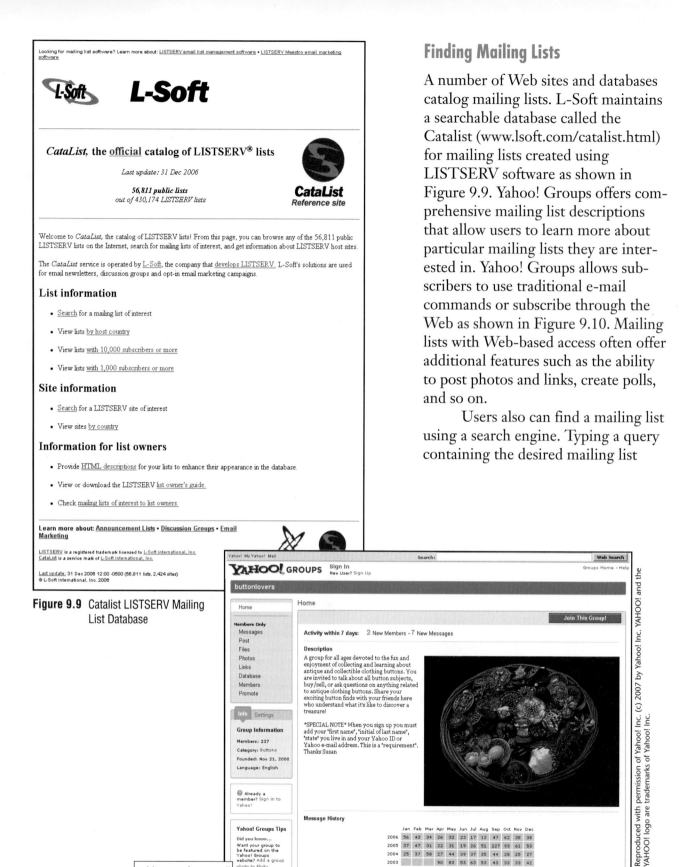

Figure 9.9 Catalist LISTSERV Mailing List Database

addresses for e-mail subscription

Web message list subscription button

Figure 9.10 Yahoo! Groups Mailing List Description

subject or topic followed by the key terms *mailing list* will often turn up search results for mailing lists related to the topic you are looking for as shown in Figure 9.11.

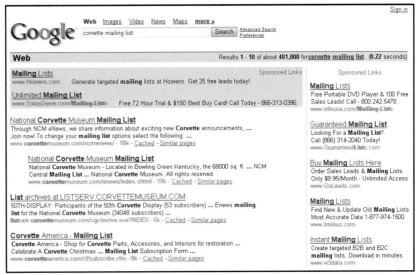

Figure 9.11 Google Mailing List Results Page

Concept

Review 1 **Electronic Mailing Lists** ●

1. Describe the different methods that can be used to read mailing list posts.
2. What is the difference between moderated and unmoderated lists?
3. How can you find mailing lists?

Skill

Review 1 **Use a Mailing List**

1. Subscribe to a mailing list by completing the following steps:
   a. Start Windows Mail.
   b. If necessary, change the message format from HTML to plain text by clicking Tools on the Windows Mail menu bar and then clicking Options. Click the Send tab and then click the *Plain Text* option in the *Mail Sending Format* section. Click the Apply button to apply the change and then click OK to close the dialog box. (*Note: If you send messages in HTML format the list server will not recognize any commands.*)

   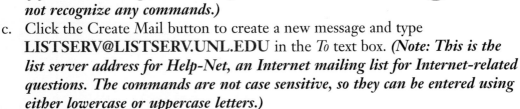

   c. Click the Create Mail button to create a new message and type **LISTSERV@LISTSERV.UNL.EDU** in the *To* text box. (*Note: This is the list server address for Help-Net, an Internet mailing list for Internet-related questions. The commands are not case sensitive, so they can be entered using either lowercase or uppercase letters.*)
   d. If necessary, remove any signature information, type **SUB HELP-NET** in the message body area, press the spacebar, and then type **anonymous**. Click the Send button to send the message when you are finished. (*Note: A dialog box will appear to let you*

   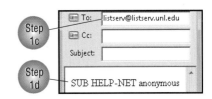

know that the message has no subject. Click OK to close the dialog box and then send the message.)

e. Wait a minute or two and then click the Windows Mail Send/Receive button to check the mail server for new messages. A command confirmation request message from the administrator of the HELP-NET mailing list should appear in your Inbox. Double-click the message listing to open the message in a new window.

f. The confirmation message contains two methods for confirming your subscription. You

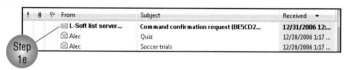

can click the confirmation hyperlink, or you can reply to the message and type **ok** in the message body. For this exercise click the Reply button, type **ok** in the message body, and then send the message.

g. Wait a minute or two and then click the Windows Mail Send/Receive button to check the mail server for new messages. You should see several new messages

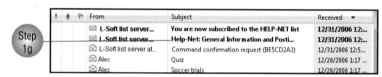

related to HELP-NET, including a message letting you know that you have been added to the HELP-NET list. Open the message titled *Help-Net: General Information and Posting Rules*. Print a copy of the message for future reference, as it contains important information on using the HELP-NET mailing list. Do not close the message.

2. Learn more about the HELP-NET mailing list archive by completing the following steps:

a. Read the entire *Help-Net: General Information and Posting Rules* message to learn about using this mailing-list, including the General Rules for Posting Messages/Replies to HELP-NET.

b. Open the *You are now subscribed to the HELP-NET list* message in your Inbox.

c. Read the contents of the message and then scroll down to the bottom of the page to find information about subscribing to the mailing list in digest form. Select and copy the SET HELP-NET DIGEST command and then click one of the LISTSERV@LISTSERV.UNL.EDU hyperlinks to open a new message window. Paste the SET HELP-NET DIGEST command in the message body and then send the message.

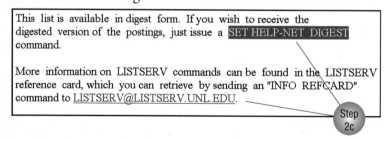

d. Wait a minute or two and then click the Windows Mail Send/Receive button to check the mail server for new messages. Open the new message describing your subscription options. Close the message when you are finished reading it.

e. Reopen the *Help-Net: General Information and Posting Rules* message. Scroll down the page until you come to the searchable archives hyperlink. Click the hyperlink to open the list archive Web page.

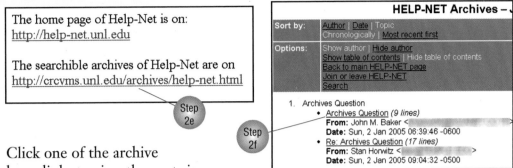

The home page of Help-Net is on:
http://help-net.unl.edu

The searchible archives of Help-Net are on
http://crcvms.unl.edu/archives/help-net.html

Step 2e

Step 2f

HELP-NET Archives –

| Sort by: | Author \| Date \| Topic Chronologically \| Most recent first |
| Options: | Show author \| Hide author Show table of contents \| Hide table of contents Back to main HELP-NET page Join or leave HELP-NET Search |

1. Archives Question
   • Archives Question *(9 lines)*
     From: John M. Baker <
     Date: Sun, 2 Jan 2005 06:39:46 -0600
   • Re: Archives Question *(17 lines)*
     From: Stan Horwitz <
     Date: Sun, 2 Jan 2005 09:04:32 -0500

f. Click one of the archive hyperlinks to view the posts in that archive. Read the posts by clicking the post subject hyperlinks. Read several archives to familiarize yourself with the mailing list.

g. Click the browser Back button to return to the List Archives page when you are finished.

3. Post to the mailing list by completing the following steps:

a. Click the <u>Post to the list</u> hyperlink at the top of the List Archives page.

b. Keeping everything you have learned about posting to the list in mind, compose a short question about something related to the Internet.

Step 3a

Archives of HELP-NET@LISTSERV.UNL.EDU

Internet Help Resource

• Search the archives
• Post to the list
• Join or leave the list (or change settings)
• Manage the list (list owners only)

c. Choose an appropriate subject and enter it in the *Subject* text box.

d. Scroll down to the bottom of the message window to click the Send button.

e. Click the <u>List Archives</u> hyperlink to open the List Archives page. Click the latest archive and look for your post. *(Note: It may take a few minutes before it appears.)*

f. Click the <u>Log off</u> hyperlink to log off the mailing list.

g. Check to see if anyone replied to your post when you receive a digest of the mailing list. You can also check the List Archives page periodically to check for any responses. *(Note: The digest should arrive within 24 hours.)*

h. Close Windows Mail and Internet Explorer when you are finished.

Step 3f

List Archives

Help-Net's Main Web Site

Subscriber's Corner
Server Archives
List Archives

List Management
List Moderation
Server Management

Help
Log off

Newsgroups

Newsgroups, also known as Internet discussion groups or forums, function like electronic bulletin boards that allow users to post and read messages. Newsgroups predate the Internet, and have their origin in a network of electronic bulletin boards known as *Usenet*—short for Users' Network. Today most newsgroups are accessed through the Internet using software programs known as newsreaders, or via a Web page interface such as the one provided by the Google Groups Web site. Many e-mail clients include a built-in newsreader,

Usenet (Users' Network) electronic bulletin board that was the pre-Internet forerunner of newsgroups; Usenet newsgroups are now available through distributed servers

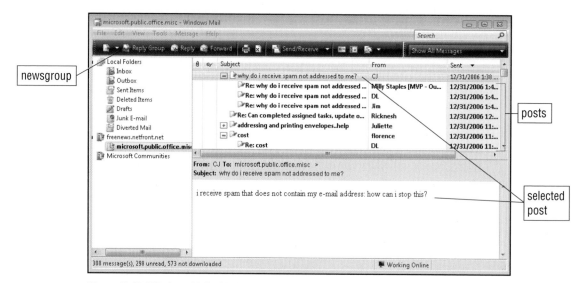

Figure 9.12 Windows Mail with Newsgroup Threads

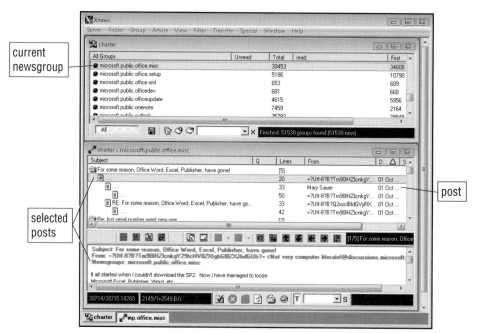

Figure 9.13 XNews Stand-Alone Newsreader

such as the Windows Mail newsreader shown in Figure 9.12. Working with newsgroups through an e-mail client is similar to working with e-mail messages. Stand-alone newsreaders such as XNews, shown in Figure 9.13, usually offer more features than e-mail client newsreaders. The user must add an account for a news server in the newsreader in order to read newsgroups. In Windows Mail, the process is very similar to the process used to add an e-mail account.

Newsgroups are handled by special servers known as news servers. Not all ISPs support newsgroups, and those that do usually do not offer access to all newsgroups, which number in the tens of thousands. Publicly accessible news servers provide an alternative for those without ISP news server service. The newzbot! Web site shown in Figure 9.14 is just one of many free services that can be used to locate publicly accessible news servers.

Newsgroups are an example of a distributed database, meaning that the contents of the database are stored on a number of different servers in different locations. When a user posts a message or article to a newsgroup, it first goes to the news server to which the user is connected. From there the contents of a newsgroup file, known as a newsfeed, will be replicated to other news servers around the world using the ***Network News Transfer Protocol (NNTP)***. During the replication process, news servers will compare the incoming data to previous data and add only new messages.

Newsgroup users subscribe to the newsgroups they want from a list of newsgroups available on the news server they are using. The subscription process is as simple as selecting a newsgroup name and then clicking a subscribe button. Once online, a newsreader can be used to download the latest posts or articles for any newsgroups to which the user has subscribed. Just as with mailing lists, users can reply to existing posts or create new posts. Once the latest posts have been downloaded, most newsreaders allow users to work offline. The user can reconnect to the Internet to send any new posts or to check for additional new posts. Although the two systems differ technically, newsgroups and mailing lists share a lot of terminology. Just as with mailing lists, a user contribution to a newsgroup is called a post or sometimes an article, a series of posts under the same topic is known as a thread, and newsgroups can be moderated or unmoderated.

Usenet newsgroup names are structured as ***hierarchies*** separated by dots. There are currently eight major top-level hierarchies as described in Table 9.1,

Figure 9.14 newzbot! Home Page

http://newzbot.com

Network News Transfer Protocol (NNTP) the protocol used for Usenet newsgroups on the Internet

hierarchies the term for Usenet newsgroup categories

Table 9.1 Big Eight Top-Level Hierarchies

Top-Level Hierarchy	Discussions Related To	Examples
comp.*	computers	comp.bugs.misc comp.databases.sybase
humanities.*	humanities	humanities.language.sanskrit humanities.lit.authors.shakespeare
misc.*	topics that do not readily fit under the other Big Eight hierarchies	misc.business.consulting misc.education.medical
news.*	newsgroups	news.admin.net-abuse.blocklisting news.announce.important
rec.*	recreational activities	rec.gardens.roses rec.games.video.saga
sci.*	science	sci.techniques.microscopy sci.space.news
soc.*	social issues	soc.women soc.support.depression.treatment
talk.*	controversial topics	talk.euthanasia talk.politics.drugs

commonly referred to as the Big Eight. A newsgroup name begins with a top-level hierarchy, such as soc.* (for social), followed by one or more lower-level hierarchies. Newsgroup names proceed from the general to the specific. For example, the newsgroup named soc.support.depression.treatment begins with the general top-level hierarchy soc, indicating that the discussion topic involves a social issue. The additional lower-level hierarchies narrow the focus of the newsgroup to make it more specific, allowing a newsgroup user looking at the soc.support.depression.treatment newsgroup name to know that it was created to discuss issues related to the treatment of depression.

The very popular alt.* top-level hierarchy was created not long after the Big Eight made their appearance. Alt (alternative) newsgroups were created to handle nonmainstream topics that were too controversial for the Big Eight. The process for creating an alt newsgroup is much simpler than the process for creating a Big Eight group and does not require approval. Alt newsgroups are so popular that they contain more messages than all the Big Eight newsgroups combined.

News servers delete posts or articles after a specified time that can vary. To address this, in 1995 a service called DejaNews began archiving and indexing newsgroup postings. DejaNews and its archives were acquired by Google in 2001 and is now known as Google Groups, as shown in Figure 9.15. Google Groups contains more than 1 billion newsgroups messages. Web sites such as Google Groups provide an alternative to using a newsreader to access newsgroups.

Figure 9.15 Google Groups

Concept Review 2 Newsgroups

1. Name two methods that can be used to read newsgroups.
2. What does the Big Eight refer to?
3. What protocol do most news servers use?

1. Add a news server in Windows Mail by completing the following steps:
   a. Start Windows Mail.
   b. Click Tools on the menu bar and then click Accounts to open the Internet Accounts dialog box.
   c. Click the Add button in the Internet Accounts dialog box.

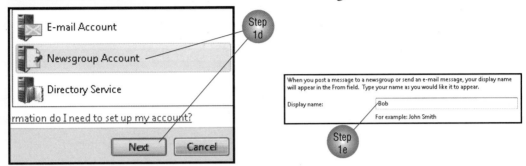

   d. Click the Newsgroup Account option and then click Next.
   e. Type your display name in the *Display name* text box and then click Next. *(Note: You do not have to use your real name.)*
   f. Type your e-mail address in the *E-mail address* text box and then click Next. *(Note: You can post anonymously by entering a fictitious e-mail address.)*
   g. Type **freenews.netfront.net** in the *News (NNTP) server* text box and then click Next. *(Note: Freenews is a free news server. Your instructor may advise you to use another news server.)*
   h. Click the Finish button.
   i. Click the Close button to close the Internet Accounts dialog box.
   j. A dialog box will appear asking you if you would like to download groups from the account you just created. Click Show Available Newsgroups, But Don't Turn on Communities to begin downloading groups. *(Note: Enabling Communities takes advantage of advanced features in Windows Mail, but requires support from the newsgroup server. The amount of time it takes to download groups depends on your connection speed. A slow connection may take several minutes.)*
   k. The Newsgroups Subscriptions dialog box will appear when the downloading is complete. Click OK to close the dialog box. If you are prompted to view a list of newsgroups, click No. *(Note: You could use the Newsgroups Subscriptions dialog box to start the subscription process, but in the next step you will learn how to open the Newsgroups Subscriptions dialog box from scratch.)*

2. Subscribe to a newsgroup and read posts by completing the following steps:
   a. If necessary, open Windows Mail.
   b. Select freenews.netfront.net in the Folder window. If a message advising you that you are not subscribed to any newsgroups in this account appears, click the No button. *(Note: When subscribing to newsgroups in the future, you can click Yes when this message appears, but you will learn another method that can be used to subscribe to newsgroups in the next few steps.)*
   c. Click Tools on the menu bar and then click Newsgroups to open the Newsgroup Subscriptions dialog box.

d. If necessary, select the All tab to see the list of all the available newsgroups.

e. Type **microsoft public** in the *Display newsgroups that contain* text box to find newsgroups with these terms. *(Note: Your instructor may tell you to select another newsgroup.)*

f. Scroll down the list of newsgroups until you come to *microsoft.public.office.misc* and then select it.

g. Click the Subscribe button to subscribe to the *microsoft.public.office.misc* newsgroup.

h. Click the Subscribed tab to see that you are subscribed to the *microsoft.public.office.misc* newsgroup.

i. Click *microsoft.public.office.misc* on the Subscribed tab and then click the Go to button to view the newsgroup posts. *(Note: The first time you do this it may take a few minutes to download the newsgroup posts.)*

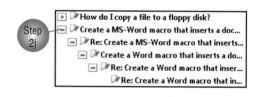

j. Click one of the plus signs next to a post to view all of the message in a thread and then click the first post to view it in the preview pane. *(Note: When you click a plus sign to expand a thread, it will turn into a minus sign. When a minus sign is clicked, an expanded thread will contract and the plus sign will display again.)*

k. Double-click the post to view it in its own window. Click the Maximize button in the title bar to expand the window.

l. Click the Next button to view the next post. Clicking Previous will open the previous post. Close the window when you are finished.

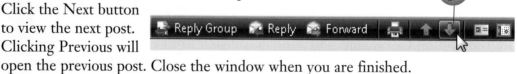

m. When being used to read news, Windows Mail displays Write Message, Reply Group, Reply, and Forward buttons. Clicking Write Message opens a New Message window where you can create a subject (thread) post. Clicking the Reply Group button allows you to send a reply to the entire group containing the contents of the selected post, while clicking Reply will send an e-mail reply to the person who wrote the post (rather than sending a newsgroup post). The Forward button can be used to forward a post to others in an e-mail message. *(Note: Ask your instructor for advice or instructions on creating a new post or replying to a previous post.)*

3. Switch between reading e-mail and reading newsgroups by completing the following steps:

a. Click the Inbox folder in the Folders window. You can now read e-mail.

b. Click *microsoft.public.office.misc* in the Folders window to return to the newsgroup.

4. Unsubscribe to a newsgroup by completing the following steps:

a. If necessary, start Windows Mail.

b. Click Tools on the menu bar and then click Newsgroups to open the Newsgroup Subscriptions dialog box.

c. Click the Subscribed tab to view the list of newsgroups subscriptions.

d. Click the *microsoft.public.office.misc* newsgroup.

e. Click the Unsubscribe button to unsubscribe to the newsgroup. *(Note: The subscription icon will be removed but the name of the newsgroup will remain. If you click the All tab and then click the Subscription tab again, you will see that the newsgroup name has been removed as well.)*

f. Click OK to close the Newsgroup Subscriptions dialog box. If prompted to subscribe to newsgroups, click No.

Web-based Forums

Web-based forums, also known as bulletin boards or message boards, are similar to newsgroups in function but the technology behind them is different. GUI Web-based forums, such as the one shown in Figure 9.16, use special software to store and handle forum data in a single server location instead of the NNTP protocol and distributed database platform used by newsgroups. Many commercial Web sites offer Web-based forums, as they are a feature that draws customers. Figure 9.16 shows a forum on the Adobe Web site, provided as a service to users of the company's Dreamweaver 8 Web page editing program.

Web-based forums offer several advantages and disadvantages compared to newsgroups. On the positive side, Web-based forums offer a number of features unavailable through newsgroups, such as the ability to enable e-mail notification when replies are made to a post as shown in Figure 9.17, the ability to use graphical emoticons, and the ability to use an avatar.

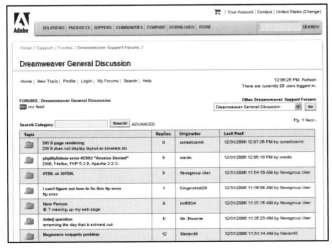

Figure 9.16 Web-based Forum

Usenet Hierarchies

The original newsgroup network known as Usenet initially employed three hierarchies to categorize newsgroups: fa.* for groups originating on the ARPANET, mod.* for moderated newsgroups, and net.* for unmoderated groups. This limited number of hierarchies eventually proved unsatisfactory and led to what has been termed the "Great Renaming" in 1987. In that year, the old hierarchies were supplanted by new, more descriptive hierarchies that allowed for better organization. Originally there were seven hierarchies, known as the "Big Seven," but with the addition of the humanities.* hierarchy in the mid-1990s the top-level hierarchies became known as the "Big Eight."

The approval process for creating a newsgroup in one of the Big Eight hierarchies is quite involved. A proposal known as a Request for Discussion (RFD) must be submitted to the moderator of news.announce.newgroups, and the RFD is then posted to news.groups as well as other newsgroups that may be relevant to the proposed newsgroup. After discussion of the RFD, the original RFD may have to be revised and resubmitted depending on the outcome. At the final stage of the process a group known as the Usenet Volunteer Votetakers (UVV) conduct a poll that will determine whether a newsgroup is approved or disapproved. The entire process can take a number of months from start to finish.

The difficult approval process and the exclusion of many controversial newsgroups topics from the original Big Seven eventually led to the creation of other hierarchies soon after the Great Renaming, chief among them the alt.* hierarchy, now the largest newsgroup hierarchy. Currently there are hundreds of different hierarchies containing tens of thousands of newsgroups. If you cannot find a newsgroup you want, you can always create your own!

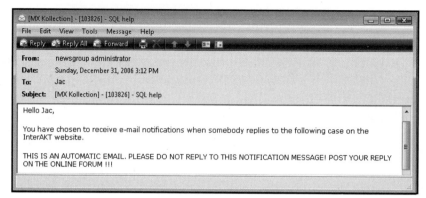

Figure 9.17 Web-based Forum Reply Notification

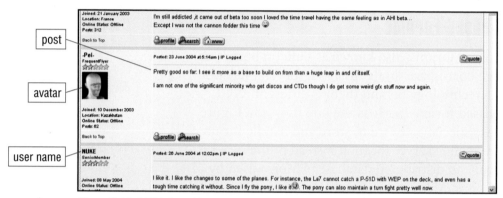

Figure 9.18 A Web-based Forum Avatar

An *avatar* serves as a graphical representation of a forum user such as the avatar shown in Figure 9.18.

On the negative side, the single server nature of a Web-based forum makes it more vulnerable to disruption compared to newsgroups stored in a distributed database. It can also be harder to locate Web-based forums because they are contained in different Web sites rather than grouped together like newsgroups. Using a Web-based forum for the first time can be confusing because there are a number of different Web-based forum software technologies in use, each with a different layout and features.

Concept Review 3 Web-based Forums

1. How do Web-based forums differ from newsgroups?
2. Name some of the advantages and disadvantages of Web-based forums as compared to newsgroups.
3. What is an avatar?

Skill Review 3 Explore a Web-based Forum

1. Read posts on a Web-based forum by completing the following steps:
    a. If necessary, start Internet Explorer.
    b. Type **discussion.monster.com/messageboards** in the Address bar and then press Enter.

c. Scroll down the page until you find the General Interest Message Boards area. Click the Current Events hyperlink to open the Current Events Message Board.

d. Scroll down the page until you see the message listings. Find a thread you find interesting and then click it.

e. Read the original message, which is at the top of the thread.

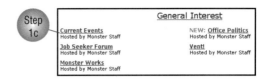

f. Scroll down the page to read a few of the replies. *(New replies are added under the last post. Therefore, the oldest posts are up top and the newest posts are at the bottom.)*

g. Click the Current Events hyperlink at the top of the page to return to the Current Events threads.

h. Use the skills you have just learned to visit other message boards sponsored by Monster.com. Navigate and read different threads so that you gain a better understanding of how to use the message boards.

2. Register so that you can post to Monster.com message boards by completing the following steps:

a. Click the Create A New Monster User hyperlink at the top of the page.

b. Fill in the Contact Info section. *(Note: Fields preceded by a red asterisk must be completed, all others are optional.)*

c. Fill in the Login & Email section. *(Note: Use a real email address if you want to be able to retrieve a forgotten password in the future.)*

d. Fill in the Career Info section and uncheck the checkbox to Create a Monster Job Search Agent

e. The Equal Opportunity/Affirmative Action section is optional, so we will skip it.

f. In the Resume Options section, choose the option for *I'll post my resume later.*

g. In the Updates & Offers section, uncheck all checkboxes.

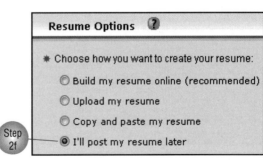

h. In the Other Information And Offers section, select No for each item, then click the Create Account button at the bottom of the page.

i. If a Monster Special Offers page appears, click the No Thanks button at the bottom of the page without filling in any part of the form.

3. Create a new post by completing the following steps:
   a. Now that your account is created, once again type discussion.monster.com/messageboards in the Address bar and then press Enter. *(Note: Typing the URL in the Address bar is the most direct route back to the message boards.)*
   b. Navigate to a message board of your choice and click the New Thread button at the top of the page.
   c. Enter a screen name so others can identify you and click the Save button.
   d. Type a subject for your new post in the Subject text box. Type your message in the large Message box. Click the Post button to post your message. *(Note: The format for creating a reply is identical, except that the subject text box is already filled in with the subject of the post to which you are replying.)*

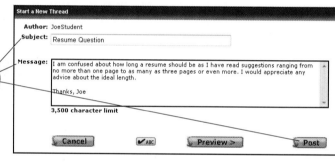

   e. Wait a few minutes and then return to the message board to which you posted and look for your post. Monster.com message forums are moderated so there will be a time lag before a post appears on a forum.
   f. Close the Monster.com Web page.

Weblogs (Blogs)

Weblogs, also referred to as web logs or blogs, are a form of personal journal or diary in Web page format. Weblog entries are referred to as posts, and each post made by a blog writer—known as a blogger—is date and time stamped so that readers know when the post was created. Posts appear in reverse chronological order, meaning that the most recent post will appear first. A blog typically displays a limited number of posts, with previous posts automatically moved to an archives section. Each post usually features a *permalink*, which is a unique URL that can be used to display an entry. Most weblogs contain a set of hyperlinks, sometimes called a *blogroll*, that link to other blogs or Web sites. Blogrolls allow bloggers to share favorite blogs with readers, but also function as a method of increasing blog traffic because many linked blogs will reciprocate linkage. Figure 9.19 shows a typical weblog layout.

Tech Demo 9-2
Weblogs

permalink a unique URL that can be used to link to blog entries

blogroll weblog section than contains links to other blogs or Web sites

Blogs can be created in several different ways. The easiest method is to use a weblog service that provides ready-made blog templates as well as hosting. Table 9.2 contains a list of free weblog providers. Many of these providers offer free weblog hosting with upgraded services available for a fee, such as Google Blogger shown in

Table 9.2 Free Weblog Providers

Provider	URL
20six	www.20six.co.uk
Blogger	www.blogger.com
eBloggy	www.ebloggy.com
LiveJournal	www.livejournal.com
tBlog	www.tblog.com
Tripod Blog Builder	blog.tripod.lycos.com
WordPress	www.wordpress.com

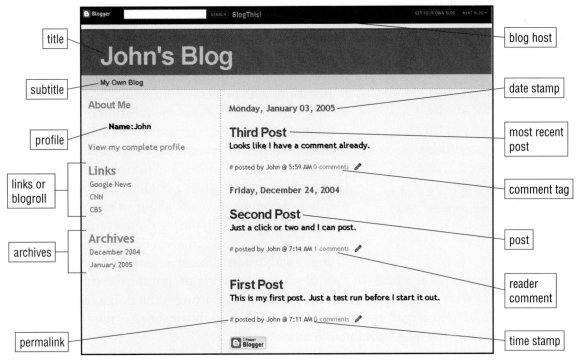

Figure 9.19 Basic Weblog Features

The Blog Phenomenon

While Web pages have been around since the advent of the Web in 1995, weblogs are a more recent development. The term *blog*, derived from web log, first gained currency in 1999. Not coincidentally, in that same year blogging was given a boost with the arrival of the first hosted weblog building tools that made it easy for anyone to start their own blog. The popularity of blogging has continued to increase dramatically to the point that the dictionary publishers Merriam-Webster named blog the number one Word of the Year in 2004. In early 2005, weblog authority and blogosphere search engine Technorati claimed to be tracking almost five and a half million weblogs, while the Pew Internet and American Life Project released survey results that indicated that 7 percent of Americans had created a blog and that 27 percent of Internet users were blog readers.

The first blogs started out as personal journal-like Web pages, with bloggers entering posts about personal observations or thoughts. Other bloggers would post links to news articles or editorials followed by their comments or observations about the linked article. Nowadays there are any number of different blog formats, including political, news, corporate, and topical blogs. More and more Americans are turning to blogs for news and information, and some observers feel that blogs pose a challenge to traditional media by focusing attention on news stories that mainstream journalists ignore. Candidate and other political blogs played a prominent role during the 2004 Presidential campaign. During the Asian Tsunami disaster in late 2004 many bloggers played a public service role by providing firsthand accounts from affected areas and helping to coordinate relief efforts. Despite the rapid increase in blogs, they are still a mystery to many—while the Pew study documented the rapid rise of blogs it also noted that some 62 percent of American Internet users were not familiar with them.

Source: Pew Survey Data, www.pewinternet.org/pdfs/PIP_blogging_data.pdf Technorati Data, www.technorati.com

TrackBack weblog feature that uses an Internet utility known as ping to create a link to a comment referenced in a comment on another weblog

Figure 9.20 Google's Blogger Free Weblog Service

Figure 9.20. Some weblog providers let bloggers use their Weblog service but host it on another site using FTP.

Blogs also can be created using stand-alone weblog software. The user installs the software on his or her computer, but must find a host server for the blog content. While requiring more knowledge than weblog services, weblog software gives the user more options for customizing the blog.

Most weblogs include comment and/or *TrackBack* features that make them a form of asynchronous communication. The two-way communication between weblogs and readers allows the creation of blogging communities, and the interconnected blogging communities are sometimes referred to as the blogosphere.

Most weblogs allow readers to comment on a post. Once a comment is made, a comment tag shows the number of comments made about an entry as shown in Figure 9.19. Clicking the tag displays the comments page. Weblog owners can also add comments to dialogue with readers. Some weblog providers offer comments as a built-in feature while others do not, but third-party comment software is available and can be added to an existing weblog. If a blogger has trouble with readers leaving abusive comments, he or she may remove or disable the blog's comment feature.

Weblogs also have a TrackBack feature, which notifies a weblog owner that another blogger has made a reference or comment to a post on the owner's weblog. TrackBack uses an Internet utility known as ping to create a link to the original blog entry as shown in Figure 9.21. Bloggers often carry on a form of dialog using the TrackBack feature.

Many weblogs as well as other Web sites now feature RSS feeds. RSS (Really Simple Syndication) is an XML format for automatically notifying people of Web site updates. Many blog readers subscribe to RSS feeds that let them know when new entries have been added to a blog. RSS feeds can be subscribed to through an RSS aggregator or reader that can be used to collect, update, and display RSS feeds. Web sites that are RSS-enabled often feature a small orange XML button that viewers can use to subscribe to the feed, but RSS feeds also can appear as hyperlinks. There are a number of different ways to subscribe to RSS feeds, but a simple method is to right-click an RSS feed button or link and then click Copy Shortcut to copy the URL of the syndicated content. The URL can then be pasted in the appropriate area of an RSS aggregator or reader.

Weblog directories such as the blogarama.com Web page shown in Figure 9.22 offer an easy way to find weblogs. A reader can search a weblog directory by category, author, title, words or phrases, or country. A search query in a search engine with search terms related to the type of weblog you are looking for with the words *blog* or *weblog* will often turn up weblogs. Many people enjoy surfing blogs by using the blogroll links found in most weblogs.

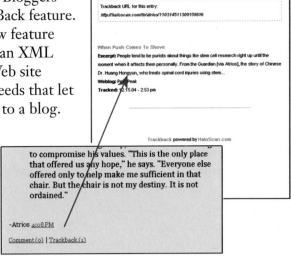

Figure 9.21 TrackBack Link and Comment

Figure 9.22 Blogarama Weblog Directory

Concept Review 4 Weblogs (Blogs)

1. Describe the typical features of a weblog.
2. What is the blogosphere?
3. What is TrackBack, and how is it used?
4. How can you find a weblog?

1. Create a weblog by completing the following steps:
   a. Start Internet Explorer.
   b. Type **www.blogger.com/start** in the Address bar and then press Enter to open the Blogger start page.
   c. Click the CREATE YOUR BLOG NOW button in the bottom right area of the page.
   d. Fill out the email address, password, display name, and word verification textboxes. The display name will be used to sign your blog posts. Be sure to check the *Acceptance of Terms* check box and then click the Continue button. ***(Note: Write down your user name and password and keep them in a safe place as you will need them to log on to Blogger in Step 2.)***
   e. Enter a title for your blog in the *Blog title* text box and a blog address in the *Blog address* text box.

   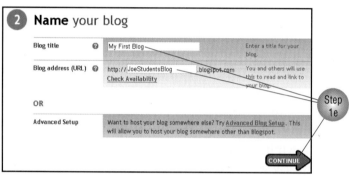

   The text you enter in the *Blog address* text box will form part of the URL that others will use to read and link to your blog. Click the Continue button when you are finished. ***(Note: Write down and store your blog URL.)***
   f. Choose the Sand Dollar template at the bottom of the page. You can view a larger version of the template by clicking on it. Click the Continue button when you are finished.
   g. You can click the START POSTING button to begin working on your blog, however you will learn how to log on to Blogger in the next step.

2. Log on to Blogger and create a post by completing the following steps:

   a. Complete Step 1b to open the Blogger start page, then click the New Blogger link at the top of the page to open the sign-in page.
   b. Fill in the *Username* and *Password* text boxes and then click the SIGN IN button to log on to your blog.
   c. Click the New Post hyperlink located in the top left area of the page.

d. Create a title for your post by typing it in the *Title* text box.

e. Type your first post in the large message body text box.

f. Click the Post Options hyperlink at the bottom of the message box and verify Allow is selected under Reader Comments.

g. Click the Publish button to publish your post.

h. Click the (in a new window) hyperlink at the top of the Web page informing you that your post was successfully published. Your blog will open in a new browser window.

i. Read your first post.

j. Click the Sign Out hyperlink to sign out of Blogger when you are finished.

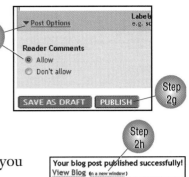

Wikis

Asynchronous document collaboration enables people to work together on documents regardless of their location. Chapter 6 contained information about one form of asynchronous document collaboration technology known as Web-Based Distributed Authoring and Versioning (WebDAV), but there are other technologies, including an increasingly popular type of Web site known as a wiki.

wikiengine the software package used to create wikis

The term *wiki* is derived from the first wiki, the WikiWikiWeb, created in 1995 by Portland, Oregon, computer programmer Ward Cunningham. Seeking a name that reflected the simplicity of his collaborative concept, Cunningham chose to name it after wiki wiki, the Hawaiian word for very quick. There are a number of different wiki variations, but core wiki features include user editability, automatic linking using the wiki naming convention of two or more capitalized words run together, and the ability to create pages without HTML. When capitalized, Wiki often refers to the original WikiWikiWeb, while the lowercase form or wiki refers to other wikis. Software that drives a wiki is known as a *wikiengine*, and there are a number of different wikiengines available.

Users create or edit wiki source text using an edit form as shown in Figure 9.23, and the wikiengine automatically renders the user-entered text into text that can be viewed using a browser during the saving

special code used to format wiki topic

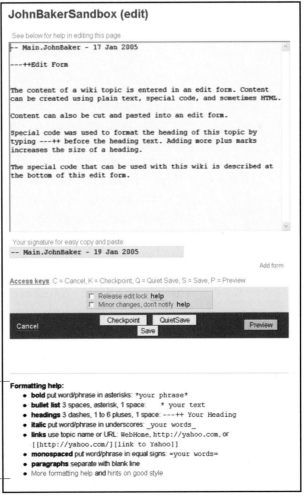

Figure 9.23 Wiki Edit Form

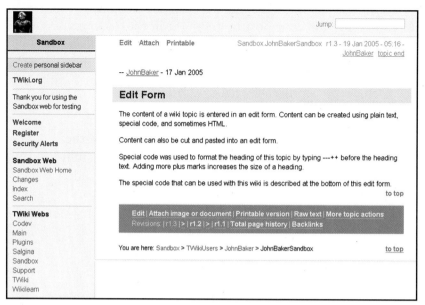

Figure 9.24 Rendered Edit Form Content Viewed in Browser

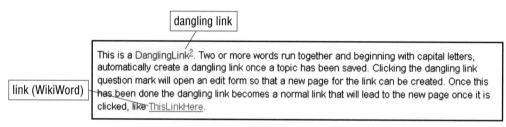

dangling link

link (WikiWord)

This is a DanglingLink[?]. Two or more words run together and beginning with capital letters, automatically create a dangling link once a topic has been saved. Clicking the dangling link question mark will open an edit form so that a new page for the link can be created. Once this has been done the dangling link becomes a normal link that will lead to the new page once it is clicked, like ThisLinkHere.

Figure 9.25 Wiki Dangling Link

process as shown in Figure 9.24. Content entries can include plain text, special wiki code, as shown in Figure 9.23, and sometimes HTML. This simplicity means that no technical or programming knowledge is necessary in order to create or edit a wiki page.

Hyperlinks known as **WikiWords** provide the main navigational method for wikis, and one of the key features of wikis is the ease with which links and new pages can be created. Creating a link in a wiki is as simple as typing two or more capitalized words linked together to create a WikiWord, such as PageTwo or AfricanBirds. When a topic is saved, wiki software automatically recognizes a WikiWord as a defined link pattern and creates a **dangling link**, which is a WikiWord followed by a question mark as shown in Figure 9.25. Clicking a dangling link opens an edit form like the one shown in Figure 9.23, so the user can create a new page. Once the user creates and saves the page, the page link will appear as an ordinary hyperlink.

Although unorthodox, creating links before a page is created helps to minimize the possibility of creating orphan documents that are unlinked to other pages. Another advantage to this method is that users can create a dangling link for a topic they think should be created, and other users can then click the dangling link to create the new topic and complete the link. Regular URLs complete with protocol, such as http://www.cnn.com, can be used to create links to pages located outside a wiki.

WikiWord wiki hyperlink created by typing two or more capitalized words with no spaces between them, as in PageTwo or AfricanBirds

dangling link a link created when a WikiWord is created and saved, appears as a hyperlink usually followed by a question mark

Most wikis have a ***sandbox*** as shown in Figure 9.26, which is an area that newcomers can use to experiment with creating and editing wiki pages. The sandbox is isolated from the other parts of a wiki, so there is no danger of doing anything that could affect other wiki components. Once new users feel comfortable, they can then leave the sandbox to work on the other pages in a wiki.

sandbox practice wiki page isolated from the other parts of a wiki so there is no danger of doing anything that could affect other wiki components

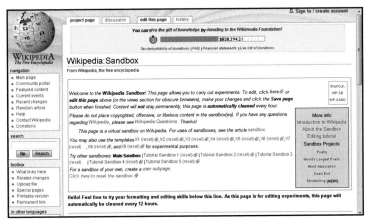

Figure 9.26 Wiki Sandbox

Wikipedia

The largest and perhaps most ambitious wiki project to date is the Wikipedia (http://www.wikipedia.org), an online encyclopedia created and maintained by voluntary contributors. In addition to the English language version, there are Wikipedias in German, Swedish, Spanish, Chinese and a number of other major languages, as well as some lesser known languages such as Catalan and Esperanto. The English language Wikipedia currently contains over 1.5 billion articles, almost thirteen times as many articles as the 2007 electronic edition of the Encyclopedia Britannica. That figure is even more impressive when you consider that the Wikipedia project only started in 2001.

While it would seem that extending an invitation to anyone to write content for the Wikipedia would be a prescription for chaos and inaccuracy, the results so far have been impressive. Wikipedia maintains what it terms a neutral point of view (NPOV) policy that urges contributors to write without

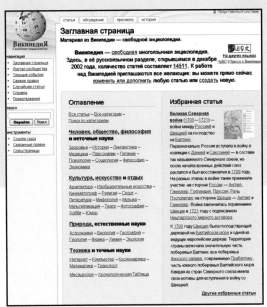

bias. In practice this means that different points of view should be reflected without any one view being advocated. In general, the NPOV policy has prevailed, although there have been "edit wars" between those seeking to promote their own views on controversial topics. Wikipedia has experienced an ongoing problem with vandalism, but so far the innate resilience of the wiki model combined with Wikipedia's devoted community of users has enabled it to deal with that issue successfully.

The success of Wikipedia has led the Wikimedia Foundation, the nonprofit operators of Wikipedia, to create a number of other wikis, including Wiktionary (dictionary), Wikisource (public domain texts), Wikibooks (textbooks), Wikiquote (notable quotations), Wikispecies (a directory of species), Wikinews (free-content news), and Wikiversity (free learning materials and activities).

Many people are surprised to learn that anyone can edit the pages in a public wiki, and wonder how wikis prevent hacking and vandalism of wiki contents. The simple answer is that there are no measures in place to prevent those activities, but the nature of wiki and the wiki community has so far prevented those issues from becoming a problem. The fact that there is little or no security makes a wiki unattractive to hackers because of the lack of a challenge. As a collaborative effort, wikis usually attract a devoted community that will usually repair any damage soon after it is detected. Past page revisions are maintained so if a page is deleted or defaced it can be restored. Persistent vandals and hackers can have their IP addresses blocked. Some wikis have restricted editing privileges in an effort to protect against malicious activity, but wiki purists argue that only public wikis that allow anyone to read or write are true wikis.

Wiki software can be used to create and host a wiki. Most wiki software is open source software, meaning that it is in the public domain and that its source code can be modified. Wikifarms such as the Xwiki.com Web site shown in Figure 9.27 offer wiki software and hosting services for those who do not have the facilities or technical ability to create and host their own wiki.

There are a number of ways to discover the different public wikis available. WikiIndex, at www.wikiindex.org, is a wiki of wikis, while Meatball offers what it calls a tour bus that stops at featured wikis at www.usemod.com/cgi-bin/mb.pl?TourBus.

Figure 9.27 Xwiki.com Web Site

Concept Review 5 Wikis

1. How do the pages in a wiki differ from the pages in an ordinary Web site?
2. What is a WikiWord?
3. What is a wiki sandbox?
4. Describe the process of creating links and new pages in a wiki.

1. Use a Wikifarm to create your own wiki by completing the following steps:
   a. If necessary, start Internet Explorer.
   b. Type **www.riters.com** in the Address bar and then press Enter.
   c. Click the <u>Make A Wiki</u> hyperlink at the top of the riters.com home page.

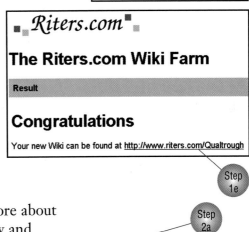

   d. If necessary, scroll down the Make A Wiki Web page until you reach the *Wiki name* text box. Type a name for your wiki in the text box and then click the create button. *(Hint: Use only letters or numbers to create your name. The use of any other characters will result in your name being rejected.)*
   e. Click the hyperlink to your wiki site when the Congratulations page appears. *(Hint: Record this URL and save it so that you can find it again.)*

2. Edit your new wiki page by completing the following steps:
   a. Read the information on the Your new Wiki page. Click the Edit button in the upper right corner of the page to begin editing it. *(Hint: You can also click the <u>EditText</u> link at the bottom of the page.)*

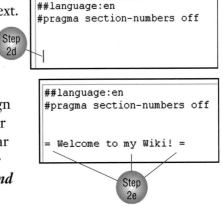

   b. Read the text in the edit form to learn more about editing your wiki. Select all the text below and including the = Your new Wiki = line and then press the Delete key to delete it.
   c. Scroll to the bottom of the page and review the special code you can use to format your wiki text.
   d. Scroll back up to the top of the edit form and place the insertion point two lines below the #pragma section-numbers off line.

   ```
   ##language:en
   #pragma section-numbers off

   |
   ```

   e. Type an equal sign (=) and then press the spacebar to create one space after the equal sign you just created. Type a heading name for your wiki. When you are finished, press the spacebar again and then type another equal sign. *(Hint: There must be a space between the starting and ending equal signs and your header text.)*

   ```
   ##language:en
   #pragma section-numbers off


   = Welcome to my Wiki! =
   ```

   f. Scroll down below the edit form and click the Preview button to preview the heading you just created. *(Hint: The preview is displayed below the edit form.)*
   g. Scroll back up to the top of the page to continue editing. *(Hint: Do not click your browser Back button or you will lose the content you just created. You may see a warning telling you that you should refrain from editing the page in order to avoid editing conflicts. If you get this message, wait until the stated time is up before you begin editing.)*

h. Place the insertion point just after your header and then press the Enter key twice to create blank lines between the header and the text you are about to enter.

i. Type an introductory paragraph for your wiki.

j. Repeat Step 2f to preview the text you just entered.

k. Press the Save Changes button located below the edit form to save the changes you just made. *(Hint: When you click the Save Changes button, you may see a new page asking you to enter some random letters or numbers in a text box before clicking the Submit button. This is a human verification system designed to prevent spam abuse. Enter the characters you see in the black box and then click the Submit button to continue.)*

l. Click the Edit button to return to the edit form. Place the insertion point after the last sentence of your paragraph and then press Enter twice to create blank lines between the paragraph and a new paragraph you are about to create.

m. Type a new paragraph below your first paragraph. Click the Save Changes button when you are finished typing.

n. Click the Diffs button located at the top right of the page. Look at the color-coded text that displays a record of the changes you have made to your wiki so far. When you are finished, click the View button at the top right corner of the page to return to the browser view of your wiki page.

3. Create a link and add a new page to your wiki by completing the following steps:

a. Click the Edit button at the top right corner of your wiki page.

b. Place the insertion point after the last sentence of your second paragraph and then press Enter twice to create blank lines between the paragraph and the link you are about to create.

c. Type a WikiWord that will serve as a link to the new topic page you are about to create. A WikiWord is two or more capitalized words run together, such as NewLink, MySecondPage, and so on.

d. Click the Save Changes button.

e. Click the WikiWord you just created. *(Note: This wiki does not display a dangling question mark as described earlier in the text.)*

f. Click the Create this page hyperlink to create a new page. *(Note: Your WikiWord appears at the top of this page to let you know that you are creating a new page for that WikiWord.)*

g. Select and delete the text in the edit form and then type a new paragraph. Click the Save Changes button when you are finished.

h. Click the FrontPage button at the top of your new page to return to the front page of your wiki.

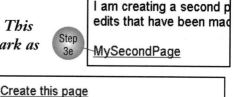

i. Click the WikiWord link you just created to test it. It should lead to the page you just created.

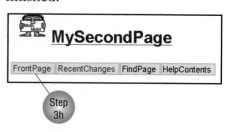

j. Continue to experiment with your wiki by adding and formatting new text and creating new pages.

k. Close Internet Explorer when you are finished.

Chapter Summary

- Administrators create mailing lists using a number of popular mailing list software programs such as Majordomo, Mailman, and LISTSERV.

- Most mailing lists offer three reading options: posts can arrive as individual e-mail messages, posts can arrive in a digest form that is an accumulation of posts over a period (usually daily) sent as one message, or posts can be viewed via a Web page.

- Most mailing lists are archived so that members can view previous postings.

- The traditional method used to subscribe or unsubscribe from a mailing list is to send a command such as HELP or SUBSCRIBE in the subject or body of an e-mail message.

- Open mailing lists allow anyone to subscribe, while closed lists restrict subscribers.

- A moderated list has a list moderator who reviews the posts to a mailing list before they are forwarded to other members.

- Before posting a message to a mailing list, you should look for any Frequently Asked Questions (FAQs) or similar documents that discuss guidelines or rules for posting.

- Newsgroups, also known as Internet discussion groups or forums, function like electronic bulletin boards that allow users to post and read messages.

- Newsgroups predate the Internet and have their origin in a network of electronic bulletin boards known as Usenet—short for Users' Network.

- Today most newsgroups are accessed through the Internet using software programs known as newsreaders, or via a Web page interface such as the one provided by the Google Groups Web site.

- Special servers known as news servers handle Usenet newsgroups using the NNTP protocol.

- Newsgroups are an example of a distributed database, meaning that the contents of the database are stored on a number of different servers in different locations.

- Usenet newsgroup names are structured as hierarchies separated by dots.

- There are currently eight major top-level hierarchies, commonly referred to as the Big Eight.

- Newsgroup posts, or articles, are usually deleted after a specified time that can vary.

- Web-based forums use special software to store and handle forum data in a single server location instead of the distributed database platform used by Usenet newsgroups.

- Using a Web-based forum for the first time can be confusing because there are a number of different Web-based forum software technologies with different layouts and features.

- Weblogs, also referred to as web logs or blogs, are a form of personal journal or diary in Web page format.

- Weblog entries are referred to as posts, and each post made by a blog writer, known as a blogger, is date and time stamped so that readers know when the post was created.

- Most weblogs contain a set of hyperlinks, sometimes called a blogroll, that link to other blogs or Web sites.

- A weblog may include a comment and/or TrackBack feature, making it a form of asynchronous communication.

- The weblog comment feature allows readers to comment on a post.

- Core wiki features include user editability, automatic linking using the wiki naming convention of two or more capitalized words run together, and the ability to create pages without HTML.

- Users create or edit wiki source text using an edit form.

- Wiki content can be entered in an edit form using plain text, special wiki code, or sometimes HTML.

- Hyperlinks known as WikiWords are the main navigational method used by wikis, and one of the key features of wikis is the ease with which links and new pages can be created.

- Most wikis have a sandbox, which is an area that newcomers can use to experiment with creating and editing wiki pages.

- Some wikis restrict editing privileges in an effort to protect against malicious activity, but wiki purists argue that only public wikis that allow anyone to read or write are true wikis.

- Most wiki software is open source software, meaning that it is in the public domain and that its source code can be modified.

- Wikifarms offer wiki software and hosting services for those who do not have the facilities or technical ability to create and host their own wiki.

Key Terms

Numbers indicate the pages where terms are first cited in the chapter. An alphabetized list of key terms with definitions can be found on the Encore CD that accompanies this book. In addition, these terms and definitions are included in the end-of-book glossary.

avatar, *290*

blogroll, *293*

dangling link, *298*

flame, *279*

hierarchies, *285*

lurking, *279*

Network News Transfer Protocol (NNTP), *285*

permalink, *293*

post, *276*

sandbox, *299*

thread, *276*

top-post, *279*

TrackBack, *294*

Usenet (Users' Network), *283*

wikiengine, *297*

WikiWord, *298*

Net ✓ Check

Additional quiz questions are available on the Encore CD that accompanies this book as well as on the Internet Resource Center for this title at www.emcp.net/Internet2e.

Multiple Choice

Indicate the correct answer for each question or statement.

1. Blogroll refers to
   a. a weblog section featuring links to other blogs and or Web sites.
   b. a weblog section that allows readers to post comments.
   c. the list of bloggers responsible for maintaining a blog.
   d. the tendency of some blogs to move vertically while users are scrolling through them.

2. Majordomo is a
   a. wikiengine.
   b. software program used to create electronic mailing lists.
   c. Web-based forum.
   d. Usenet newsgroup.

3. Previous posts to a mailing list or forum are stored in
   a. storage vaults.
   b. post files.
   c. archives.
   d. post safes.

4. Posts to a mailing list are sent to the list
   a. server address.
   b. address.
   c. owner address.
   d. administrator address.

5. Web-based forums
   a. use the NNTP protocol and are stored in distributed databases.
   b. use special software to store and handle forum data in a single server location.
   c. are a server-free form of asynchronous communication.
   d. do not allow the use of avatars.

6. A wikiengine
   a. refers to the software used to create wikis.
   b. refers to software that can speed up or accelerate wikis, making them easier to use.
   c. is a type of robot used to automatically gather data for a wiki.
   d. periodically scans a wiki for viruses.

7. A mailing list digest
   a. is a condensed form of a mailing list.
   b. is a mailing list summary.
   c. is an accumulation of posts compiled and sent as one message.
   d. contains posts on a variety of different topics.

8. Newsgroups
   a. are made available through distributed databases.
   b. feature news articles from news sources around the world.
   c. are a read-only form of asynchronous communication.
   d. allow subscription by invitation only.

9. The protocol used to distribute newsgroups over the Internet is
   a. NNTP.
   b. UUCP.
   c. NTP.
   d. IP.

10. Newsgroup names are composed of
    a. categories.
    b. hierarchies.
    c. name segments.
    d. newsnames.

True/False

Indicate whether each statement is true or false.

1. Permalinks are links that can be used to link to blog entries.
2. A subscription command to a mailing list should be sent to the list server address.
3. Top-posting refers to typing a response above what was written in a previous post and is considered bad style.
4. WikiWords cannot be used to create new pages in a wiki.
5. Newsgroups are usually available only through a single database.
6. A closed mailing list restricts subscribers to those meeting certain requirements.
7. A flame is an abusive post or message.
8. Moderated mailing lists or forums do not review posts.
9. Messages to a mailing list or forum are referred to as posts.
10. Old posts to mailing lists and forums cannot be retrieved.

Virtual Perspectives

1. Discuss your favorite asynchronous communication method and explain why it is your favorite. Are other asynchronous communication methods more suitable in certain situations? If yes, discuss those situations.

2. Wikis are popular tools for collaborative Internet projects. Unlike other Internet technologies, wikis employ little or nothing in the way of security. Wiki proponents say that the number of good people using wikis outnumbers the number of bad people and that most wikis function pretty well—with fewer disruptions and irritations than other technologies such as mailing lists, newsgroups, e-mail, and so on. However, some wikis have felt it necessary to add editing restrictions and login requirements in an effort to deal with malicious users. Discuss your feelings on the future of wikis. Will they continue to thrive, or will they eventually be forced to adopt some of the restrictive security measures used by other Internet technologies in order to survive?

Internet Lab Projects

Project 1
Add a Profile to Your Weblog

1. Start Internet Explorer and log on to the blogger.com blog you created in Skill Review 4.
2. Click the Edit Profile hyperlink on the Dashboard page.
3. If necessary, click the *Share my profile* option to enable it.
4. Scroll down the page until you come to the *General* section. Enter your birthday information and the URL for your home page if you have one.
5. Scroll further down to the *Location* and *Work* sections and enter that information.
6. Type profile information in the *Extended Info* section text boxes.
7. Press the SAVE PROFILE button when you are finished.
8. Click the Dashboard hyperlink to return to the Dashboard.
9. Click your blog hyperlink.
10. Click the View hyperlink to view your blog.
11. Click the View my complete profile hyperlink to view the profile you just created.
12. Click the EDIT YOUR PROFILE button if you need to edit your profile.

Project 2 Create Links for Your Blog

1. Choose three Web pages that you will link to from your blog. Write down the complete URL for each Web page.
2. Start Internet Explorer and log on to your blog.
3. Click the Manage Posts button at the top of the Dashboard. *(Hint: The Manage Posts hyperlink is next to a small gear icon.)*
4. Click the Edit hyperlink to the left of your blog title.
5. If necessary, scroll down in the message box to the end of your blog post, click after the last sentence, and press Enter twice to create a new line.
6. Type a descriptive word or phrase for your first URL, like **CNN**.
7. Select the text you just typed and click the Link button in the toolbar above the message box.
8. In the URL textbox, type the full URL, including the *http://* part. For example, you may type **http://www.cnn.com**. When you are done typing, click OK. Your text is transformed into a hyperlink.
9. Click after the new hyperlink, press Enter, and type a descriptive word or phrase for your second URL.
10. Select the text you just typed and click the Link button in the toolbar above the message box.
11. Enter your second URL in the URL textbox, including the *http://* part, and click OK.
12. Click after your second hyperlink, press Enter, and create your third hyperlink.
13. If necessary, scroll to the bottom of the page and click the Publish button.
14. Click the View Blog hyperlink to view your blog with your new edits.
15. Test the links by clicking them. Use the browser Back button to return to your blog each time you test a link.

Project 3 Create a Wiki Tutorial

Use the wiki you created in Skill Review 5 to create a tutorial for any one of the five Internet technologies covered in this chapter. Describe the technology, explain how it works, and provide examples of what it can be used for. Make liberal use of hyperlinks (WikiWords) within your wiki tutorial. For example, any terms you use should be created as WikiWords, and the WikiWords should link to new pages containing definitions along with any other related information. You should also add links to material located outside your wiki where relevant. Use the formatting that is available to make your pages attractive and easy to read.

Internet Research Activities

Activity 1
Explore Blogs

Blogs were frequently in the news in 2004, so much so that ABC News declared bloggers "People of the Year." However, at the same time the Pew Internet and American Life Project found that more than 65 percent of American Internet users had never heard of the term. Research the blog phenomenon and then write or type a short paper on an aspect of blogging that you find interesting or noteworthy.

Activity 2
Create a Comparison Table for Asynchronous Communication Methods

Use the information you have learned in this chapter as well as information you gather from Internet research to create a comparison table that describes the advantages and disadvantages for each of the different asynchronous communication methods you learned about in this chapter. For each method include at least two URLs for sites that can be used to locate examples of each method. For example, Yahoo! Groups can be used to locate mailing lists, Google Groups can be used to locate newsgroups, and so on.

Activity 3
Net Challenge

Visit the Wikipedia main page at http://wikipedia.com and click the English hyperlink (or a different appropriate language hyperlink for yourself). Click the Anyone Can Edit hyperlink in the top left area of the page (under Welcome To Wikipedia) and read the Wikipedia:Introduction page to learn more about Wikipedia. Click the Learn more about editing hyperlink at the top of the page. Explore the various links to learn more about creating and editing Wikipedia pages. When you are finished reading, click the Sandbox hyperlink to visit the Wikipedia sandbox. Use the sandbox to practice editing a Wikipedia page. Once you feel comfortable editing in Wikipedia, return to the Learn more about editing page and reread the material contained in the your first article link. Pick a topic and write an article for wikipedia once you are sure you understand the process. Check back periodically to see if your article has been edited or deleted.

Alternate activity: Edit or contribute to an existing Wikipedia article.

Chapter 10
Synchronous Communications

Learning Objectives

- Define the role and function of synchronous communication.

- Demonstrate how Internet Relay Chat (IRC) works.

- Explain how instant messaging (IM) clients work and identify different IM features.

- Explain video conferencing.

- Explain how to use Windows Live Messenger for video chat.

- Describe Voice over Internet Protocol (VoIP) and use a VoIP program to place computer-to-computer phone calls.

Living on the Net

When Bob first heard about Internet Relay Chat (IRC), he thought it sounded a bit complicated. It was somewhat daunting at first, but after downloading the program and trying it out he found that using it was easier than he thought it would be. It was a real novelty for Bob to be able to communicate through the Internet in real time, even though conversations were conducted using a keyboard.

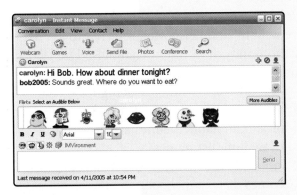

Soon after using IRC for the first time, Bob and Carolyn started using an instant messaging (IM) program to stay in contact when they were both online. They soon found that IM was addictive, and sometimes they had to control the urge to send messages in order to make sure they could get any work done. What Bob found most amazing was the steady increase in IM client capabilities—whiteboarding, program sharing, file sharing, even voice and video conversation.

The most amazing Internet communication feature that Bob has used to date has been Voice over Internet Protocol (VoIP). Both Carolyn and Bob use a VoIP freeware program to make computer-to-computer calls to friends and family around the world. The best part about it is that the calls are free unless they want to call people using regular phones.

The Internet communication methods mentioned above are examples of synchronous communication. Synchronous communication occurs in real time (back and forth), unlike the asynchronous methods you learned about in Chapter 9 that involve a significant time lag or delay between messages. Asynchronous and synchronous Internet communication methods can be packaged together to create Web conferencing or collaboration tools that allow people to work together on documents while communicating in real time, even though they may be located thousands of miles apart.

Internet Chat

Tech Demo 10-1
Internet Chat

In the early days of the Internet, chat consisted of synchronous text-based conversations, with participants using their keyboards to send messages back and forth. Internet technology has improved to the point that Internet chat now encompasses voice and voice with video conversations. Even with the availability of Internet audio and video technologies, text-based chat is still very popular, and millions of people around the world use Internet Relay Chat (IRC) client programs or Web-based chat sites to engage in conversation.

Internet Relay Chat (IRC)

Internet Relay Chat (IRC) the first open Internet protocol that enabled users to engage in real-time text conversations over the Internet

Internet Relay Chat (IRC) was created by a Finnish graduate student named Jarkko Oikarinen in 1988. It was the first open Internet protocol that let people engage in real-time text conversations, and it still enjoys a large following. To hold an IRC conversation a user must have an IRC client program installed on his or her computer. IRC client programs connect to IRC servers that form networks. IRC networks exist independently, so users on one network cannot converse with users on other networks. Table 10.1 shows the top 10 IRC networks in terms of the number of users.

Conversations in IRC are held in channels, often referred to as chat rooms. An IRC network can carry thousands of different channels. The IRC client prefaces the names of channels carried on the IRC servers in a network with a pound sign (#) as shown in Figure 10.1, while prefacing local channels that exist only on one server with an ampersand (&). IRC channel names are usually organized around topics, but channel names are often not as self-explanatory as newsgroup and mailing list names.

An IRC user can quickly and easily create his or her own channel. The person who creates a channel becomes the channel operator, but channel operators can invite other channel participants to become channel operators. Channel operators have the responsibility for seeing that a channel runs smoothly and they have the option to temporarily or permanently ban a user for any reason. Each IRC user takes on a nickname, known as a nick in IRC. An at sign (@) precedes the channel operator's nick in the list of nicks using a channel. The channels in a network's channel list change constantly as channels close when there are no participants and new channels

Table 10.1 Top 10 IRC Networks

Rank	Network	Users	Channels	Servers
1	QuakeNet	212,478	197,410	43
2	IRCnet	124,123	60,680	45
3	Undernet	115,422	47,771	27
4	EFnet	101,049	41,196	58
5	Rizon	39,446	4,932	1
6	DALnet	33,534	16,081	40
7	GameSurge	31,586	64,190	20
8	UniBG	25,799	16,126	39
9	WebChat	21,885	5,546	6
10	Aitvaras	18,511	20,335	15

Source: http://irc.netsplit.de/networks

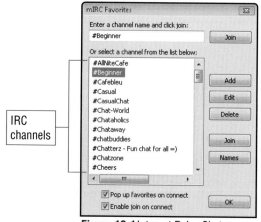

Figure 10.1 Internet Relay Chat (IRC) Channel Listing

are created. An IRC user also can contact another user to carry on a private conversation, but IRC's primary purpose is to enable group conversations.

Some GUI IRC clients feature command buttons, but many clients still require users to enter commands with the keyboard. (The user enters the command in a text box in the IRC client window and then presses Enter to execute the command.) Table 10.2 lists some common IRC commands, all of which begin with a forward slash (/).

A shareware program called mIRC is currently one of the most widely used IRC clients for Windows operating systems. mIRC installation is straightforward, and the only information the user must enter when logging on to a server includes a user name, an e-mail address, the desired nickname, and a nickname alternative. The alternative nick will be used if your first choice is already taken when you enter a channel. The required information is entered using an Options dialog box that appears once mIRC installation is complete as shown in Figure 10.2. The setup dialog box can also be used at a later time to choose an IRC network for logon.

Once the mIRC user connects to an IRC server, a dialog box will display a list of channels available on the server as shown in Figure 10.1. The user can join a channel by typing the pound sign followed by the channel name and then pressing the Enter key, or by double-clicking the channel listing. The name of the channel and the number of people in the channel appear in the channel window title bar. The nicks for the users currently in the channel appear in the list at the right side of the channel window. The topic, instructions, terms of use, and other information related to a channel often appear at the beginning of the welcome notice as shown

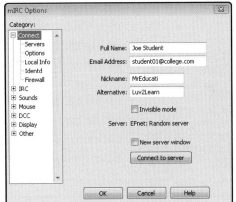

Figure 10.2 mIRC Options Dialog Box

Table 10.2 Common IRC Commands

Action	Command	Example
change nick	/nick [new nick]	/nick bobbalouie
find nick info	/whois [nick]	/whois mallrat
invite someone to join you on another channel	/invite [nick] [#]	/invite mallrat #beginners
join a channel	/join [#]	/join #beginners
leave a channel	/leave [#]	/leave #beginners
let participants know you will be away	/away [message]	/away back in five
list of channels	/list	/list
prevent someone from talking to you	/ignore [nick] [#]	/ignore bozo #beginners
quit IRC	/quit [message]	/quit see you next time!
remove user from a channel (only by channel operators)	/kick [#] [nick]	/kick #beginners bozo
send a private message	/msg [nick] [message]	/msg mallrat what's up?
let participants know you have returned after using the /away command	/away	/away

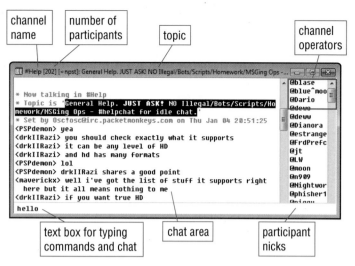

channel name

number of participants

topic

channel operators

text box for typing commands and chat

chat area

participant nicks

Figure 10.3 mIRC Channel Window

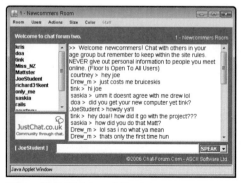

Figure 10.4 DALnet IRC Chat Netiquette Guide

Figure 10.5 Web-based Chat Window

in Figure 10.3. *IRC robots* or bots used to automate routine channel functions often generate the initial channel information.

The ongoing channel conversation appears in the large text box, and as the conversation continues, the contents will move down. Use the scroll bar located near the right side of the channel window to scroll up and down the conversation. The user contributes to a conversation by typing in the text box at the bottom of the mIRC channel window, as shown in Figure 10.3, and then pressing the Enter key.

It is a good idea to watch a conversation for a while before jumping in so that you understand what is going on and do not interrupt. Follow basic netiquette rules to avoid offending other channel participants. Most IRC networks provide Web page netiquette guides specifically designed for IRC users as shown in Figure 10.4. Form is not as important as content, so chat is often entirely in lowercase and spelling errors are expected and accepted.

Chat rooms are notorious for content that may be considered inappropriate by many. The channel operator determines what content is acceptable. Due to the uncensored nature of chat rooms, many of the sites are unsuitable for children and many parents use parental control software to restrict the chat sites their children can access. People also may misrepresent themselves in chat rooms, and with no means of verification, it is usually not a good idea to make arrangements to meet chat participants in person.

Web-based Chat

Web-based chat allows users to access some IRC networks and other private networks via a Web browser to engage in text-based chat, and sometimes voice and video chat. Web-based chat does not require the installation of special software, and there is no need to know or use any special commands. However, a user can open only one channel or chat room at a time with Web-based chat, whereas IRC clients can keep multiple channels open at the same time. Web-based chat graphical interfaces differ, but the basic features will be familiar to IRC users and include channel headers, a participant nick list, a text window for the chat conversation, and a text box for typing as shown in Figure 10.5. Many business Web sites use Web-based IRC chat to provide customer support for their products and services.

Some Web sites use Web-based chat to host live event chats, where experts or celebrities field questions submitted through a Web-based chat room. Many news Web sites such as CNN and the BBC periodically host live event chats. Notices about live event chats include information such as the date and time for the event, how participants can log on to chat, and guidelines for submitting questions. Figure 10.6 shows a chat invitation for a live event hosted by the National Association of Teachers of Singing. Once a live event chat has been conducted, the Web site that hosted the event usually makes a transcript available, such as the live event chat transcript shown in Figure 10.7.

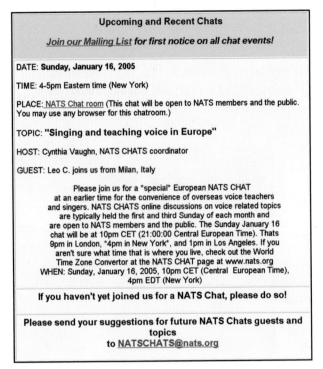

Figure 10.6 Live Event Chat Invitation

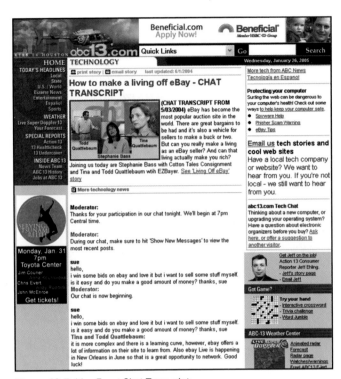

Figure 10.7 Live Event Chat Transcript

Concept Review 1 Internet Chat

1. Describe how Internet Relay Chat (IRC) works.
2. Can people connected to different IRC networks carry on conversations?
3. What is a nick?
4. What is a channel operator?

Skill Review 1 Use Internet Relay Chat

1. Download and install an Internet Relay Chat program by completing the following steps:
   a. If necessary, start Internet Explorer.
   b. Type **www.mirc.com/get.html** in the Address bar and press Enter.
   c. Locate the mIRC download area for Windows operating systems and click the hyperlink for the server closest to your location.

d. When the File Download – Security Warning dialog box appears, click the Run button.

e. Once the download is complete, the Internet Explorer – Security Warning dialog box may appear again warning that the publisher could not be verified. Click the Run button to begin the installation process. *(Note: This message means that the publisher of the software has not attached a digital signature to the software. Because mIRC is a well-known and trusted software publisher, and you are downloading the software directly from the mIRC download site, you do not have to worry about its origin.)*

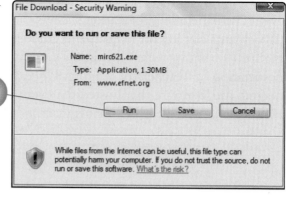

f. If the User Account Control dialog box appears, click Allow.

g. Click Next when the installer dialog box appears.

h. Click the I Agree button when the License Agreement dialog box appears.

i. Click the Next button when the Choose Install Location dialog box appears. *(Note: Ask your instructor if the default destination folder is acceptable. If necessary, change the folder by clicking the Browse button to browse and locate the appropriate folder.)*

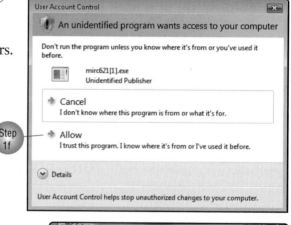

j. Click the Next button when the Choose Components dialog box appears to install mIRC with the default components.

k. Click the Next button when the Choose Start Menu Folder dialog box appears to create a Start Menu folder for mIRC in the default location.

l. Click Next when the Select Additional Tasks dialog box appears to have the installer perform the default operation of backing up existing files and creating a desktop icon for mIRC.

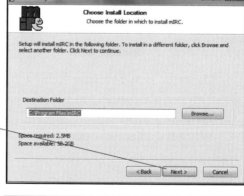

m. Click the Install button when the Ready To Install dialog box appears to continue installing the software.

n. Check the *Run mIRC* and *Read mIRC help file* check boxes in the dialog box that lets you know the installation was successful and then click the Finish button.

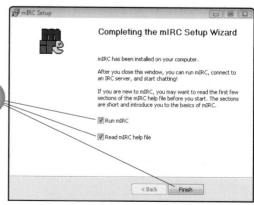

o. Read through the Help file by clicking the different topic hyperlinks. Print topics you are interested in. Close the Help window when you are finished.

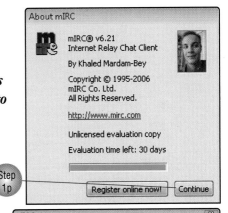

p. Click the Continue button in the About mIRC dialog box. *(Note: mIRC is a shareware program that requires registration and payment within 30 days. If you want to use the program beyond that period, you can register and pay for it later. This dialog box will appear each time you open mIRC and let you know how many days remain in the evaluation period.)*

q. With the *Connect* category selected, type your name, e-mail address, nickname, and alternative nickname in the appropriate textboxes. If necessary, uncheck the *Invisible mode* check box.

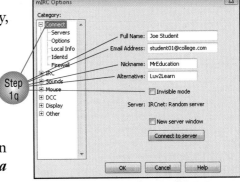

r. Click the *Server* category in the *Category* list and then click the IRC Server your instructor recommends, then click Select to save your selection and automatically return to the Connect category.

s. Click OK.

t. Click the Connect button in the toolbar to connect to an IRC server. *(Note: If you have a problem connecting to a server, click Tools on the mIRC menu bar and then Options to reopen the Options dialog box. Use the Option dialog box to repeat Step 1r and try a different server.)*

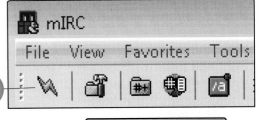

u. If the Windows Security Alert dialog box appears informing you the Windows Firewall has blocked the program, click the Unblock button.

2. Use mIRC to chat by completing the following steps:

a. When mIRC connects to an IRC server a channel window will appear. Double-click the *#Beginner* channel to enter that channel, or type the channel name in the text box (typing the pound sign is optional) and click the Join button. *(Note: Your instructor may ask you to open another channel.)*

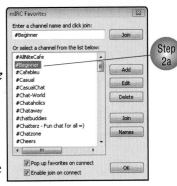

b. Lurk for a short period and then type **Hello** in the text box at the bottom of the channel window. Press Enter to add what you just typed to the conversation.

c. Continue to converse as appropriate by typing your replies in the channel window text box and pressing the Enter key.

d. Type **/whois** followed by a space and then type one of the nicks from the nick list. Press Enter to find more information about the person behind the nick. *(Hint: The whois information will appear in the Status window, which may be hidden by the channels windows you are using. If so, click the server button located on the switchbar below the mIRC toolbar. To return to the channel window, click the button with the channel name that appears on the switchbar.)*

e. Return to the channel window and type **/leave** followed by a space, type the channel name, and then press Enter to leave the channel. *(Note: Do not forget to type # before the channel name.)*

f. Type **/quit** followed by a space in the status window text box area and then press Enter to leave the IRC server.

g. Click File on the mIRC menu bar and then click Exit to close mIRC.

h. Close Internet Explorer.

Instant Messaging

Instant messaging (IM) in its most basic form resembles IRC in that it uses a client program connected to a server network to enable real-time text conversations. The principle difference between the two is that the focus of IRC is on group conversations carried on in channels or chat rooms whereas instant messaging is primarily used for one-on-one private conversations as shown in Figure 10.8. However, group IM conversations are possible.

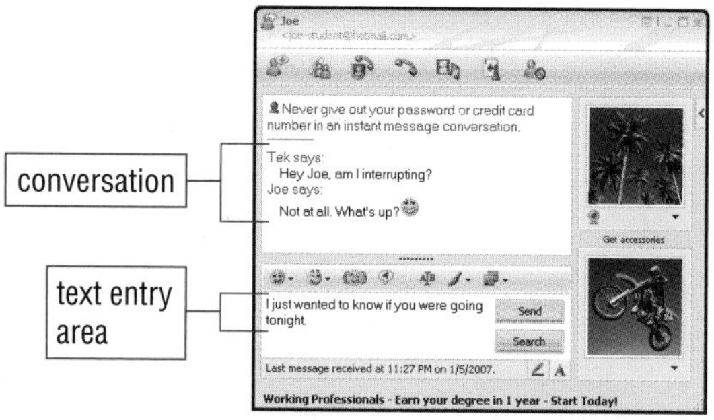

ICQ (I Seek You) and America Online were the first to offer instant messaging, but they now have competition, with the largest competitors being Windows Live Messenger and Yahoo! Messenger. An increasing number of people are discovering the convenience of IM, with a recent survey finding that 42 percent of Internet users in the United States are regular IM users. Of that group, 24 percent use IM more than e-mail, so it is possible that one day IM might supplant e-mail as the most popular Internet application.

Most IM clients can be downloaded as freeware. Windows XP came with a pre-installed instant messaging client called Windows Messenger. However, Windows Vista does not include a messaging client. Microsoft offers the new Windows Live Messenger as a free download for XP and Vista users. Windows Live Messenger is meant to replace Windows Messenger on XP.

Most IM clients by default open when the computer starts up and then automatically log on to the Internet once a connection is detected. To be able to start conversations, IM users create contact lists of friends and acquaintances with whom they wish to correspond as shown in Figure 10.9. To simplify the task of getting friends to join an IM service, most IM clients feature a command that can be used to invite friends to install the client and register with the service to carry on conversations as shown in Figure 10.10.

When an IM client connects to the Internet, it contacts an IM server and lets the server know that the user is online. It also passes the names on the user's contact list to the server, so that the server can check to see if any of those contacts are online. The IM server returns user status information to the IM client, so that the IM client can display the status of each contact as shown in Figure 10.9. The server also lets those contacts that are online know that the user just came online, as well. An IM user can then select an online contact to begin a conversation in a separate window as shown in Figure 10.8. When a user goes offline, his or her IM client notifies the IM server so that it can notify other contacts that the user has gone offline. There are times when users do not want to be interrupted, so most IM clients enable a user to indicate that he or she is busy, away from the computer, and so on, as shown in Figure 10.11. Most IM clients also feature an ignore or block command that enables a user to ignore messages from anyone he or she wishes to avoid.

Figure 10.8 Windows Live Messenger Conversation Window

conversation

text entry area

instant messaging (IM) synchronous Internet communication method that uses a client program connected to a server network to enable real-time text conversation

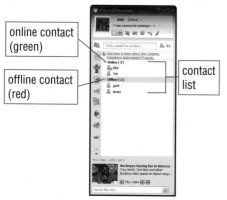

online contact (green)

offline contact (red)

contact list

Figure 10.9 Windows Live Messenger Contact List

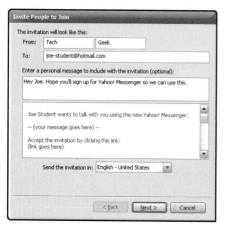

Figure 10.10 Yahoo! Messenger Invitation Window

One of the drawbacks to instant messaging is that a number of incompatible protocols are in use. For example, ICQ, one of the first instant messaging programs, works only for conversations with other people running the ICQ client software on the ICQ network. This limitation is becoming less problematic with the more popular IM clients. Currently, Windows Live Messenger users can chat with Yahoo! Messenger users and vice-versa. Some IM clients enable conversations across different networks, but to date no instant messengers operate across all IM networks. For that reason, many people run several IM clients to stay in contact with people on different networks.

Most IM clients feature graphical emoticons as shown in Figure 10.12 that the user can insert into any message to make the emotion behind a text communication clearer. The latest IM clients now offer a number of different synchronous and asynchronous communication features in addition to real-time text chat, including chat rooms, voice chat, webcam, file sharing, whiteboard applications, e-mail, phone dialing, and streaming information such as news, stock market quotes, and even weather information as illustrated in Figure 10.13.

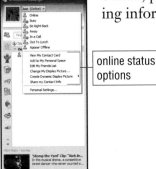

online status options

Figure 10.11 Windows Live Messenger Online Status Options

Figure 10.12 Graphical Emoticon Selection in Windows Live Messenger

Figure 10.13 Weather Information Displayed in Yahoo! Messenger

Instant Messaging 3-D Avatars

One of the difficulties inherent in any text-based conversation lies in correctly gauging the emotion or feeling behind what is being written. Real-life face-to-face interactions offer visual and auditory clues that assist with this task, but when these are absent, misunderstandings often arise. When chat first appeared, users created character-based smilies, or emoticons, to address this problem. These character-based clues were soon supplemented by the graphical emoticons now available as menu items in most IM clients.

Although emoticons are helpful in conveying the emotion behind any statement, they are still a poor substitute for face-to-face interaction. To address this shortcoming and to make IM conversations more lifelike, several companies—including IMVU

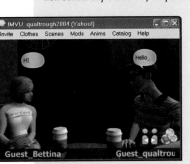

and America Online (AOL)—now offer graphical 3-D avatars that mimic human expressions and movement.

To use the IMVU avatar, the user starts a conversation in an IM window. The IMVU 3-D avatar program then invites the conversation participant to a 3-D conversation. Once the user accepts the invitation, each participant's 3-D avatar appears in his or her IMVU windows. The users type directly into the IMVU window, and the text appears in cartoon-like bubbles emanating from their avatar's heads.

While the IMVU program is free, the company plans to make money by offering additional wardrobes and other features that will allow users to customize their avatars. AOL has similar ideas, and charges a small fee for their 3-D avatars called SuperBuddie. It is still too early to tell if 3-D avatars will become a big hit, but as the technology that drives them improves and the avatars become more realistic, odds are they will prove popular.

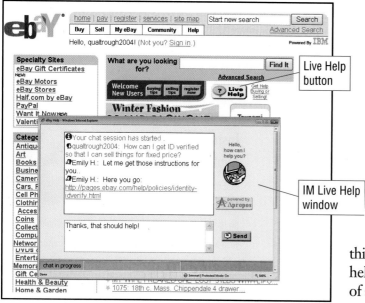

Figure 10.14 e-Bay Instant Messaging Help Window

Instant messaging offers a number of different business applications. Many companies save money by using instant messaging instead of phone calls. Web-based instant messaging is also increasingly used for one-on-one customer support, such as eBay's help service shown in Figure 10.14. To use the service, an eBay customer clicks a help button on the eBay home page. Once the customer enters his or her eBay ID or e-mail address, an instant messaging window appears, and an eBay assistant will answer questions. A major advantage of this method compared to traditional telephone help is that the customer can print a transcript of any conversation for future reference.

IM users should be aware that any conversation may be vulnerable to interception by unauthorized parties, so it is not a good idea to exchange confidential information such as passwords or account numbers. IM users also should keep in mind that conversation partners can save a transcript of any conversation, so they should be careful about saying anything that could be embarrassing if revealed to a third party. Many companies archive their IM and e-mail traffic for a period of years in order to comply with legal requirements, such as the financial reporting requirements of the Sarbanes-Oxley Act of 2002. Instant messages are the target of viruses, so IM users should make sure that their virus protection software is set to scan IM messages. Finally, criminals have used IM to perpetrate a number of different scams, so users should be very careful when talking to anyone whose identity they are unsure of.

Concept Review 2 Instant Messaging

1. Describe how instant messaging works.
2. What is a contact list?
3. What precautions should you take when using instant messaging?
4. What are some of the other features that IM clients offer besides text-based conversation?

Skill Review 2 Use an Instant Messaging Program

1. Download and Install Windows Live Messenger. *(Note: Check with your instructor before completing this section as Windows Live Messenger may already be installed on your computer. If that is the case, skip to the next section.)*
   a. Click Start and then click Windows Live Messenger Download. Internet Explorer launches and opens the Windows Live Messenger download page. You may be prompted to connect to your ISP by entering your username and password.

b. Click the Get It Free button.

c. At the File Download dialog box, click Run to download and install the program without saving it.

d. Internet Explorer warns you before running the installation program. In the Security Warning dialog box, click Run.

e. In the Windows Live Messenger Wizard dialog box, click Next to begin the installation.

f. Read the information in the Terms of Use and Privacy Statement dialog box. Select the option stating *I accept the Terms of Use and Privacy Statement* and click Next.

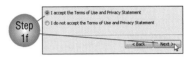

g. In the Choose Additional Features and Settings dialog box, be sure to uncheck all check boxes, then click Next. Checking any of these boxes would result in changes being made to the default behavior of your computer or Internet Explorer. For the purposes of this tutorial, we will install Windows Live Messenger without any additional features or settings.

h. If the User Account Control dialog box appears, click Continue. User Account Control in Windows Vista prohibits unauthorized users from making certain changes to the computer, such as installing software.

i. At the *Windows Live Messenger has been installed* dialog box, click Close.

j. Exit Internet Explorer. The Windows Live Messenger window should now be visible.

2. Create a .NET Passport. *(Note: Check with your instructor before completing this topic to find out if you need to create a new .NET Passport, if your instructor has an account created for you, or if you may use your personal .NET Passport if you have one. If you need to create a .NET Passport account, complete the following steps. If you do not need to create a .NET Passport account, skip ahead to the next section.)*

a. If Windows Messenger has already been set up for a user with a .NET Passport account, Windows attempts to log on the user with the e-mail address of the .NET Passport. You may be prompted for your password if the password has not been stored.

b. If necessary, click Start, click All Programs, and click Windows Live Messenger to launch the program.

c. Click the Get a new account hyperlink at the bottom of the Windows Live Messenger window.

d. Internet Explorer opens the Windows Live ID sign-up page. (You may need to provide your username and password to sign in to your ISP.) Click the Sign Up button.

e. Type your desired name in the Windows Live ID text box and click the Check Availability button to see if that username is available.

f. If your desired name is not available, type a different name and click the Check Availability button again. Continue this process until you find a name that is available. Once you have decided on a name and verified it is available, write it down on a piece of paper followed by *@hotmail.com*. You will later sign in to

Windows Live Messenger using an email address consisting of the name you just used followed by "@hotmail.com". This e-mail address is your .NET Passport.

g. Continue to fill out the rest of the sign-up form and click the I Accept button to create your account.

h. When the Congratulations page appears, exit Internet Explorer. The Windows Live Messenger window will once again be visible.

3. Use Windows Live Messenger.

a. If necessary, click Start, click All Programs, and click Windows Live Messenger to launch the program. Windows Live Messenger may be configured to automatically sign you in if it was previously installed. If you are automatically signed in, skip the next step and proceed to step c.

b. Enter your .NET Passport, password, and click the Sign In button. *(Note: If you have a Hotmail or MSN account, you already have a Passport—sign in by typing your e-mail address and password.)*

c. If a Windows Security Warning dialog box appears saying the Windows Firewall has blocked the program, click the Unblock button.

d. For the remaining steps you will be working with your instant messaging partner. Decide between you and your partner which student will add the other as a contact and only one student should complete steps e–f.

e. At the top of the Windows Live Messenger window, click the Add a Contact button.

f. In the Instant Messenging Address textbox, type the e-mail address of your partner, then click the Add a Contact button at the bottom of the window. You are returned to the main Windows Live Messenger window where you will see your new contact listed.

g. The student that did not add the contact should complete this step. At the Windows Live Messenger dialog box informing you that *[student name]* has added you to his/her contacts list, click OK to accept *Allow this person to see when you are online and contact you* and *Add this person to my contact list.*

h. In the *Online* section of the Windows Messenger window, double-click the e-mail address of the student with whom you have been partnered. A Conversation window opens in which you type message text to send and read the other person's replies.

i. With the insertion point positioned in the message text box at the bottom of the Conversation window, type **Instant messaging is fun!** and then click the Send button. The other student receives an alert on his or her computer as soon as the message is received.

j. Send a few more messages back and forth to each other.

k. When you are finished using Windows Live Messenger, click the Close button on the Conversation window title bar.

l. Click the Windows Live Messenger – Signed In icon on the taskbar next to the current time and then click *Sign Out* at the pop-up menu.

Vista Remote Assistance

Almost everyone has at one time or another experienced the frustration of trying to solve a computer problem by enlisting the help of a friend or expert over the phone. While this can sometimes produce good results, it often ends in failure because the person trying to assist is forced to guide the person seeking help through the process of diagnosing and solving a problem without being able to see or handle their computer.

Windows Vista provides a remedy for this dilemma through a feature called Remote Assistance. With Remote Assistance, a computer user needing help (referred to as the ***novice***) can use Windows Live Messenger to give permission to another user (referred to as the ***expert***) to take control of his or her computer via a network or Internet connection, as in Figure 10.15. The person taking control can then directly analyze and repair any problems as if he or she were sitting in front of the remote computer, as in Figure 10.16.

Figure 10.15 Requesting Remote Assistance from Windows Live Messenger

novice the user requesting help
expert the user providing help

Here is how Remote Assistance might work with two people named Rikki and Jordan. Rikki wants Jordan to help with a software problem, so Rikki starts Windows Live Messenger and establishes contact with Jordan. Rikki then clicks the Request Remote Assistance option under the Activities menu to send an invitation to Jordan. Once Jordan accepts the invitation, a Remote Assistance interface will open in her screen. At the same time, a dialog box will appear in Rikki's screen asking him to confirm that he gave permission to Jordan to view his screen and chat. Once Rikki gives his OK, Jordan can view Rikki's screen but cannot make any changes. To take control of Rikki's computer, Jordan needs to request permission by clicking a Take Control button at the top of her Remote Assistance window. Once Rikki OKs that, Jordan can control Rikki's computer as if it were her own and try to solve the problem. Rikki and Jordan can converse using a special Remote Assistance window that appears on both of their desktops. To take advantage of Remote Assistance, the user must make sure that the Vista firewall is configured to allow Remote Assistance by opening the Windows Firewall dialog box, clicking the Exceptions tab, and then verifying that there is a check mark in the *Remote Assistance* check box. There are other things that can affect the ability to use Remote Assistance, so if you run into problems, you may need to check other firewall and security settings or consult your network.

Figure 10.16 Remote Assistance

Concept Review 3 Remote Assistance

1. Describe a situation where you might ask for Remote Assistance.
2. What benefits does Remote Assistance offer over more traditional methods of support, like the telephone?

Skill Review 3 Use Remote Assistance

(Note: In this exercise, you will be working with a partner. Make sure you know your partner's Windows Live Messenger ID so you can start a conversation. Before you begin, decide who will play the part of the novice requesting assistance and who will be the expert offering assistance.)

1. If necessary, start Windows Live Messenger and sign in using your e-mail address and password.

2. Begin a chat conversation with your partner and make sure you each contribute at least one line to the conversation.

3. *Novice completes this step:* Click the Activities icon in the message window toolbar and select Request Assistance.

4. *Expert completes this step:* Click the <u>Accept</u> hyperlink in the message window.

5. Wait while Remote Assistance loads. The expert will receive a notice asking to wait for the novice to accept the connection.

6. *Novice complete this step:* Click Yes in the Windows Remote Assistance dialog box to allow the connection.

7. The Remote Assistance windows loads in both computers and the session has begun.

8. The Novice should move the mouse, drag windows around, and open a program. The Expert should see these actions in the Remote Assistance window.

9. *Expert complete this step:* Type a few lines in the Message Entry box at the bottom left area of the Remote Assistance window to start a chat conversation, then press Enter or click the Send button.

10. After the novice replies, type a few more lines each to continue the conversation.

11. *Expert complete this step:* Click the Take Control button in the toolbar and wait until the novice accepts.

12. *Novice complete this step:* Click Yes in the Windows Remote Assistance window to allow the expert to control your computer.

13. *Expert complete this step:* Read the message in the pop-up window and take careful note that pressing the Escape key will cause you to lose control. Click the OK button.

14. *Expert complete this step:* Begin to move the mouse in the Remote Assistance window, drag windows, or launch a program. Be careful not to close the Windows Remote Assistance chat window on the novice's computer or your session will end.

15. Both the expert and the novice can now move the mouse and control the novice's computer, but only one should move the mouse at a time to avoid confusion.

16. *Novice complete this step:* Click the Stop Sharing button in the Windows Remote Assistance toolbar to stop the expert from having control. The expert can still see your screen but can no longer control the mouse.

17. ***Expert complete this step:*** Read the message in the pop-up dialog box explaining that you no longer have control over the novice's computer, then click the OK button.

18. Either person should click their Disconnect button to end the session. It doesn't matter who clicks it.

Step 18

Step 18

19. If necessary, click OK to confirm the disconnect, then close the Windows Remote Assistance window.

Vista Remote Desktop

Remote Desktop is similar to Remote Assistance in that it allows a user in front of one computer to control a remote computer. The difference between Remote Desktop and Remote Assistance is that with Remote Desktop, there is only one person involved. Remote Desktop is useful if someone has to access their own computer remotely. For example, imagine you are at school or at work and need to access a file on your home computer. Rather than getting in the car, driving home, accessing the file, and driving back, simply start Remote Desktop on the computer at school or work and connect directly to your home computer. The home computer screen will go blank so others in the house can't see what you are doing. The computer being controlled remotely must be running Windows XP Professional, Windows Vista Business, or Windows Vista Ultimate. All editions of Windows XP and Vista can act as the controlling computer without installing addi-

tional software as they come with the Remote Desktop Connection software built-in. Users of earlier versions of Windows down to Windows 95, and even Macintosh users, can download the connection software for free on the Microsoft Web site to allow them to control an XP Professional or Vista Business or Ultimate computer. As the download page changes from time to time, it is best to search the Microsoft Web site for ***rdp client*** in order to find the connection software download for your system. It takes some basic networking skills to make Remote Desktop work properly behind a firewall, so while it is included with Windows for free, some users find it easier to purchase third party software like Symantec's pcAnywhere or pay for an online service like GoToMyPC.com that offers similar functionality with fewer technical demands on the user.

Figure 10.17 Video Conferencing

Video Conferencing

Video conferencing, sometimes referred to as teleconferencing, employs audio and video technologies to allow two or more people to engage in a real-time conversation in which all parties can see each other as shown in Figure 10.17. The first video conferencing services using dedicated telephone lines or network connections were introduced in the 1970s and were very expensive. The prohibitive cost meant that only large businesses and educational institutions could afford to use them. As the technology has developed installation costs have come down, but the charges for using the multiple Integrated Services Digital Network (ISDN) phone lines necessary for traditional video conferencing remain high and are billed on a costly per-minute basis.

video conferencing computer applications that allow two or more people to engage in a real-time conversation in which all parties can see each other

With the increasing availability of high-bandwidth Internet connections and the development of more effective compression technologies, video conferencing has begun migrating to the Internet, leading to desktop video conferencing transmitted over the Internet using personal computers. Although ISDN video conferencing still has the edge as far as audio and video quality, Internet protocol (IP) video conferencing offers some advantages that ISDN cannot match. Perhaps the most important advantage is that IP video conferencing permits Web collaboration capabilities through a single Internet connection that allows the easy incorporation of Internet-based content. For example, web-based video conference participants can view and work with presentations, documents, e-mail, and so on. Another very important advantage that IP offers is the low cost of most Internet connections compared to the high connection costs for dedicated video conference lines. Most observers expect IP to dominate the video conferencing market in the future as the technology steadily improves.

Figure 10.18 Webcam

To engage in desktop video conferencing, participants need computers equipped with sound cards, video cards, a webcam, a headset or separate microphone and speakers, the appropriate software, and a broadband Internet connection. Although video conferencing can work with dial-up connections, the low bandwidth usually produces poor audio and video that can make the experience frustrating. Most computers sold today come equipped with sound and video cards, so the only hardware outlay usually involves the purchase of a webcam that perches on top of a computer monitor like the one shown in Figure 10.18 and a headset consisting of earphones and built-in microphone like the one pictured in Figure 10.19.

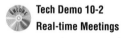
Tech Demo 10-2
Real-time Meetings

Figure 10.19 Headset

While many video conferencing packages are targeted to commercial users, home and small business users can choose one of a number of free video conferencing options, including services offered by the major instant messaging clients such as Windows Live Messenger and Yahoo! Messenger.

Because these services usually offer a one-on-one connection, this type of feature is usually referred to as video conversation or chat. Setting up a video conversation with an IM client is almost as simple as sending an instant message if both the parties have the required hardware and software and are connected to the same service. In Windows Live Messenger, a video conference can be initiated from the main Messenger window by right-clicking an online contact and choosing Video > Start a Video Call from the pop-up menu as in Figure 10.20. If you are already in a conversation with a contact, click the Start or Stop a Video Call button on the toolbar as in Figure 10.21. An invitation to start a video conversation will be sent to the conversation participant. Once the participant accepts the invitation, webcam video will appear in a separate area inside the conversation window, allowing each participant to see the other through their webcams as shown in Figure 10.22. The Video Call feature enables audio as well, so participants can engage in a normal conversation while viewing each other. A conversation participant will see a small picture of their own webcam view below the larger picture from the other participant's webcam.

Figure 10.20 Start a Video Call from the Main Messenger Window

Figure 10.21 Start a Video Call from the Current Conversation

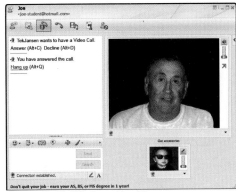

Figure 10.22 Windows Live Messenger Video Conversation

Concept Review 4 Video Conferencing

1. What is needed in order to have a desktop video conference?
2. What advantages does IP video conferencing have over ISDN video conferencing?

Skill Review 4 Use Windows Live Messenger for Video Chat

(Note: To complete this exercise, both participants must have a computer equipped with sound and video cards, a webcam, and a headset or separate microphone and speakers. Both computers must run Windows Vista.)

1. If necessary, start Windows Live Messenger and sign in using your e-mail name and password.
2. Send a message to one of your online contacts telling him or her that you would like to have a video conversation.
3. Click the Stop or Start a Video Call button on the toolbar to send an invitation to your contact. Once your contact accepts the invitation by clicking the Accept hyperlink in his or her conversation window, webcam video will appear on both your screens. *(Hint: If you experience any problems with the audio or video, stop the conversation by closing the conversation window, opening Windows Live Messenger, clicking the menu icon in the top right corner of the title bar, pointing to Tools, then clicking Audio and Video Setup to open the Audio and Video Setup wizard. The wizard will take you through the process of checking your audio and video settings. Once any problems are resolved, repeat Steps 1–3 to begin a new conversation.)*

Step 3

4. Adjust the size of your web-cam video window by clicking on the arrow in the bottom right corner of your video window, pointing to Size, and selecting the desired size.

5. Adjust the speaker and microphone volume by sliding the slider bars up or down as appropriate.

6. Carry on a short conversation. While you are conversing, you can use the conversation window to exchange messages, play games, or start other activities from the various toolbar buttons.

7. When you are finished, click the Start or Stop a Video Call button on the toolbar to stop the video call but remain in a text conversation, then close the conversation window.

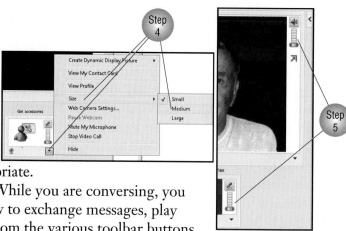

Voice over Internet Protocol (VoIP)

Voice over Internet Protocol (VoIP) or IP telephony involves the transmission of voice telephone calls over the Internet. To accomplish this, the analog audio signals used by ordinary telephones must be converted into digital signals that can travel across the Internet before being switched back into analog signals at the receiving end. While early VoIP technologies suffered from a number of faults—including poor sound quality, echoing, and frequent drop-outs—it has improved to the point that some VoIP services now offer superior sound quality compared to regular telephone service.

As you learned in Chapter 1, *Understanding the Internet*, the packet-switching technology used by the Internet provides a much more efficient method of transmitting data compared to the circuit switching used by plain old telephone service (POTS). This factor helps make VoIP calls much

Voice over Internet Protocol (VoIP) technology that facilitates the transmission of voice telephone calls over the Internet

VoIP in Business

The potential savings and convenience offered by VoIP has not escaped the attention of many large businesses equipped with their own high-speed networks. Using VoIP to handle voice communications over these networks instead of analog lines can provide considerable savings and offer organizations more control over communication infrastructures. The potential savings offered by VoIP have led Boeing, Ford, Bank of America, and a number of other large businesses to ink deals linking their offices with IP phones. An innovative real-life example of a VoIP business application was recently provided by McDonald's when that company announced the trial use of VoIP to link drive-through window order-taking processes at nine of its Southern California restaurants. McDonald's hopes to save money by using VoIP to consolidate order taking in a remote call center, an undertaking that would be prohibitively expensive using regular telephone service.

As a relatively new technology, VoIP is still experiencing teething problems, but in most cases, problems lie with the networks carrying VoIP rather than the VoIP technology. Network problems that slow data communication are a disaster for VoIP, causing high latency, dropouts, and other problems that can make calling an unpleasant experience. The biggest potential threat to VoIP in the United States is posed not by technology, but by possible changes to the current regulatory environment. At the moment, VoIP providers are exempt from the taxes applied to analog telephone services. Traditional telecoms threatened by VoIP are pushing for VoIP providers to be placed under the same regulatory classifications in order to even the playing field. If that happens, it would drive up the cost of VoIP and possibly delay implementation, but in the long term most industry observers are confidant that VoIP will eventually entirely replace voice calls over circuit-switched networks.

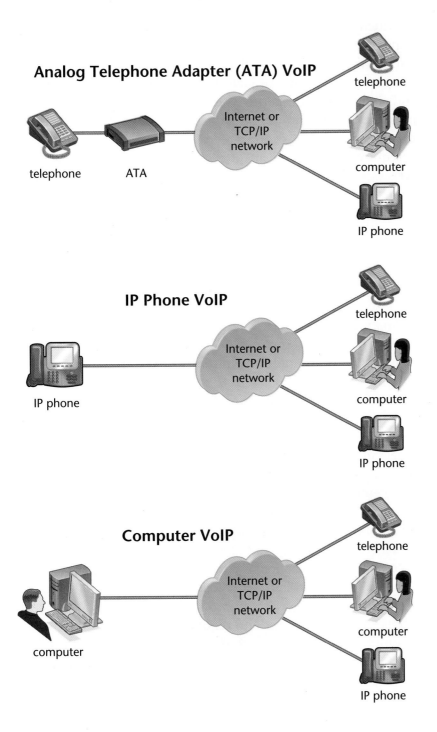

Figure 10.23 VoIP Connection Methods

cheaper than regular phone calls handled by traditional telephone service providers, and computer-to-computer VoIP calls can often be made for free.

There are three main VoIP connection methods in use at the consumer level as illustrated in Figure 10.23. Normal telephones can be used for VoIP calls by connecting them to an analog telephone adaptor (ATA) that converts analog signals to digital signals. The ATA, about the same size as an external modem, plugs directly into an Internet connection using an

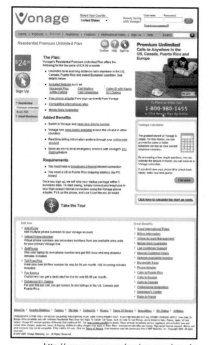

http://www.vonage.com/services_premium.php

Figure 10.24 VoIP Service Provider
Service Plan

IP phone telephone that plugs
directly into the Internet or into a
computer connected to the Internet
in order to permit VoIP phone calls

softphone a screen-based GUI
interface used by some VoIP
applications that emulates the
appearance of a telephone or telephone keypad

Figure 10.25 Skype Softphone
Interface

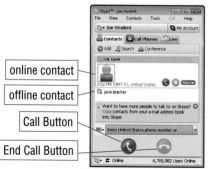

online contact

offline contact

Call Button

End Call Button

Figure 10.26 Skype Contact List

Ethernet jack or an RJ-11 phone jack to connect to a VoIP server provided by a VoIP service. VoIP phone calls can then be made to regular telephones, computers running VoIP software, or to an IP phone. VoIP service providers like Vonage, AT&T, and others usually charge a flat rate for calls within the United States and Canada, and charge very competitive per-minute rates for calls to other countries as shown in Figure 10.24. If an ATA adaptor is connected to a computer that is connected to the Internet, no special software is required because the adaptor communicates directly with a VoIP server.

IP phones, sometimes called hardphones, contain ATA hardware and like ATA adaptors plug directly into an Internet connection using an Ethernet jack or an RJ-11 phone jack to connect to a VoIP server. Another similarity with ATA adaptors is that if an IP phone is plugged into a computer that is connected to the Internet, no special software is required as the IP phone communicates directly with a VoIP server. Many IP phones can also work as a regular phone using ordinary telephone lines if desired.

Computer-to-computer VoIP connections use software to make calls from one computer to another computer, from a computer to a regular telephone, or to an IP phone. Computers used for VoIP need to have a full-duplex sound card installed so that users can talk and hear at the same time just like they can in an ordinary telephone conversation. Computer-to-computer VoIP users can speak and hear using a microphone and speakers or a headset. Computer-to-computer VoIP software features a *softphone*, which is a screen-based GUI interface that emulates a telephone or telephone features as shown in Figure 10.25. The softphone can dial regular telephones and IP phones, while computer–to–computer VoIP calls are usually made by selecting online user names from a contact list.

Skype is one of the most popular computer VoIP programs in current use. Available as freeware, Skype can be used to make computer-to-computer VoIP calls anywhere in the world free of charge. Skype makes money by charging for calls made to regular telephones. Skype users can buy credit online that will be deducted when they make calls to regular telephones. Calls to regular telephones are made using a softphone keypad interface as shown in Figure 10.25, or by using a USB telephone connected to a USB port.

Making a computer-to-computer call using Skype is very similar to using an IM client, and in fact, Skype can be used for instant messaging in addition to making phone calls. Once the user installs Skype and registers a Skype Contact name, he or she can add other Skype Contact names to his or her contact list. To make a phone call, the user double-clicks a Skype Contact from a list of online Skype users as shown in Figure 10.26. Skype features sound effects that sound just like a regular phone connection, so when placing a call users will hear the phone ringing or a busy signal if unlucky. A call recipient's computer will ring to alert him or her about incoming calls as well. Current Skype versions cannot receive phone calls from regular telephones, but Skype promises that this drawback will soon be eliminated in upcoming releases.

Concept Review 5 Voice over Internet Protocol (VoIP)

1. What is VoIP, and how does it work?
2. Describe the different methods that can be used to make VoIP telephone calls.
3. What is a softphone?
4. What does a full-duplex sound card allow computer users to do?

Skill Review 5 Use VoIP to Make Phone Calls

(Note: Ask your instructor if you have permission to download and save files to your computer or network location. If you do not have permission, ask you instructor where you should save the file you download for this exercise. To use VoIP to make phone calls, your computer must contain a full-duplex sound card and be equipped with a microphone and speakers or a headset.)

1. Download a free VoIP software program by completing the following steps:
   a. If necessary open Internet Explorer.
   b. Type **www.skype.com** in the Address bar and then press Enter to open the Skype home page.
   c. Click the Download Skype Now button in the middle of the page. *(Note: Web pages change, so if you do not see the download button in the middle of the page, look for it in another location on the Skype home page.)*
   d. When the download page appears click the Download Now button.
   e. Click the Run button in the File Download - Security Warning dialog box to start downloading the program.
   f. Once the download has completed, a User Account Control dialog box may appear asking for permission to continue the installation. If so, click Continue.
   g. Close any other applications that are open on your computer, select your language from the list, check the box indicating you have read and accept the license agreement and privacy statement, then click the install button.

   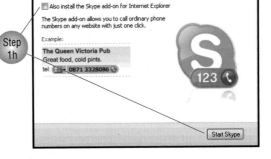

   h. Uncheck the box for installing the Internet Explorer add-on, then click the Start Skype button.
   i. Enter the information in the appropriate textboxes in the Skype - Create Account window to create your Skype account. A red asterisk (*) marks any field where an entry is required. Click Next and enter the appropriate information in the remaining fields. Make sure the *Sign Me in When Skype Starts* check box is checked. Click

the Sign In button when you are finished.

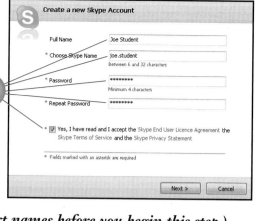

j. When the Skype - Getting Started guide appears, click the Start button at the bottom of the dialog box to begin a short tour of basic Skype tasks. When you are through with the tour, click the Finish button to close the guide.

2. Add contacts to Skype by completing the following steps:

(Note: Obtain your classmates' Skype Contact names before you begin this step.)

a. With the Skype window open, click the Add Contact button to add contacts. *(Hint: If the Skype window is not open double-click the Skype button on the taskbar to open it.)*

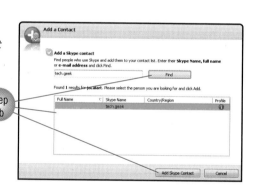

b. Use the Add a Contact window to enter a Skype Contact name in the text box. Click the Find button to verify the Skype user exists, then click the Add Skype Contact button. A message box will appear allowing you to send a welcome message to your new contact. Type a message and click OK. *(Note: An e-mail message will be sent to the contact letting that person know that you are adding him or her to your contact list so that viewing the contact and initiating a call is possible. You should receive similar messages from your classmates. Click the OK button to give your permission.)*

c. Repeat Step B to add another contact or click the Close button if you are finished adding contacts.

3. Make a Skype computer-to-computer call by completing the following steps:

a. If necessary, click the Skype window Contacts tab to see if any of your contacts are online.

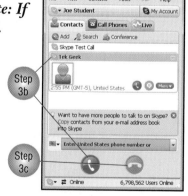

b. Double-click an online Skype Contact or select a contact and click the green Call button to begin a call. *(Note: If you are being called you will hear a ringing sound. Click the Green telephone to answer the call.)*

c. When you finish with a call, click the red End Call button to hang up. *(Note: The End Call button will not appear red until a call is active.)*

d. Minimize Skype to minimize it to the taskbar.

Chapter Summary

- In the early days of the Internet, chat consisted of synchronous text-based conversations, with participants using their keyboards to send messages back and forth.

- Internet technology has improved to the point that Internet chat now encompasses voice and voice with video conversations.

- Internet Relay Chat (IRC) was the first open Internet protocol that let people engage in real-time text conversations on the Internet.

- IRC client programs connect to IRC servers that form networks. IRC users must be on the same network in order to communicate.

- Conversations in IRC are carried on in channels, often referred to as chat rooms.

- The person who creates a channel becomes the channel operator.

- Channel operators have the responsibility for seeing that a channel runs smoothly, and to assist them in that task their powers include the ability to temporarily or permanently ban users for any reason.

- Follow basic netiquette rules to avoid offending other channel participants.

- Because of chat's uncensored nature, many chat rooms are unsuitable for children. Many parents use parental control software to restrict the chat sites that their children can access.

- Web-based chat allows users to use their Web browser to access some IRC networks and other private networks to engage in text-based chat, and sometimes voice and video chat.

- Advantages of Web-based chat include that it does not require the installation of special software and does not require the user to know or type any special commands.

- With Web-based chat only one channel or chat room can be open at a time, whereas IRC clients can keep multiple channels open at the same time.

- Web-based chat operators sometimes host live event chats where experts or celebrities field questions submitted through a Web-based chat room.

- Instant messaging (IM) in its most basic form is similar to IRC in that it uses a client program connected to a server network to enable real-time text conversations.

- The principle difference between IRC and IM is that the focus of IRC is on group conversations carried on in channels or chat rooms, whereas IM is primarily used for one-on-one private conversations.

- By default, most IM clients open when a computer starts up and then automatically log on to the Internet after detecting a connection.

- To be able to start conversations, IM users create contact lists of friends and acquaintances with whom they wish to correspond.

- One of the drawbacks to IM is that a number of incompatible protocols are in use.

- The latest IM clients now offer a number of different synchronous and asynchronous communication features in addition to real-time text chat.

- IM users should be aware that any conversation may be vulnerable to interception by unauthorized parties, so it is not a good idea to exchange confidential information such as passwords or account numbers.

- Video conferencing, sometimes referred to as teleconferencing, employs audio and video technologies to allow two or more people to engage in a real-time conversation in which all parties can see each other.

- With the increasing availability of high-bandwidth Internet connections and the development of more effective compression technologies, video conferencing has begun migrating to the Internet, leading to desktop video conferencing transmitted over the Internet using personal computers.

- Although ISDN video conferencing still has the edge as far as audio and video, quality Internet protocol (IP) video conferencing offers some advantages that ISDN cannot match.

- To engage in desktop video conferencing, participants need computers equipped with sound cards, video cards, a webcam, a headset or separate microphone and speakers, the appropriate software, and a broadband Internet connection.

- While many video conferencing packages are targeted to commercial users, individual and small business users can employ a number of free video conferencing options, including services offered by the major instant messaging networks such as Windows Live Messenger and Yahoo! Messenger.

- Setting up a video conversation with an IM client is almost as simple as sending an instant message if both the parties have the required hardware and software and are connected to the same service.

- Voice over Internet Protocol (VoIP) or IP telephony involves the transmission of voice telephone calls over the Internet.

- While early VoIP technologies suffered from a number of faults—including poor sound quality, echoing, and frequent dropouts—it has improved to the point that some VoIP services now offer superior sound quality compared to regular telephone service.

- Normal telephones can be used for VoIP calls by connecting them to an analog telephone adaptor (ATA) that converts analog signals to digital signals.

- IP phones, sometimes called hardphones, contain ATA hardware and, just like ATA adaptors, plug directly into an Internet connection using an Ethernet jack or an RJ-11 phone jack to connect to a VoIP server.

- Computer-to-computer VoIP connections use software to makes calls from one computer to another computer, to a regular telephone, or to an IP phone.

- Computers used for VoIP need to have a full-duplex sound card installed so that users can talk and hear at the same time, just as in an ordinary telephone conversation.

- Computer-to-computer VoIP software features a softphone, which is a screen-based GUI interface that emulates a telephone.

Key Terms

Numbers indicate the pages where terms are first cited in the chapter. An alphabetized list of key terms with definitions can be found on the Encore CD that accompanies this book. In addition, these terms and definitions are included in the end-of-book glossary.

expert, *323*

instant messaging (IM), *318*

Internet Relay Chat (IRC), *312*

IP phone, *330*

IRC robot, *314*

novice, *323*

softphone, *330*

video conferencing, *326*

Voice over Internet Protocol (VoIP), *328*

Web-based chat, *314*

Net Check

Additional quiz questions are available on the Encore CD that accompanies this book as well as on the Internet Resource Center for this title at www.emcp.net/Internet2e.

Multiple Choice

Indicate the correct answer for each question or statement.

1. E-mail is an example of
   a. asynchronous Internet communication.
   b. VoIP communication.
   c. synchronous Internet communication.
   d. Internet chat.

2. Internet Relay Chat (IRC)
   a. features channels that people can use to engage in group conversations.
   b. was the first instant messaging client.
   c. is an example of a serverless Internet communication method.
   d. is now rarely used.

3. IRC channel operator nicks are prefaced by a(n)
   a. forward slash (/).
   b. back slash (\).
   c. at sign (@).
   d. pound sign (#).

4. IRC channel names are prefaced by a(n)
   a. forward slash (/).
   b. back slash (\).
   c. at sign (@).
   d. a pound sign (#).

5. One difference between Web-based chat and chat using an IRC client is that
   a. Web-based chat users can only open one channel at a time.
   b. IRC client users can only open one channel at a time.
   c. Web-based chat users cannot use nicks.
   d. IRC client users cannot use nicks.

6. Most instant messaging programs
   a. can be downloaded as freeware.
   b. can be downloaded as shareware.
   c. are not available for downloading.
   d. must be installed using a CD.

7. An expert computer user can connect to a novice's computer by using:
   a. IRC.
   b. mIRC.
   c. Remote Assistance.
   d. an IP Phone.

8. IP phones are sometimes referred to as
   a. softphones.
   b. hardphones.
   c. analog phones.
   d. cell phones.

9. A softphone is
   a. a type of telephone used with notebook computers.
   b. an IP phone that can only receive calls but cannot make them.
   c. a screen-based interface that emulates a telephone or telephone features.
   d. another name for an ATA.

10. Full-duplex sound cards
    a. let people talk and listen at the same time when conducting a conversation using VoIP.
    b. must be installed in pairs on each computer to let people both talk and listen when conducting a conversation using VoIP.
    c. are necessary in order to use an instant messaging client.
    d. are a type of sound card that comes complete with built-in microphone.

True/False

Indicate whether each statement is true or false.

1. IP phones cannot make calls to regular phones.
2. IRC commands begin with a back slash (\).
3. IRC robots are used to automate routine IRC channel functions.
4. One of the drawbacks to VoIP is that packet-switching is not a suitable method for transmitting phone calls over the Internet.
5. One drawback to instant messaging clients is that there is no way to indicate that you do not want to be bothered.
6. IRC channel operators cannot invite other users to become channel operators.
7. Instant messaging clients generally only feature text-based chat.
8. Remote Assistance allows a computer user to view the desktop of a remote system and interact with it as if she was sitting at the remote computer.
9. Almost all instant messaging clients allow conversations with people on other IM networks.
10. Synchronous Internet communication makes real-time back and forth communication possible.

Virtual Perspectives

1. In the United States, VoIP service providers are not subject to the same regulations that govern traditional telecommunications providers, thus allowing them to avoid paying many taxes and tariffs. Supporters of VoIP say this is necessary in order for this fledgling technology to get off the ground, while detractors feel that VoIP service providers are being allowed an unfair advantage. Research this subject and then express your opinion on this issue.

2. Instant messaging has become increasingly popular, so much so that surveys show that many people are using IM at work for nonbusiness purposes. Schools are also finding it hard to prevent students from using IM when they should be participating in other activities. What kind of controls, if any, do you think should be placed on IM usage in schools and in the workplace? How would you enforce any rules that you might suggest?

Internet Lab Projects

Project 1

Save a Transcript of an IM Conversation

1. If necessary, open and sign on to Windows Live Messenger.
2. Send a message to one of your online classmates on your contact list.
3. Engage in a short text conversation with your classmate.
4. When you are finished conversing, click the Show Menu button towards the right of the title bar, point to File, and click Save As. If a dialog box appears informing you the conversation will be saved in rich text format, click OK.
5. Use the Save As dialog box to browse and locate a folder that the transcript will be saved to.
6. Click the *Save as type* down-pointing arrow and select *Text Document* to save the transcript of your conversation in text format.
7. Type a name for the transcript in the *File name* text box and click the Save button. If a dialog box appears warning you about your selected format, click OK.
8. Minimize or close the conversation window.
9. Open Notepad and locate and open the transcript file you just saved. *(Note: You can also view the transcript in Word because it can open and display text files.)*

Project 2

Use Windows Live Messenger to Send a File or Photo

1. If necessary, open and sign on to Windows Live Messenger.
2. Send a message to one of your online classmates on your contact list.
3. Click the Share Files button in the toolbar, then click Send a Single File.
4. Use the Send a File dialog box to browse to and select a file or photo that you want to send. After selecting the file, click the Open button to close the dialog box and send the file.
5. Your classmate will have to accept your invitation to send the file before it will be sent. Once the invitation is accepted, you will receive an acceptance notification and the transfer process will begin.
6. Go to your classmate's computer and see how the transferred file looks in the conversation window. A hyperlink to the location of the transferred file will appear in the conversation window. Click the hyperlink to open the file.

Project 3

Use Skype to Make a Conference Call

1. Find two or three of your classmates who are willing to hold a conference call with you.
2. Open Skype and make sure you are signed in.
3. If you have not added your friend's names to your Skype Contact list, follow the instructions contained in Skill Review 5, Steps 2a–c to add them now.
4. Check to see that your contact list shows that your classmates are online. If not, remind them to start Skype and sign in.
5. Select one of your online contacts, press the Ctrl key, and then select the other online contacts that you want to participate in the conference call. A maximum of four people can participate in a conference call.
6. Click the green call button at the bottom of the Skype window to start the call.
7. When everyone answers, you can begin your conversation.

8. To end the conference, click the End Call button at the bottom of the Skype window.

9. When the End the Conference confirmation dialog box appears, click the Yes button to end the conference.

Internet Research Activities

Activity 1
Research Internet Chat and Instant Messaging Security Issues

Asynchronous communication methods such as Internet chat programs and instant messaging clients offer convenience but also can compromise security if the appropriate steps are not taken. Conduct Internet research to learn more about the security issues involved with these forms of communication, and then write or type a short paper outlining the issues and describing any steps users can take to avoid problems.

Activity 2
Explore More About Instant Messaging Clients

Research the different features offered by Windows Live Messenger, Yahoo! Messenger, and one other IM program, and then create a table comparing the features using a format similar to the following table:

Features	IM 1	IM 2	IM 3
Video	✔	X	✔
Voice	✔	✔	✔
File Transfer	✔	✔	✔

Activity 3
Net Challenge

Learn more about using Windows Vista Remote Desktop by reading the Vista Remote Desktop sidebar in this chapter. When you are finished, log on to the Internet and find a tutorial that steps you through configuring your home computer to accept Remote Desktop connections. When you get home, configure your computer as per the tutorial. When you get back to school, attempt to connect to your home computer through Remote Desktop. *(Note: As always, make sure you have backed up important data and created a Restore Point before making any changes to your home computer. You may want to have the tutorial you found approved by your instructor before making any changes that could harm your home computer.)*

UNIT 3

Emerging Trends

IM Vulnerabilities

Not all emerging trends are positive developments. An example is the rapid emergence of malware targeting instant messaging clients. This threat, estimated to be increasing by 50 percent a month in early 2005, parallels the rapid increase in the popularity of this mode of synchronous communication. Because IM clients operate in real-time, they can spread viruses around the globe many times faster than e-mail, so the threat is very real. While many Internet users are aware of the dangers of e-mail viruses, they remain ignorant of the fact that Instant messaging programs are vulnerable as well. As a result, many fail to take preventative steps that could offer protection. IT journal InfoWorld estimates that while 85 percent of organizations are estimated to be using IM, only 5 percent have proper security in place. To avoid problems, IM users should avoid clicking on unfamiliar URLs or downloading files from unknown sources, and make sure they have the latest Windows updates and current antivirus software installed. Since many IM viruses hack Buddy lists, IM users should exercise extra vigilance with any messages from friends that ask them to click URLs, visit Web sites, or download attachments.

Sources: Cathleen Moore, "IM viruses: The next big threat?" www.infoworld.com/article/05/02/11/HNimvirus_1.html
Daniel Thomas, "IM viruses increase by 50 percent a month." www.vnunet.com/news/1162017
Robert Vamosi, "IM viruses finally come of age." http://reviews.cnet.com/4520-3513_7-6072173-1.html

Revolutionary Blogs

The Chinese government strictly controls all forms of communication in an effort to control what the Chinese people can see and hear, but these efforts are being undermined every time a new Internet technology appears. According to the BBC, some 50,000 Chinese government employees monitor Internet traffic. Blogs are the latest technology to play a role in circumventing restrictions and providing an outlet for expression. Within the space of two years, their number has grown from 1,000 to over 600,000. To avoid being blocked, an Adopt a Chinese Blogger program is being developed to distribute blogs on servers located beyond the reach of Chinese authorities.

Source: Kevin Anderson, "Breaking down the Great Firewall." http://news.bbc.co.uk/2/hi/asia-pacific/4496163.stm

Integrating Real-Time Communication

Although there are any number of Internet-based real-time communication methods available, many of them are incompatible. Nowhere is this problem better illustrated than in the case of instant messaging systems. Until recently, Microsoft Messenger users were unable to send and receive messages to and from those using Yahoo! and

AOL IM services. In early 2005, Microsoft launched Office Communicator 2005 in recognition of the need for better integration of real-time communications. Aimed at enterprises (a buzzword covering businesses and other large organizations), Office Communicator 2005 will support Yahoo! and AOL IM services when used with Microsoft's Live Communications Server 2005 with a Service Pack installed. Communicator 2005 also integrates land-line, VoIP, and mobile phone services. In 2006, Microsoft announced the upcoming release of Office Communicator 2007, due out in the second quarter of 2007.

Sources: Yardena Arar, "Microsoft Launches New Real-Time Communications Tools." www.pcworld.com/news/article/0,aid,119940,00.asp
http://office.microsoft.com/en-us/communicator/FX101729051033.aspx

From Blog to Vlog?

If you have just gotten used to blogs, get ready for a related phenomenon with an even stranger name—the vlog. Vlog is short for video blog, which in turn is short for video web log. Vlogs are similar to ordinary blogs except that they use video as their primary means of communication rather than as the occasional blog enhancement. Still in their infancy, it is possible to create a vlog using conventional blogging software, but vlog software is now available that makes creating vlogs far easier. A vlog software program called Vlog It! (www.seriousmagic.com/products/vlogit), lets users convert their scripts into an onscreen teleprompter that they can read from just like professional newscasters. The software also makes it easy to insert still pictures, video, and sound clips at script-designated times. Vlog It! also features video editing tools that can help make a vlog look as professional as a network newscast. While there are relatively few vlogs at the moment, their growth is set to take off as broadband access increases.

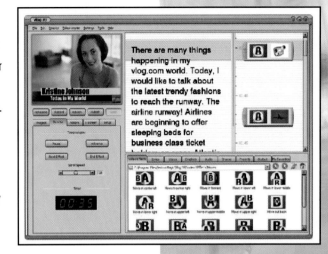

Sources: www.seriousmagic.com/products/vlogit/, www.msnbc.msn.com/id/7226225/

E-mail Future under Attack?

The very elements of e-mail that make it a success—its openness, simplicity, and availability, lead some to think that its future is threatened. The various threats to e-mail posed by spam, viruses, and fraudulent use such as phishing attacks have been estimated to cause some $15 billion annually in personal losses, and that figure is rising as threats proliferate. While e-mail security measures are constantly being implemented, the forces behind the threats adapt just as rapidly. The problem has gotten so bad that many e-mail users are restricting their use of this otherwise convenient communication method. Attachments are often the victim of this increased vigilance, with many businesses and consumers no longer daring to open them. Some businesses are even considering a return to using conventional mail, on the assumption that the increased cost and slower speed would be counterbalanced by increased security. One of the keys to countering e-mail threats is the ability to prevent e-mail senders from disguising their identities, and Microsoft, Yahoo!, and AOL are working together to create a caller ID-like e-mail technology that will make doing that impossible. Whether this effort will be successful remains to be seen, but the overall track record of preventive efforts is not good. Despite a number of different efforts to control it, in mid-2005 64 percent of e-mail was spam, up from 58 percent just a half year ago at the end of 2004.

Source: www.usatoday.com/tech/news/2004-06-14-email_x.htm

Discussion Questions

1. Do you think governments have a right to control Internet content? If you agree, describe the circumstances under which you feel control is appropriate. If you disagree, explain your position.

2. Are blogs a temporary fad or are they here to stay? What about video blogs (vlogs)? Do you think they will catch on or will they turn out to be a novelty that does not become mainstream?

3. Do you think that efforts to counteract e-mail threats will ultimately be successful, or are these futile efforts in a battle that will eventually be lost? Describe what you would do to end threats to e-mail communications.

4. The variety of different mutually incompatible instant messaging systems provide an example of the kind of situation that makes some people think that new product developers should be required to make their systems compatible with other systems. State whether or not you agree with that sentiment, and describe what steps, if any, you would take to resolve incompatibility issues.

APPENDIX A

Mozilla Firefox

The Mozilla Firefox Web browser has proven so popular since its November 2004 release that it has gained about 30% of the browser market, converting a large percentage of Internet Explorer users. The wide-spread acceptance of Firefox is due in part to its reputation as a more secure browser platform than that offered by Internet Explorer 6 and also due to innovative ideas such as tabbed browsing, a Download Manager, Live Bookmarks, and other features that make using Firefox a pleasure for many.

Figure A.1 shows the Firefox default browser layout. The menu bar commands are the same as those featured in Internet Explorer 6 with the

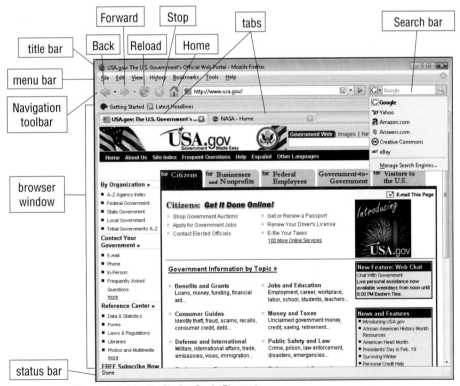

Figure A.1 Mozilla Firefox Basic Elements

exception of the History and Bookmarks commands. Clicking the History command will display a list of recently visited Web sites, as well as Back, Forward, and Home commands. The Bookmarks command is equivalent to the Favorites button in Internet Explorer. The Firefox Search bar located at the right side of the Navigation toolbar features the Google search engine by default, but clicking the down-pointing arrow displays a list of other search engines and references sites. Additional sites can be added to the list by clicking the Add Engines command from the list as shown in Figure A.1. Firefox newcomers can click Help on the menu bar and then For Internet Explorer Users to access information geared toward Internet Explorer users, including information on terminology differences, importing Favorites and other settings, Firefox features, and keyboards shortcuts as shown in Figure A.2.

Switching over to Firefox is easy, and Firefox takes users through the steps necessary to transfer Favorites (Bookmarks), cookies, passwords, and other settings from the user's previous browser during the installation process. These items can be transferred at a later date by clicking File on the menu bar and then Import, which opens the Import Wizard shown in Figure A.3.

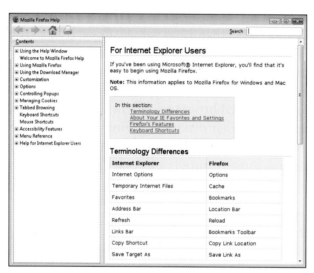

Figure A.2 Firefox for Internet Explorer Users Page

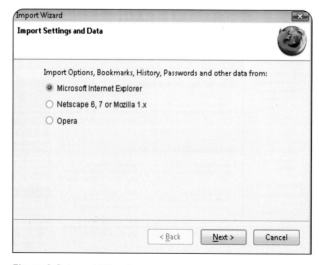

Figure A.3 Import Wizard

Tabbed Browsing

Tabbed browsing lets Firefox users open more than one Web page at a time in the same browser window. Each open page is indicated by a tab at the top of the browser window as shown in Figure A.1. A new tab can be opened by clicking File on the menu bar and then New Tab, by double-clicking an empty space on the Tab bar, by pressing Ctrl + T, or by right-clicking an empty space on the Tab bar and then clicking New Tab from the shortcut menu. Tabs can be closed by clicking File on the menu bar and then Close Tab, pressing Ctrl + W, or right-clicking a tab and clicking Close Tab. Tabs help to keep a desktop free from the clutter of multiple open browser windows.

Live Bookmarks

Firefox lets users save RSS news and blog headlines as live bookmarks. Once an RSS live Bookmark has been saved, it can be reopened to display the latest RSS headlines as shown in Figure A.4. To save a live Bookmark, look for the orange RSS icon to the right of the Location bar as shown in Figure A.4. Clicking the icon will display a Subscribe To ToolTip if more than one feed is available from the current Web site. Clicking a feed listing will open a Web page with a Subscribe Now button that can be clicked to open the Add Live Bookmark dialog box. The Name text box can be used to rename the feed if desired, and the down-pointing arrow at the right of the Create in text box can be clicked to display a short list of Bookmarks that can be used to store the feed. Clicking the arrow button located to the right of the down-pointing arrow expands the Add Bookmark dialog box so that it display a scrollable list of all Bookmarks. The dialog box can also be used to create new Bookmarks.

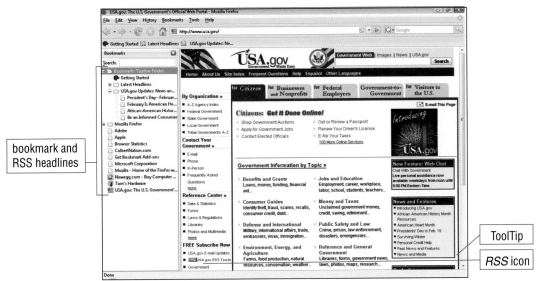

Figure A.4 Live Bookmark RSS Headlines and Orange *RSS* Icon

Download Manager

The Download Manager shown in Figure A.5 lets Firefox users manage past and current file downloads with a single dialog box. The Download Manager also offers a number of different management tools, including the ability to pause and cancel downloads, to display a completed download's folder location, to remove download records, and to retry downloads. The Download Manager opens automatically when files are downloaded. It can be opened manually by clicking Tools on the menu bar and then Downloads or by pressing Ctrl + J. Download Manager options can be changed using the Options dialog box. The Options dialog box can be opened by clicking Tools on the menu bar and then Options. Download options can be access from the Main category of the Options dialogue box as shown in Figure A.6.

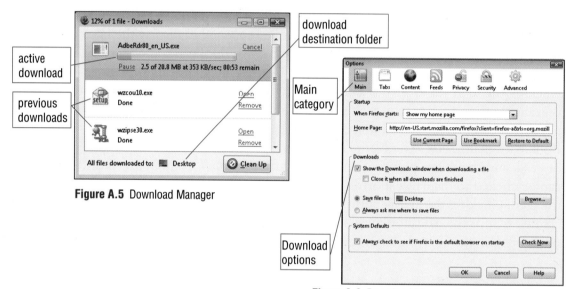

Figure A.5 Download Manager

Figure A.6 Download Manager Options Dialog Box

Skill Review 1 Install Mozilla Firefox and Conduct a Search

1. Download and install the Mozilla Firefox Web browser by completing the following steps:
   a. Start Internet Explorer.
   b. Type **www.getfirefox.com** in the Address bar and then press Enter.
   c. Click the <u>Download Firefox - Free</u> link at the top of the page. *(Note: If you are using a Mac OS X or Linux system, click the <u>Other systems and languages link</u> located just below the <u>Download Firefox - Free</u> link. Scroll down to the English language browser listing and then across to the Mac OS X or Linux Download links. Click the appropriate Download link. Subsequent steps may differ from those described below.)*
   d. Click the Save button in the File Download dialog box when it appears. Use the Save As dialog box to navigate to the folder you will use to save the file and then click Save. *(Note: The length of time the download process takes will vary depending on your connection speed.)*

e. If necessary, click the Close button when the Download complete dialog box appears.

f. If you have permission to install the program, open Windows Explorer, find the Firefox Setup file, and then double-click it to begin the installation process. If an Open File - Security Warning dialog box appears, click the Run button.

g. If the User Account Control dialog box appears, click Continue. Then click Next to proceed with the installation.

h. Click the *I Accept the terms of the License Agreement* option and then click Next.

i. Click the *Standard* option and then click Next.

j. The Install Complete window will appear once the installation is complete. Click Finish to close the window and start Mozilla Firefox. ***(Note: If the Import Wizard dialog box appears, click the* Don't import anything *option unless instructed otherwise. If the Default Browser dialog box appears, click* No *unless instructed otherwise.)***

2. Conduct a search using Mozilla Firefox by completing the following steps:

a. If necessary, start Firefox by clicking Start, clicking All Programs, clicking Mozilla Firefox, and then clicking Mozilla Firefox.

b. Search for the CNN Web site by typing **CNN** in the Search bar and then pressing Enter.

c. Open the CNN.com Web site by clicking the CNN.com listing on the Google results page.

d. Create a new tab by clicking File on the menu bar and then New Tab.

e. Open a new Web page in the tab you created by typing **news.bbc.co.uk** in the Location bar and then pressing Enter.

f. Click the CNN tab to switch back to the CNN.com Web page.

g. Bookmark the CNN.com page by clicking Bookmarks on the menu bar and then Bookmark This Page.

h. Click the arrow button located to the right of the *Create in* text box to expand the Add Bookmark dialog box.

i. Click the New Folder button.

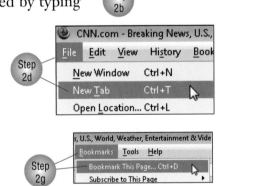

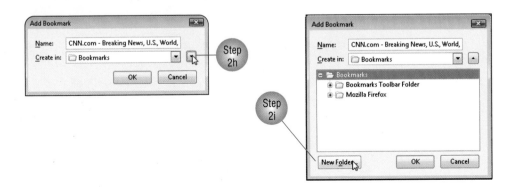

j. Name the new folder *News* and then click the OK button when you are finished.

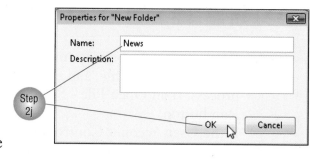

k. The folder you just created will be displayed and automatically selected in the Add Bookmark dialog box *Create in* text box. Click the OK button to close the Add Bookmark dialog box.

l. Click the BBC tab to display the BBC Web page.

m. Look for the orange RSS icon to the right of the Location bar and click it.

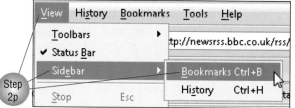

n. Click the Subscribe Now button.

o. Use the Add Bookmark dialog box to create a new folder named RSS Feeds, and save the BBC RSS feed to that folder. Click the OK button when you are finished.

p. Click View on the menu bar, point to Sidebar, and then click Bookmarks.

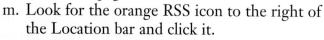

q. Scroll down to the RSS Feeds folder you created and then click the plus sign (+) next to the folder icon.

r. Click the plus sign (+) next to the BBC News folder to display the list of current RSS headlines.

s. Click one of the headlines to display that page in the browser window.

t. Close Firefox by clicking File and then Exit.

GLOSSARY

A

Abilene backbone the Internet backbone used by Internet2

absolute document path document path containing all the information needed to link to a document located on another server, beginning with the protocol and ending with the file name

accelerated Internet an Internet technology that uses standard modems and POTS lines to connect to the Internet, but employs compression and caching technologies to increase throughput and provide speeds up to five times faster than standard dial-up connections

access point a radio device used to connect a wireless device to a peer network or a wireless LAN to a wired LAN

acronym a word formed from the first letter of each word in a phrase, such as LOL for "laughing out loud"

ActiveX control a set of Microsoft programming/scripting language technologies that expand Internet Explorer capabilities; ActiveX controls are often referred to as a type of plug-in

Address bar browser bar that displays the IP or URL address of the currently displayed Web page and enables the user to browse to other URLs

advanced search pages search engine pages that feature additional search options used to conduct complex searches

adware (advertising supported software) a software application that can display advertising banners while the program is running or via some other triggering mechanism

analog electronic signals that are sent in continuous waves, as opposed to digital signals that contain binary data consisting of ones and zeroes

analog telephone adaptor (ATA) an adaptor that converts analog signals to digital signals so that a regular telephone can be used for VoIP communication

anchor tags paired HTML tags used in conjunction with an HREF attribute to create a hyperlink in a Web document

animated GIF a type of GIF image file that creates an illusion of motion by instructing a browser to load two or more images in succession

anonymous FTP server an FTP server open to the public, usually allowing log on using *anonymous, guest,* or *ftp* as the user name and a user's e-mail address as a password

antivirus program software that can be used to scan a computer to detect any malware that may be present

application a computer program that performs a specific task or function

archive a collection of stored data, such as mailing list or forum posts

ARPANET the first packet-switched computer network

ASCII mode FTP transfer mode used for text files

Asymmetric Digital Subscriber Line (ADSL) DSL connection providing differing bandwidth rates for downloads and uploads

asymmetric encryption encryption method that uses paired private and public keys for encryption and decryption (also known as public-key encryption)

asymmetrical an Internet connection that offers different bandwidths for uploading and downloading, usually offering slower uploading bandwidth

asynchronous document collaboration Internet communication that enables people to work together on documents regardless of their location

attachment a document attached and sent with an e-mail message

authentication refers to the process of verification

AutoComplete Internet Explorer feature that stores previously entered information so it can be matched against text being entered in form fields in order to speed up the data entry process

avatar graphical representation of a forum user

B

Back button button on the Internet Explorer Standard Buttons toolbar that moves back through previously displayed Web pages so that a Web page can be retrieved and displayed in a browser

backbone a high-speed line that forms the major pathway for a network

backdoor payloads virus payload that allows unauthorized access to a computer

bandwidth a value that expresses the maximum amount of data that can be transmitted through a communications link over a given time frame, such as 2.5 Mbps

behavior blocking antivirus program tool that looks for behaviors that are typical of malware

Big Eight the eight major Usenet newsgroup top-level hierarchies, originally the Big Seven

binary mode FTP transfer mode for nontext files

biometric authentication a cutting-edge technology that enables a computer to use biological features such as fingerprints, speech, or even iris patterns to verify a user's identity

bit rate the number of bits used per second to record samples

bitmap an image file type that stores image information as a grid composed of tiny picture elements, known as pixels

blended threat threat that use a combination of different types of malware

blogger someone who maintains a weblog or blog

blogosphere the interconnected blogging community

blogroll weblog section than contains links to other blogs or Web sites

Bluetooth a wireless personal area networking technology that uses radio waves to connect devices within a range of about 30 feet

Boolean logic a type of algebraic logic that employs expressions using operators

Boolean operators single word logical expressions used in Boolean logic, such as AND, OR, and NOT

bridge tap device used on POTS lines that can impair DSL signals

broadband usually refers to Internet connections offering bandwidth higher than the 56 Kbps offered by dial-up access

broadband over power line (BPL) an Internet connection technology that delivers Internet data over electrical power lines and into homes

browser a software program that enables the user to view the different materials available on the portion of the Internet known as the World Wide Web

browser extensions programs that extend the function of a browser

browser window the area of a Web browser where Web page content appears

brute force attack an attack that aims to overcome a password-protected computer or network by systematically trying different combinations of letters and numbers until the correct password is discovered

buffering a streaming technique in which an initial portion of a broadcast downloads before a streaming broadcast starts playing, creating a buffer or store that the player can draw on to compensate for differences between transmission and playing rates

byte a unit of measurement equal to eight bits

C

cable Internet Internet service delivered over the coaxial cable used to convey television signals into homes or businesses

cable modem modem used in cable Internet systems

cable modem termination system (CMTS) device at a cable TV office that connects users to an Internet backbone

cache to store or save, such as the pages cached in a search engine database

Carrier-Sense Multiple Access with Collision Detection (CSMA/CD) access method used by Ethernet networks to avoid frames colliding with each other if nodes transmit frames at the same time

Cascading Style Sheets (CSS) a method for specifying how an HTML document should be displayed; it can be contained in a separate document or inside an HTML document

case sensitive a program that is case sensitive will distinguish between capitalized (uppercase) and uncapitalized (lowercase) words

cellular phone networks digital telephone networks that use a network of cells containing a radio transmitter and control equipment to carry phone signals

central office (CO) telephone company office that provides telephone service to end users through a connection referred to as the last mile

certification authorities (CA) independent certification bodies that issue digital certificates

channel headings alternate name for IRC channel names

channel operator the responsible party in IRC chat rooms for seeing that a channel runs smoothly

channels chat rooms used in IRC networks

chat synchronous Internet communication that allows real-time conversation

chat room a channel or location in IRC or Web-based chat programs that people use to engage in group conversations related to a topic or subject

circuit switching a method for transmitting data using single telephone circuits (lines) connected through a central switchboard

Classless InterDomain Routing (CIDR) a method for conserving IP addresses; also known as *supernetting*

client a computer or device on a network

client/server network a network in which computers or devices (clients) are linked to a central computer known as a server

closed mailing list mailing list that restricts subscribers to those meeting certain requirements

clustered results search hits organized by category or similarity

coaxial cable cable that supports high bandwidth and is resistant to interference because it contains a grounded shield

codec a compression technology used to compress and decompress audio files

command-line FTP client programs FTP client programs that feature an interface in which the user types simple commands such as get, put, and so on

computer network two or more computers linked together so that they can communicate and share resources

confirmation message e-mail message confirming successful subscription to a mailing list or similar type of forum

contact list a list of contacts maintained in IM clients and other synchronous Internet communication applications

cookie a small text file that Web sites can place on a computer to help a Web site server recognize previous visitors in order to customize the viewing experience

copyright legal protection afforded to creative ideas and expressions

cracker a computer expert who attempts to penetrate or hack protected computers or networks with criminal intent, such as to steal or destroy information

crawling term used to describe the process used by spiders to search the Internet for documents

cyber crime crimes committed using the Internet

D

dangling link A link created when a WikiWord is created and saved; appears as a hyperlink usually followed by a question mark

data corruption a virus payload that damages or even removes data from a computer; also known as *deletion payload*

dedicated GUI FTP client program a stand-alone GUI FTP client program that is not part of another program

dedicated line a telephone line that is separate from the public telephone network and is for the exclusive use of the organization leasing the line

deep Web the portion of the Web that is generally beyond the reach of search engine spiders

denial-of-service (DoS) attack attack that paralyzes a computer network by bombarding it with traffic in the form of packets of useless information

desktop video conferencing video conferencing using desktop computers and an Internet connection

dial-up Internet access Internet connection method using a standard telephone modem over POTS telephone lines

digest compilation of posts sent to a mailing list

digital electronic signals contain binary data consisting of ones and zeroes, as opposed to analog signals that are continuous waves

digital certificate a means of verifying that a public key belongs to the person who claims to own it

digital signature encryption method that allows an Internet user to confirm that a digitally signed message originates from the person claiming to have sent it, and that the contents of the message have not been altered

Digital Subscriber Line (DSL) an Internet technology capable of providing high-speed Internet service using POTS twisted-pair wires

diplexer component of a cable modem used to asymmetrically assign downstream and upstream traffic to certain frequencies

directories the folders on an FTP server are referred to as folders or directories depending on the FTP client software being used

Discrete Multitone (DMT) Modulation a method of dividing the frequencies in a twisted-pair wire into 256 frequency bands of 4.3125 kHz

distributed database a database stored on a number of different servers in different locations

distributed denial-of-service (DDoS) attack DoS attack that uses a Trojan horse to download a small program onto an unsuspecting Internet user's computer so that the computer can be one of many computers used to take part in a DDoS attack

document relative path document path used to link to documents that are located in the same folder as the document containing the hyperlink

Domain Name System (DNS) a system for mapping a domain name to an IP address

dotted decimal notation a method of expressing IP addresses in decimal format

download a process in which files are received via the Internet

drilling down connecting directly to the databases and other types of content not indexed by search engines in order to access the deep Web

DSL Access Multiplexer (DSLAM) a DSL device that receives customer connections and concentrates them into a single connection to an Internet backbone

Dynamic HTML (DHTML) utilizes a combination of HTML, Cascading Style Sheets (CSS), and JavaScript to enable users to create dynamic Web pages

E

edit form form used to create new pages in a wiki

electronic mailing list topic-focused e-mail-based discussion environment

e-mail (electronic mail) a method for sending and receiving messages and attachments through the Internet

e-mail address an address used to designate the recipient of an e-mail message, consisting of a user name or local part and a domain name separated by the @ symbol

e-mail client a software program used to used to compose, send, and receive e-mail messages, such as Windows Mail or Eudora

e-mail servers special servers designed to handle e-mail traffic

embed tag Netscape-style plug-ins use the <embed> tag to insert media and JavaScript for communication

emoticons keyboard character combinations used to communicate emotions and avoid misunderstandings in text communications

encryption the process of scrambling text or data into an unreadable format that cannot be unscrambled without the use of a key

Ethernet a networking technology used to create LANs

eXtensible HTML (XHTML) combines HTML 4.01 elements with the syntax used by XML, a SGML-derived metalanguage

extranet an intranet that shares a portion of its resources with users outside the intranet

F

fair use refers to provisions of U.S. copyright law that permit the use of some copyrighted material for criticism, commentary, news, parody, personal use, and so on

Favorites Center button button under the back/forward buttons that opens the Favorites Center to display Favorites, Feeds, and History

Favorites list list of saved URLs that can be organized for the quick retrieval of frequently visited Web pages

fiber-optic cable cable composed of strands of optically pure glass or plastic used to transmit data through beams of light that bounce off the reflective walls of the cable

file compression utilities programs that use algorithms to reduce the amount of redundant or repeated data in a file

file servers computers that store information on a network

File Transfer Protocol (FTP) a program developed for the ARPANET that provided a standard means of transferring files

filtering the process of including or excluding certain information to create a complex search

firewall hardware and software buffers that prevent unauthorized access to a network

first generation cellular (1G) the first generation of cellular phone networks that used analog technology

fixed wireless Internet service wireless Internet connection that broadcasts signals from a tower to an end user's antenna at a fixed location

flame an abusive e-mail message or post

flame war the back and forth sending of abusive messages that can escalate out of control

Forward button button on the Internet Explorer Standard Buttons toolbar that moves forward through previously displayed Web pages so that a Web page can be redisplayed in the browser

freeware software that developers make available for free distribution and use

frequently asked questions (FAQs) a document created to prevent people from asking the same questions over and over again

FTP client software software that enables a client computer to use FTP to transfer files to and from an FTP server

FTP host address the URL or IP address used by an FTP server, such as ftp.wsftp.com or 156.21.4.25

FTP server software software that enables a computer to act as an FTP server

FTP session an FTP connection established between a client and a remote host

Full Screen view an expanded browser view that hides toolbars and menus

full text indexing process in which search engines save the entire contents of a Web page

full-duplex sound card a sound card that allows users to talk and hear at the same time when using audio applications

G

general search question search question that seeks contextual or background information

getting a file downloading a file

GIF image lossless image format that is the most commonly used image format on the Web

gigabit a unit equal to 1,000 megabits

gigaPOPs (gigabit Point of Presence) Internet access points used to connect to Internet2, supporting data transfer rates of 10 gigabits per second (Gbps)

graphical user interface (GUI) a computer interface (window element) that uses graphics instead of text

group a collection of e-mail addresses saved under a single group name for convenience in addressing e-mail messages

GUI (graphical user interface) FTP client programs FTP client programs that provide a point-and-click interface that lets users input commands via buttons or menus, or by dragging and dropping files

H

hacker a computer expert who attempts to penetrate or hack protected computers or networks for fun

handoff term used to describe the way cell phone signals are seamlessly passed from one cell to another

hashing a mathematical process (used during digital signature creation) that condenses the contents of a message to a few lines called a message digest

header in packet switching, the method used to identify a packet's source, its destination, and its relationship to other packets

headset a microphone and earphone combination worn on the head

Help Internet Explorer feature that provides a searchable Help topic database

helper application stand-alone program, such as Microsoft Word or Excel, that can open to display content downloaded by a browser

hertz (Hz) a unit of frequency equal to one cycle or wave per second

heuristic scanning antivirus program tool that looks for general malware characteristics rather than specific characteristics such as a signature

hierarchies the term for Usenet newsgroup categories

High Bit-Rate DSL (HDSL) DSL technology that provides symmetrical Internet data transmission using two phone lines

History button button on the Internet Explorer Standard Buttons toolbar that the user can click to display a list of previously visited Web sites in the Explorer bar

History list list of previously visited Web pages automatically stored in the Favorites Center

Home button button on the Internet Explorer Standard Buttons toolbar that displays the default browser home page in the browser window when clicked

home page the gateway or index document for a Web site

host a computer or device connected to a network

hot zone wireless network coverage that extends beyond typical hotspot coverage

hotspot a public location with readily accessible wireless networks coverage

HTML interpreter a browser program that interprets and displays content containing the HTML markup language

https (Hypertext Transfer Protocol over Secure Socket Layer) protocol used for SSL transactions

hybrid search engine search tool that combines search engine and subject directory features

hyperlink text (hypertext) or objects (hypermedia) linked to other text or objects in Web documents

hypertext text that contains links (hyperlinks) to other documents

HyperText Markup Language (HTML) computer language used to design Web documents

HyperText Transfer Protocol (HTTP) protocol enabling communication between a client and file servers

I

IEEE 802.11 (IEEE 802.11a, IEEE 802.11b, and IEEE 802.11g) wireless radio frequency specifications used in wireless networking, also known as Wi-Fi

IEEE 802.16 wireless specification referred to as WiMAX

indexer search engine program that sorts the words contained in or related to the Web page and organizes them in a database

information theft payloads virus payloads that steal information from a computer

instant messaging (IM) synchronous Internet communication method that uses a client program connected to a server network to enable real-time text conversation

Instant Search Box search box to the right of the address bar allowing instant searches of Internet search engines

integrated services digital network (ISDN) a dial-up Internet technology that integrates voice and data services by creating multiple digital channels in a single telephone wire, allowing the simultaneous use of several devices at the same time

intellectual property creative ideas and expressions that are afforded legal protection such as copyright or trademark protection

interactive Internet content that accepts viewer input to control the viewing experience

interlacing enables an image to display gradually as it downloads into a Web page

internal search engine search engine that searches the contents of a Web page or site rather than the entire Web

Internet the global network of networks that connects computer networks around the world

internet two or more networks joined together

Internet Access Provider (IAP) a company or organization that only provides access to the Internet

Internet backbone the core or central network that forms the Internet

Internet Message Access Protocol (IMAP) an incoming mail protocol where e-mail messages are read and manipulated on the server without downloading them to a local machine

Internet Protocol (IP) address an address that identifies the node and the network to which a device is attached so that the other computers and devices can find it and communicate

Internet Protocol Version 4 (IPv4) a protocol providing for 32-bit IP addresses

Internet Protocol Version 6 (IPv6) a protocol providing for 128-bit IP addresses, also known as IP next generation (IPng)

Internet Relay Chat (IRC) the first open Internet protocol that enabled users to engage in real-time text conversations over the Internet

Internet Service Provider (ISP) a company or organization that provides Internet access and other services such as Web development and hosting

Internet2 a university-led research and development consortium founded in 1996 to develop new technologies and applications for the Internet

intranet a private TCP/IP network used within companies or organizations

IP next generation (IPng) a new version of the IP protocol that vastly expands the number of IP

addresses that will be available to cope with the growth of the Internet

IP phone telephone that plugs directly into the Internet or into a computer connected to the Internet in order to permit VoIP phone calls

IRC client program program that enables users to use the IRC protocol to engage in real-time chat

IRC robot robot used to automate routine IRC channel functions

IRC servers servers that form the networks that support Internet Relay Chat

J

Java applet small application (program) created using the Java programming language

JavaScript a scripting language used to make HTML pages interactive

JPEG image lossy image format that supports more than 16 million colors and is the best Web image format for photographs

K

keyboard shortcut a quick command input method that enables a user to press a function key such as F1 to choose a command

keyframes important reference-point frames used in Flash animations

keywords significant or important words used to form search queries

kilobit a unit equal to 1,000 bits

kilobyte (KB) a unit equal to 1,024 bytes

kilohertz (kHz) a unit equal to 1,000 hertz (Hz)

L

last mile telephone company term referring to the last portion of any telephone connection from a central office (CO) to an end user

latency the time between the transmission and reception of data across a network, usually measured in milliseconds (ms)

limited edition software stripped-down versions of regular software programs; registration and payment will enable previously inaccessible or inactive features and tools once the product is licensed

Links bar an Internet Explorer toolbar that provides a quick method for accessing frequently viewed Web pages

list address the e-mail address that mailing list posts are sent to for distribution to other list members

list manager (administrator address) the e-mail address for the manager or administrator of a mailing list

list moderator someone who reviews the posts to a moderated mailing list before they are forwarded to other members

list server address the e-mail address to which mailing list commands are sent

live event chats news events where experts or celebrities field questions submitted through a Web-based chat room

live streaming Internet audio and video broadcast that occurs live as an event happens

load coil device used on POTS lines that can impair DSL signals

local area network (LAN) a network within a single building or adjacent buildings with a maximum coverage area of approximately half a mile

lurking reading mailing list or forum posts without actively participating by making posts

M

mailing list software program software used to create an electronic mailing list

malware short for *malicious software*, malware refers to any program or computer code deliberately designed to harm any portion of a computer system

media access card (MAC) component of a cable modem that handles the interface between network protocols

media players software programs and portable players that can play audio and sometimes video files

megabit a unit equal to 1,000 kilobits (Kb)

megahertz (MHz) a measurement of signal frequency; one megahertz is equal to 1,000,000 hertz (Hz)

message digest the result of a message being hashed

message header the *From*, *To*, *Cc*, *Bcc*, and *Subject* information in an e-mail message; the New Message window includes text boxes for entering header information

message rule rule created to automate e-mail processes for incoming e-mail, such as directing incoming messages to specified folders or blocking e-mail from specified e-mail addresses; works only with POP3 mail server accounts

meta search engine search engine that searches the contents of a Web page or site rather then the entire Web

meta tags HTML tags, located in the header section of a Web page's HTML document, that contain title, description, keywords, and other document-related information

metropolitan area network (MAN) networks connecting a metropolitan area

microbrowser the small Web browser in hand-held devices

mirror site a server that duplicates the content of another server to help take some of the load off the more heavily trafficked Web sites

modem a device used to send and receive signals over analog telephone, digital, and cable lines

moderated refers to mailing lists or forums that use a moderator to review posts before they are forwarded to other list members or displayed in a forum

MP3 audio file format short for MPEG Audio Layer 3, the most popular audio file format in use on the Internet today

multicast data transmission method in which copies of source data are made as close to the recipient as possible, thereby conserving bandwidth

multimedia the use of more than one type of media on a Web page, such as any combination of text, graphics, animated graphics, video, audio, or even hypertext

Multipurpose Internet Mail Extensions (MIME) protocol used to handle attachments to e-mail messages

Musical Instrument Digital Interface (MIDI) audio file format digital audio format that contains musical instructions rather than an actual sound recording

N

natural language the language used in conversational or everyday speech

nested search query a search query containing some Boolean operators in parentheses to indicate the order in which Boolean expressions should be evaluated

netiquette the rules for good behavior when communicating through the Internet; a term created by combining *Internet* and *etiquette*

Netscape-style plug-in a plug-in developed by Netscape

network access point (NAP) connection that allows ISPs or IAPs to connect to an Internet backbone

network address translator (NAT) a program used to change private IP addresses into permitted IP addresses that can travel on the Internet

network interface card (NIC) computer card used to connect a computer or device to a network

Network News Transfer Protocol (NNTP) the protocol used for Usenet newsgroups on the Internet

network operations center (NOC) an office that provides Internet services

network overhead bandwidth absorbed by network operation needs and inefficiencies

news server special server used to handle newsgroups

newsfeed the contents of a newsgroup file that is replicated to other news servers

newsgroups a type of electronic bulletin board that allows users to post and read messages

newsreader a software program used to read newsgroups

nicks nicknames in IRC

node a computer or device connected to a network

NSFnet computer network created by the National Science Foundation to connect non-ARPANET networks

O

object tag ActiveX controls use the <object> tag and VBScript for communication

OC-1 cable fiber-optic cable that supports bandwidth capacity of 51.84 Mbps

OC-3 cable fiber-optic cable that supports bandwidth capacity of 155.52 Mbps

off-topic post post that is not related to a list or forum topic

on-demand streaming audio and video Internet broadcasts available on user request from archived material

online service provider (OSP) a type of Internet service provider that offers content and services only to members and usually requires special software that is unique to the OSP, for example AOL and CompuServe

online storage services companies providing remote storage space on servers the user can access online

open architecture philosophy the ARPANET's commitment to open architecture meant that other networks did not need to change their internal protocols to connect with the ARPANET

open mailing list mailing list that allows anyone to subscribe

P

packet switching a data transmission method where large chunks of data are divided into packets that can travel along any number of different circuits until the packets are collected and the data reassembled in its original form at the destination

packets segmented data transmitted through packet switching

Page button grants access to many commands such as copy, paste, save as, and zoom

page ranking process used by most search engines in which search hits are ranked by relevance

parental control software software that enables parents to control the Internet content that children can access to prevent the children from viewing inappropriate content

payload the malicious action that will be performed by the virus

peer-to-peer network a network in which computers are linked directly to one another

permalink a unique URL that can be used to link to blog entries

personal area network (PAN) network used to connect an individual's computer devices

personal certificate digital certificate used to confirm a personal identity

Personal Digital Assistants (PDAs) multipurpose handheld computer devices used to accomplish personal organization functions

phishing an online scam that tricks Internet users into believing that they are being contacted by a legitimate and well-known company

phrase search a search for an exact combination and order of words in a search engine, conducted by placing quotation marks around a phrase or word combination

pixel the smallest unit of information contained in a bitmap image

plagiarism the act of representing someone else's words, writings, or findings as your own

plain old telephone service (POTS) the standard telephone service found in last mile connections to most homes

plug-ins small programs or program modules that work within a browser

plug-ins folder a browser application folder where plug-ins are stored

PNG image image format that offers interlacing and transparency and produces smaller file sizes than the GIF or JPEG formats

polymorphic virus a virus that changes with each replication

port computer doorway used for various activities, such as FTP, connecting to the Internet, and so on

post message sent to mailing lists, newsgroups, forums, and similar discussion areas

Post Office Protocol 3 (POP3) an incoming mail protocol where the user's e-mail client connects to a POP3 server and downloads the messages stored on the server to the local computer

preview pane section of the Windows Mail window that displays a preview of the message currently selected in the message list

Print button button on the Internet Explorer Standard Buttons toolbar that prints the current Web page using the current print settings

private key a key that can be used to decrypt a message

program sharing computer applications that allow two or more parties to share a computer program through the Internet

protocol a set of rules that enables computers to communicate

proxy server a firewall function that handles page and data requests so that the requesting computer or computer network never comes into direct contact with remote computer systems

public domain software software that is freely available because the author or authors have specifically stated that it is in the public domain and not copyrighted

public key keys used in asymmetric encryption that are made public for use by anyone wishing to send an encrypted message to a public key owner

pulsing zombie type of DDoS attack that is intermittent and aims to degrade rather than shut down a service

putting a file uploading a file

Q

query a request for information typed in a search engine search text box

query processor a search engine component that compares the content of a search query to the contents of the search engine index to produce a list of relevant documents

Quick Tab visible only when multiple tabs are open; displays thumbnails of pages open on tabs

R

Rate Adaptive DSL (RADSL) DSL technology that enables modems to adjust their speed according to the length and quality of a telephone line in order to improve transmission quality

read receipt an automated receipt that lets an e-mail message sender know when a message was read by a recipient

Really Simple Syndication (RSS) an XML format for automatically notifying people of Web site updates

refining a search the process of modifying a search to improve the results

Refresh button button on the Internet Explorer Standard Buttons toolbar that refreshes the browser window display by submitting a new Web page request when clicked

results page Web page displaying the results of a search query in a search engine

ripping the process of extracting tracks from audio compact discs (CDs) and saving them to a computer

root folder the top folder (directory) on an FTP server

router a computer device that determines the paths that packets take

RSS aggregator (or reader) a program that can be used to collect, update, and display RSS feeds

RSS Feeds list list of subscribed RSS Feeds available from the Favorites Center

S

sampling rate measures how frequently samples of an audio waveform are recorded per second

sandbox practice wiki page isolated from the other parts of a wiki so there is no danger of doing anything that could affect other wiki components

satellite Internet a wireless Internet connection method that broadcasts Internet data by satellite

scalable when an image can be enlarged or reduced without suffering a loss in quality

scroll bars vertical or horizontal bars that appear in a browser window if a displayed Web page is wider or longer than the browser window; scroll bars can be used to move the browser window contents up and down and sometimes left and right

search engine Web site that uses software tools to index the contents of the Web so that information can be located and retrieved

search hit search results containing information related to a search query

search logic the logical processes used by search engines to match the information they index to the contents of a search query

search syntax conventions the individual ways that search engines interpret or accept logical processes, such as the use of paired quotation marks to indicate a phrase search

second generation cellular (2G) the second generation of cellular phone networks that used digital technology

second-and-a-half generation (2.5G) an improvement to 2G cellular that uses packet switching and offers greater bandwidth (56 Kbps) and supports limited Internet capability such as e-mail and simple Web browsing

Secure Sockets Layer (SSL) an encryption protocol used to ensure the security of financial transactions and other private activities conducted over the Internet

security updates Microsoft updates also known as patches that repair system vulnerabilities as they become discovered

server a computer that provides services to other computers, such as handling requests and sharing resources that may be located on the server

shareware software made available at no cost but requiring registration and payment at the end of a limited trial period

Short Message Service (SMS) a method for sending short text messages through cellular phones

signature a name and address or other personal information automatically appended to the end of an e-mail message

Simple Mail Transfer Protocol (SMTP) the protocol used to send e-mail messages

softphone a screen-based GUI interface used by some VoIP applications that emulates the appearance of a telephone or telephone keypad

spam the online equivalent of the junk mail delivered by the postal service

specific search question search question that seeks facts or details

spider automated program used by search engines to "crawl" the Internet looking for Web pages and other documents

splitter a filter used on telephone lines to separate the low-end frequencies used to carry voice signals from the higher frequencies used for DSL signals

spoofing disguising an e-mail or Web site so that it appears to come from a well-known or trusted company

spyware any program that is used to gather user information without their knowledge

stand-alone weblog software software that can be used to create blogs

Standard Buttons toolbar a toolbar of Internet Explorer command buttons

status bar Internet Explorer bar that displays the loading and security status of the current Web page

stealth dialing disconnects a user from his or her dial-up ISP and reconnects the user to another ISP charging exorbitant rates

stemming the ability of some search engines to search for the root words or partial form of keywords, as well as the keywords themselves

Stop button button on the Internet Explorer Standard Buttons toolbar that stops a URL request when clicked

stop words extremely common words and characters such as *the, in, for, to, #,* and *&* that search engines ignore to keep search results hits to a manageable level and to increase the speed of any search

streaming audio a method used to deliver audio over the Internet by transmitting audio (and more recently video) data in such a way that it can play as soon as it arrives, avoiding the necessity of downloading the entire file before playback

string two or more keywords in a search query

subject directory a search tool that contains links to Web sites and pages organized in hierarchically arranged subject categories

subject header a short line included at the top of an e-mail message that enables recipients to glance at the message list and know the topic of a message before opening the message

subject-specific search engine search engine that narrows the focus of the Web content they index by dealing with a single subject or field

subnetting a method that sets aside special IP addresses for intranets

surface Web the portion of the Web that can be indexed by search engines and subject directories

Symmetric DSL (SDSL) DSL technology that provides identical upload and download bandwidth, but cannot support simultaneous voice transmission

symmetric encryption encryption method that employs a private key that is shared between parties who wish to encrypt their communication

symmetrical an Internet connection that offers the same bandwidth for uploading and downloading

synchronous communication real-time back and forth Internet communication, such as chat, instant messaging, VoIP, and so on

T

T1 cable a type of telephone line containing two twisted-pair wires with a bandwidth of 1.544 megabits per second (Mbps)

T3 cable a type of telephone line containing 28 T1 lines with a bandwidth of 44.746 Mbps

Tab displays a web page in the browser window; multiple tabs can be open at once

Tab List visible only when multiple tabs are open; displays a list of all open tabs

TCP/IP (Transmission Control Protocol/Internet Protocol) paired protocols that handle the breakdown of data into packets and ensure that packets are delivered and then reassembled in the correct order

telco-return cable modems type of cable modem used on cable systems with limited channel capacity that uses telephone lines for upstream data

tele-immersion the ability of an individual to experience being somewhere other than his or her actual location

Telnet a program developed for the ARPANET that enables users to access remote computers (hosts) and work with files and programs

text shortcut letters or numbers used to imitate the sound of a phrase

third generation cellular (3G) the latest version of cellular technology capable of providing high speed data rates, therefore supporting full Internet access, including streaming video

thread a series of posts on the same subject

threat any event that could potentially violate the security of a computer system

throughput the actual amount of user data that a network can transmit per second

title bar bar at the top of every application window in Windows that lists the name of the program in the window, and sometimes the name of the current document or page

Tools button offers commands to configure simple security and privacy settings

top-level domain (TLD) the rightmost portion of the domain name (for example, .com), sometimes referred to as an extension

top-level hierarchies the highest level of Usenet newsgroup hierarchies; the first hierarchy in a newsgroup name

top-post the act of typing a response above what was written in a previous post rather than below it

TrackBack weblog feature that uses an Internet utility known as ping to create a link to a comment referenced in a comment on another weblog

trademark a legally registered name, slogan, or symbol used to identify a product or service in order to distinguish it from competitors and to create recognition

transparency an empty area in an image that allows the background color of a Web page to show through the image

Trojan horse a type of malware that hides or disguises itself as a harmless or legitimate program

tuner component of a cable modem that that sends and receives signals to and from a modulator and demodulator

tween frames the frames located between keyframes in Flash (and other) animations

twisted-pair cable two insulated copper wires twisted around each other in a continuous spiral to form a single telephone line, commonly used in POTS last mile service

U

unicast data transmission method in which a copy of the source data must be created for each recipient, a process that uses a lot of bandwidth

Uniform Resource Locator (URL) a method for locating documents on TCP/IP networks that incorporates domain names by providing the path to a document or location on the Internet

unmoderated refers to mailing lists or other type of forums in which posts are not reviewed

upload a process in which files are sent via the Internet

Usenet (Users' Network) electronic bulletin board that was the pre-Internet forerunner of newsgroups; Usenet newsgroups are now available through distributed servers

V

variable bit rate encoding (VBR) digital recording technology that features a continuously changing bit rate that increases or decreases depending on the complexity of the content being encoded

VDSL gateway device that converts data received by a DSL modem into pulses of light that can travel through fiber-optic cables

vector-based animation animation method that uses mathematical values to describe images instead of saving them in individual frames

Very High Bit-Rate DSL (VDSL) DSL technology that provides download speeds of up to 52 Mbps

video conferencing computer applications that allow two or more people to engage in a real-time conversation in which all parties can see each other

virtual private networks (VPNs) a method used by some extranets to operate through the Internet using encryption to maintain privacy and security

virus a self-replicating form of malware that is spread from computer to computer using another file or program as a host

virus definitions a dictionary file used by antivirus software to identify known viruses

virus signature a string of binary code that is unique to a virus, also known as its fingerprint or pattern

Voice over Internet Protocol (VoIP) technology that facilitates the transmission of voice telephone calls over the Internet

W

WAV audio file format uncompressed digital audio file format developed by Microsoft

Web site certificate digital certificate used to confirm that a Web site is secure and genuine

Web-based chat alternative to using IRC client that allows the use of a Web browser to access some IRC networks and other private networks to engage in text-based chat, and sometimes voice and video chat

Web-based forum a type of forum that uses special software to store and handle forum data in a single server location instead of the NNTP protocol and distributed database platform used by Usenet newsgroups

webcam small digital camera designed to take photos and video images for transmission over the Internet

webcasts audio and video broadcast over the Internet

weblog a form of personal journal or diary in Web page format

weblog directory directory that can be used to find weblogs

weblog service a service that provides ready-made blog templates as well as hosting

webmail Web-based e-mail that provides an e-mail account accessible through any Web browser

wide area network (WAN) a network that links LANs and extends over a much wider geographic area, which could be a city, state, or even country; the Internet is the largest example of a WAN

wiki a type of Web site with pages that can be edited by viewers

wikiengine the software package used to create wikis

wikifarm service that offers wiki hosting

WikiWord wiki hyperlink created by typing two or more capitalized words with no spaces between them, as in PageTwo or AfricanBirds

wildcard symbols symbols that by convention can be used in some search engines to find stems or partial forms of a keyword; common wild card symbols are ? and *

Windows Contacts Windows folder that stores contact information, including e-mail addresses that can be used to address messages in Windows Mail. Usually located at C:\Users\<username>\Contacts.

Windows Mail e-mail client that comes bundled with Windows

Wired Equivalency Privacy (WEP) 128-bit encryption method used to ensure wireless security

Wireless Application Protocol (WAP) an internet protocol designed for the small screens found on hand-held devices

Wireless Fidelity (Wi-Fi) a term for the IEEE 802.11series of wireless specifications created by the Wi-Fi Alliance

Wireless Markup Language (WML) the language used to display information displayed in microbrowsers

wireless networking a network where computers connect using radio waves

workstations term for computer on a LAN

World Wide Web (WWW or the Web) an Internet application that enables users to access hyperlinked Internet resources using Web browsers

worm a form of malware that spreads through network connections without the need for a host program

X

xDSL collective reference to the different members of the family of DSL services available, such as ADSL, HDSL, VDSL, and SDSL

Z

zip file an archive that contains one or more compressed files

zombie a computer hijacked to take part in a DDoS attack

INDEX

IP phones, 330
Ipswitch FTP client programs, 184
IPTV (Internet Protocol Television), 224
IRCnet, 312

J

Java, 17
Java applets, 204, 221, 223
JavaScript, 14, 17, 204, 221, 222–23
Jet Propulsion Lab's Interplanetary Network (IPN), 24
Joint Photographic Experts Group (JPEG) images, 183, 209, 210

K

Kartoo.com, 199
Keyboard shortcuts, 123
Keyframes, 224
Keyword queries, 149–50
    refining, 150–51
Keywords
    in defining search questions, 147
    meta tag, 137
Kilobit, 37
Kilobyte (KB), 38
Kiss.exe, 68
Knopf, Jim, 190

L

Language options, 156–57
LANS (local area networks), 19, 20–21
Last mile telephone company, 34–35
Latency, 39
    for cellular Internet connections, 52
    by Internet connection type, 39
Leased lines, 46
Level 3 Communications, 35
    Internet backbone for, 35
Licklider, J. C. R., 4, 5
Links bar, 124
Linux, 40

List address, 278
List moderator, 278
LISTSERV, 276
List server address, 278
LISTSERV software, 280
LiveJournal, 293
Live streaming, 218–19
Load coils, 44
Local area networks (LANs), 19, 20–21
Local machines, 172
Lock the Toolbars command, 117
LookSmart, 140
Lossless compression, 183
Lossless formats, 214
Lossless technologies, 213
Lossy formats, 214
Lossy technologies, 183, 213
Love Bug virus, 67
    Address Book hijacking method used by, 67
L-Soft, 280
Lurking, 279
Lycos mail, 263

M

MAC (media access card), 46
Mac operating system (OS) X, 40
Macromedia, 224
Macromedia Director, 225
Macromedia Dreamweaver, 225
Macromedia Flash, 225
Mail.com, 263
Mailman, 276
MailWasher, 88
Majordomo, 276
Malware, 66–68, 86, 98
    blended threats, 68–69
    countermeasures, 69–73
        antivirus programs, 70–71
        behavior blocking, 71
        heuristic scanning, 71
        service patches and updates, 69, 72–73
        signature scanning, 71
    Microsoft decision tree in distinguishing, 66
    Trojan horses, 68
    viruses, 67, 69
    worms, 67–68, 69
Massive Multiplayer Online Games (MMOGs), 206
McAfee SpamKiller, 88

McAfee VirusScan, 70
Media access card (MAC), 46
Media and file format search options, 156
Media players, 203
Megabit, 37
Melissa virus, 67
Message boards, 289
Message rules, 255, 256
    dialog box, 256
Meta search engines, 140
Meta tags, 137
    keywords, 137
Metropolitan area network (MAN), 19
Mget command, 175–76
Microbrowsers, 52
Microsoft, 77, 218
    malware decision tree in distinguishing malware, 66
    Windows Defender, 90
Microsoft Outlook, 240
Microsoft Xbox, 206
MILNET, 4
MIME (Multipurpose Internet Mail Extensions) types, 204–205
    file name extensions and, 204
MIRC, 313
Mirror site, 188
MIVA, 140
MLA Style Manual and Guide to Scholarly Publishing, 161
MMOGs (Massive Multiplayer Online Games), 206
Modems, 40
    cable, 40, 45–46
    internal, 40
    ISDN, 40
    xDSL, 40
Moderated mailing lists, 278
Modulator, 45
Morris worm, 67
Mosaic browser, 16–17, 17
Mouse-over events, 222
Moving Picture Experts Group (MPEG), 215
Mozilla, 104
Mozilla Firefox, 17, 98, 104, 105, 177
Mozilla Thunderbird, 240
MP3 audio file format, 215–16, 216
MP3 VBR audio format, 216
MPEG (Moving Picture Experts Group), 215

Credits

Chapter 1: p. 3, top, courtesy of U.S. Internal Revenue Service; p. 3, lower right, Courtesy of www.brighthand.com; p. 9, Figure 1.6 © ICANN, used with permission; p. 11, Figure 1.7, Photo copyright © Dan Murphy. Used with permission; p. 17, upper image, courtesy W3.org, http://www.w3.org/People/Berners-Lee/Overview.html; lower right Step 4. Google™ screen capture ©Google Inc., reprinted with permission; p. 22, sidebar image, © Copyright 1994-2005 Motorola, Inc.; p. 22, Figure 1.20, © 2004-2005 Koninklijke Philips Electronics N.V.; p. 23, Figure 1.21, Courtesy of Internet2®. **Chapter 2:** p. 33, lower left, ©2000 Eyewire Inc.; p. 40, Figure 2.8, Copyright 2003 NetComm Limited; p. 44, Figure 2.10, Copyright © 2005 D-Link Corporation/D-Link Systems, Inc.; p. 44, Figure 2.11, Copyright © 1998-2005 Net to Net Technologies, Inc.; p. 46, sidebar image, © Copyright 1994-2005 Motorola, Inc.; p. 52, Figure 2.20, © 1992-2005 Cisco Systems, Inc.; p. 53, Figure 2.21, Copyright © 2002 Siemens; p. 53, Figure 2.22 © 2005 Bluetooth SIG. **Chapter 3:** p. 68, Figure 3.2, Special permission to use a screen capture of the URL http://www.cert.org © 2006 Carnegie Mellon University, in this publication is granted by the Software Engineering Institute; pp. 68-69, Microsoft product screen shots reprinted with permission from Microsoft Corporation; p. 70, Figure 3.3, used with permission by Trend Micro; p. 81, Figure 3.16, courtesy of thawte, Inc.; p. 83, Figure 3.21, ©2005 Microsoft Corporation. **Chapter 4:** p. 104, Figure 4.1, Microsoft product screen shots reprinted with permission from Microsoft Corporation; p. 106, Figure 4.2, from firstgov.gov; p. 116, , 4.19 and 4.20 from firstgov.gov. **Chapter 5:** p. 133, middle, Google™ screen capture ©Google Inc., reprinted with permission; p. 135, Figure 5.1, image courtesy of Lycos, Inc.; p. 136, Figures 5.2 and 5.4, Google™ screen capture ©Google Inc., reprinted with permission; p. 137, Google™ screen capture ©Google Inc., reprinted with permission; p. 139, Figure 5.8, screen capture from Consumer Product Safety Commission; Figure 5.9, screen capture courtesy of healthonnet.org; p. 140, Figure 5.10, ©2007 InfoSpace, Inc. All rights reserved; p. 141, Figure 5.12, screen captures courtesy of FDA.gov; p. 143, Figure 5.15, courtesy of about.com; p. 145, Figure 5.16, courtesy of BrightPlanet Corporation; p. 146, Figure 5.17, Google™ screen capture ©Google Inc., reprinted with permission; p. 150, courtesy of Ask.com; p. 151, Figure 5.19, Google™ screen capture ©Google Inc., reprinted with permission; p. 152, Figure 5.20, reprinted by permission of Infopeople, which is supported by the U.S. Institute of Museum and Library Services under the provisions of the Library Services and Technologies Act, administered in California by the State Librarian; p. 155, Figure 5.22, top image Google™ screen capture ©Google Inc., reprinted with permission; p. 156, Figure 5.24, Google™ screen capture ©Google Inc., reprinted with permission; p. 157, Figures 5.26, 5.27, 5.28, Google™ screen capture ©Google Inc., reprinted with permission; p. 163, Figure 5.29, screen captures used with permission from the Landmark Project. **Chapter 6:** p. 180, top screen capture, Microsoft product screen shots reprinted with permission from Microsoft Corporation; p. 182, first and second screen captures, courtesy of InternetSoft Corporation; p. 184, left screen capture © Glub Tech, Inc., used with permission; p. 187, Figure 6.16, courtesy of tucows.com; p. 188, images courtesy of tucows.com; p. 190, Figure 6.21, Screenshot of the FileAnywhere.com website used by permission. FilesAnywhere.com is the brainchild of "Dallas Maverick", Mark Cuban. **Chapter 7:** p. 203, lower right, Courtesy of Apple Computer, Inc.; p. 203, screen capture courtesy of virginmegastores.co.uk; p. 210, Figure 7.9, Courtesy NASA/JPL-Caltech; p. 211, Figure 7.10, permission Jet Propulsion Laboratory; p. 213, courtesy of freeimages.co.uk; p. 216, Figure 7.16, Courtesy of Apple Computer, Inc.; p. 217, Figure 7.18, screen capture courtesy of Apple Computer, Inc.; p. 219, Figure 7.20 courtesy of National Public Radio; p. 220, top 3 images, courtesy mididb.com; p. 223, Figure 7.24, courtesy of javascriptkit.com. **Chapter 8:** p. 239, middle image, reproduced with permission of Yahoo! Inc. © 2007 by Yahoo! Inc. YAHOO! and the YAHOO! logo are trademarks of Yahoo! Inc, bottom image, Google™ screen capture ©Google Inc., reprinted with permission; p. 264. Figure 8.27, Google™ screen capture ©Google Inc., reprinted with permission, Figure 8.28, reprinted with permission scc.net a BPSI.net company. **Chapter 9:** p. 275, screen capture courtesy of allaboutjazz.com; p. 276, Figure 9.1, Microsoft product screen shots reprinted with permission from Microsoft Corporation; p. 276, Figure 9.2, courtesy of land-rover.team.net; p. 277, Figure 9.3, courtesy of land-rover.team.net; p. 278, Figure 9.7, courtesy of land-rover.team.net; p. 280, Figure 9.9, courtesy L-Soft International, Inc.; p. 281, Figure 9.11, Google™ screen capture ©Google Inc., reprinted with permission; p. 285, Figure 9.14, used with permission from newsbot.com; p. 286, Figure 9.15, Google™ screen capture ©Google Inc., reprinted with permission; p. 289, Figure 9.16, used with permission from Adobe; p. 294, Figure 9.20, Google TM screen capture © Google Inc., reprinted with permission; p. 295, screen capture used with permission from blogarama.com; p. 299, Figure 9.26, courtesy of wikipedia.org; p. 300, Figure 9.27, used with permission from xwiki.com. **Chapter 10:** p. 315, lower image, courtesy of mirc.com; p. 316 and 317, images courtesy of mirc.com; p. 330, Figure 10.24, used with permission from Vonage; p. 326, Figure 10.17, Copyright CORBIS; p. 326, Figure 10.18, Copyright Jose Luis Pelaez, Inc. / CORBIS.